Rural Writing

Rural Writing:

Geographical Imaginary and Expression of a New Regionality

Edited by

Mauricette Fournier

Cambridge
Scholars
Publishing

Rural Writing:
Geographical Imaginary and Expression of a New Regionality

Edited by Mauricette Fournier

This book first published 2018

Cambridge Scholars Publishing

Lady Stephenson Library, Newcastle upon Tyne, NE6 2PA, UK

British Library Cataloguing in Publication Data
A catalogue record for this book is available from the British Library

Copyright © 2018 by Mauricette Fournier and contributors

ISBN (10): 1-5275-0643-6
ISBN (13): 978-1-5275-0643-5

TABLE OF CONTENTS

LIST OF FIGURES AND TABLES

Introduction

From Regionalist Literature to Literature of the Regionality

Mauricette Fournier

The region is then a topos, a place for argumentation from which the discourse of regionalism — the anamnesis of a traumatic loss — can begin
—Roberto Maria Dainotto

A sign of the contemporary porosity of the social sciences and humanities, researchers of various nationalities, from two main disciplinary fields, geography and literature, have contributed to the present book, centered on the writing and representations of the rural space and regionality. This interdisciplinary dialogue is a continuation of the epistemological Spatial Turn generated by postmodern criticism which, since the years 1960-1970, has endeavored to rehabilitate the place, on the one hand of narratives, on the other hand of space. Globalization and the awareness of the spatial transformation of the world has led the human and social sciences, like literary studies, since the 1980s especially, to carry out a "Spatial Turn" (Soja, 1989; Lévy, 1999) and to consider that space is fundamentally a component of the complexity of the social. At the same time, the geography, discipline of space, made a "cultural turn", which led it to take an interest in literature, individual and collective representations of the world or spatial imaginaries, first in the Anglo-Saxon world (Tuan, 1978; Pocok, 1988), before extending to Francophone research (Lévy, 1989; Brosseau, 1996; Dupuy, 2009).

This "geographical turn" has had an impact on the outlines of the different academic disciplines, as well as on their reciprocal relations. The general interest in spatiality has allowed for rapprochement, a dialogue between geography and literature (Brosseau and Cambron, 2003; Bédard and Lahaie, 2008). Thus, for twenty years, a new literary geography has emerged, diffused by the works of Franco Moretti (2000 and 2008), Bertrand Westphal (2007 and 2011), Michel Collot (2011). This is further illustrated by the increase in collective publications (Lévy, 2006; Tissier, 2007; Rosemberg, 2007; Dupuy and Puyo, 2014 and 2015; Madoeuf and Cattedra, 2012; Fournier, 2016 ; Peraldo, 2016).

Literature and geography are therefore linked. The novel in particular appears as an instrument of knowledge allowing by the detour of fiction to explore the real. At this prism, literary geography has often chosen to observe the urban universe (Madoeuf and Cattedra, 2012) according to the preferences of the writers of the last century. Although, corollary of urbanization, many artists (writers, painters…) seized, as early as the nineteenth century and most of the twentieth century, the city as object and scene of their reflection on a world under construction, it has not been the same for rural areas.

It is clear that, with some exceptions, until recently the countryside's representations have been shaped by the writings of a ruling class (Bergounioux, 2014). Thus the production conditions explain largely the symbolic appropriation of rural areas by various ideologies. The regionalist literature, with a predominantly ruralist coloring, was important in France during the Third and Fourth Republics (with authors like Henry Pourrat, Jean Giono, Marcel Pagnol filmography), but also well represented in other countries (*e.g.* José María de Pereda in Spain, or Patrice Lacombe in Canada, or Verga and Federigo Tozzi in Italy). "*Regionalism* [writes Francis Langevin (2010)] *sought to reorganize the system of attribution of authority between a region considered peripheral (to the global marginal influence), and a center (with overdetermined global influence)*". Anne-Marie Thiesse (1991 and 1993) showed how these literary demonstrations were, in France, skillfully recovered for various purposes by political discourse: it was a question of repatriating, into the national "central" imagination, the peripheral regions, whose symbolic attachment remained fragile for historical reasons.

In recent decades, however, beside the "country novels" or "terroir novels" that follow in line with the rustic trend initiated in the nineteenth century and meet real popular success given the importance of printing, more demanding productions have emerged. These writings often fed by a sense of loss and the end of a certain agricultural lifestyle also explore the contemporary reconstructions of rural areas, little publicized. They redefine a new "regionality" (or a new "provinciality") a term recently used by Francis Langevin (2010), as less militant and certainly less connoted in its nostalgic links to the land. Various researchers have begun to analyze the expressions of this new "regionality": Sylviane Coyault (2002) for France, Stuart Taberner (2004) for Germany, Liesbeth Korthals Altes and Manet van Montfrans (2002) in the Netherlands, etc. As a follow-up to this research this book proposes to revisit the rural areas and their representations in contemporary writings, in popular and legitimate cultures, in order to draw a global landscape of current countrysides and new regionality.

By "writings" we mean literature in all its forms - novels, autobiographies, tales (chapter 10), songs (chapters 5 and 11) - but also audio-visual productions (chapters 9, 13, 14, 15 and 16). The book is divided into four parts. The first has for object to present an overview of the new literary expressions, in connection with the transformations of rural areas in various parts of the world. The following two parts illustrate two particular geographical areas, the French Massif Central and the Francophone America (Quebec, Acadia), concerned both by the same problems of contemporary representations of a new regionality, sobering to identity issues, authenticity, transmission of the memory and values in a globalized context. The last part focuses on it more in a particular genre, detective stories, in novels and on screen, investing more and more rural areas (here from Italy, Outer Hebrides, Russia, Québec) to give them new representations.

Rural textuality: permanence and transformation of peripheral areas

The first part of this book concerns the rural textuality, the continuities and transformations that affect peripheral areas, which are increasingly often described by contemporary writers. The first chapter starts on an observation: scholars of the social sciences and literati, who have focused their research on the geo-literary approach, often contrast "high" literature with the popular terroir novel. This contrast continues to be very topical, particularly in the French context. **Marina Marengo** does not propose to demonstrate the supremacy of the neorural novel over the terroir novel, or indeed the opposite. Instead, she attempts to understand how two very different literary forms have contributed to building the spatial imaginary of rural France (whether in terms of peasants and rural society of the past or right up to the present) which underlies current European agricultural policies and/or the promotion of French rural heritage.

As in France, in the last decade, several Iberian writers have dedicated part of their literary production to the representation of the rural space and their writings reflect the deep changes that have transformed the land during the 20th century. **Maria Dasca** shows that writers such as Francesc Serés (1972), Ramon Erra (1966) and Joan Todó (1977) have developed a critical view of the present rural milieu by which they overcome the traditional ideological opposition between rural and urban space. The goal of her paper is to examine the representation of these contemporary marginal spaces, some of which were troubled by the Spanish Civil War or the end of the communist era in Eastern Europe. She focuses on the role of memory in the creation of emotional realities related to personal and collective identity.

The study of the literary representation of rural Spain continues with the contribution of **Joan Tort Donada** and **Rosa Català Marticella** who seek to provide an overall vision of the idea of rural in the works of Josep Pla, generally considered to be the writer that has made the widest and most meaningful contribution to Catalan contemporary literature. Josep Pla defined himself as a farmer, because of his own family background. In fact, the works of Josep Pla suggest two directions explored in this essay. They appear on the one hand, as a key for discovering the contemporary meaning of the countryside and the rural world, not only in Catalonia and Spain, but also in the European context, and, on the other hand, as a tool for tackling, in a creative manner, the great questions and challenges the rural world must face in the second decade of the twenty-first century – that is to say, in the era of globalization.

This part is concluded with an article devoted to Lebanon from the study of the novel *Poste restante* by Hanan El-Sheikh. Although the work of this author is an ode to the city of Beirut, the presence of the campaign, embodied by the Bekaa, holds a special place. Even plagued by drug trafficking – it is a haven of peace, opposed in all respects to the danger of the constantly bombarded Lebanese capital. The writing of the author reinforces the sensitive dimension compared to rural areas, dimension that **Nora Semmoud** and **Florence Troin** try to highlight, especially via the translation by the narrative maps. The novel thus reflects a particular relationship to war-torn areas. They are the extreme images of some socio-spatial concepts discussed by geography (fragmentation, border) and – of particular interest to us – the marginalized spaces. The underlying idea of this paper about "Poste restante" is that the war exacerbates the emotional relationship to space. The work, thus forcing the trait of the dimensions of the lived and perceived spaces, gives special light on this input of geography.

To conclude, **Mauricette Fournier** proposes a reflection on the contribution of literature to the territorial sciences (in particular geography and anthropology). She is based mainly on two stories, *Espèces d'espaces* by Georges Perec and *Miette* by Pierre Bergounioux, to show how these writers participate in redefining spatiality and regionality.

New expression of regionality in the French Massif Central: literary revival in search of authenticity

This section, dedicated to the French Massif Central, starts on a paper by **Antoine Marty** and **Mauricette Fournier** who study the setting diachronic perspective representations of the Ardèche mountains in the song "La Montagne" (The Mountain) written by the French singer Jean Ferrat in 1964 and the current website of the Monts d'Ardèche Regional Natural Park. They want to highlight the relations between geographical imaginary and the territorialization process of space and mutual co-construction between representations and dynamics animating the territory. The comparison of the geographical imaginary carried by the two media (song and website) can highlight the systemic evolution of space: from the end of the rural society and the rural exodus to a development of tourism and recreational, to an idealization of the past which gives back an attractiveness to the territory and capitalizes on a territorial identity perceived as strong and rich.

The three following contributors have chosen to analyze *Pays Perdu,* by Pierre Jourde, a book published in 2003 that became "known" for its poor reception, and more widely the work of its author on the issue of authenticity. This short narrative has been nurtured by his knowledge of his family's land, in Lussaud, a hamlet in Auvergne, where about twenty peasants reside, an ageing population that lives modestly from traditional farming, a tradition on the verge of extinction. Pierre Jourde's text presents the reader with not only a series of portraits, but also with anecdotes and reflections on peasant life, its roughness and beauty. Jourde's tribute was not appreciated by all the inhabitants, and some felt contempt and indiscretion. Therefore, in 2005, they greeted him with insults, threats and blows. Ten years after the publication that severed the author's relationship with his former neighbors, Pierre Jourde published a text with a biblical title, *La première pierre* (2013). In this essay, the Parisian iconoclastic critic expresses his self-criticism partly questioning his writing, partly convincing his reader of the legitimacy of his pictorial ode to the "lost country".

Based on several works of Pierre Jourde, *Pays perdu* (2003) and *La première pierre* (2013) in the first place, but also *Géographies imaginaires* (1991)*, La littérature est un sport de combat* (2015)*,* etc., the analysis of **Annie Jouan-Westlund** investigates the various power dynamics at play in the autobiographical work positioning the author as an authority figure over the farmers who inspired his characters. While debating the author's claim to an "authentic" piece of literature, the study analyzes the impact of the farming community's social structure and its media coverage on *Pays perdu*'s reception. This exploration of the multiple textual and non-textual fictional representations leading to a misunderstanding of the text, addresses the limits of creative freedom when the expectations of "rural" readers are not fulfilled and the "city" writer, like Pierre Jourde, is considered a traitor.

For his part, **Jérôme Cabot** aims at reconsidering the novel in order to define its aesthetic, anthropological and social dimension, and to study, also, why the inhabitants that it portrays received it badly. He finds that contrary to conventional local color literature, in *Pays perdu*, the description of Lussaud is based on a blurring of space-time landmarks which breaks away from the homotopic consensus and celebrates a "smooth space", complicated with conflicting geographical references, pre-industrial anhistoricity, legends and myths. For the author, the text gives nobility to the little hamlet, in a mock-heroic manner which raises the common everyday life up to epic, turns humble people to heroes, makes prosaicness aesthetic, and gives a metaphysical sense even to the cow dung. This paradoxical eulogy produced an unacceptable text, which exhumes the dead and converts the oral memory, its secrets and its taboos, into written Literature. Thus, *Pays perdu* was intrinsically doomed to offend, trapped by the difficulties of any non-native literary speech.

Finally, **Pierre Couturier**, geographer, addresses the question of the relationship between literature and social sciences from the writings of Pierre Jourde. He finds that in *Pays perdu*, Pierre Jourde binds in a same feeling of loss, beings and places. Subsequently, taking a reflective look at his novel, Pierre Jourde develops the link between the loss and the "sense of place", which leads him to the question of authenticity in literature. Pierre Jourde comes to assimilate the search for authenticity rather than the "typical" that hides the truth. The paper examines to what extent this allows literary viewpoint to inform and enrich the debate within the social sciences between supporters of authenticity as analytical category and those who confined it to a native class.

New expression of regionality in francophone America: tensions between memory to transmit and values to share

This second part with regional character leans on documents highly varied (novels, movies, tales, even toponymical inventions) to explore new expressions of the regionality in francophone America (Quebec and Acadia).

Marie Pascal is based on two classic novels – *Séraphin, Un homme et son péché* (Claude-Henri Grignon: 1933) and *Le Survenant* (Germaine Guèvremont : 1945), to study the theme of rurality, enhanced here in two of its main aspects: the Catholic religion on the one hand, and the family on the other. The two literary characters – both eponymous – illustrate the fragility of rurality, however rooted on secular beliefs and habits and are very well adapted for the screen on the edge of a new century and therefore, for a new public. Indeed, the two directors (Charles Binamé: 2002; Éric Canuel: 2005) enhance, develop, and worsen the literary characters' transgressive aspects through several crucial sequences of their filmic adaptations. In doing so however, they but accentuate the implacability of rural life which in the end leads to the failure of the two figures of marginality. The paper proceeds to these questions: how is the rural order represented in the two novels and how do the different types of transgressions – intratextual through the study of marginality and extratextual through the directors' additional scenes – only accentuate the fact that rural life will endure.

Pierre-Mathieu Le Bel and **Aurore Mirloup** studied the case of the Municipality of Saint-Élie-de-Caxton, Quebec, interesting by its contemporaneity and its commercial success. This town has seen its destiny change following the success of the work of the storyteller, poet and writer Fred Pellerin. Since the early 2000s, the work of Pellerin served as a lever for development for the municipality. A tourist trail has been created associated to his tales, supported by maps and audio guides on which the visitors hear the author himself narrate traditional myths, historical anecdotes and his own inventions. This author can be considered as creating a link between a secular rural oral memory and the contemporary urban reader. Pellerin's tales become a mediator between locations. The paper studies the narrative processes mobilized by Pellerin to see how texts create a specific geography. Then it explores how the texts content is instrumentalized by local actors as they use literary tales to value isolated rural areas, and which aspects of the socio-spatial representations are adopted by visitors.

For her part **Marie-Laure Boudreau** is interested in Acadia, a rural French settlement in the New World that had well-defined borders. Following the "Great Deportation" of 1755, its people have been scattered throughout Europe and the Americas. As a result, its official borders on the map dissolved. Today, people still identify as "Acadians", even if there is no clear geographic boundaries defining Acadia's territory. Where is "Acadia" today? If most people who identify as Acadians live in rural areas, there are also those who live in urban areas. Acadians, who share cities with antagonistic Anglophone communities (such as Moncton, New Brunswick) or live as "exiles" in other North American cities, often long for a rural home. Drawing on concepts borrowed from Yi-Fu Tuan about conceptual appropriation of a territory, this article explores place names and landscape description in Acadian contemporary songs as an attempt to localize a place called "Acadia".

Finally, **Ekaterina Isaeva** analyses a peculiarity of language: the use of periphrasis for secondary naming of Quebec place names. Periphrasis as a process of language and discourse while accentuating the expression of the text presents a new image of the object as it holds additional information. In the case of place names, the first information about it often falls into oblivion in the collective memory. And the secondary naming is used in the media today, titles and / or signboards. Periphrasis replaces toponym with a pictorial expression containing more words and thus more information. The reason for the creation of a periphrastic toponym is in the desire of individuals identifying themselves with the same language and culture to present an important place's quality shared by everybody. The periphrastic toponyms are not only rich in expression but contain judgments of the world and oneself. In this context, Quebec periphrastic place names represent an undeniable scientific interest in verbal-cultural approach.

Noir in the countryside: rural areas in detective novels and crime films

Alessandra Bonazzi recalls that the strategy of the writer Andrea Camilleri for avoiding the so-called "disenchantment with the world" is to construct for one's characters a land made up of different parts, shaping and structuring a land based on reality. But she describes what happened during the nine seasons (from 1999 to 2013) of the televised version of the detective novel series featuring Inspector Montalbano as the progressive voiding and systematic "cleansing" of the "half-made-up places" that form the settings of the novels written by Camilleri. The very human clutter of the "invented land" was transformed into a silent empty landscape. With a sort of hyperbole the landscape established its independence first from the novel and then from the action, becoming a stage whose function was the (global) reconstruction of an imagined Sicilian geography. Thus the paper looks on at the broadcasting of a progressive transformation of the landscape into a geographical imagination irreducible to reality, though quite effective for their very concrete repercussions on reality itself.

In her paper **Oksana Dognon** tries to distinguish the opposition of the rural side to the big city in Russian Mafia cinema, as well as its influence on the viewer. She shows that the influence of the rural appears to be the benefactor to the Russian Criminal protagonist: the rural often turns a hard personality of the criminal into a human being, as is illustrated by the example of the film "Boumer" which shows the representation of the rural and its influence on the evaluation of the four criminal friends. The originality of the Russian mafia cinema genre was, in some cases that it was produced and performed by former criminals: for example Vitaly Demochka, a former criminal, became a producer and an actor, a peculiarity of his story, that he transferred his real life into the movie. Thus, the former members of his criminal group have become actors in his film "Spets" and heroes of his novel "Special".

Franck Chignier-Riboulon was interested in the work of Peter May, a Scottish novelist, now living in France. Among his detective stories, the Lewis trilogy takes place in the Outer Hebrides, a far west archipelago, separated from the Scottish Mainland by a dangerous strait, The Minch. Isolated for centuries, Gaelic culture has survived until now in these islands. In his books, Peter May makes comparisons between the 50's and 60's with nowadays. The author shows how May plays with former decades to present changes and continuities, overall in cultural aspects. By showing religious behaviors or the black skies of the archipelago, the writer helps readers to re-discover a world away, a despised territory. Moreover, the paper explains how May has tried to restore the image of Gaelic culture, associated for a long time with under-development and a backward world, and, finally, participated in a renewal movement for a very weak Gaelic culture and a still poor people.

In his paper about *Sous les vents de Neptune* [*Wash this Blood Clean from my Hand*] by Fred Vargas (2004), **Christophe Gelly** focuses on the only novel in which this French detective fiction writer places her recurring investigator, superintendent Adamsberg – a character whose traits are very much indebted to a whole tradition of French crime fiction – in a foreign environment, namely in Ottawa where he is being trained on DNA profiling. The aim of his study is to show how the image of Canada is reconstructed on an imaginary level, noticeably as far as language is concerned, which enables the author to depict her character's investigation and method quite differently from the way they appear in her other novels. In this outlook, Christophe Gelly first examines the issue of realism in the novelistic representation and then focuses on the question of language as a symbol for otherness. These topics are examined according to their specific meaning in the poetics of the genre specific to Fred Vargas.

References

Bédard, Mario et Lahaie, Christiane (dir.). 2008. « Géographie et literature », *Cahiers de Géographie du Québec,* 52, n°147, 150 p.

Bergounioux, Pierre. 2014. *Exister par deux fois,* collection Essais, Fayard, 295 p.

Brosseau, Marc. 1996. *Des romans-géographes.* Paris, L'Harmattan, (coll. Géographie et cultures), 246 p.

Brosseau, Marc and Cambron, Micheline. 2003. « Entre géographie et littérature : frontières et perspectives dialogiques », *Recherches sociographiques,* vol. 44, n° 3, p. 525-547

Collot, Michel. 2011. « Pour une géographie littéraire », n° 8, LHT, Dossier, publié le 16 mai 2011 [En ligne], URL : http://www.fabula.org/lht/8/8dossier/242-collot

Coyault, Sylviane. 2002. *La province en héritage. Pierre Michon, Pierre Bergounioux, Richard Millet.* Genève, Librairie Droz, coll. « Histoire des idées et critique littéraire », 289 p.

Dainotto, Roberto Maria. 2000. *Place in Literature: Regions, Cultures and Communities,* Cornell University Press, 178 p.

Dupuy, Lionel. 2009. *Géographie et imaginaire géographique dans les Voyages Extraordinaires de Jules Verne : Le Superbe Orénoque (1898).* Thèse de géographie, université de Pau et des Pays de l'Adour, 332 p.
http://jules-verne.pagesperso-orange.fr/These_Lionel_Dupuy.pdf

Dupuy, Lionel and Puyo, Jean-Yves (ed.). 2014. *L'imaginaire géographique. Entre géographie, langue et littérature,* Presses de l'Université de Pau et des pays de l'Adour : coll. Spatialités, 427 pages

Dupuy, Lionel and Puyo, Jean-Yves (ed.). 2015. *De l'imaginaire géographique aux géographies de l'imaginaire. Écritures de l'espace,* Presses de l'Université de Pau et des pays de l'Adour : coll. Spatialités, 175 pages

Fournier, Mauricette (ed.). 2016. « Géographie, littérature, territoires », *Territoire en mouvement,* 31/2016 [https://tem.revues.org/3767]

Fournier, Mauricette (ed.). 2016. *Cartographier les récits.* Clermont-Ferrand, Presses Universitaires Blaise Pascal, collection CERAMAC, n° 35, 242 p.

Korthals Altes, Liesbeth and van Montfrans, Manet (ed). 2002. *The New Georgics. Rural and Regional Motifs in the Contemporary European Novel.* Amsterdam, Rodopi, coll. "European Studies", 244 p.

Langevin, Francis. 2010. « Un nouveau régionalisme ? De Sainte-Souffrance à Notre-Dame-du-Cachalot, en passant par Rivière-aux-

Oies », *in* Sébastien Chabot, Éric Dupont et Christine Eddie (ed.) « Narrations contemporaines au Québec et en France : regards croisés », *Voix et Images*, vol. 36, n° 1, (106) 2010, p. 59-77.

Langevin, Francis. 2010. « La régionalité chez Hervé Bouchard, Éric Dupont et François Blais », in Zuzana Malinovská (dir.), *Cartographie du roman québécois contemporain*. Prešov (Slovaquie), Acta Facultatis Philosophicae Universitatis Prešovensis, coll. « Monographia » (n°112), p. 36-53.

Lévy, Bertrand. 1989. *Géographie humaniste et littérature : l'espace existentiel dans la vie et l'œuvre de Hermann Hesse (1877-1962)*. Thèse de doctorat, Ed. Le Concept moderne, Genève, 400 p.

Lévy, Bertrand. (ed.). 2006. « Géographie et littérature », *Le Globe. Revue genevoise de géographie*, n°146, 160 p.

Lévy, Jacques (ed.). 1999. *Le tournant géographique : penser l'espace pour lire le monde*. Paris, Belin, 398 p.

Madoeuf, Anna and Cattedra, Raffaele. 2012. *Lire les villes, Panoramas du monde urbain contemporain*. Tours, Presses universitaires François Rabelais, Collection Villes et Territoires, 374 p.

Moretti, Franco. 2000. *Atlas du roman européen, 1800-1900*. Paris, Seuil, 235 p. [Atlante del romanzo europeo: 1800-1900, Giulio. Einaudi, Turin, 1997].

Moretti, Franco. 2008. *Graphes, cartes et arbres : Modèles abstraits pour une autre histoire de la littérature*. Paris, Les Prairies ordinaires. Coll. « Penser/Croiser », 142 p. [Graphs, Maps, Trees, Londres, Verso, 2005].

Peraldo, Emmanuelle(dir). 2016. *Literature and Geography. The Writing of Space throughout History*, Cambridge Scholars Publishing, 490 p.

Pocok, Douglas C. 1988. "Geography and Literature". *Progress in Human Geography*, vol. 12, p. 87-102.

Rosemberg, Muriel (dir). 2007. « Le roman policier. Lieux et itinéraires, numéro thématique », *Géographie et Cultures*, n° 61, 143 p.

Soja, Edward. 1989. *Postmodern Geographies: The Reassertion of Space in Critical Social Theory*. London: Verso Press, 266 p.

Taberner, Stuart (ed). 2004. *German Literature in the Age of Globalisation*. Birmingham, University of Birmingham Press, coll. "The New Germany in Context".

Thiesse, Anne-Marie. 1991. *Écrire la France. Le mouvement littéraire régionaliste de langue française entre la Belle Époque et la Libération*. Paris, Presses Universitaires de France, 320 p.

—. 1993. « La littérature régionaliste en France (1900-1940) », *Tangence*, n° 40, mai 1993, p. 49-64.

Tissier, Jean-Louis (dir). 2007. « Géographie et littérature », *Bulletin de l'Association des Géographes français*, vol 84, n° 3, p. 243-368.

Tuan, Yi-Fu. 1978. "Literature and geography: implications for geographical research", *in* David Ley et Marwyn S. Samuels (ed.), *Humanistic geography – Prospects and problems*. Chicago, Maaroufa Press, p. 194-206.

Westphal, Bertrand. 2007. *La Géocritique, Réel, Fiction, Espace*. Paris, Éditions de Minuit, 278 p.

—. 2011. *Le monde plausible. Espace, lieu, carte*. Paris, Éditions de minuit, 254 p.

PART 1:

RURAL TEXTUALITY:
PERMANENCE AND TRANSFORMATION
OF PERIPHERAL AREAS

CHAPTER ONE

FROM THE RURAL "TERROIR" TO THE "NEORURAL" NOVEL: THE CONTRADICTIONS AND COMPLEMENTARITIES BETWEEN POPULAR AND HIGH LITERATURE IN CONTEMPORARY FRANCE

MARINA MARENGO

The countryside: one territory, many territories

Today as in the past, the countryside and rural areas have often been the subject of interest not only for researchers, geographers in particular, but also of many writers. Nineteenth century French campestral literature is a classic example and George Sand is one of its better-known exponents. His works have been part of French children's literature for well over a century. There were numerous literary works, mainly novels, connected to realism, naturalism and verism particularly between the mid-1800s and the early 1900s, which left an important mark on the literary world with regard to ruralism. These authors produced works which became the subject matter of important scientific studies. Nonetheless, some of the early 20th century novels were classified as popular (Thiesse 1993 and 2000), mainly consisting of literary sagas and *terroir* novels (a specific term relating to France and Québec[1]). Scholars and literati have rarely appreciated or even respected these works. Over the last few decades, as if in complete contrast to popular literature, a new strand of

---

[1] The Quebecan fictional genre is defined "du terroir" and it all but disappeared when urbanisation and the urban lifestyle took hold. In recent years it has made a comeback in Quebec, but with a new concept of terroir, which is both rural and urban.

neorural novels has developed in France. The writings of Michon, Bergounoiux, Lafon, to name a few, have received recognition from "high" literature, resulting in a renewed contrast between the different genres of literary fiction in France.

Setting aside the French literary diatribes, Unesco's list of World Heritage Sites bears witness to the renewed interest in rural contexts on a global level. Embedded in this current "race" towards heritisation is an ancient concept, somewhat overused and emptied of profound meaning: the *terroir*. Although today it refers mainly to vineyards and wine production, its origins trace back to the French Middle Ages. From a spatial point of view, *terroir* corresponds to *finage*, that is, the municipal territory. A definition was agreed on in 2010 shared by scholars and local actors in the territory. The *terroir* is

> [...] defined as the delimited geographical space where a human community, throughout its history, has built a collective intellectual knowledge of production based on a system of interaction between the physical and biological environment as well as a collection of human factors. The socio-technical paths are defined over time and are specific to it and in practical terms they are established by conferring a reputation to the typicality and singularity of the specific geographical area (Fanet 2010, 4).

Rural literature: diatribes about a very "hexagonal" phenomenon

The two types of novel mentioned above, actually show the two sides of the same coin, despite their profound differences. The *terroir* novel, consecrated by the affirmation made by the *Ecole de Brive* and the *Salon du livre de Brive-la-Gaillarde*[2], is characterised by the abundance and redundancy of words and the linearity of the writing. Its success with the general public has not prevented it from being considered as an inferior genre. The *terroir* has often been made into a film version or television series, bringing fame and greater literary success, but distancing it further form the "real" rural literature. Nevertheless, the two types of literature are

---

[2] *Foire du livre de Brive-la-Gaillarde* was created in 1973. It began as a local event and has now become an international phenomenon, which takes place in a small provincial French town and brings together writers, poets, critics, journalists, scholars and people of letters. Following the success of Claude Michelet's literary saga, set in a small town near Brive, a group of authors who do not consider themselves terroir writers, but rather as literary writers of the local context.

undoubtedly complimentary. The likes of Michon and Bergounioux lead us to the essence of the French countryside, where we go in search of these basic elements of an agricultural and rural world, which represent our origins and our deepest socio-cultural roots, even though they have completely changed over the past century. The *terroir* constitutes the hard core of contemporary heritage processes, in a context where traditional rurality has all but disappeared, and the modern form of rurality has to fend off the onslaught of the urban way of life and production.

Popular literature, in spite of being considered a minor genre, has helped to define the spatial imaginary of France, largely due to the fact that these novels are compulsory reading books at secondary school. Moreover, those who are not accustomed to reading, like the inhabitants of the terroir themselves, usually find this type of literature much more approachable. Furthermore, as they are essentially literary sagas, the time span is greater and the transformation of certain features can be fully appreciated, namely: landscapes, local communities and specificity of the farms − from small landowners and share farming with multiple crops to the large farming industries specialised in monoculture or selective animal husbandry. All this without the authors of the *terroirs* considering themselves as real literati, despite receiving literary awards and general acclaim. Claude Michelet serenely stated in his autobiography, *J'ai choisi la terre*: "When the newspaper I worked for closed, I still had the writing itch [...] I kept it up and was drawn toward the novel" (2005, 152).

This ongoing lively debate between literati, as well as high and popular literature, has also had other effects, namely: the identification of new territorial subjects and the instruments to study them, promotion of the local environment and a greater consideration of the contents of projects and processes regarding territorial and cultural marketing in the local context.

Geographical and literary reflections on the terroir and popular literature

Pierre Ouellet points out that

[...] *terroirs* offer numerous perspectives, head on or sideways, which add a gravitational pull to one's viewpoint like a stone in freefall. We must take advantage of this because the *terroirs* disappear and our view will be exhausted (1996, 171).

A traditional geographer, like Maurice Le Lannou, had also previously maintained that,

> [...] the so-called "localised" novel[3] allows us to perceive facts with greater sensitivity, whereas systematic science simplifies and deforms these facts through its processes of classification and risks becoming just a scientific document. [...] The key to its usefulness lies in the description, in the topography of the agricultural landscape (1967, 36).

Jean-Louis Tissier, considering all the literary works as a whole, wrote:

> The literary environment is [...] much more than a huge field of "monocultural" text with a poor yield. There are different literary varieties and genres, which establish privileged relationships with the territory. Geographers have not been particularly sensitive to these differences, thus becoming consenting victims of the hegemony of the novel (1992, 240).

Researchers, mainly geographers, have been distanced further by the linearity of the descriptions of popular literature. Only Michel Chevalier, when referring to the *terroir* novel, sustains that

> [...] many passages are like "parts" of an anthology, similar to the arrival of a tractor in the hamlet in 1950. One can perceive [...] the evolution of the town, which is not only depopulated, but stripped of its noteworthy residents and tradesmen and replaced by commuters and second homes, thus condemning traditional rural society. [...] It is a shame that no geographer has seriously considered using these literary works (2001, pp. 113-114).

As far as the neorural novel is concerned, it is able to represent the essence of the phenomenon using fewer words and thanks to the "rarefied" writing style, using metaphors and complex narrative techniques, unheard of in scientific texts. Marc Brosseau described this genre as a geographical description without the description (2008). The two types of literature are equally important for researchers, particularly with reference to the rural environment and the processes of change over the last century. The literary works chosen for this part of the analysis regarding the geo-literary approach, give us an insight into the transformation of the landscapes, local communities, the running of the farms as well as the types and methods of production. The analysis will also look into the transformations

---

[3] In this period the concept of terroir had not been appreciated and enhanced from a geographical point of view and there was no talk of heritisation.

resulting from the mechanisation and industrialisation of agriculture, as well as the changes brought about by the European Common Agricultural Policy (C.A.P.).

The combined contribution of these literary works gives us an understanding of how they have contributed to building and transmitting the spatial imaginary of rural areas, whether in terms of the traditional past or the ultramodern present. Nevertheless, it should be noted that from a methodological point of view, the literary quotes in this paper are not used to illustrate the analytical reflections on just one concept, but rather to create a point of discussion regarding the conceptual categories that are being analysed.

A cross-section of the traditional rural world

The plotlines of both neorural and *terroir* novels, take us

[...] to Corrèze and Creuse. Or in Dordogne [...] Somewhere down there, on the edge, of course, but right in the centre: swallowed boundaries [...] It is all about new continents, just drifting [...] places lost in time, as time too is lost, strange upside-down places, rare spaces in danger of extinction, breeds of bastard places (Ouellet 1996, 166).

These places, their boundaries lost, are often indecipherable, not only because they are marginal, but also due the fact that they are so imbued with the vital essences that have allowed entire generations to reach us, but in a form that is no longer clear or legible. In the past:

They ploughed only where the plough was able to churn the soil and until the land became steep. The rest was left as pastureland or moorland, if the grass didn't grow. It is difficult to imagine it now. Only by looking at postcards of the region dating back to the beginning of the century, can you get an idea of what it was like (Bergounioux 1995, 89)[4].

---

[4] The literary quotations in the text refer to the following editions of the novels: Bergounioux, Pierre. 1995. *Miette*. Paris: Gallimard-Folio. Lafon, Marie-Hélène. 2009. *L'annonce*. Paris: Gallimard-Folio, Michelet, Claude. 1979. *Des grives aux loups*-Volume 1. Paris: Robert Laffont, and 1980. *Des grives aux loups. Les palombes ne passeront plus*-Volume 2; 1990. *Des grives aux loups. L'appel des engoulevents*-Volume 3; 1998. *Des grives aux loups. La terre des Vialhe*-Volume 4. The last three published in Paris by Robert Laffont-Pocket.

As well as this osmotic relationship with the land, there was another relationship, between landowner and peasant, which was regulated by a share-cropping contract:

No one knew where they came from, they weren't from the area. They had arrived eight years before, it seems they came from the Brive region, some thirty kilometres away. Foreigners [...] Share-croppers, who cultivated the three hectares of the notary's farm fairly well: two cows, six sheep, a pig and some chickens. They lived poorly, spoke little, and did not get involved in the town life of Saint-Libéral-sur-Diamond. And everyone distrusted them (Michelet 1979, 15).

The lives of poverty led by the peasants sometimes justified petty theft from the landlord's share of the crops. Even poaching was widespread, a source of extra family income, as well as an important source of protein in their poor diet:

[...] many did not forgive him for remaining the incorrigible poacher of his childhood. Everyone knew he still laid traps, but no one had ever caught him in the act. It was obvious he was a fraudulent hunter, but from knowing it to actually catching him in the act [...] the gamekeeper and the Ayen gendarmes had failed miserably to do so (ibidem, 83).

In other areas, small properties were common, passed down generation after generation and carrying specific obligations: "Baptiste had inherited the property, the 1930s house, most of the land and the obligation to look after them" (Bergounioux 1995, 16). For this reason there was always someone in the family who was leaving, voluntarily or not. "They said that Adrien had always preferred craftwork to agriculture [...] He left the town to look for work in Paris" (ibidem, 16-17).

There were also many small family properties, built up over the centuries, using the strategy of marriage (Fel 1992). As they grew progressively, they were often characterised by fragmented land, which made the farming more difficult and laborious:

As the only son of Mathieu-Édouard and Noémie Vialhe, he had inherited the main part of the current property, eight hectares patiently collected generation after generation by a dynasty of Vialhe, who had passed down the land, knowledge, and the name Edouard, given to all the first born sons. He had added another hectare to the existing eight when he returned from military service. His wife, Léonie, had brought a dowry of two hectares of good fields in 1859. A year later, their son, Jean-Edouard, was born and he in turn had helped them greatly with the farming work. He had also made an excellent choice, when he married, at the age of twenty-eight, the young Marguerite, ten years his junior, as beautiful as a flower and a dowry of four hectares of high quality fields (Michelet 1979, 26).

The progressive growth and fragmentation of these properties over one or more municipalities, made it necessary to name every plot of land.

Pierre-Edouard loved this immense stretch of land, he felt at home in these fields. He knew everyone by name, at least the ones belonging to the Vialhe. Over there was the Long field with its old oak trees, down there, next to the Caput hill, was the Peuch field, a little further away, the Malides – a wheat field –, still further, the Perrier field and at the very end, hidden by Puy Blanc, was the Big Field, sown with rye. The boy even knew who the other fields belonged to, where the boundary stones were, and he also knew the owners, share-croppers and tenants who worked there. [...] The Vialhe family with their fifteen hectares, eight cows, twelve sheep, two goats ad three sows, were among the most important landowners in the municipality. Only the properties of the notary, the castle and a few share-cropping properties owned by people from Terrasson, Ayen and Objat were larger than their farm (ibidem, 17-18).

The reputation of a rural family built up over several generations has been summarised in and exemplary way by this literary description.

Changes in the French countryside in the 20th century

A great change took place in the French countryside at the beginning of the nineteen hundreds, as in the rest of Europe.

It is no longer possible, after 1920, to live as Miette has, to live as those who had been in the position she now occupied for the last three thousand years. Machinery had to be bought. A new, more spacious, two-storey house will be built, still in granite though. It will be a hundred paces away from the original house where the date of its construction, 1610, is inscribed on the lintel" (Bergounioux 1995, 92).

The younger generation of farmers at the beginning of the 20th century were innovative, not only for purchasing or hiring mechanical farming equipment, but also for using "exotic" fertilizers, such as guano, or even chemicals, alongside the traditional manure: "Jean-Édouard, was gaining independence from old Edouard's paternal authority [...] He was the first one to use chemical fertilizers, with such expertise as to earn the respect of everyone" (Michelet 1979, 75).

The agricultural innovations in the first decades of the century were remarkable in every area, from the crop rotation techniques to the fertilisation of the land. In addition, agricultural consortiums came into being where farmers could obtain what they needed at controlled prices and receive advice about agriculture and machinery: "Thanks to Jean-Édouard's willingness and expertise, he set up an agricultural consortium, where most of the farmers came for their supplies" (ibidem, 73). These factors— the use of fertilizers, choosing selected seeds, changing to different crops, purchasing new equipment —have all changed the way we perceive farming, thus facilitating the progressive transition from subsistence agriculture to market farming.

Small farms based on polyculture usually integrated with some form of animal husbandry, depending on the local culture and traditions. Farm animals required an initial investment, often with the help of a small agricultural loan, which helped to build up a solid additional income to the purely agricultural one:

> It is pretty easy to buy two sows and eight sheep, or even some farming tools […] the repayment is never more than the proceeds from the sale of four beautiful pigs a year! So, seeing as we will have two sows, there will be a dozen pigs for us to sell! (ibidem, 410).

This additional income was partly reinvested in the farm: "[…] they had just sold six of the ten lambs born to the sheep, the remaining four were females which they wanted to keep to increase the size of the flock" (ibidem, 439).

In the division of family labour, it was usually the woman's work to look after the animals, including taking them to pasture, a task often shared with the children. Peasant women throughout the ages have integrated agricultural revenue with these activities, whether breeding silkworms, fattening up the family's pigs, sheep and cows or feeding the farmyard animals: "Nicole […] looked forward to milking time, caring for the fragile udders and the new-born calves, which were sold when only three-weeks old" (Lafon 2009, 36). In some cases these activities were limited to ensure that the family had the necessary amount of animal protein in their diet, but in other cases, the women's skills brought in a decent supplementary income:

> She had just finished tending to the cows and a smell of the pen spread around the room. She put down the pail of milk on the table. "Help me to put the pot for the pigs on the fire". She got up and grabbed the huge

cooking vessel full of kitchen leftovers, turnips, bran and water and hung it
on the chain (Michelet 1979, 30).

The care of the animals was on top of the routine housework and the
usual help in the fields: a peasant woman's work was never done.

The countryside is abandoned: demographic and functional emptying

Profound changes took place at the beginning of the 20th century, such
as a progressive and inexorable mechanisation and modernisation of
agriculture, the world wars and the socio-economic changes they caused,
which focused on the industrialisation of Western Europe. These are few
of the reasons contributing to the significant demographic and functional
losses in some areas of countryside in continental Europe (Kostrovicki
1980). In addition to the exodus, was the factor of the ageing population,
and directly related to this a lack of initiative.

There were 1092 inhabitants in 1900; 979 in 1914, and 701 now. One of
the grocers had to close down his shop. Only two of the four carpenters
who worked here before the war were left and they were struggling to
make a living, just like the three remaining builders. Nobody had replaced
the miller and everyone knew that the old notary would close his office at
the end of the year. The small share-croppers were disappearing
everywhere, unable to survive on just two or three hectares. The land was
abandoned and grew wild. The agricultural consortium languished. As for
the fairs, reopened thanks to the tenacity of the Léon family [...] by the
look of things, soon there would be only one a month (Michelet 1979, 401-
402).

It should be remembered that between the two world wars, the
mentality of the younger generation had changed dramatically; they no
longer wanted to invest their energy in the family businesses:

[...] refusing to bow to the despotic head of the family, they packed their
belongings and left. Having fraternised with comrades-in-arms coming
from urban areas, they realised that there were other ways of earning a
living than working the land. They had not only shared cheap wine and
tobacco, but also ideas, comparing their lifestyles, jobs and wages (ibidem,
387).

In this way the countryside lost a part of its youngsters of working age.

In one year, eight youngsters between the ages of sixteen and twenty, left the town, attracted by the jobs and salaries in the city. This year, for the third year running, the deaths in the municipality outnumber the births (ibidem 1980, 370).

Furthermore, in just over fifty years, the level of education of the inhabitants of rural areas had progressed from basic literacy, if any at all: "[…] the mayor had chosen Jean-Édouard as his deputy, mainly because he could read and write" (ibidem 1979, 27), to a bachelor's degree in agronomy of the fourth generation of the 20th century.

Dominique […] was attending the Grignon school, from which he hoped to qualify as an agronomist. Pierre-Edouard had been proud of his grandson from the start, so the day on which Dominique received his first diploma, his grandfather presented him with the twenty-franc Napoleon coin, the same one his own grandfather had given him, when he had obtained his elementary school-leaving certificate on 11 July 1902 (ibidem 1980, 420).

Many changes were facilitated by the evolution of mobility, largely due to the advent of the railway: "The inauguration of the railway line between La Rivière-de-Mansac and Saint-Libéral-sur-Diamond took place on 31 July 1909" (ibidem 1979, 191-192). Electric rails were replaced by diesel trains, although less prestigious, they still ensured the mobility of people and goods from the countryside to the regional urban centres. However, strategies tied to the cost effectiveness of the railway service, soon defined rural and mountain lines as "dead wood", leading to their closure.

During a sad town council meeting, the permanent cancellation of the locomotive, which had replaced the train since 1924, was announced. This decision had been taken for economic reasons. The line, which had opened Saint-Libéral to the world at the turn of the century and brought with it fairs, markets and foreign business, was now in deficit. Without it, Saint-Libéral would return to its isolation and obscurity. The bus service they promised could do nothing for the tons of plums, cherries, peas and beans produced in the municipality that had to be transported to Brive or Objat. They would have to take to the road again with their carts, in the middle of the night to reach wholesale market in time. Alternatively, they would have to buy a truck, but no one had the means (ibidem 1980, 92-93).

In just a few decades, even the most basic services disappeared in the rural areas, partly due to this demographic exodus, but also to the completely altered way of life. As the shops closed, their place was taken by the street-food traders, who came into the town regularly to supply the basic goods and foodstuffs to the inhabitants:

> He had started his rounds fifteen years before. In the beginning he only sold cheese, sausages, cured hams and the like, then as time went on his clients asked for some meat, after the butcher's closed down, and then some fish when it was available. He then added bread to his stock, again on the request of his clients, because the baker only delivered on Saturday. (ibidem 1998, 62).

This is an essential service for all those, especially the elderly, who "[…] do not have a car or work in the city and can't reach the shopping centres and malls which are popping up around the city, like mushrooms after an autumn shower, but far away from Saint-Libéral" (ibidem).

Moreover the crucial role of religion had disappeared. The old parish priests had either passed away or retired and they were not replaced.

> Even the priest became itinerant, like the street-food seller. He officiated in several parishes and only gave mass in Saint-Libéral every fifteen days or for funerals. After the theft in the church […] the Ministry of Culture, after nearly three years deliberation, ordered the church to be locked not only at night, but also during the day (ibidem, 62-63).

These profound changes have often relegated a culture, a way of life and production, dating back thousands of years, to a mere folkloristic expression.

The most recent changes: CAP issues and the implosion of the bygone rural world

Despite the efforts and investments of the farmers, agricultural and economic policies have increasingly made agricultural work less desirable.

> When he worked the land, he would never be able to achieve such a result, to cleanse the land in such a way, to tame it […] notwithstanding these fantastic changes and all the care and fertilising, the land could stand it no longer. It had nourished several generations of Vialhe, as well as previous generations of all those that had cultivated the land for tens of centuries. Now, year after year, it was incapable of providing for those who cultivated it. And yet they looked after it better than ever. The land was tired of producing more and more, ceaselessly. What was considered the yield of a lifetime, only ten years ago (and unthinkable fifty years ago) was now thought of as a mediocre result, just enough to cover the costs of

production. In actual fact, it was a senseless headlong rush in a stupid and ridiculous race, which Jacques had to continue if he wanted to survive. Like hundreds of other farmers, he had been forced to succumb to the rules of intensive farming. Producing more and more in an attempt to compensate for the stagnating and sometimes falling revenue by increasing the volume of production (ibidem 1990, 43).

The C.A.P. (European Common Agricultural Policy) has done much to influence European farmers (Bryant and Grillotti Di Giacomo 2007):

Above all, we must understand that the European minions, influenced by the Americans, considered a property like the one owned by Vialhe, however good it may be, as a dead weight which they were not prepared to sustain. Their only aim was to see that small farmers, whose work was of no interest to anyone, disappeared. Anyone who denied this was a liar and an imposter (Michelet 1990, 99).

The new conditions of life and above all work, have caused irreversible changes in the countryside in France and Europe:

His great grand-uncles had bought the farm, it had a history, but it would end with him. The current situation gave him no other choice. Farms were being grouped together and the land joined into one single property, but even so, it was difficult for a family with children to live in dignity (Lafon 2009, 45-46).

This was due to the fact that

Farmers fell into serious debt by buying more powerful materials and equipment and constructing huge farm buildings [...] So if there was a downturn in the value of their production, the cost of calves, milk, or both, the farmer found himself alone, having to face an enormous mountain of debts (ibidem, 46-47).

The consequence of these social, territorial, demographic, economic and cultural transformations was that "Nothing will be passed down, continued, perpetuated. There will be no successor for the Fridières farm" (ibidem, 77).

There could have been some hope of continuity if agricultural policies had been more flexible:

[...] that imported, unwanted boy [...] clearly had the skills. The animals sensed it [...] he had done some research at school about the traceability of agricultural products [...] Nicole and his uncles [...] realised that in times gone by and in other circumstances, with his vocation and atavism, Eric would have made an excellent farmer (ibidem, 142).

However, it was too late: the changes were too violent and radical, discouraging all those who sought a solution changes were discouraged those who sought a solution of continuity.

The only way to survive these imposed changes and achieve satisfactory results was, and still is to this day, to produce a high quality, niche product:

> [...] think about setting up a high-quality livestock farm. One that becomes a point of reference among breeders. Aim for a top notch product, you can do it because you have the skills and know. You are a good animal breeder (Michelet 1990, 311).

Niche and high-class products and a short distribution chain: literary fiction captures with great clarity the only remaining way that farmers can survive in marginal rural areas.

Rural and literary outlook

The more farsighted farmers and landowners had already understood these processes of change and had organised themselves accordingly:

> He would be the last to work the land with total devotion. He had understood that the end was near [...] when he inherited it from his father. As the first-born, he realised that the bond which had lasted three thousand years, and of which he was the embodiment, would be broken after he had gone. The hills were getting ready for a long lonely journey, abandoned by man (Bergounioux 1995, 114).

The path taken by the French countryside as described in this paper, followed the trend which took place throughout Europe in the last century. Neo-rurality now reigns in the countryside and is supported by a concerted effort to enhance the value of local areas. It is an effective reality, which has prevented the emptying of our countryside. Nevertheless, we must not underestimate the urban influence, the reference model of "outsiders". There is a high risk of "museification" of the countryside, as well as the predominance of stereotypes tied to cultural and territorial marketing. Alongside these territories, managed according to an urban blueprint, are those cultivated by farmers that are increasingly detached from the land and forced to follow an industrial approach based on productivity.

A middle ground has gradually spread in recent decades, with the great success of organic farming, the traceability of foodstuffs, locally sourced products and the "slow-food" lifestyle. In addition, there has been the complimentary input of new projects focusing on green and cultural tourism:

> It is unthinkable to just wait passively for the death of the town in such a beautiful region, so welcoming, where you eat maybe too much, but so well. [...] Because here you will find all that is "local", the landscape, everything you want! We have to target tourists. They are everywhere and we must find a way to make them come here. Seeing as they all think they are great photographers, we have to cajole them [...] we need something specific to attract them to our area. For example, the most beautiful photos of our town, church or old houses (Michelet 1990, 267-268).

These new opportunities were followed by itineraries, walks and other cultural initiatives arising from these literary works or their authors. They began to take root in those areas where the demographic and functional emptying had seemed relentless they do not attract huge crowds, but they have successfully managed to maintain and transmit values, knowledge and skills rooted in the local sphere (Fournier and Bordessoule 2014). A constructive and productive way to avoid forgetting territories that would otherwise be abandoned to oblivion

Primary sources

Bergounioux, Pierre. 1995. *Miette*. Paris: Gallimard-Folio.

Lafon, Marie-Hélène. 2009. *L'annonce*. Paris: Gallimard-Folio.

Michelet, Claude. 1979. *Des grives aux loups* - Vol. I. Paris: Robert Laffont.

—. 1980. *Des grives aux loups. Les palombes ne passeront plus* -Vol. II. Paris: Robert Laffont-Pocket.

—. 1990. *Des grives aux loups. L'appel des engoulevents*-Vol. III Paris: Robert Laffont-Pocket.

—. 1998. *Des grives aux loups. La terre des Vialhe*-Vol. IV. Paris: Robert Laffont-Pocket.

—. 2005. *J'ai choisi la terre*. Paris: Robert Laffont-Pocket.

Other references

Berque, Augustin. 1995. *Les raisons du paysage*. Paris: Hazan.

Brosseau, Marc. 2008. "L'espace littéraire en l'absence de description: un défi pour l'interprétation géographique de la littérature". *Cahiers de géographie du Québec*, Volume 52: 419-437.

Bryant, Christopher R., and Maria Gemma, Grillotti Di Giacomo, eds. 2007. Proceedings of the International Colloquium "Quality Agriculture: historical Heritage and environmental Resources for the integrated Development of Territories", Genova: Brigati, 2007.

Chevalier, Michel. 2001. Géographie et Littérature. *Société de géographie de Paris*. Hors série number 1500 bis.

Fanet, Jacques. 2010. "Terroir, climat e sol". In Proceeding of "VIII International Terroir Congress", 3-7. Soave-Verona: Proceedings session 4-3 (www.terroir2010.entecra.it).

Fel, André. 1992. "Paysans français. Modèles et auto-portraits". *Géographie et cultures*, Number 1: 119-128.

Fournier, Mauricette, and Eric Bordessoule. 2014. "Les 'villages du livre': un modèle sans label". In *Labellisation et mise en marque des territoires*, edited by Mauricette Fournier, 581-602. Clermont-Ferrand: Presses Universitaires Blaise Pascal, CERAMAC 34.

Kostrowicki, Jerzy. 1980. *Geografia dell'agricoltura: ambienti, società, sistemi, politiche dell'agricoltura*. Milano: Angeli.

Le Lannou, Maurice. 1967. *Le Déménagement du territoire. Rêveries d'un géographe*. Paris: Seuil.

Ouellet, Pierre. 1996. "Le roman de la terre. Millet, Michon, Bergounioux". *Liberté*, Volume 38: 165-177.

Thiesse, Anne-Marie. 1993. "La littérature régionaliste en France (1900-1940)". *Tangence*, Number 40: 49-64.

—. 2000. *Le roman du quotidien. Lecteurs et lectures populaires à la Belle Époque*. Paris: Seuil.

Tissier Jean-Louis. 1992. "Géographie et littérature". In *Encyclopédie de géographie*, edited by Antoine Bailly, Robert Ferras and Denise, Pumain, 217-239. Paris: Economica.

CHAPTER TWO

REPRESENTING THE LAND IN CURRENT IBERIAN LITERATURE

MARIA DASCA

> "The field that you are standing before
> appears to have the same proportions as your own life"
> (Berger 1991, 205)

Preview: fictionalizing space

At the turn of the twenty-first century rural space became one of the epicenters of contemporary fiction. Banished by modern imagery which had dominated the urban space, it has gradually gained strength in the narrative of authors such as Francesc Serés and Joan Todó, whose work involves a major thematic renewal. At the center of their novels we find the world issued from the current crisis. Their literary references, however, belong to the Spanish and Catalan prose tradition of the twentieth century – as they say themselves, they are indebted to Josep Pla, Gaziel, Jesús Moncada, Camilo José Cela and Juan Benet, among others, all great describers of the landscapes of the peninsula. Their literature sets out from the fictionalization of family spaces, in their cases on the periphery of Catalonia. For Serés, it is the Franja d'Aragó, the strip of land between Aragon and Catalonia. And for Todó, it is the lands of the Ebre delta on the border between Catalonia and the Valencian Country.

The space they describe is a countryside which, as in the Berger quote at the beginning of this article, seems to have the same proportions as the life of the characters who mould themselves to it and identify with it. In that sense, it becomes a space related to the profound knowledge of its inhabitants, who can talk about it through their own words, readings and experiences.

This article proposes a closer look at the rural imagery in Serés and, to a lesser degree, that of Todó. In the work of both authors, space has a key role. Their literature brings to mind the concept of *space* from the Latin *spatium* (applied to that which can be measured in strides) and, at the same time, it can refer to an interval or a path, one portion of a longer extension. In their fiction, space includes portions of a known and trodden land which can provide modernity. Serés and Todó treat space in its most local form: talking of landscapes or places (specific points in the space). As Berger would suggest, no landscape exists without the 'I': "[w]hen we 'see' a landscape, we situate ourselves in it. If we 'saw' the art of the past, we would situate ourselves in history" (Berger 1972, 11). The space they describe in their work is not natural; it is social and, basically, ontological. It is designed from the viewpoint of the people and the groups that are situated within it and, more specifically, of the narrative voice which projects it and which, as Berger says, gives it "proportion".

Of the work by Serés (Saidí, 1972), our interest lies in the novels *Els ventres de la terra*, *L'arbre sense tronc* and *Una llengua de plom* (included in the trilogy *De fems i de marbres*, 2003), and the collection of short stories, *La pell de la frontera* (2014)[1]. In the trilogy, several stories relate individuals to the territory by constructing a collective memory and giving the story a mythical dimension. The book talks of the profound changes that occurred in the land of Saidí during the twentieth century, including the Spanish Civil War, and gradual depopulation which began in the 1960s. The author focuses on the changing relationship between the landscape and its people, and follows the way the physical mutations cause irreversible changes in its history and, on the rebound, in memory.

La pell de la frontera, on the other hand, focuses on the present. Serés includes different stories centered on the changes that took place in the Franja with the massive arrival of immigrants from the Maghreb and Sub-Sahara. In total, there are fourteen texts written over a period of ten years (2003-2013), and inspired by real people. All of them have passed through a space (the village of Saidí and its surroundings) which, for the author, is both familiar and strange, modifying it completely, and making it incomprehensible.

At the center of Serés's literature, there are vital changes in that their modification (individual and collective), in turn, signifies an adaptation in the perception of reality and the narration's tempo. As the writer explains: "In Saidí, the town where I was born, the landscape imposes itself in a greedy manner and, with the landscape, a determinated concept of passing

---

[1] English translations of titles of works by Serés are: *Els ventres de la terra* (The bellies of the earth), *L'arbre sense tronc* (The tree without a trunk), *Una llengua de plom* (A leaden tongue) (included in the trilogy *De fems i de marbres* – Of manure and marble), and *La pell de la frontera* (The skin of the border).

the time." (Serés 2012, 174). The two books offer a complementary view of a single phenomenon: the living conditions of the people (native and emigrant in the trilogy, immigrant in the collection of short stories) in the territory. The places that form the center of relationships between the people are the road, the fields, the farmhouse, the barns and the bars.

In *L'horitzó primer*[2], Joan Todó (La Sénia, 1977) fictionalizes his return to his native village. After graduating and trying out different jobs, the main character spends the summer in the village, where he has been invited to read the opening speech for the village fête. The book was published in chapters in the magazine *L'Avenç,* and recreates the different rituals by which the co-inhabitants spend their vacations: from discussions in the cafés to the bull running. His return, forced by a lack of resources and work, is the main theme of the book, but it also includes parts of an essay on the history of the village, its characters and institutions. Other themes present are the Spanish Civil War, the *maquis* resistance, discotheques and the gradual decline of the furniture industry which had been the main economic force in the area.

The topography of the area is associated with the horizon in the title (The first horizon), and the lines of the ridges which mark and delimit the border with Aragon: "Entre l'horitzó clos de les muntanyes properes i l'horizó obert, però calitjós, de la costa, és com si dominés el primer" (Todó 2013, 97). *Horitzó,* according to the author, is also a very versatile term in hermeneutics since it relates to a prejudice-free interpretation without any *a priori* ideas. The way that Todó tackles the rural space (lived in and rediscovered) is therefore a free view and one that is charged with history. As a line by Segimon Serrallonga referred to in the text suggests: "la llibertat té llocs, o no ho sabies?" (Todó 2013, 56). His freedom in the end is based on the ultralocal character of the place and in its specificity. This uniqueness depends on the locals' perception, because, according to Simmel, "the mood of the landscape [...] is one pertaining to *just this* particular landscape" (Simmel 2007, 28).

The works of Serés and Todó are not unusual in the current Catalan literary imaginary. Artists like Perejaume and novelists such as Marta Rojals (with *Primavera, estiu, etcètera,* 2011) and Ramon Erra (with *Desfent el nus del mocador,* 2008) have created a solid and incisive work in anthropological and creative descriptions of ways of being (and living) in the village, the place of origins. Their current positioning involves an updated view of Catalan rural life, highly influential, and moving beyond the pictorial and literary romantic tradition. Between them, Serés and Todó offer a complex and personal x-ray of the economic crisis (which has

---

[2] English translation of the title *L'horitzó primer* (The first horizon).

directly affected their generations) and its consequences in the everyday life of the people.

Erra's narrative, on the other hand, recreates certain kinds of rural life, profoundly affected by the changes (physical, economic and ideological) that have shaken Europe over the last thirty years. He is interested in a "visceral" rurality (the author's own adjective) which critics have situated in the postindustrial and postmodern era. Erra explores the lives of marginal characters, placing them in a highly-diversified space that can be found at any point of the Western worldview. And he does so under the (recognized) influence of the Russian and Czech narrative tradition, echoing elements from the stories of Nikolai Gogol, Boris Pilnyak, Isaac Babel and Anton Chekhov, such as the treatment of the ellipsis and the absurd, metaliteral references, and the interrelationships between stories, as well as the linguistic hedonism and the eroticism in the narrations of Bohumil Hrabal.

The space described by these writers is also the *espace vécu* that Armand Frémont considers "révélateur des identités régionales" (Frémont 1976, 14). It is a social space related to the psychological values given to places and which unite people through material links. It is a heterogeneous and combinatory space made up of an "ensemble de relations qui définissent des emplacements irréductibles les uns aux autres et absolument non superposables" (Foucault 2001, 1574). In Serés, the play between the relations that make up the story (and the related landscape) is based on the adoption of an interview format or the resource of using a plurality of voices. In Todó, on the other hand, the play is based on splitting the narrator into a 'You' Writer and Central character, who compete for legitimacy of authorship. At the same time this strategy enables him to build the story, which is described as if it were articulated by his own double.

The way these two writers tackle the fictionalization of the Franja, and the lands of the Ebre, is inseparable from two characteristics that Soja observes in the novel: "an explicitly geographical as well as historical configuration and projection." (Soja 1989, 23). In the construction of a landscape that has been lived in there are several factors, such as collective memory, that give it voice and form, and the historical events that have made it a transit point, subject to alternating waves of emigration and immigration. In that sense, the way it is formed comes from the changes introduced in the spatial and temporal perceptions of modernity: "Modernization [...] is a continuous process of societal restructuring that is periodically accelerated to produce a significant recomposition of space-time-being in their concrete forms, a change that arises primarily from the historical and geographical dynamics of modes of production." (Soja 1989, 27).

The identification between the characters and places means that these historical and geographical changes (determined by the economic logic of capitalism) have a profound effect on the individual, to the point where their relationship with the space becomes problematic. In Serés, the characters belong to places but if they abandon them, the places reject them. Returning involves verifying irreversible changes within them and assuming a process of no return:

> Ja no és casa meva. Vaig viure-hi a dispesa. El teu lloc no és aquí, em repetia sempre la mare quan anava a veure-la; el meu lloc no és aquí, em repetia jo. Sempre hi vaig viure amb un sentiment de provisionalitat que des de petit m'ha acompanyat en tot el que he fet. Res del que he fet ha estat per durar. [...] Ja no és casa meva, i el vidre verdós i translúcid de la porta de baix ja no mostra l'ombra de la mare que obre des de fora. Mostra una uniformitat de color espantós i solitari. La porta té un color que mai no havia tingut (Serés 2003, 79-80).

The relationship of the 'I' with the space, and its (always unmistakable) inadequacy, reappears in Todó, in a work which, as mentioned above, emerges from and justifies itself in the physical return to the place of origin:

> Quan avui dia la gent asseguda al voltant d'una taula folrada amb tovalles de paper recorda la vida aquí, mentre pels camps s'entén el gemec dels grills i les txitxarretes, després que els anys hagin diluït els motius per marxar, amb els inconvenients del present més vius a la memòria, en forma d'angoixes i neguits urgents, el record inventa un paradís perdut on fins i tot els tricornis es tornen entranyables. Cert o no, comences a adonar-te que tornar-hi és impossible. ¿Què és ser d'un lloc? Cada dia, cada mes, cada any que passes lluny d'ell et modifica, te n'allunya. I alhora aquell lloc t'ha dibuixat, d'una manera que la gent de fora percep millor que tu mateix; si ets tu la teua memòria, i la memòria és el relat que et justifica, milers de detalls invisibles procededeixen del lloc on vas nàixer. Com un malnom que et persegueix (Todó 2013, 128).

Rural space

Before analyzing the works of Serés and Todó, we have to ask ourselves what we mean by *rural*. *Rural*, from the Latin *rus* (*field*), is that which "has a place, which occupies a space". Rural space, consequently, would be everything related to the space of the countryside, which it occupies and where it has its place. In the case of the literature in question it is a post industrial rurality, the result of the gradual economic decline of the second half of the twentieth century.

The works by Serés and Todó invert the process in which urbanization of the rural world becomes the basis for the myth of industrial progress. That process, seen by Soja as being an illustrative metaphor for the need of capitalism to *spatialize* in order to reproduce essential relations of production (Soja 1989, 50), enters into crisis. According to Soja, "What distinguished capitalism's gratuitous spatial veil from the spatialities of other modes of production was its peculiar production and reproduction of geographically uneven development via simultaneous tendencies toward homogenization, fragmentation and hierarchization" (Soja 1989, 50).[3]

The fictionalized landscape is partly the result and reaction of that homogenization, fragmentation and hierarchization. With the end of the myth of the progressive city, from the 1970s, the nineteenth century bourgeoisie also disappeared. The loss of the city's privileged centrality and its identification as a political and consumer space (Resina 2012, 12) becomes problematic. This situation, however, is reversed on with the end of the twentieth century. Depopulation in Saidí began during the 1960s, until it received unexpected waves of immigration at the start of the twenty-first century: "[Hi] arribava la gent d'arreu, com hi arribava el món" (Serés 2014, 108). But it was a change that he thought did not alter the occupied landscape and one which illustrated the transitory essence of human life: "Els llocs s'acaben ocupant, al final som nosaltres els que estem de pas." (Serés 2014, 93). There is a moment when the flow stops and becomes blocked.

As Serés reports, the countryside becomes an excluded space, invisible to the media. On becoming an object of representation it is recognized in accordance with the function it has always had: a center of material production, primary source of work and resources for survival. Unlike the city, what conditions the rural habitat is its identification with "a tempo and scale of transformation that goes hand in hand with the generational relay in a human community and can be absorbed through ordinary processes of social and personal adaptation." (Resina 2012, 12).

---

[3] Soja's analysis is based on Lefebvre's theory of "landscape produced by modernity". This space is "homogeneous for various reasons; manufacture of elements and materials [...] methods of management and control, surveillance and communication [...] this homogeneous space is fragmented: lots and parcels. Reduced to crumbs! [...] With a rigid hierarchy: residential areas, commercial areas, leisure areas, areas for the marginalized, etc." (Lefebvre, 2013, 210).

The transformation of these rituals is central to Serés's writing, where the countryside is a humanized space resulting from the work of humans. The three titles in the trilogy show the inextricable link between the land and the people, whether through anthropomorphization: *Els ventres de la terra* (The bellies of the earth) and identification with nature: *L'arbre sans tronc* (The tree without a trunk), or through the symbolic metaphorization of the spoken word *Una llengua de plom* (A leaden tongue). To an extent, the thematization of the world of work is related to one of the most common ideas in Serés's writing (which can also refer to the neorealist literature of the 1960s): the inherent effort of the struggle for human survival. In that material and physical relationship the fatigue associated with experience is perceived: "estic malalt d'experiència" (Serés 2003, 116), "la vida dels altres" (Serés 2003, 117) weighs on me, repeats one of the voices in *Els ventres de la terra*.

In Serés's work, scenes where the characters are absorbed in their contemplation of a landscape in decline, and in unstoppable deterioration, are frequent. The final balance of this meditative observation on the process of extinction is clear: only the matter – an arid land void of biological remnants – remains and equates to incipient spatial differences: "La merda nodreix la ciutat com els fems peixen la terra." (Serés 2003, 231). In stating the antithesis between the ephemeral – manure – and the enduring – marble – the title of the trilogy itself synthesizes what we have just said. In contrast, the landscape encountered by more recent immigrations is, in short, a "[p]aisatge degradat", with no protection or security, with "deixalles dins meu" (Serés 2014, 73) and where "no saps on comença la ruïna i on acaba la brutícia" (Serés 2014, 159).

In an almost cartographic approach to the physical description of the landscape, Serés's literature relates to the pictorial desire to reaffirm that which is visible in painting. The very concept of *landscape* grants authority to what is *visible* in that it presupposes an experience on the ground, a view that seeks to discern and understand. Serés copies visual language when it comes to specifying an appearance that is both personal and ethereal and which is expressed through the medium of images. That is why there are so many photographs in it. The old photographs (blurred and with unrecognizable faces) capture biographical or historical moments which are capable of synthesizing lives and which, over time, have become non-narrative vestiges: only appearances; mute instants in which to sustain a fragile memory of a collective nature. Or images which situate individuals in the course of an unalterable future:

> aquesta és l'herència que has rebut, el reconeixement que tota aquesta desferra és solament una aparença, la visió diària que sota el cresp tèrbol

dels anys passats, sota el tel volvós d'aquest batibull, hi ha alguna cosa que s'esdevé en el temps travessant des de lluny l'esgavell, quelcom d'una noblesa excessiva que tiba en la mateixa direcció que ho fan els fils que et mouen, que mous, on ets lligat (Serés 2003, 317).

As Viestenz states, "Serés postulates that the core of representing one's own geographical space through a particular form, whether it be cinematic or novelistic, derives from a relationship with structures erected by member of other cultural groupings" (Viestenz 2012, 151-2). This is well exemplified by the description of the Monegros desert, which is compared to the spaces in Westerns, a *topos* that is both individual and collective:

El món s'acabava als Monegres, que encara eren meus. Em pertanyien de la mateixa manera que em sol pertànyer una part dels límits que habitem. Els abastava i m'incloïen perquè allà hi havia el final del món conegut i l'inici de la història. De la història amb majúscules, de l'origen de tots els mals, l'escenari d'una guerra civil que era el punt [de partida] de totes les coses trencades, que arriben fins avui. Era el lloc dels temps sense temps, la guerra s'instal·lava en una època llunyana però a la vegada intensament viva, constant, present (Serés 2014, 193).

The space of the desert is also the place which shows the failure of human activity. The Monegros was populated during the period of Franco until it started to lose demographic and economic weight and returned to waste land. With the crisis, erosion would not become just a physical but also an anthropological phenomenon: "*Crisi* vol dir 'migració', vol dir que arriba un punt que els pobles es tornen irrecuperables, que la desertització no és tan sols un fenomen geològic." (Serés 2014, 199).

Todó, for his part, sees landscape as a detailed tapestry with distinguishable geographical elements comparable with the profiles of certain animals:

Per a tu, aquest tapís té un dibuix concret, la línia de moles, tosses i serrats que es veu des del terrat de cals teus pares. Un amfiteatre blavós, aplanat contra el cel, que de xiquet perfilaves una vegada i una altra en els teus blocs de dibuix, afinant obsessivament la línia sinuosa que arrenca sobre el campanar de Rossell, el poble veí, s'allarga per la Lloma del Gegant, cau al Coll de les Tones, s'arrodoneix a la Roca del Migdia abans d'aixecar-se en una petita graonada i, després de passar per la Tossa, s'enfonsa en la vall de la Sénia, s'aixeca novament, com un onatge congelat, cap a la serra de Pallerols i mor a la dreta dels Tres Castells, de camí cap al Mas de Barberans (Todó 2013, 13).

It is a landscape presented as a "sinuous line" similar to the lines of a drawing, which is presented to the viewer as if it were an "amphitheatre", in front of which the narrator, following it with his eyes, proceeds to assign names. Finally, it is also a mobile nature which "s'allarga" (elongates), "s'arrodoneix" (becomes rounded), "s'enfonsa" (sinks) and "s'aixeca" (rises up). In the midst of this "diffuse" geography (Todó 2013, 15), which depends of the random arrangement of infrastructures is the village of La Sénia.

Unlike the fiction of Serés which, as we have seen, takes as his theme the world of work, Todó describes the locality as a village that has "sempre ha tendit a ser un poble embadalit, tancat en si mateix" (Todó 2013, 40). The tedium of the summer months (when the main character arrives) accentuates the sense of sleepiness.

At the same time, the landscape delimits the vital expectations of La Sénia's inhabitants, among which the main character feels *dépaysé*. Therefore, the horizon of the village (and its limits) is also the horizon that decides the friends of the narrator's generation:

> Rere els seus gestos endevines un horitzó molt determinat, descobreixes que mentre tu no hi eres, mentre anaven passant els anys que us semblaven idèntics, desaparcebuts sota el pas de cada dia, heu sofert tots una transformació [...]. El seu univers gira al voltant dels fills. Dels estris de la llar, de les prestacions dels automòbils, dels preus de les coses, de les petites intrigues per surar a la feina i dels fitxatges del Barça; totes les alteracions metereològiques que envolten aquest contou amenaceu aquests camps sembrats on ell fa la seva vida, aquestes terres que ara, de cop, veu assetjades per una maltempsada (Todó 2013, 41).

A space of words and memory

Writing about rural space, and more specifically about the experience of seeing and living in rural space becomes, in the works of Serés and Todó, the main topic of the story. There is a kind of self-reflection there which is expressed in relation to the writing process and the questions and vacillations involved in the treatment of something that has already been seen and experienced. The (visual and verbal) code is the object of reflection on beings in the world. That also ratifies the fictional centrality of space. Perec refers to this in a description which, like Serés, relates the task of the writer to that of the land surveyor:

> L'espace commence ainsi, avec seulement des mots, des signes tracés sur la page blanche. Décrire l'espace: le nommer, le tracer, comme ces faiseurs des portulans qui saturaient les côtes de noms de ports, de noms de caps, de

noms de criques, jusqu'à ce que la terre finisse par ne plus être séparée de la mer que par un ruban continu de texte. L'aleph, ce lieu borgésien où le monde entier est simultanément visible, est-il autre chose qu'un alphabet? (Perec 1974, 21).

The literary space is therefore also linguistic space. In *De fems i de marbres* the language serves, adamically, to name and control the world and make it apprehensible. Furthermore, language gives coherence to a reality which is fragmented from epistemological and physical point of view. The first part of the trilogy (*Els ventres de la terra*), with its collective protagonism, explores different moments in twentieth century rural life. The countryside is the center of it and is also seen as a leitmotif, a transmitter, of life and memory:

En la meva memòria els camps de blat són tots els llocs i les baules són els altres, els que han viscut amb mi en cadascun dels moments en què he tingut vida, els que tinc ara ordenats curosament, com una commemoració de fets que són baules, el cinema, la taverna, la granja, la ciutat i el mercat (Serés 2003, 138).

In *L'arbre sense tronc* the main character is Assís, who learns languages in the marketplace and uses them as a vehicle for naming things and exchanging them. He goes to the city to carry on studying and get a good command of them in the same say that man tries to control the earth: "Estudiï llengües, i no deixi que les llengües l'estudiïn a vostè", he is advised by a mentor (Serés 2003, 212). Although he now knew the names for urban things, city life disorientates him. The first-person discourse of the narration, from the mouth of a character who makes language his profession, focuses on what he can say, because it is what he knows: it is the result of his sensory experience of the world. Landscapes, smells, cries. But it is the way he sees landscape that marks the starting point for his reflection on the world, the tiny microcosmos in which he lives, made up of "fields" and "earth". He tells his wife about it:

Mira tot el blat que es veu des d'aquest turó, Maria, com oneja. Diries que s'assemella a tots els blats, diries que és el mateix blat de sempre, el rònec dels primers anys i l'espès de quan es van posar els regadius, i també el que va començar a canviar de fesomia quan van portar tractors, el sembrat per on passejàvem quan tornàvem de la ciutat a veure els pares. El mateix blat de sempre damunt la mateixa terra i, tanmateix, no res, tot de caps que es mouen ensems, no res, això és el que som, no res (Serés 2003: 312).

The main character in *Una llengua de plom* is a land surveyor. Again, contact with the rural space occurs from what is measurable and palpable.

More than just the maps (Serés's literature is full of cartographies), man is also required to try to interpret them:

> ¿Què diuen els plànols? No diuen res, els plànols, res no diuen quan tot es parla en una llengua estranya i àdhuc el més migrat dels senyals s'amaga rere la sorda faiçó de la Vall, aquesta extensió de plantes seques i erms deixats créixer salvatges [...] Els plànols no són el terrer, res no es pot traduir. Els camins que t'ensenyen els plànols estan, en realitat, coberts de malesa, d'herbes que es vinclen fins al mig del camí (Serés 2003: 319, 321).

These fictionalized places are also spaces with which humans have to come to an agreement, and this takes them into a battle (a job) that is won with the acceptance of human perishability and the limitations of human knowledge to understand and comprehend them. Faced with the non-places of Marc Augé we can also find anthropological places: identificational, relational and historical, all heavily charged with memory. These places participate in the production of a sense which is the basis of ontological knowledge: "In its productive role, and as a producer, space (well or badly organized) becomes part of the relations of production and the forces of production" (Lefebvre 2003, 208).

In Serés, it is only the voices of the natives that allow us to enter deeper into the reality of the landscape. They are the depositaries of collective thought, inherited from a univocal and foreseeable interpretation:

> es tractava de no canviar el sentit que sempre havien tingut la casa i la família vers allò que havia de fer aquí al món, el nom, el món, la paraula, tot plegat constituint una veritable unitat que mai no podria trencar-se, i que més enllà del lloc on jo o els meus descendents fóssim tot s'havia de perpetuar, les coses que passen, passen perquè han de passar, no pot ser d'altra manera (Serés 2003, 293).

With the crisis, verbal comprehension of the world is called into question in *La pell de la frontera*. This book acts in counterpoint to *De fems i de marbres* insofar as it portrays the present of the last decade, a period characterized by the inherent uncertainty of liquid societies. Only the nature of the world seems to respond to a certain regulation: "El gran ecosistema que ens abraça a tots, encara que pensem que el nostre és el que compta, aplanarà altra vegada el paisatge i la història, com si res no hagués passat." (Serés 2014, 168). Faced with that, literature is just a volatile sketch (a gesture?): "Escriure era com intentar descriure un núvol que canvia de forma fins que desapareix" (Serés 2014, 304).

In Todó, as well, the instability of language is the result of the instability of the landscape, situated in a "tercera perifèria" (third periphery) "oblidada generalment pels polítics i els discursos oficials" and characterized by a particular linguistic diversity (Todó 2013, 56):

> És la tercera perifèria que vas anomenar tu al pregó, sense identitat fixa, extramurs de les essències que unifiquen el col·lectiu, oblidada. En aquest territori, de fet, fins i tot el llenguatge és inestable: fas una passa i ja has xafat una isoglossa. [...] El llenguatge es replega com una pell al dedins d'un colze, cada cosa té dos o tres noms, cada paraula tres o quatre formes diferents (Todó 2013, 97-8).

A space of knowledge

"¿[B]uscan los hombres, a través del paisaje, aquello que no son?" wondered Claudio Guillén (1998, 98). The landscape shapes man and man projects himself onto it, in a relationship that involves self-recognition in relation to the world. This is expressed, again, by Guillén:

> se nos hace difícil no considerar muchos paisajes como entornos nuestros, reales o inminentes, aunque no estemos en ellos, o bien simbólicamente como vías de reconocimiento de nuestra situación en el mundo. Así, el paisaje es la vez omisión y conquista del hombre. En el paisaje el hombre se vuelve invisible, pero no su mirada y acaso su construcción de un sentido (Guillén 1998, 98).

As we will see, this "construction of sense" is based on the use of certain poetical images, which have "un dynamisme propre" (Bachelard 1958, 2). In *De fems i de marbres* knowledge comes from the symbolical subjectivization of the outside reality. Stories are constructed *in media res*, in retrospective temporal movement. There are two processes for subjectivizing space: humanization and identification with the landscape (a theme that was introduced in the previous point) and the use of memory and recollection. In terms of memory, as Jean Yves and Marc Tadié remind us (Tadié 1999, 15), it is affective (and therefore a carrier of emotions) and imaginative (involving a reconstructive factor). Therefore, emotions with a transforming burden are associated with and shape the story. At the same time, memory, according to Resina, involves a "sense of identity, which can be defined at two separate moments of consciousness – whether it be the subject that it present to itself or the community that renews itself through intergenerational making present of its central values and wisdom" (Resina 2012, 14). That is why it is an element that makes it possible to transcend individual identification and to facilitate the intergenerational transmission of knowledge, thereby constructing that sense of identity.

Serés conceives of writing as a kind of anagnorisis through which he positions himself (and positions 'the other') in a time and a place, and interrogates himself about the uncertain nature of reality. Moreover, in *La pell de la frontera* he denounces the paradox that, at a time of irreversible changes, protection and security seem to be under the control of the giant food corporations dedicated to transgenics, storage and conservation. The arrival of the "gent d'arreu" (Serés 2014, 108), from a world that goes past leaving sediments, is seen as a necessity with an enormous human cost. It is "el món [que] ja no s'aturava enlloc" (p. 68), made up of Senegalese, Malians, Guineans, Nigerians and Moroccans, who have arrived "perquè nosaltres no perdéssim el món de vista" (Serés 2014, 72).

The unstoppable flow of life, and the problems in talking about it and creating interest in it, are centered in a reflection when the 'I' is seen to be obliged to constantly reformulate itself – it is born and ends in every book (Serés 2014, 299). The author constructs "[...] històries minúscules, desplaçades i desencaixades, parcials, arraconades, vaporoses, difícils de descriure i possiblement mentideres, errònies." (Serés 2014, 108). Faced with a tribal mentality, we find the perishable reality of each character's voice, problematic in its ineffability: "Tot l'ordre del començament s'ha desfet en el xerrar" (Serés 2003, 254).

The collective dimension of the story, however, is called into question in Serés when the narrator talks of the radically solitary dimension of the human condition, whether in the countryside (where amoral familism is practiced), or in the city (where anomie occurs). The origin of the community itself (explained in "Ser", the oldest story in *De fems i de marbres*, with a fictitious date of 1893), denies the unifying capacity by including incest. The structure of the work tends to gradually emphasize the feeling of isolation of the individual, with numerous references to abandoned land.

Many of the characters find themselves in a liminal situation which underlines the so-called "border paradox" (Certeau 1990, 186-187); in other words, the idea that anything which is separated is simultaneously united by the thing that separates it. The title *La pell de la frontera* is a beautiful example of this. Skin, as a frontier, isolates and brings us together. The solitude of the characters is accentuated in that sense by the solitary condition that distinguishes them, on the one hand, from the group and, on the other, from the process of de-ruralization which they are indirectly witness to. In the story, the resulting secularization is relative; it does not include desacralization because it does not have a transcendent dimension.

In *L'horitzó primer,* knowledge of the place is based on the invocation of historical and legendary figures (like the Tiger of the Maestrat – Ramon Cabrera – and 'la Pastora'), the observation of the territory and, more specifically, a succession of scenes that are descriptive of the day-to-day, such as the weather. So the summer-autumn continuity corresponds to the description of the shaping of the weather in the landscape, and it allows the cyclical passing of time to become established. These descriptions are focused on changing and ethereal phenomena, which modify the perception of the landscape and introduce sensorial tones: "Els crepuscles són una brasa vermella, atiada pel vent de l'endemà. Una difusa olor de fum d'olivera repta el carrer" (Serés 2013, 117). The scene described is embellished through the metaphorization of subtle elements such as the clouds and the sun:

> Enguany fa uns dies de juliol estranys, amb núvols que cobreixen el cel, burells i inflats, però que després se'n van sense deixar anar cap gota d'aigua. La llum canvia a cada moment, i els turons es cobreixen d'un tapís sinuós d'ombres corbades, que sembla que juguin amb les línies de l'horitzó. A cada nuvolada hom pensa que ja està, que ha arribat el xàfec, que l'aigua és aquí; després comencen a aparèixer clapes de blau, el sol travessa com un ganivet de foc la llana grisa del cel i comença a rostir una carena, envaint-ho tot a poc a poc (Todó 2013: 39).

Conclusions

The rural literature explored in this article is characterized by its specific and experienced nature. Located on border territory, the writing is stimulated by the desire to reformulate spaces in continual transformation, either through the use of characters with whom the reader can identify, or through moveable phenomena such as time. In that sense, the stories commented on typify a sector of contemporary creation that has as its center the peripheral space around the big metropolis (Barcelona, in the Catalan case). They are narrations that turn circles around anodyne characters, valuable for their stories, centered in the world of work and daily survival. Films like *Petit indi* (2009), by Marc Recha, and fictional documentaries such as *La plaga* (2013), by Neus Ballús share this focus. Their works recreate a hybrid space in permanent mutation, crossed by the roads, rivers and fields. They form self-sufficient territories, with their own rules, where alternative communities and atypical families spring up.

Their survival depends on their empirical knowledge of the rural reality. In the midst of the global era, Serés's and Todó's view of rural life remind us of the importance and the relief of what is local (and on which, according Cliffort Geertz, depends social knowledge), or the power of evocation of the place, associated with its literature, its history and memory. All of this marks a very interesting space of transition, similar to the way in which Majorcan writer Emili Manzano concluded his book *Pinyols d'aubercoc*: "Demà me'n vaig. Tendré una altra pell. No tan enfora com per mudar de llengua, però a bastament com per mudar d'accent. La meva llengua haurà de tocar altres racons de la boca per dir certes paraules..." (Manzano 2008, 125-126). With this "canvi de llengua" (change of language) these writers build imaginary places, which imply a "generatrice" conception of the space and, to conclude, the configuration of a singular poetic (Grassin 2000, XII).

References

Bachelard, Gaston. 1958. *La poétique de l'espace*. Paris : Presses Universitaires de France.
Berger, John. 1972. *Ways of Seeing*. London: British Broadcasting Corporation and Penguin Books.
—. 1991. *About Looking*. New York/London: Random House/Vintage.
Certeau, Michel de. 1990. *L'invention du quotidien. 1. Arts de faire*. Paris : Gallimard.
Erra, Ramon. 2008. *Desfent el nus del mocador*. Barcelona: La Magrana.
Grassin, Jean-Marie. 2000. "Pour une science des espaces littéraires". *La géocritique. Mode d'emploi*. Limoges : Presses Universitaires de Limoges, I-XIII.
Guillén, Claudio. 1998. *Múltiples moradas: Ensayo de literatura comparada*. Barcelona: Tusquets.
Frémond, Armand. 1976. *La région, espace vécu*. [Paris] : Presses Universitaires de France.
Foucault, Michel. 2001. "Des espaces autres". *Dits et écrits (1954-1988)*. 2nd vol. Paris : Gallimard.
Lefebvre, Henri. 2003. "Preface to New Edition (from *La production de l'espace*, 1986)". *Key Writings*. Edited by Stuart Elden, Elizabeth Lebas and Eleonore Kofman. New York/London: Continuum, 206-213.
Manzano, Emili. 2008. *Pinyols d'aubercoc*. Barcelona: L'Avenç.
Perec, Georges. 1974. *Espèces d'espaces*. Paris : Éditions Galilée.

Resina, Joan Ramon. 2012. "The Modern Rural". *The New Rural. An Epistemology of Transformed Space*, edited by J. R. Resina, William R. Viestenz. Madrid: Iberoamaericana/Vervuert, 7-25.

Rojals, Marta. 2011. *Primavera, estiu, etcètera.* Barcelona: La Magrana.

Serés, Francesc. 2003. *De fems i de marbres: trilogia.* Barcelona: Quaderns Crema.

—. 2014. "That". *The New Rural. An Epistemology of Transformed Space*, edited by J. R. Resina, William R. Viestenz. Madrid: Iberoamaericana/ Vervuert, 7-25.

—. 2014. *La pell de la frontera.* Barcelona: Quaderns Crema.

Simmel, Georg. 2007. "The Philosophy of the Landscape" [1913], *Theory, Culture & Society*, 24 (7-8), pp. 20-29.

Soja, Edward W. 1989. *Postmodern Geographies: The Reassertion of Space in Critical Social Theory.* London/New York: Verso.

Tadié, Jean Yves & Marc. 1999. *Le sens de la mémoire.* Paris: Gallimard.

Todó, Joan. 2013. *L'horitzó primer.* Barcelona: L'Avenç.

Viestenz, William R. 2012. "De mots a terra: Linguistic Ruin in Francesc Serés's *L'arbre sense tronc*". *The New Rural. An Epistemology of Transformed Space*, edited by J. R. Resina, William R. Viestenz. Madrid: Iberoamaericana/Vervuert, 139-155.

CHAPTER THREE

JOSEP PLA'S RURAL WORLD: A 'PHILOSOPHY OF LIFE'?

JOAN TORT-DONADA AND ROSA CATALÀ-MARTICELLA

Introduction

This chapter seeks to provide an overall vision of the 'rural' concept in the works of the Catalan writer Josep Pla (Palafrugell, province of Girona, 1897-1981). Some of his essays, specifically those describing the rural landscape and rural world and written between 1940 and 1970, are extensively used as our primary source of information. Pla's works have been chosen as he is generally considered the writer to have made the widest and most meaningful contribution to Catalan contemporary literature. He was, essentially, a descriptive writer who evoked in many of his essays the landscape of his homeland. Furthermore, Pla defined himself as a farmer (*pagès* in Catalan, 'a man of the soil'), because of his own family background, in keeping with the idea that this occupation involves a particular way (both pragmatic and transcendent) of understanding life and culture. In fact, the works of Pla suggest two directions of study, directions that we have explored on other occasions and which we intend, to some degree, to return to here: on the one hand, his work as a key to discover the contemporary meaning of the rural world not only in Catalonia and Spain but also in other parts of Europe; and, on the other, his work as a tool to tackle, in a creative manner, the great questions and challenges the rural world faces in this the second decade of the twenty-first century – that is to say, in the era of globalisation.

At the heart of this chapter is a main section in which we explore the interactions between *landscape* and the *rural world* in Josep Pla's work, two central concepts in his writing and the object of constant reflection throughout his work. In this section we raise a number of questions that we consider fundamental to our understanding of Pla. Not so much as a subject in their own right, but rather as substantive pillars of his literary universe: the perception of the environment in terms of its landscapes, the pre-eminence of the rural world in this perception and the understanding of agrarian practices in terms of their "utility" and of the figure of the farmer as a permanently active creator of landscape. Before this main section, we offer a brief biographical note about Josep Pla and another about his literary style, which some critics have called "synthetic realism" or "poetic realism". We conclude the chapter with some final reflections, as a means of summarizing the main ideas raised throughout the discussion.

Josep Pla: a biographical note

Josep Pla was born in 1897 in Palafrugell, a small town (of just 7,100 inhabitants in 1900) in the province of Girona, lying in the extreme north-east of Spain. This town is the capital of the district or *comarca* of the Baix Empordà, the geography of which was to have a marked impact on all that he was to write. Born into a family of small rural landholders, throughout his life he fiercely defended his ties to the land and the family's farming traditions; yet, he never dedicated himself to farming. The first few years of his life were spent in this his birthplace: a truly rural setting that was to influence greatly the writer's personality. In 1907 he went to Girona to begin his secondary schooling. In the autumn of 1913 he moved to Barcelona, and enrolled at the Law Faculty of the University. He began writing for local magazines, and in 1918 set out on his career as a journalist. In 1919, he started work as a press correspondent for various newspapers, and spent long periods in France, Italy and England. For a brief period, he became active in local politics, and was an elected representative in the *Mancomunitat* (the name given to what is today the autonomous government of Catalonia). In 1925 he saw the first of his many books published: *Coses vistes*, which, according to the critics, showed very early indications of a highly original literary style, and which, with the years, would leave its indelible mark on modern Catalan literature (Fuster 1976).

The following books also date from this early period: *Rússia* (1925), *Cartes de lluny* (1928), *Francesc Cambó* (1928-30) and *Madrid: l'adveniment de la República* (1933). Pla actively participated in the events of these times as a political journalist, but in July 1936 he was to go abroad, not returning to Barcelona until 1939. The Civil War was to represent a turning point in his life. From 1940 until his death (1981), Pla's life was to revolve around his farmhouse or *masia* in Catalan, in

Llofriu, a place that he only ever abandoned sporadically in order to set out on one of his great journeys. In his home, isolated from the world, he worked intensively and wrote prolifically, both for the press and his own books. The following are just some of the works that date from this period, *Guia de la Costa Brava* (1941), *Viatge en autobús* (1942), *Un senyor de Barcelona* (1945), *Els pagesos* (1952) and *Homenots* (1958-62). In 1966, the publication of his Complete Works was set in motion, reaching completion in 1986 with the publication of his forty-fifth book. He died in April 1981, in his *masia*, having completed one of the richest and most extensive bodies of literary work in the history of Catalan literature: the volumes of his Complete Works, amounting to more than 30,000 pages, attest to the magnitude of his contribution. Among these books one genre stands out, that of the essay, which Pla used in developing a work in which the exploration of the memory becomes the primary axis of reflection (Xavier Pla 1997).

Pla's ties with the rural world throughout his life are apparent – directly and indirectly; explicitly and implicitly – in all his work. But perhaps it is in his 1952 essay – *Els pagesos* – where the author expresses most clearly this personal attachment, to the point of presenting it as his "philosophy of life" (Tort, and Paül 2008). A paragraph from this book captures this idea perfectly:

> My world is the world of the *pagesos*. I am a man of farming stock. All my family on my father's side have always lived in a *masia* (...) in the Empordà, since before the Council of Trent. On my mother's side, this farming background is equally deep-rooted. (...) What's more, I have spent the second part of my life in the house of my ancestors in the Empordà in constant contact with the land and the people who live there. (...) There is no specific literary, sociological or economic reason to account for my contact with the rural world (...): it is due simply to the fact that I form a basic part of it, that I am a microscopic element within this vast human magma (Pla 1975, 263-264).

Pla's literary style: synthetic realism (or *poetic realism*)

Among critical studies of the work of Josep Pla, that of Joan Fuster (Fuster 1983; first edition 1966) is considered a classic. Here, we wish to take this as our main point of reference, together with a short chapter this author also dedicates to Pla (Fuster 1976, 257-62). Overall, his reflections concerning the literary ideas of the Catalan writer, and his art of writing and of describing, as well as his conception of realism, are of great use to us in developing our argument here.

Fuster claims that Pla took on the occupation of writer based on a simple premise, or perhaps not so much a premise as an imperative: "To explain oneself and make oneself understood" (Fuster 1976, 258). Later, Pla himself offers us more clues as to how he believed this objective could be achieved: "The first duty of a writer is to observe, describe and capture the period he has been born into. All this is infinitely more important than any useless, sterile attempts to achieve a wild, primeval originality"[1]. For Fuster, Pla belongs without any question to the line of 'realist' writers: "[Pla] only accepts that literature which is based on what is *real* and he seeks in the *real* the emotion that delights. What Pla called 'reality, that marvellous, enormous, mysterious reality that surrounds us and which we never tire of exploring' has to be, he writes, the object of the writer's lucid investigations" (Fuster 1983, 25). Seen in this way, writing (or the "practice of writing") essentially becomes a way of being aware of this "marvellous", "enormous", "mysterious" (and we would add "highly complex") reality that surrounds us. Ultimately, this is the underlying rationale of *synthetic realism*: the literary model to which Josep Pla's writing is constantly associated, according to Fuster. In the specific model of synthetic realism, Fuster reasons, "the writer is not a mirror [...], but a man; that is, a point of view, a temperament, a talent, a sensitivity. The greatest achievements of literary realism are imbued with the personality of their authors: reality is played out in the book, in each case, selected, adjudged and reorganised by the man that describes it and reflects on it." (Fuster 1983, 68).

In our view, the literary concept of *synthetic realism*, in the terms in which it has been outlined, offers interesting possibilities for application in the field of geography. In fact, this is nothing new, to the extent that we believe *synthesis* – understood in the grammatical sense of "composition of a whole" (Real Academia Española 1984, II, 1249) continues to be an operation or method that is genuinely linked to the work of the geographer. Suffice it to note in this regard that if in the previous paragraph we were to replace the word "writing" with "geography" and "writer" with "geographer", the reflections of Pla and Fuster alike would continue to make complete sense. While we await the opportunity to develop these ideas further, we would like to insist here on one specific idea that goes a long way to summarizing our contention: if we agree with Nicolás Ortega (Ortega 1987) regarding the *cultural* focus of geographical knowledge – a focus that sees the task of the geographer as one of "knowing how to see" and which concerns itself equally with the "object" and "subject" of this knowledge, then we can conclude that geography

---

[1] Pla, quoted in Fuster 1976, 259.

should converge in multiple ways with literature as it seeks to account for the world. After all, is this not what geographers have tried to do for centuries, in spite of the "subjective bias" that their worldview might have conveyed?

Landscape and the rural world in the work of Josep Pla: two closely related concepts

The landscape is widely present in the work of Josep Pla. Scholars of his output recognise essentially two central themes in his literature: *people* and *landscape*. This should come as little surprise, for an author who sees his work as a "global chronicle" of the society and the times in which he lived. "I have wanted to describe the country of my time": this sentence, almost a principle, and one that Pla wrote in the prefaces to some of his travel books, is quoted by Joan Fuster as being defining of Pla's personal worldview (Fuster 1983, 19). Probably, it sums up, in the most succinct way possible, his way of seeing both literature and life.

Pla studied the landscape because he was interested in everything he saw, indeed, in everything that he could perceive with his senses. In the words of Fuster, "his curiosity – the curiosity of the writer – explores the world with its antennas always alert, and the landscapes and people, however different from his own, have for him the infallible seduction of life, of any form of life. And he does not ignore them. He can turn anything into a subject for his writing" (Fuster 1983, 75). The appreciation he transcribes is notable, since it serves as a measure of the potential that the "landscape dimension" can have in his work; especially, if we accept the maxim that everything that fits in the human gaze can be landscape. At one point, Pla writes that "The Empordà is before anything else a landscape" (Pla 1988, 204). And if we agree that this corner of Catalonia is, in many ways, his main focus of interest, we can understand that in the writer's particular gaze of this land lies latent a lesson of deeply experienced geography (Tort, 1992).

Pla makes copious use of the word landscape. On occasions, he will repeat it two or three times on the same page. But often, without actually mentioning it, he is able to compose extraordinarily vivid landscape paintings. Consider this example of the *comarca* (or district) of the Maresme:

> If with the tremor of the waves to our backs we head inland up into the little valleys formed by the falling mountain slopes, we find such sunny spots, reigned over by a sense of calm, so peaceful and idyllic, so heavily

scented with the plants of the south, an air so silent and clear, that they are like delicious oases. These spots are usually small, enclosed, endearingly intimate. Sometimes a tiny village can be found huddled up in the small hollow of a valley (Pla 1976, 759).

Whether the word 'landscape' appears in the text or not is perhaps largely irrelevant. But given that we are dealing with Pla, and with a literature of the characteristics of Pla's, we believe that it is anything but irrelevant. Its use, generally intentional, attracts our attention because it is not usual, at least not in ordinary literature. And it can be significant of the "centrality" of this theme in his work. It is worth noting, in this regard, that in some of his guides and travel books certain sections make explicit reference to this very question. But it is important that the reader is not taken in by appearances. On one occasion, Pla writes:

> The people of the Empordà never speak of the landscape and avoid – out of delicacy, I suspect – any such intellectual conversation to avoid being taken for dullards. The landscape forms part of the conversations that only those of a certain kind of people can have – people who, in short, that are unhappy and of little substance (Pla 1988, 206).

The paradox is more than evident. At the theoretical level it appears that for Pla any discussion of the landscape is something elitist and highbrow. Perhaps there is some truth in this, above and beyond any attempt at irony. But what is very clear, given the "landscape content" of a significant part of his literary output, is that Pla does speak of landscapes. And he does so in a very significant way, if we consider his whole body of work. It is an aspect that, from the perspective of our analysis, we consider essential to stress.

How does Pla approach the treatment of such a fundamental concept as landscape in his work? To what extent does his particular approach to the landscape shed light on his worldview as a writer, and on his particular conception of rural life? These are questions that we address below, examining a number of key statements which allow us take a systematic approach to the study of the fundamental thinking of Josep Pla on these subjects.

The rural landscape as the landscape *par excellence*

Pla frequently fixes his gaze on rural settings. As such, we can speak of a certain "centrality" of the rural landscape in his work. On the one hand, we can identify this as his environment of reference, as he himself reveals on occasions. But, on the other, the rural landscape is also the landscape of his dreams: "One of the things that would give me most pleasure would be one day to own a house and a garden, a cabbage patch, a cherry tree and a cow" (quoted in Fuster 1983, 36). In addition, this "centrality" is also related to the fact that towns and cities instil within him a sense of distrust. Some of his thoughts on Barcelona allow us to perceive the echo of this particular personal predisposition:

A human mass that possesses not so much a diamond edge as a purely biological power of absorption – the aspirations of a gigantic sponge (Pla 2013, 61).

[In Barcelona] everything is very different, in terms of life's immediate claims everything is bigger and more important, but I find little that appeals to me (Pla 2013, 320).

However, these feelings of mistrust for the urban life of Barcelona do not prevent him from often showing a genuine fascination for the capital of Catalonia.[2] And, in general, he has a quite open-minded opinion of the city, especially, compared with certain nationalistic sentiments in the rest of the territory in which Barcelona is presented as the "danger to be combatted". Regardless of these considerations, what seems clear throughout his work is that the landscape is a concept that takes shape as he leaves the city and enters into the rural world[3]:

The original reason that led the city of Olot to extend its local boundaries was its landscape, so often painted, written and sung about (Pla 1976, 803).

The city [Figueres] is clean and hospitable. I go to see the plain of the High Ampurdan from Castle Hill. A magnificent sight: an incomparable, entrancing, beautiful landscape. What wondrous sky, sea, and land! (Pla 2013, 237).

---

[2] For example, in the following extract: "Barcelona is the capital of Catalonia. From the most distant times, the weight of Barcelona's history has had such a bearing on Catalonia and on the lands with which it shares a language that nothing that has happened in this city has left them unaffected. Barcelona has an enormously strong gravitational pull. With each passing day it will grow stronger. With each passing day this becomes clearer" (Pla 1976, 733-4).

[3] Although not always. In the first pages of his *Guia de Catalunya* he tells us, for example: "We will visit an infinite number of urban and agrarian landscapes" (Pla 1976, 733). It could be said that, throughout his work, he applies the word *landscape* preferably, but not exclusively, to rural settings.

From the beach of Sa Bauma the old town [of Tossa], with its towers and walls, dominates this splendid picture. Behind the beach there is a small lovely landscape of orchards, carob, pine and almond trees (Pla 1976, 49).

In all three cases he provides 'picture postcard' descriptions of the towns and cities, but the countryside that surrounds them is explicitly *landscape*. The distinction, however, is no obstacle to our experiencing the extraordinary descriptive powers of the author captured in these urban paintings: the "intra-urban" landscape and the sites occupied by the cities. This can be appreciated in the following texts about Palma de Mallorca and Palamós:

And the streets are still silent. The streets of the palaces and courtyards where the years pass in a sweet drowsiness of exquisite peace, as if only vaguely lived in. As you walk, you sense a nostalgia for a life that is escaping us, a life that draws breath from this intuition and foreboding. In these hidden, solitary streets, the city offers us it noblest, most solemn profile, its stone embellished by the miraculous touch of time (Pla 1976, 388-9).

Palamós is a well located town. It sits in the bottom of a bend of a fabulously elegant bay, on high ground reaching out a little into the sea. In the gentlest point in the bend lies the port, while its houses line up along the shore, looking west and south. The houses perch on top of the promontory. From a distance the town has a certain coherence, centred around the church tower, in front of the sea (Pla 1988, 701).

In fact, Pla was fascinated by general city panoramas. Specifically, he wrote that "The urban geometry, which when seen close up tends to be horrible, profits greatly when seen in all its panorama" (Pla 2013, 248). It is worth noting that Pla often takes pleasure in the differences in perception derived from "the change of scale". In the following texts about Palafrugell and Sóller, we also find indications of this:

[In the outskirts of Palafrugell:] Each vineyard has a pit for making sulphur and a shack. These urban elements scattered across the land humanise the landscape and make it more companionable (Pla 2013, 218).

The landscape around Palafrugell is dotted with small houses and shacks. It is a well-furnished landscape, full of life (Pla 2013, 275).

Something truly delightful to behold are the houses in the village of Sóller, literally buried in a world of plant life, their roofs emerge from amidst the thick of the orchards and all the slopes of the surrounding mountains display an explosion of greenery. The town itself, the streets of Sóller, are lined with trees, and in some places the plane trees are so boastful you would believe them to have been transported here from some town in the centre of France (Pla 1976, 474).

The agrarian landscape as a "useful landscape"

In Pla's work, among what we generically identify as rural landscapes, the "agrarian" landscape dominates all others; that is, the landscapes specifically linked to agrarian activities are the ones he cares for most. The reason for this seems to lie in the fact that only landscapes that generate some kind of wealth can be described as beautiful (Fuster 1983, 62) And for Pla, who presented himself to the world as a *pagès*, as "a man of the land", the landscape that generates wealth *par excellence* is the agrarian landscape. The following excerpt is eloquent in this regard:

> Gardens are beautiful. Orchards are adorable. They are, moreover, perfectly adapted to the times we live. The most beautiful landscapes are those born of a utilitarian beauty, which are edible, with their roots in Roman law and personal liberty (Pla 1976, 763).

We transcribe below a selection of texts describing different agrarian landscapes. The author undertakes the descriptions with elegance and sensitivity, transmitting to the reader a real sense of joy:

> On these springtime evenings one of the things that lifts me – that distracts me, I mean – is the sight of the allotments on the outskirts of towns. They are wonderfully kept and exquisitely cultivated. [...] These little plots are full of the coolness of the earth. The soft green leaves, coursing with sap, bring calm and repose to the mind. This plentiful harvest combats the painful light of the declining day (Pla 2013, 54-5).

> The small house, centred on El Canadell beach, is clean and pleasant but makes me uneasy when I enter. [...] There is a little front garden with a wrought-iron fence and a small orchard in the back. The orchard has two or three trees laden with the tastiest greengage plums (Pla 2013, 125).

> Here we find a great landscape [referring to the plain of the Alt Penedès]. It never descends into elegance, it remains at all times solid, useful and serious. It is a landscape that we can only ever conceive of in terms of the cultivation of the land in one of its most intelligent forms (Pla 1976, 1025).

Changes to the agricultural landscape are accepted only reluctantly, but always with the criterion of their utility as a fundamental reference[4]:

> The iron structures being put up everywhere to support windmills are horrendous. They look awful beside the old, run-down houses belonging to small farmers. They don't fit the landscape at all. But that is the extent of it. In Saharian territory, water – a drop of water – is a blessing from God (Pla 2013, 137).

> Close to town we see the iron windmills they are installing almost everywhere for irrigation. They aren't exactly pretty, but they are useful. In a country which such a dearth of useful things, this has to be a prime consideration (Pla 2013, 277).

In some places, the agrarian landscape is virtually consecrated: "In the moonlight, from the garden porch, you can see the geometrical lines of cultivated terraces: the land's orderly patterns." (Pla 2013, 273). This is, when all is said and done, the apex of his existence.

The farmer as *creator* of landscape

In this general framework in which the agrarian landscape takes the leading role, the farmer or *pagès* logically occupies a pre-eminent position. In philosophical mood, Pla once said, paraphrasing Montaigne, that man occupies an insignificant place on earth (Pla 2013, 50). But this belief is qualified in other fragments of his work; in particular, when he explicitly defends the *pagès* as a key figure and creator of the landscape.

It is worth emphasising at this point that the word *pagès* has the same etymological root as *país* (country) and *paisatge* (landscape), all derived from the Latin *pagus*.[5] In Catalan territory, above and beyond the

---

[4] In general, this criterion prevails in Pla's mind, even outside specifically agrarian landscapes. Speaking, for example, about Sant Carles de la Ràpita and the possibilities of exploiting Els Alfacs as a port, he explains: "They tell me it is the largest natural port of the Mediterranean and that it would hold all the naval fleet. But for the time being, it has only a geographical utility: Sant Carles was also a small port for disembarking goods from the delta and from further inland: rice, salt, carob and oranges. [...] It offers a marvellous panorama but one quite lacking in utility" (Pla 1976, 1111).

[5] The word *pagus* is essentially equivalent to "the land", understood as the basic support for life and human activities (and, therefore, for agriculture). The term has entered the Romance languages with the modern meaning of "the highest political jurisdiction" or "state". But in languages such as Catalan (*país*), French (*pays*) and

etymology of the term, the *pagès* is a figure endowed with particularly deep meaning, a meaning that Pla captures and develops extensively in his book entitled *Els pagesos*. Here, it is very clear that the *pagès*, active subject of *pagus*, is the builder of the landscape; essentially, because over the generations he has transformed the *pagus*.

The significance of the figure of the *pagès* derives from the fact that Pla sees the world by taking the "human measure" as his fundamental reference (Fuster 1983). Pla seeks humanised landscapes, landscapes that are a reflection of the forms of humanisation. A short excerpt, in which the author describes small details in the area around Palafrugell, is expressive of this:

> There were vines, other crops, and fields of alfalfa. The pine and olive groves gave a little style to and somehow lightened the landscape where man had made such a heavy mark (Pla 2013, 59).

This point of view is also perceptible in his description of a deeply humanised landscape, that of the Maresme, which in Pla's day offered a rich agrarian mosaic:

> This [the Maresme] is an excellent Catalan *comarca*. Normal, equable, balanced. Perfect order reigns. This order is the work of careful calculation; it obeys a plan of physical output. This order coincides with – or produces – a higher order of landscape beauty and harmony of which the *pagès* might not suspect he is the author, but which fascinates its creators and those who contemplate its utilitarian harmony. [...] The Maresme honours a country; it serves an excellent tradition (Pla 1976, 763).

The humanised landscape, created by the *pagès*, is here "ordered", "useful", "beautiful", "harmonic", "adorable", etc. Interestingly Pla stresses that the *pagès* might not be aware of his own creation.[6] As can be appreciated, Pla makes constant references to Roman law, the legal basis of a complex system for regulating relations between land, landowner and farmer. Indeed, for the author, to speak of the *pagès* and of his *paisatge* is, essentially, to speak of the Roman world:

Occitan (païs) it maintains, along with the latter, the original meaning of "the land" (Coromines 1979-1989, VI, 166).

[6] The idea of the agrarian landscape as an "anonymous" landscape is constant in Pla, who always referred to himself as a *pagès* (Pla 1975, 10).

> I speak of the *pagesos* of the country, of Catalonia, a class that is constituted basically of Roman traditions, Roman law, the feudal contract, the peasant revolts caused by the breaking of the feudal contract and the freedom of contract ushered in after the French Revolution. This is a two-thousand-year-old assemblage projected onto the cultivation of the land (Pla 1975, 73).

He considers Roman law the creator of the property of the *pagès* and, consequently, of the land parcel mosaic. In this sense, for Pla "landscape mosaics" are much more beautiful than the landscapes of *latifundista* monoculture; it is, no doubt, a personal conception, but one that is deeply rooted in the agrarian landscapes that surrounded him and in the typical farm run by the *pagesos* in his *comarca*:

> People who pass through the Empordà, from outside the *comarca*, fall in love with the work that the *pagesos* do here each year. It is a work of prodigious beauty, so much so that it is the decisive factor in its surprising appearance. Countries that practice monoculture boast merely panoramic landscapes of crushing monotony. If monoculture is practiced on large estates, any interest in these landscapes – besides that of an economic nature – is highly precarious. The Empordà is a *comarca* that tends – and I stress tends – towards small properties. This tendency is perhaps most visible in the 'Empordà *petit*' than in the lands that lie beyond the Ter, where you still can find properties of a certain size (Pla 1988, 35).

Far from limiting himself solely to the *pagès* of the Empordà, Pla also refers to this figure in relation to other territories. Two examples, one about Mallorca the other about Ibiza, are especially illustrative of this:

> The Mallorcan *pagès*, tenacious, hard-working and intelligent, preserves the landscape of this country in a state of fertile order and, therefore, of great beauty (Pla 1976, 349).

> The *pagès* of Ibiza displays an essential sentiment: his love of the land, his affective ties for the ownership of his land (Pla 1976, 675).

The excerpt referring to Ibiza captures Pla's way of understanding the *attachment* of the *pagès* to his land. It is ultimately a relationship in which his affective ties merge with his ties of ownership. For Pla, half *pagès*/half writer, this is abundantly clear. Familiar with the agrarian history of Catalonia, and with the work of Vicens Vives, Pla knows that the abolition of feudal servitudes and the right to own land have been the greatest milestones in the history of Catalan agriculture. For Pla, *pagès*, landscape and property are indivisible concepts.

Final Reflections

At a conference in Barcelona, in 1991, Peter Gould offered the following reflection: "As human beings, we are all geographers, in the same way as we are all historians and philosophers, that is, individuals capable of thinking consciously about our existence in a given space and time". Interestingly, he illustrated this reflection with an explicit reference to Josep Pla, "the great Catalan writer who knew so well the ties people have with places and the land"; and he specifically highlighted Pla's deep understanding of the rural world, most clearly reflected in his book *Els pagesos*, to which we have referred at various points throughout our article (Gould 2000).

Pla is a leading author in Catalan literature, and his essentially descriptive work contains many elements of interest for the geographer. As a writer-geographer (in line with Peter Gould's assessment), Josep Pla has undoubtedly had an important influence on the construction of the territorial image of Catalonia throughout the twentieth century. His books were extremely popular and were widely read during his life; today, he continues to be read. His books fix or consolidate some of the images, myths and symbols of the contemporary Catalan landscape. Among these, as we have seen throughout our analysis, is the generic image of rural Catalonia; a preeminent image in his work, despite the fact that already in Pla's lifetime Catalonia was, for the most part, an urban country.

In this context, it is interesting to note that Pla's ideas about the rural world and its farmers, far from merely reproducing well-worn images or offering up a simple conventional outline, are a consistent system of thought in their own right. In other words, they reveal what might be identified as "a philosophy of life". And they make quite evident his awareness of the transformations that the countryside and the rural world have undergone everywhere in the world since the mid-twentieth century. This can be seen quite clearly in the selection of fragments from *Els pagesos* reproduced below:

Ancient life has passed into history. The *pagesos* today are very different from those half a century back: isolated, impervious, absent, satisfied within their narrow limitations. Everyone today wishes to have access to the conveniences of life, the pleasures of living. The *pagesos* are no different in this respect from any other class of people (Pla 1975, 191).

People speak of absenteeism and the migration away from the land. We should have no false illusions. This phenomenon is inevitable as long as the living conditions of the *pagès* continue to be, as they are in general, unpleasant (...). The material conditions of life transform human mentality. When this transformation cannot be resolved by normal means, it is resolved by abandoning the land and freedom (Pla 1975, 211).

It is, in short, a very similar diagnosis to that offered by John Berger, a writer, like Pla, fascinated by the richness and intrinsic diversity of rural culture in the broadest sense of the term; conscious also of its inexorable transformation and defender, ultimately, of its *memory* (a guardian of this culture in the process of disappearing the world over) as a last resort in preventing the loss of an irreplaceable heritage: "To make sense of the rural world, it is essential to know what the farmers know; to understand the instincts they have acquired, their immense power of observation and the wisdom they possess. All this is being destroyed just when the world needs it most"[7].

References

Primary sources

Pla, Josep. 1975. *Els pagesos*. Barcelona: Destino.
—. 1976. *Tres guies*. Barcelona: Destino.
—. 1983. *El quadern gris*. Barcelona: Destino.
—. 1988. *El meu país*. Barcelona: Destino.
—. 2013. *The Gray Notebook*. New York: The New York Review of Books. Translation by Peter Bush.

Other references

Coromines, Joan. 1979-1989. *Diccionari etimològic i complementari de la llengua catalana*. Barcelona: Curial Edicions.
Fuster, Joan. 1976. *Literatura catalana contemporània*. Barcelona: Curial Edicions.
—. 1983 [First Edition: 1966]. "Notes per a una introducció a l'estudi de Josep Pla". *In* Pla, Josep. *El quadern gris*, 11-83. Barcelona: Destino.
Gould, Peter. 2000. "Pensar como un geógrafo. Una exploración en la geografia moderna". Scripta Nova. *Revista Electrónica de Geografía y Ciencias Sociales*, 78: 1-17.
Kapuscinski, Riszard. 2002. *Los cínicos no sirven para este oficio. Sobre el buen periodismo*. Barcelona: Anagrama.
Ortega, Nicolás. 1987. *Geografía y cultura*. Madrid: Alianza Universidad.

---

[7] Berger, quoted in Kapuscinski 2002, 117.

Pla, Xavier. 1997. *Josep Pla. Ficció autobiogràfica i veritat literària*. Barcelona: Quaderns Crema.
Real Academia Española. 1984. *Diccionario de la llengua española*. Madrid: Espasa Calpe.
Tort, Joan. 1992. "La literatura com a font de recerca geogràfica: notes sobre la significació de l'Empordà en l'obra de Josep Pla". *Revista de Geografia*, XXVI: 57-66.
Tort Joan, and Valerià Paül. 2008. "From economical marginality to cultural marginality: the crisis afflicting the farmer's world as reflected in the writings of Josep Pla". *The global challenge and marginalization*, edited by Márcio M. Valença, Etienne Nel, and Walter Leimgruber, 117-132. New York: Nova Science Publishers.

Acknowledgements

Sincere thanks are due to Iain Kenneth Robinson for his linguistic assistance in the text.

This paper has been prepared in the context of the Research Project CSO2012-39564-C07-06, supported by the Ministerio de Economía y Competitividad, and carried out within the research group GRAM, supported by the government of the Generalitat de Catalunya (2014SGR 825).

Chapter Four

The Hidden Side of *Poste Restante. Beyrouth*: A View of the Lebanese Countryside in Wartime

Nora Semmoud and Florence Troin

Introduction

The novel *Poste restante. Beyrouth*[1] lends itself clearly to a study of literary geography. Space is present throughout – either the city of Beirut or the Bekaa Valley – giving a densely woven texture to the author's intense relationship with the places where the novel is set during a period of war (1975-1990). However, it is above all a question of "connivance", as defined by Sautter (1979) and developed by Gervais-Lambony (2007). For us, this involves exploring place identity through a convergence of our areas and objects of research in the Arab world and the literary works of authors who have used them as a setting for their narratives. In this case, it also concerns similarities between concepts of social geography and the literary school to which the novel appears to belong, based on realism and a critique of society.

As in studies of rural geography, the novel highlights the classic dynamics experienced by rural areas today, except that the socio-spatial reorganizations and life-style changes occur more rapidly and in unprecedented ways in a context of war. We propose two overlapping ways of reading Hanan El-Cheikh's text. The first involves the light shed by the depiction of places in the novel (Rosemberg 2007) on the geographical processes of socio-spatial marginalization/de-marginalization and the ensuing hierarchical structure. The dynamics of these war zones, both rural and urban, are created through extreme events, corresponding to

---

[1] Cf. reference to Primary Source.

the ultimate form of certain socio-spatial concepts of geography, such as fragmentation, isolation, and the closure of borders. The second way of reading the novel concerns the significant ways that these regional reorganisations are experienced in a time of war. The novel depicts a specific relationship to places that have been devastated by war, like the lives of the women and men who had the courage to remain there. This notion of courage and attachment to places (Beirut, Bekaa, Lebanon) lies at the heart of the novel and gives particular force to the epilogue. The war (loss of human life and the material and symbolic destruction of places) clearly intensifies the author's emotional relationship with particular places, in a sort of desperate search for what has been lost (previous life, material possessions, social relationships, etc.). The novel is constructed around six letters, providing a vehicle not only for realism and social critique, but also an autobiographical account, punctuated by the melancholic blues of Billie Holiday.

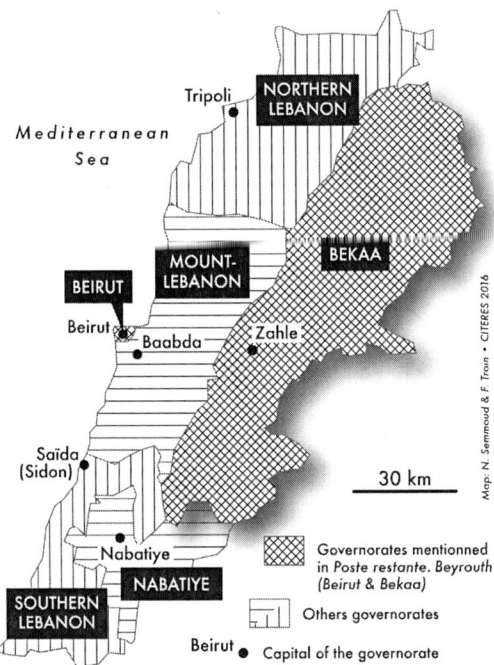

Figure 4.1 The governorates of Lebanon and the location
of Beirut and the Bekaa in the country. (Map: N. Semmoud & F. Troin 2016)

These two ways of reading the novel will be illustrated first in relation to the Bekaa Valley, the "beloved land" of the author, and then through the interrelationships between Bekaa and Beirut (See Figure 4.1).

Bekaa during the war: marginalisation and "renaissance"

Hanan El-Cheikh does not name the village in the Bekaa Valley where she was born, but her descriptions, both of the landscape and the way it has changed, correspond in many aspects to the analyses of this geostrategic region, with its small and medium-sized towns and villages, made by Bennafla (2006), Flateau (2013), Verdeil and Velut (2005) and Verdeil (2007). As explained above, our aim is to identify analogies between the geographers' view and the literary narrative, notably its sensorial aspect.

A marginalized area

Poverty and the predominance of rural activities make Bekaa a marginalized area, relative to a country that is more than 80% urbanized (Bennafla 2006). With very little support, farming in Bekaa has survived largely thanks to the use of poorly paid Syrian workers. In the novel, the difficult living conditions of the people in the author's home village are illustrated by the story of a ten-year-old child who lost his hand while sorting rubbish in a place where there was a bomb.

> He goes onto the tip and sorts the rubbish… He puts the items into separate bags, I mean the old things in one, glass bottles, plastic bottles, *Nido* tins, empty cans in the other…. It's better for him than going at night to the cemeteries to look for gold teeth, like the others (p. 124).

However, as stressed by Bennafla (2006), the Bekaa Valley has a strong strategic dimension due to its position between Syria and Lebanon. The author suggests that the development of the region is heavily influenced by geopolitical factors. Likewise, Verdeil and Velut (2005) see the Bekaa Valley as the ideal place to understand the rapidly changing political landscape to which Hanan El-Cheikh refers in her novel. We will see below how the agricultural landscape has changed, and the paradoxical effects of war on this strategic region, which is one of the most affected.

> The typically Mediterranean agricultural landscape observed in central Bekaa gives way to sparsely vegetated areas of steppe in the north of the

valley and on the arid Anti-Lebanon foothills, which are used as pastureland for goats and sheep (Bennafla 2006).

The agricultural landscape, depicted in small brush-strokes by Hanan El-Cheikh, does not seem to have been particularly marked by the stigmata of war. The author's emotional, indulgent and mythologizing description appears to be at odds with that of geographers. Is this a form of self-protective denial?

> Some villages have been destroyed, but the weather-beaten stones suggest that these ruins are old and that it is the work of nature. [...] It does not appear that the war has touched the village, that it has brought the roar of cannons and rockets, even if some walls bear the scars (p. 127-128).

Figure 4.2 The Bekaa Valley. (Photo: B. Dewailly 2004)

Cannabis is one of the main crops of the region. It was introduced in the 1920s in the dry, isolated areas in the north, and production developed significantly during the civil war to fund the militia. According to Flateau (2013), processing laboratories have continued operating, despite American pressure in the 1990s to eradicate the cultivation of cannabis and opium poppies in Bekaa. Flateau explains that, in addition to local production, the "morphine base" from Afghanistan and Turkey is processed into heroin in Bekaa. Likewise, the cocaine base that reaches Lebanon from Africa or the Mediterranean countries is processed in the villages in southern Bekaa. "The activities related to the manufacture of resins and to the laboratories producing heroin and cocaine are manna for the political stakeholders – the militia – challenging the authority of the State. Bekaa has thus become a global hub in the drug economy. Drug distribution then becomes part of the political system." (Flateau 2013).

The novel provides a clear description of the functioning of this economy, which was already flourishing during the war. Hanan El-Cheikh paints a subtle picture of the links between this economy, the warring factions, and its place in transnational drug trafficking networks.

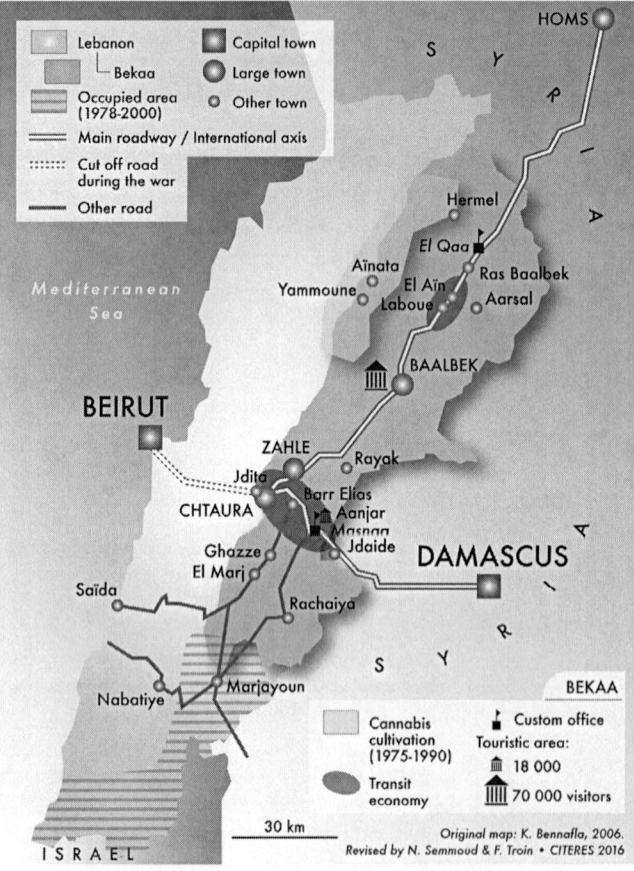

Figure 4.3 Economy in the Bekaa (cannabis cultivation) during the war. (Map: N. Semmoud & F. Troin 2016, according from K. Bennafla 2006).

They use the most up-to-date techniques to prepare, package and transport the hashish. All the young people think only of being part of their circle when they see them getting into their private helicopters, with their (…) gold or diamond rings, and their belts of guaranteed pure crocodile (p. 146).

An American car is parked in front of a doorway, and a hashish plant grows as tall as a tree [...]. It's Oum Kamel; cultivating hashish is now her only interest, and she constantly looks back with regret: 'Ah! If only we had known hashish in those days! We were mad to plant courgettes and aubergines' (p. 167).

Have you seen the trees that are now only stumps? Have you seen the poppies instead of fruit trees? Everything has changed (p. 200).

There is also a convergence between the approaches of geographers and the literary narrative regarding the way that the Bekaa Valley, like the country, is split along religious lines, reflecting a spatial fragmentation linked to community and religious diversity. Thus, in the novel, the war spares neither the city of Beirut nor the Bekaa Valley; the economic issues and struggles for power in these areas led to the same strategies of separation and control by militia protecting the interests (particularly economic) of the large Lebanese clans.

According to Flateau (2013), the people living in the centre and north of the Bekaa Valley are Christian, those in the south-east are Druze, those in the south Sunnites, and towards Baalbeck they are Shi'ite, together with Syrian workers and Palestinian camps. The author's village is undoubtedly in this sector. "Zahleh is thus a Christian bastion and a university centre, but it is increasingly challenged by Chtaura, the large economic centre of the region, and a crossroads towards Syria". Like the above-mentioned geographers, the author considers this mosaic as a powder keg, with undoubted repercussions on community tensions in the rest of Lebanon.

The numerous effects of this "balkanisation" are described in the novel, particularly in Beirut, but we can assume that the author's view of the Bekaa is filtered by the traumas arising from these separation strategies. People, of all faiths, were forced to move, leading to a real sense of uprooting (Bourdieu, and Sayad 1964).

My presence among my friends no doubt reminded them of a reality they wanted to forget. For them, everything had changed, where they worked, their home, everything except their car! Here, they had to recognize what was really happening in Lebanon. They were living in these new houses and in these neighbourhoods that meant nothing to them, even if some of them had grown up there (p. 354).

The people seem to be disoriented, faced with the substitution of their old spatial identities by religious identities that assigned them to places that did not have the same meaning for them. The protagonists of war swept away the interfaith communities, replacing them with spatial community groups justified mainly by security.

After that, we only really felt safe at home; it was the only place where we
didn't have to be careful about what we said, or to apologize for or justify
the crimes committed by members of our community (p. 354).

Paradoxical representations are found within each micro-territory; on
the one hand, a mutual stigmatisation, as if to prove the equation "living in
one's own community means security, the opposite is dangerous", and on
the other, a mutual over-idealisation that seems to relate to the concept of a
lost paradise.

In the West, you've got everything: wheat, flour, oil, spare parts for
washing machines and fridges… (p. 362).

[My grandmother] asked me if East Beirut was really the jewel that people
say it is, shining with all its restaurants and nightclubs (p. 354).

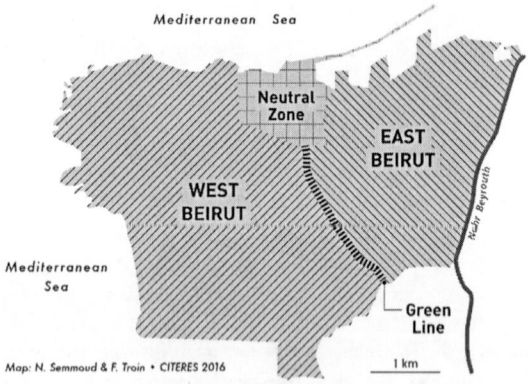

Figure 4.4. The partition of Beirut. (Map: N. Semmoud & F. Troin 2016)

In her own way, Hanan El-Cheikh depicts these community tensions in
Bekaa, notably through the position of her Shi'ite family, large
landowners, in relation to the new local political powers that overturned
the old social order. Her grandfather's land is used for combat training by
young Palestinian Fedayeen from the village, revolutionaries inspired by
Nasser's nationalisation of farmland in Egypt. The family is thus faced
with the dilemma of asking the armed militia to protect their land, with the
risk of being at the mercy of the community and political group to which
the militia belong.

Hanan El-Cheikh depicts this fragmentation from her own experience,
and in particular from the difficulty of getting to the Bekaa Valley by car.

I used to react violently, as if these road-blocks opened my eyes and revealed the full horror of the truth: Lebanon had been divided into small states and autonomous zones; some had a clear plan in mind, and the current situation was nothing but a result that the warring parties' calculations had not anticipated (p. 127).

But she also shows the paradoxes of this fragmentation, describing the porous nature of the borders and the way they are crossed in Beirut and in the Bekaa Valley, through a relative agreement in the productive areas (Tratnjek 2011). In Beirut, the people who cross from one sector to the other, clandestinely and by devious means, sometimes taking life-threatening risks, recreate the links between the two sectors.

This fragmentation, linked to the history of Lebanon and exacerbated by the civil war, has taken a drastic turn with the armed conflict in Syria, as analysed by Bennafla (2006): "If Bekaa is a zone of muted confrontations between local political parties, between foreign powers, and between Syrian political clans, it is also an area of confrontation between community groups. Like the Lebanese territory as a whole, the region is a patchwork of disparate groups, regularly torn apart by internal tensions."

Metamorphoses

The changes in the Bekaa Valley during and after the war have been extensively analysed by geographers specialised in this issue. For example, Bennafla (2006) observed that the end of the Lebanese civil war was marked by renewed agro-industrial activity in the valley, notably with vast cattle and poultry farms, taking advantage of the franchise system, the availability of land, and funding by the Lebanese diaspora[2]. In the novel, these dynamics were already at work during the civil war. The author describes them in detail, through the changes that she observed and the experiences of people in her home village.

This time, we weren't greeted by my grandfather's fields, but by a sign for a hairdressing salon. A hairdresser here? Impossible […]. A sweet factory! A bank! A chicken farm! A restaurant! The Café de la Source! On three floors! Villas!... Grandmother, do you think it is still our village? A bank! Two banks! (p. 129).

---

[2] According to Verdeil (2007), 200,000 people left the country as a result of the conflict.

In this way, she shows the growth of the service sector in her village and the role of the Lebanese diaspora in the changes; after making money abroad, they return to invest in their home village, which is where their new social position is most effective, because they are recognized by their community. "[…] Hamad Jaafar made his fortune in Kuwait; on his return, he opened a factory, and his brother a restaurant." (p. 129).

The new light shed by the novel, compared to the analyses of geographers, concerns particularly the upheaval in the social order, reflected in the drop in status of some landowner families, including the author's, and the rising status of former farm workers. From their humble background, these families became rich thanks to the drug economy or their allegiance to the warlords, or by working abroad. The author's family is one of a small number of middle-class landowners who stayed in Lebanon, choosing not to align themselves with the warring parties to defend their interests. The author's comments about her family's marginalisation carry an underlying criticism of the Lebanese middle-class who took advantage of the conflict to make money.

> What can I say? The only thing on which everyone in this country agrees is money, from the informers to the militia, including the Israelis (p. 314).

> My grandfather hasn't forgotten how [that family] became one of the richest in the village, and even in the region. Their ancestors were simple mule-drivers […]. Through their ingenuity, some of them made a name by smuggling tobacco, and then hashish during the war. Overnight, the whole family started spending money like there was no tomorrow. The women were forbidden from picking up camel droppings and cow-pats for the fire […]. Far from criticising the family, the villagers were proud to belong to the same region, the Bekaa Valley, proud to see them take part in the political game […]. [The family] developed its own field of action, created a militia to protect them, its routes and its agents who had become increasingly active in drug-trafficking (p. 145).

The social hierarchies linked to the power struggle between the parties of the civil war seemed to have replaced the traditional relationships of power between the landowning middle class and the other social groups.

Hanan El-Cheikh's narrative highlights sensorial aspects, often invisible to the geographers' eyes, and explores the temporality of despair, like Camus in *La Peste*[3]. The present maintains painful relationships with the past and seems to erase the future. Faced with the plague of war and

---

[3] Cf. reference to Primary Source.

the ever-present prospect of death, Hanan El-Cheikh is totally in the present, but constantly conjures up the past, with melancholic and painful nostalgia. She is unable to see the future, because she can see no end to the dramatic present. The present that should fade is omnipresent; the past and her nostalgia make her suffer, and the future does not exist.

Figure 4.5. The end of the traditional agricultural activity.
(Photo: B. Dewailly 2004)

Nostalgia (Rey 2005, 1007), from the Greek *nostos* "home-coming" and *algos* "pain", is defined in psychopathology as a depressive state linked to an obsessive yearning for the homeland, and in common parlance it is a wistful recollection of the past, a desire to return to former times […]. Ever-present in the narrative, this nostalgia, described as wistfulness, melancholy and sadness, could have been pathological and disabling if Hanan El-Cheikh had not also made use in her narrative of collective memory, as defined by Halbwachs (1950).

Like Halbwachs, Hanan El-Cheikh associates personal memory (her own) with that of the group (her family and friends), fuelling it with representations of the past, linked to possibilities offered by the present, and ultimately using it to build a sense of identity. In this way, she updates ancient forms, adjusting the representations of the past on which people define their relationships with others, with where they live, with themselves, with their own identity. The author thus accepts the loss of her grandparents' social status, but above all uses it as a critique of the changes that affect social relationships with the countryside.

Bekaa/Beirut: inextricably linked

In the novel, the Bekaa Valley and Beirut are powerful, interconnected mirror images of each other. The two places experience the same processes of division and the same paradoxes. Here, the literary narrative largely matches the analyses of geographers. For example, Bennafla (2006) observes that Bekaa boosted its transit economy (trade, banks, catering, services) during the war, by taking advantage both of the marginalisation of Beirut due to bombing and of its situation as the interface between Lebanon and Syria. This flourishing economy continued after the war with construction, in spite of the revival of Beirut and the coast. According to Bennafla (2006), it demonstrates the attachment of the Lebanese living abroad to their home villages, where they build more or less grand houses, occupied for part of the year.

Identification and rooting

The narrative makes extensive reference to the notion of identification with the homeland – and the symbolic sense of rooting that it implies, both for those who have left (for Beirut or abroad) and those who remain. The author expresses these notions through letters and by declaring her love to the land, as if to her lovers. She starts a letter addressed to Bekaa with "My beloved land". The personification of the village and the love she bears it are totally conflated with her feelings towards her grandfather.

> My grandfather sat down heavily, as if he carried you [the land] both on his shoulders and in his heart. [...] But when he had to leave you to go to college in Beirut, he couldn't bring himself to do it. The sparrows and the partridge were the first to call him to you, and he became as skilful a hunter as his father (p. 132-133).

The narrative also highlights the interconnections between Beirut and Bekaa through the reputation of her family and grandfather in Beirut. It appears that the social position of large families in Beirut is determined by their landowner status in Bekaa.

> You gave birth to my family, penetrated its most intimate secrets. You whispered its name so that it would echo across the mountains, valleys and plains, from telegraph pole to telegraph pole, until it reached Beirut (p. 121).

> My grandfather's name was known as far as Beirut, like Sursock, Beydoun and other Lebanese families whose names were used to designate streets in

the city or one of its neighbourhoods. [...] Grandmother moved away from you, but your roots were firmly planted in her. That is why she only gave half of herself to the town: one eye, one nostril, one hand; everything that had to do with Beirut was temporary, at the very least, marginal (p. 136).

However, the author's intimate relationship with the land is ambivalent; on the one hand, the difficulty of living in a country, a town and a village scarred and ravaged by war, where staying on involves a daily struggle, and on the other hand, a poetic vision of the place (Sansot 1999, Bachelard 1957).

[...] the noise of the street interrupted my train of thought, showing me how I had become completely absorbed by the war (p. 285).

Merely staying in Beirut during these last years was in itself a full-time job (p. 293).

The sensorial aspects expressed by Hanan El-Cheikh, not only affectivity, feelings, sensations, the imaginary, and memory, but also colours, smells, etc., inevitably give a sense of the poetry of place.

To shed philosophical light on the issue of the poetic image, we need a phenomenology of imagination. In other words, a study of the phenomenon of the poetic image when the image emerges in the conscious mind as coming straight from the heart, the soul, from human existence as it is experienced (Bachelard 1957, 11).

Paradoxically, the author creates poetic images of areas that have been devastated. If the poetic image reflects the depth of the psyche (Bachelard 1957, 7), we can assume that the author's poetic imagination serves to provide distance and to protect herself from an apocalyptic reality. In the same way, she uses humour, mockery and derision. "And when a rocket went through our house, we just laughed and said we would gut it and stuff it with rice like a courgette!" (p. 131).

Bekaa is also described as a safe haven compared to Beirut. The author feels safer there, and, in spite of the changes that have affected the village and the effects of the war, it remains a haven of peace, with its timeless landscapes and colours, as well as the profound values and meaning of belonging to a clan that had not succumbed.

Micro-regions and ethnogenesis

According to Tratnjek (2011), it is essential to take a territorial approach in order to understand the restructuring of the social relationships and spatial practices of people living in a war zone. As analysed by geographers and depicted in the literary narrative, war restructures specific territorialities, discontinuities, enclosures, mobility constraints, etc. However, the novel also shows the porosity of the borders and the clandestine social interactions in both Bekaa and Beirut.

In Beirut, the people who cross clandestinely and deviously from one sector to another, sometimes taking life-threatening risks, manage to recreate the links between the two micro-territories. "They run through this empty space that separates the two zones of a single town. Where are they running? Are they fleeing from an ogre?" (p. 345).

The famous green line that serves as a frontier remains porous, because it is crossed every day by a large number of people, notably to go to work, in spite of being an odious and dangerous no man's land. "In fact, some people go to work in the other sector of the town, taking their files or their lunch with them" (p. 345).

These daily migrations represent forms of breaking down or crossing frontiers, but they are confronted by shifting checkpoints.

> There were fixed road-blocks and others that moved according to circumstances; getting through depended on the mood of the guards, on the objectives of one or other militia, or on the political situation that changed from day to day (p. 351).

In a study of the territorial effects of urban wars in Brazzaville, Dorier-Apprill (1995) shows the links between the geography of ethnic groups in their homelands, and the repercussions of electoral divides on the distribution of the population in the town, particularly as the major political parties pursue the same spatial identity strategy in the capital as in the rest of the country. This similarity in socio-spatial organisation between the capital and the rest of the country can also be observed in the relationship between Bekaa and Beirut described in the novel.

Dorier-Apprill (1995) also highlighted two notions that seem in some way to match the spatial representations described in the literary narrative. The first concerns micro-territories or district-territories, which are reminiscent of the establishment of the militia in the districts controlled by the checkpoints, which, according to Tratnjek (2011), create spatial discontinuities between areas and involve a differentiation strategy, by segregating inhabitants in areas where they feel safe. Related to micro-territories, the second notion concerns phenomena of ethnogenesis. In the case of Brazzaville, Dorier-Apprill (1995) explains that the violence between the two main warring factions is not a resurgence of old tribal antagonism, but seems to be based on two forms of ethnogenesis stemming from urban modernity and used injudiciously by parties competing to establish their local hold in the capital. The study focuses on the political use of the identity aspect of civil war, through invented identities. In Congo, identity issues are crystallised in the town rather than in the more neutral and federating regions, whereas in Lebanon, a similar ethnogenesis exists in the Bekaa Valley and in Beirut.

These territorial signs indicate community and political allegiance, and are found both in the Bekaa Valley (road-blocks, military camps, statues or portraits of leaders) and in Beirut (checkpoints); they also show the influence of local political parties set up on religious lines, notably Hezbollah, which is firmly entrenched in the northern Shi'ite zones of Bekaa and East Beirut.

Conclusion

Poste restante. Beyrouth clearly comes within the scope of literary geography. There are frequent spatial representations, giving consistency to the author's intense relationship with the many places described in the narrative. It expresses a particular relationship with places that, like the women and men living there, have been devastated by war, providing an extreme image of certain socio-spatial forms that come within the domain of geography, such as fragmentation, frontiers, etc.

While there are many analogies between the geographers' approach and the literary narrative, the latter provides a perspective that is often lacking in geography, namely the sensory experience of space and its accompanying representations. The brutality and speed of change brought about by war, the shortages and loss, the painful nostalgia, violence, etc., highlight the emotional relationship of individuals with these areas during a period of war. Far from being metaphysical, this phenomenological approach shows the emotional relationships with the material reality of the place, the political and power struggles that shape it, and the social and political structure of Lebanese society. In this way, the author reveals phenomena that often remain unseen.

Primary sources

Camus, Albert. 1972 (1947). *La Peste*. Paris: Gallimard. Folio n° 42.

El-Cheikh, Hanan. 1995, *Poste restante*. Beyrouth, Arles : Actes Sud. Babel [French translation]. Original edition: *Barîd Bayroûth*, 1992, Cairo, Dâr al-Hilâl.

Secondary Sources

Bachelard, Gaston. 1957. *La Poétique de l'espace*. Paris : Quadrige/PUF.

Bennafla, Karine. 2006. "La Bekaa (Liban) : un espace géostratégique", *Mappemonde*, n° 81, 01-2006. http://mappemonde.mgm.fr/num9/lieux/lieux06101.html [consulted on the 10th of march 2016].

Bourdieu, Pierre, and Abdelmalek Sayad. 1964. *Le Déracinement. La crise de l'agriculture traditionnelle en Algérie*, Paris : Minuit.

Dorier-Apprill, Elisabeth. 1995. "Brazza ville. Des quartiers pour territoires ?" *La Nation et le territoire. Le territoire, lien ou frontière ? Tome 2*, edited by Joël Bonnemaison, Luc Cambrézy, and Laurence Quinty-Bourgeois. Paris : L'Harmattan.

Flateau, Cosima. 2013. "La Bekaa, un territoire stratégique sous influence". *Les clés du Moyen-Orient* (on the web). http://www.lesclesdumoyenorient.fr/La-Bekaa-un-territoire-strategique.html [consulted on 25th of march 2016].

Gervais-Lambony, Philippe. 2007. "Nouvel espace, nouvelle littérature. Écrire les suburbs de Johannesburg. Remarques autour du recueil d'Ivan Vladislavic". *Bulletin de l'association des géographes français (BAGF)*, 2007-3, 275-285.

Halbwachs, Maurice. 1950. *La Mémoire collective*. http://dx.doi.org/doi:10.1522/cla.ham.mem1

Rey, Alain ed. 2005. *Le Robert. Dictionnaire culturel*. Paris.

Rosemberg, Muriel. 2007. "Introduction". *Géographie et cultures*, n° 61.

Sautter, Gilles. 1979. "Le paysage comme connivence". *Hérodote*, n° 16.

Tratnjek, Bénédicte ed. 2011. "Les civils dans les conflits armés", *Les Champs de Mars*, n° 21. Paris : La Documentation française.

Verdeil, Éric. 2007. "Le bilan des destructions". *Liban, une guerre de 33 jours*, edited by Franck Mermier, and Elizabeth Picard, 12-21. Paris : La Découverte.

Verdeil, Éric, and Sébastien Velut. 2005. "Liban-Syrie : les cartes du changement", *Mappemonde*, n° 80, 04-2005. http://mappemonde.mgm.fr/num8/articles/art05402.html

CHAPTER FIVE

RELIRE LA SPATIALITE ET LA REGIONALITE AVEC LES ECRIVAINS CONTEMPORAINS – APPORTS DE GEORGES PEREC ET PIERRE BERGOUNIOUX AUX SCIENCES DU TERRITOIRES

MAURICETTE FOURNIER

Les relations complexes littérature et sciences sociales

Très longtemps, la narration et l'explication ont été associées dans les œuvres de l'humanité, y compris pour ce qui relève des sciences du territoire. Ainsi la géographie, par exemple, aurait-elle été, avance André Ferré (1953), « un genre littéraire depuis Strabon ». Cependant, la construction des sciences humaines et leur institutionnalisation, à partir du XIXe siècle, ont conduit à dissocier la littérature, dès lors perçue seulement comme fiction, de l'écrit scientifique reposant désormais sur la présentation des faits, un protocole rationnel d'analyse... même si certains rares « savants » ont encore tenté « *de concilier, dans une même recherche art et sciences* » (Jablonka, 2014, p. 91) à l'image du géographe Élysée Reclus, rédigeant à la première personne des ouvrages de vulgarisation tel *Histoire d'une montagne*.

À partir des années quatre-vingt, cette représentation de « l'imaginaire savant » a commencé à être contestée. Par ailleurs, la lecture des sociologues, en premier lieu de Pierre Bourdieu (1998), a aussi invité à reconsidérer le déterminisme de la « région » sur les mentalités, les comportements, les destinées d'une génération, surtout après la première guerre mondiale. Tout récemment, diverses expériences ont tenté de réconcilier le couple littérature-sciences sociales : en témoignent, en France, le lancement de la collection « *Raconter la vie* » du sociologue

Pierre Rosanvallon[1] ou le manifeste de l'historien Ivan Jablonka (2014).
Pour illustrer la fécondité du croisement de ces regards, nous proposons
d'expliciter l'importance des apports de (certains) écrivains contemporains
pour les sciences du territoire en développant quelques exemples, en
particulier la découverte de la spatialité avec l'œuvre de Georges Perec et
une meilleure compréhension de la régionalité (Langevin, 2010b) avec
celle de Pierre Bergounioux.

Quand les géographes découvrent la spatialité avec Georges Perec

C'est officiellement en juin 1978, soit quatre ans après la publication
d'*Espèces d'espaces*, que la géographie académique rencontre Georges Perec.
Pour la – encore jeune – revue *L'Espace géographique*, qu'il a fondée en 1972
avec Roger Brunet dans le but de diffuser les apports de la *new geography*
anglophone, Philippe Pinchemel rédige un éditorial enthousiaste dans lequel il
enjoint ses collègues à se dépêcher de lire Perec.

> Parce que nous vivons dans un monde cloisonné, il y avait peu de chances
> que l'avant dernier livre de Georges Perec, *Espèces d'espaces* […] apparût
> dans les comptes rendus de nos savantes revues ; pensez donc : un écrivain,
> un romancier, étranger à la tribune géographique.
> Surtout Georges Perec ne s'interroge pas sur la géographie, il ne
> s'abîme – pas dans la méditation épistémologique ; terrien, – il ne met
> même pas en doute l'existence de la surface et de l'espace terrestres. Bien
> au contraire, tout son livre est une célébration de cet espace terrestre, de
> l'espace géographique, célébration intelligible, tonique, joyeuse.
> Car Georges Perec a rencontré l'espace, les espaces et, qu'il le veuille
> ou – non –, qu'il le reconnaisse ou non, le voici habité par l'esprit
> géographique (lequel, doté d'une majuscule, souffle où il veut, on le sait,
> évitant de préférence les professionnels).[…]
> Alors, géographes qui vivons de la géographie, dépêchons-nous de lire
> Perec et mettons-nous à l'écoute d'un authentique géographe, d'autant plus
> authentique qu'il ignore son état et donc que le doute et l'incertitude ne
> l'habitent pas. (Philippe Pinchemel, 1978).

Une coïncidence frappante entre la publication d'*Espèces d'espaces* et le renouvellement de la géographie

L'engouement de Philippe Pinchemel pour les écrits de Georges Perec
s'explique par le fait que la discipline était en train de changer de

---

[1] http://raconterlavie.fr/collection/

paradigme. Il réalise que l'écrivain opère spontanément une mise en littérature des thèmes de la « nouvelle géographie » qu'il souhaite alors promouvoir. Ses œuvres rencontrent et illustrent ce changement de paradigme épistémologique. C'est bien parce qu'il n'est pas géographe que Georges Perec, comme le souligne Philippe Pinchemel, « *ne s'interroge pas sur la géographie,* [qu'] *il ne s'abîme – pas dans la méditation épistémologique* », qu'il peut explorer l'espace dans une « *célébration intelligible, tonique, joyeuse* ». Cette grande liberté d'artiste lui a permis de livrer, ainsi que le conclura Michel Lussault, « *une des plus importantes contributions qui soient à la réflexion consacrée à la spatialité humaine* » (Lussault, 2003, p. 702). De fait, expose Roger Brunet dans son dictionnaire critique,

> [...] l'espace géographique est une acquisition récente. L'expression n'était guère employée jusqu'à la fin des années 1960, hors quelques audaces (J. Gottmann, puis J. Labasse), et de l'anglophonie. On connaissait les régions, non l'espace, ni les espaces. (Brunet, 1992, p. 195).

C'est pourquoi Roger Brunet rappelle avoir fondé la revue *L'Espace géographique* en 1972 pour faire acte « *d'un défi scientifique militant* » (Brunet, 1992, p. 195). Une dizaine d'années plus tard, se livrant à leur tour à l'exercice de rédaction d'un *Dictionnaire de la géographie et de l'espace des sociétés*, Jacques Lévy et Michel Lussault donnent une lecture plus précise de ce moment de rupture épistémologique. Pour les auteurs, dans la géographie dite classique, fondée par Vidal de la Blache et qui a prévalu jusqu'aux années soixante, le concept d'espace n'avait pas donné lieu à un véritable « *travail d'approfondissement théorique* ». Si bien que, poursuivent-ils, « *à partir des années 1960-1970, d'aucuns ont, peu à peu, dénoncé cet assourdissant mutisme de la géographie,* [...] *impasse dans laquelle se complaisaient les zélateurs de la géographie classique* » pour redéfinir la discipline autour de cinq grands axes : production de l'espace, analyse spatiale, systémisme, espace vécu et représentations, territoires et territorialité (Lévy et Lussault, 2003, p. 325-326).

Pour comprendre la rupture épistémologique qui a marqué l'histoire de la géographie française au début des années soixante-dix, il faut aussi souligner le rôle du contexte institutionnel qui a accéléré le changement dans les pratiques de la recherche en sciences humaines, tout particulièrement en géographie, ainsi que l'ont analysé Olivier Orain et Marie-Pierre Sol (2007). Ces derniers relèvent que, jusque-là très individuelles, celles-ci sont devenues, dès lors, plus collectives grâce à une procédure incitative mise en place par le Centre National de la Recherche Scientifique (CNRS), les Recherches Coopératives sur Programme (RCP).

Ces nouvelles procédures ont permis la mise en relation, autour de projets, de toute une nouvelle génération de géographes qui avait en commun des préoccupations réflexives. Au cœur de ces « méditations épistémologiques », le concept d'espace a pu être exploré dans diverses directions.

En 1970, démarrent deux de ces RCP. La première, intitulée « Les systèmes d'organisation de l'espace », est coordonnée par Roger Brunet. La seconde, « Les structures régionales du Midi de la France et de la Catalogne », réalisée sous la houlette de Bernard Kayser à Toulouse, donnera lieu, en 1978, à une publication aux éditions du CNRS, *Espaces périphériques : études et enquêtes dans le Midi de la France et en Catalogne*, qui présente en exergue une citation de Georges Perec. En 1973, c'est la RCP « Espaces vécus et civilisations » qui voit le jour, conduite par Armand Frémont. Elle débouchera, en 1976, sur un colloque dont les actes, *Espaces vécus et civilisation*, seront édités en 1982. En 1976, Armand Frémont publie à titre personnel *La région, espace vécu* qui deviendra un ouvrage de référence. La même année, Philippe Pinchemel, grâce à la création de la RCP « Histoire et épistémologie de la géographie », entame l'inventaire du vocabulaire de la discipline qui fait écho, notamment, aux recherches lexicales menées à partir du terme « espace » dans les RCP précédentes. Il n'est donc pas surprenant que cette quête de syntaxe l'ait conduit à découvrir *Espèces d'espaces*.

L'espace de Georges Perec : un nouveau programme pour la géographie

La révolution proposée par Georges Perec commence par le choix d'une écriture particulière, une écriture fonctionnelle, volontairement « plate », sur le modèle des guides de voyage auxquels l'auteur fait explicitement référence : « *Plutôt que visiter Londres, rester chez soi, au coin de sa cheminée et lire les irremplaçables renseignements que fournit le Baedeker (édition de 1907)* » (Perec, 1974, p. 127). Georges Perec a l'intuition que les guides révèlent certaines pratiques de l'espace, ainsi que le démontrera Claire Hancock (2003). Pour l'écrivain, décrire minutieusement les lieux permet de porter sur eux un regard neuf.

Si Georges Perec s'intéresse aux *espèces d'espaces*, il se soucie peu de la géographie. Ses références, très variées, sont essentiellement artistiques, principalement littéraires, secondairement cinématographiques et picturales, parfois musicales.

A contrario, les références aux sciences sociales sont à peu près absentes d'*Espèces d'espaces,* à une rare exception : « *Marcel Mauss « Les techniques du corps » in Sociologie et Anthropologie, p. 378* » (Perec, 1974, p. 38). Quant à la géographie, elle se trouve réduite à sa dimension scolaire, trop souvent associée à une simple nomenclature. À plusieurs reprises, Georges Perec évoque ses souvenirs de classe pour critiquer le lexique géographique de l'époque, ce vocabulaire « scientifique », qui lui paraît inapte à traduire un espace changeant et la spatialité de l'individu.

Type de références	Mentions dans le texte
Références littéraires	Raymond Queneau (p. 94, p.103, p.119 etc.) / Jules Verne (p. 34, p. 127, p. 153, p. 167) / Jorge Luis Borgès (p. 26, p. 68, p. 69) / Italo Calvino (p. 158) / Paul Eluard (p. 17-18) / Lewis Caroll (p. 10) / Marcel Proust (p. 31, p. 47) / Gustave Flaubert (p. 130-131) / Stéphane Mallarmé (p. 164) / Stendhal (p. 167) / James Joyce (p. 168) / José-Maria de Heredia (p. 35) / Léon Tolstoï (p. 68) / Helmut Heissenbüttel (p. 69)
Références cinématographiques	*L'homme qui dort* (p. 110) / *La grande illusion* (p. 147) / *King Kong* (p. 105) / *2001 – Odyssée de l'espace* (p. 168) / *La planète interdite* (p. 73) / Katherine Hepburn (p. 154)
Références picturales	*Le songe de Sainte Ursule* de Carpaccio (p. 50) / Tableaux de Magritte (p. 69) / Gravure d'Escher (p. 69) / *Saint Jérôme* par Antonello de Messine (p. 171) / Renoir et Sisley (p. 44) / Portrait de Philippe Melanchthon par Lucas Cranach
Références musicales	*Maria-Thérésa* de Joseph Haydn (p. 68) / Jean-Sébastien Bach (p. 45)

Figure 5.1 Principales références de Georges Perec dans *Espèce d'espaces*.

Espace inventaire, espace inventé : l'espace commence avec cette carte modèle qui, dans les anciennes éditions du *Petit Larousse illustré*, représentait sur 60 cm² quelque chose comme 65 termes géographiques, miraculeusement rassemblés, délibérément abstraits : voici le désert, avec son oasis, son oued et son chott, voici la source et le ruisseau, le torrent, la rivière, le canal, le confluent, le fleuve, l'estuaire, l'embouchure et le delta. [...] Simulacre d'espace, simple prétexte à nomenclature.
—Georges Perec, 1974, p. 26-27.

[...] à Saint-Chély-d'Apcher (le nom – beaucoup plus surprenant quand il est énoncé que lorsqu'il est écrit – de ce chef-lieu de canton de la Lozère s'était pour des raisons que j'ignore, ancré dans ma mémoire depuis ma classe de troisième [...].
—Georges Perec, 1974, p. 49.

J'ai appris beaucoup de choses à l'école et je sais encore que Metz, Toul et Verdun formaient les Trois-Évêchés.
—Georges Perec, 1974, p. 137.

Si Georges Perec semble peu s'intéresser à la géographie académique de son époque, avec *Espèces d'espaces*, essai intuitif, il propose sans le savoir un « programme » aux géographes. Ce programme peut se lire dans l'organisation même de l'œuvre : les chapitres qui la composent (La page / Le lit / La chambre / L'appartement / L'immeuble / La rue / Le quartier / La ville / La campagne / Le pays / L'Europe / Le Monde / L'espace) soulignent l'importance de l'emboîtement des espaces, ce qui constitue un enjeu majeur de la nouvelle géographie qui émerge alors. L'ouvrage interroge également nombre de problématiques que la géographie va développer ultérieurement : la spatialité, l'appropriation des lieux (le territoire comme espace approprié), le sens de l'habiter, incluant le projet d'habiter un non-lieu (aéroport par exemple). Cette idée sera testée par les écrivains Julio Cortazar et Carol Dunlop (1983) avant d'être prise à rebours par l'anthropologue Marc Augé (1992), puis revisitée, par exemple, par Boris Grésillon qui se propose, en 2008, d'explorer les terrains délaissés par la géographie

ces "espèces d'espace", pour citer Georges Perec – friches industrielles ou urbaines transformées en lieux de culture, SquArts d'artistes, terrains-vagues accueillant troupes de théâtre et de cirque [pour réhabiliter l'ensemble de ces nouveaux lieux de culture] en tant qu'objet géographique (Grésillon, 2008).

Georges Perec insiste également sur l'idée de construction de l'espace, à savoir que l'espace n'est pas un *continuum*, mais un espace construit par la fermeture, produit par la propriété, rencontrant ainsi, par exemple, les travaux de Roger Brunet sur *Les phénomènes de discontinuité en géographie* (1968). Il montre aussi que la construction de l'espace relève tout autant de l'imaginaire, de la représentation que chacun peut se faire des lieux, en fonction de son vécu et de sa position.

Toutes ces thématiques sont, par une sorte d'effet miroir, illustrées par la manière dont Georges Perec évoque l'espace rural. Dans *Espèces d'espaces,* il ne consacre qu'un bref chapitre à « *la campagne* » qui démarre par l'affirmation suivante *:* « *Je n'ai pas grand-chose à dire à propos de la campagne : la campagne n'existe pas, c'est une illusion* » (Perec, 1974, p. 135). Cependant, s'il affirme que l'espace rural est pour lui « *un pays étranger* » (Perec, 1974, p. 136), il n'en demeure pas moins vrai qu'il en a bien une représentation mentale qui lui permet de décrire des modes de vie, des façons d'être, un type de relations sociales, bref une territorialité et une spatialité spécifiques.

> Pour la majorité de mes semblables, la campagne est un espace d'agrément qui entoure leur résidence secondaire, qui borde une portion des autoroutes qu'ils fréquentent le vendredi soir quand ils s'y rendent, et dont, le dimanche après-midi, s'ils ont quelque courage, ils parcourront quelques mètres avant de regagner la ville où, pendant le reste de la semaine, ils se feront les chantres du retour à la nature. [...] j'aime être à la campagne : on mange du pain de campagne, on respire mieux, on voit parfois des animaux que l'on n'a pratiquement pas l'habitude de voir dans les villes, on fait du feu dans les cheminées, on joue au Scrabble ou à d'autres petits jeux de société. On a souvent plus de place qu'à la ville, il faut le reconnaître, et presque autant de confort, et parfois autant de calme. [...] Pour commencer, on aurait été à l'école avec le facteur. Bien sûr, on connaîtrait tout le monde et les histoires de tout le monde.
> —Georges Perec, 1974, p. 135-139

Les destins de l'œuvre : une appropriation académique

Signe tangible de la patrimonialisation académique de l'apport de l'écrivain, Georges Perec est très présent dans les ouvrages de référence de la discipline (dictionnaires de géographie ou anthologies de textes fondateurs). Michel Lussault lui consacre ainsi plus de deux pages dans le *Dictionnaire de la geographie et de l'espace des sociétés* (2003), dont la publication sera saluée par Gildas Simon comme « *une géographie mode emploi* » dans le compte-rendu qu'il en fera pour les *Annales de géographie*, appréciant le « *très bel article sur Georges Perec comme illustration du lien entre géographie et littérature* » (Simon, 2004, p. 645). Philippe Pinchemel, Marie-Claire Robic et Jean-Louis Tissier dédient quant à eux une page à Georges Perec en fin de leur ouvrage, *Deux siècles de géographie française, choix de textes* (1984*)*, dans lequel l'écrivain côtoie Michel Serres et Julien Gracq. Et si, dans le dictionnaire de Roger Brunet, Robert Ferras et Hervé Théry, *Les Mots de la géographie*, aucune notice n'est explicitement dédiée à Georges Perec, sa présence s'affirme toutefois par des citations : ainsi est proposé, dans la rubrique « espace vécu », l'extrait suivant d'*Espèce d'espaces :*

> ça ne ferait pas une vie … ça créerait un espace familier, ça susciterait un itinéraire, mais ça ne serait jamais qu'un aménagement douceâtre de la nécessité, une manière d'enrober le mercantile » (Brunet et al., 1993, p. 195).

En quatre décennies, les géographes francophones se sont donc largement appropriés l'œuvre de l'écrivain Georges Perec.

L'apport des récits à la compréhension anthropologique du Massif central

La littérature « régionaliste », dite parfois « de terroir », apparue à la fin du XIXe siècle dans un contexte militant (le mouvement des félibriges en est l'une des manifestations les plus caractéristiques) avait pour ambition de faire revivre le passé du monde rural et cédait souvent au lyrisme du terroir (Thiesse, 1991 et 1993).

> Le genre traditionnellement apparié aux zones rurales – le roman régionaliste – apparaît vers le milieu du XIXe siècle, au moment précis où la terre, déchue du rôle économiquement dominant qui était le sien, devient la campagne. Le capitalisme supplante la société féodale. C'est à la ville que se transportent les nouveaux acteurs du procès de production, bourgeois et prolétaires, et les écrivains qui se font les interprètes des nouveaux rapports sociaux. La littérature régionale participe du caractère subalterne, désormais, de l'économie rurale. (Bergounioux, 2014, p. 18).

Se distingue désormais une littérature contemporaine, qui a un rapport plus distancé au terroir et à son histoire, que l'on pourrait nommer littérature de la « régionalité » ou de la « provincialité » (Coyault, 2002 ; Langevin, 2010a et 2010b). Ce courant est actuellement très largement représenté en France par des auteurs originaires du Massif central, même s'ils vivent maintenant le plus souvent dans la région parisienne, comme Pierre Bergounioux, Richard Millet, Pierre Michon, Marie-Hélène Lafon, Pierre Jourde, Renaud Camus...

Cette deuxième partie propose de mettre en regard les connaissances sur les structures familiales développées par les diverses disciplines des sciences humaines avec des récits. On s'attardera, en particulier, sur celui de Pierre Bergounioux, *Miette,* pour montrer comment l'auteur contribue à éclairer les ressorts de la structure anthropologique dominante dans le Massif central français, la famille souche ou autoritaire et sa transformation.

La redécouverte des travaux précurseurs de Le Play

Dès la fin du XIXe siècle, le sociologue français Frédéric Le Play (1806-1882) avait proposé un schéma d'interprétation permettant d'expliquer la variété des structures familiales observables en Europe, en s'appuyant sur les différences dans le mode de répartition des héritages et les principes coutumiers (Le Play, 1871 ; Wittmann, 1941). L'intérêt des travaux de Le Play est d'avoir établi une première géographie des modes de vie et des valeurs qui leur sont associées. Il avait en effet reconnu trois principaux types d'organisations anthropologiques, la famille instable, la famille patriarcale et la famille souche, s'étendant chacune sur des espaces spécifiques. Comme le relèvent Hervé Le Bras et Emmanuel Todd, il « *donnait une clé de différenciation non biologique de l'humanité* » (Le Bras et Todd, 1981, p. 26) à une époque où dominaient – et pour encore longtemps – les seules approches historicistes de l'évolution des sociétés.

Les travaux précurseurs de Frédéric Le Play ont commencé à être redécouverts à partir des années soixante par des chercheurs d'horizons disciplinaires différents (droit, histoire, sociologie, anthropologie, géographie) aussi bien en France qu'au Royaume-Uni. Parmi ces « redécouvreurs » s'intéressant à l'étude des structures familiales (ou des systèmes familiaux selon la terminologie employée par certains auteurs) est à souligner la contribution de plusieurs historiens de la famille dont le britannique Peter Laslett (1969) et le français Emmanuel Le Roy Ladurie (1972), qui auront une grande influence dans la formation académique d'Emmanuel Todd, lequel va se consacrer, pendant plusieurs décennies, à approfondir – et vulgariser – la connaissance sur ces structures anthropologiques (Todd, 1983, 1984, 1990, 1999; 2011), parfois en collaboration avec le démographe Hervé Le Bras (1981, 1986, 2013).

Comme Frédéric Le Play, Emmanuel Todd a l'intuition que les structures familiales, qui se sont cristallisées dans les sociétés rurales, sont porteuses de valeurs et de normes, parfois explicites, mais le plus souvent implicites, profondément ancrées dans les inconscients collectifs, les *habitus* selon Pierre Bourdieu. Les idéologies ainsi constituées se manifestent largement dans tous les domaines de la vie des sociétés (systèmes juridiques, économiques, politiques, etc.), y compris, après la disparition des sociétés paysannes pré-modernes dans lesquelles elles se sont construites. Dès lors, Emmanuel Todd va s'attacher à montrer de manière systématique, à l'échelle de la France, de l'Europe, puis du Monde, les corrélations entre les structures anthropologiques et les systèmes agraires dans un premier temps, puis leurs manières spécifiques de s'adapter à la modernité (alphabétisation, industrialisation) et leurs orientations préférentielles sur le plan politique.

Le point de départ pour établir une première classification des structures familiales présentes en Europe est relativement simple et facile à observer. Elle s'appuie sur deux couples de valeurs *a priori* antagonistes : autorité/liberté et égalité/inégalité (fig n°1). Si l'enfant adulte marié quitte le foyer de ses parents pour en fonder un nouveau, c'est le principe de liberté qui est valorisé : par extension, cette vision libérale des rapports familiaux s'étend aux relations entre les individus dans la société. *A contrario*, si l'enfant adulte marié continue à vivre avec ses parents, le principe d'autorité est prédominant. Par ailleurs, si la pratique de l'héritage consiste en un partage équitable entre tous les descendants, on peut avancer l'hypothèse d'un attachement des individus et des sociétés au principe d'égalité. *A contrario*, si la norme est l'indivisibilité du patrimoine et sa transmission à un seul descendant, ou encore l'absence de règle successorale, on pourra en déduire l'acceptation d'un principe d'inégalité.

Le croisement de ces couples de valeurs permet de définir les quatre principaux types de structures familiales présentes en Europe : la famille nucléaire absolue, la famille nucléaire égalitaire, la famille communautaire et la famille souche ou autoritaire. Cette typologie sera affinée ultérieurement pour aboutir, par exemple en France, à un système de neuf modèles familiaux que nous ne préciserons pas ici (Le Bras et Todd, 2013).

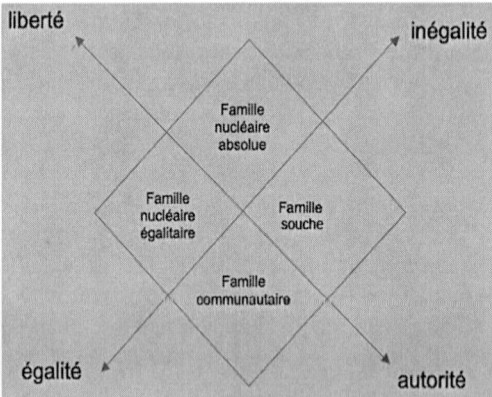

Figure 5 2. Définition des quatre types de structures familiales présents en Europe selon les valeurs qui leur sont attachées (selon E. Todd)

La famille souche ou autoritaire et les sciences sociales

Du fait de son fort degré de particularisme, mais aussi de sa répartition géographique (les périphéries européennes qui correspondent souvent à des espaces où le sentiment identitaire est très développé, tels que l'Écosse, la Catalogne, le Pays basque, l'Occitanie, l'Alsace, etc.), c'est surtout la famille souche ou autoritaire, encore appelée « système à maison », qui a suscité l'intérêt des sciences sociales. Les caractéristiques de la société occitane ont ainsi été particulièrement bien documentées, à commencer par celle des Pyrénées, étudiée par Frédéric le Play (1871), puis, un siècle plus tard, par Pierre Bourdieu (1962), Louis Assier-Andrieu (1981) ou encore un collectif de chercheurs du CNRS (Augustins *et al.*,

1986). Celle du Massif central n'a pas été en reste. La Margeride a ainsi été explorée par Élisabeth Claverie et Pierre Lamaison (1982) ou encore par une équipe de scientifiques menée par André Fel et Lucien Gachon qui a décrit la société locale comme une « démocratie paysanne », ou encore une « oligarchie paysanne » (Fel et Gachon, 1983).

Consensuelles, les sociétés autoritaires se manifestent finalement par des pratiques sociales égalitaires. Refusant un principe de différenciation des individus fondé sur les statuts socio-économiques, elles s'efforcent de réaliser une intégration verticale de la collectivité » (Fournier, 2014, p. 360).

Tous ces travaux ont montré que, dans ces régions préciputaires, les règles successorales reposaient sur un principe simple : le patrimoine, en particulier la maison et les terrains agricoles, était intégralement transmis à un héritier (parfois à une héritière) unique dans le but d'éviter la fragmentation de l'héritage.

La famille-souche repose essentiellement sur la cohabitation du couple de l'héritier unique avec ses parents et sur la transmission inégalitaire du patrimoine familial, constitué par la maison elle-même et l'ensemble des terres et des biens qui permettent à l'unité domestique de vivre. (Chamoux, 1987, p. 242).

À un seul autre enfant (cadet ou cadette) est offerte la possibilité de se marier en dehors de la maison, les unions de l'héritier(e) et du (de la) cadet(te) donnant lieu à des stratégies matrimoniales et des jeux d'alliances complexes entre familles des territoires concernés (Claverie et Lamaison, 1982). Enfin, dans le système traditionnel, les autres membres de la fratrie pouvaient rester vivre dans la maison auprès du couple héritier à condition de ne pas se marier.

La coutume successorale reposait en effet sur le primat de l'intérêt du groupe auquel les cadets devaient sacrifier leurs intérêts personnels, soit en se contentant d'une dot, soit en y renonçant tout à fait lorsqu'ils émigraient à la recherche d'un emploi, soit en passant leur vie, célibataires, à travailler sur la terre des ancêtres à côté de l'aîné » (Bourdieu, 1962, p. 38).

Beaucoup de chercheurs ont observé que, à l'échelle régionale, le « système à maison » génère un degré élevé de conscience historique, d'où découlent un fort attachement au territoire et un fort sentiment identitaire qui peuvent se manifester par des revendications régionalistes. Rappelons que « Vivre et travailler au pays » a d'abord été le slogan des terres occitanes. Emmanuel Todd, quant à lui, comme un certain nombre d'autres chercheurs en sciences sociales, considère que le système de valeurs porté par la famille souche repose principalement sur un principe de hiérarchisation des individus (certains seront héritiers, d'autres pas) et, par extension, des groupes. En accordant une place prépondérante au déterminisme anthropologique, cette lecture distanciée et plutôt mécanique de ce type d'organisation familiale, l'a conduit à penser que le système, insuffisamment porteur d'universalité, était intrinsèquement archaïque, incapable de s'adapter à la modernité, contrairement à la famille nucléaire égalitaire. Cette interprétation a été au moins partiellement contredite, par la réalité sociale et politique et par les récits plus nuancés qu'ont donnés les écrivains contemporains des mécanismes d'évolution de ce type de sociétés.

La famille souche ou autoritaire dans les récits contemporains

À partir des années soixante, et surtout soixante-dix, paraissent des « romans rustiques d'un nouveau genre [publiés par] de vrais ruraux » (Fel, 1992), originaires de différentes régions françaises : Ephraïm Grenadou pour la Beauce (*Grenadou paysan français*, 1966), Pierre-Jakez Hélias pour le pays bigouden (*Le cheval d'orgueil*, 1975), Émilie Carles dans les Hautes-Alpes (*Une soupe aux herbes sauvages*, 1977), Léonce Chaleil dans la vallée du Gardon (*La mémoire du village*, 1977). Tous ces récits témoignaient d'une paysannerie en pleine transformation, dont certains annonçaient déjà la disparition. Cette *Fin des paysans* (Mendras, 1967), de portée générale, Marie-Hélène Lafon en dressera quarante ans plus tard la chronique pour le Massif central dans son roman *Les derniers indiens* (2009).

Certains de ces récits étaient l'œuvre de fils ou filles de paysans, originaires des espaces d'extension d'une forme de famille « à maison », qui avaient connu une promotion sociale par l'école, jusqu'à devenir eux-mêmes enseignants. Ainsi en est-il de Pierre-Jakez Hélias et d'Émilie Carles et, une génération plus tard, de Marie-Hélène Lafon, fille d'agriculteurs du Cantal, et de Pierre Bergounioux. Le modèle est connu, parfois décrié par les autochtones eux-mêmes. Ainsi Alain Chany, dans *Une sécheresse à Paris*, l'associe-t-il « *à celui d'une jeunesse d'origine modeste, destinée à un avenir professionnel qui ne fait plus rêver, l'usage rétribué des mots (instituteurs)* » (Fournier, 2014, p. 356), tandis que Pierre Bergounioux en souligne discrètement le mécanisme d'acculturation opposant la singularité chère aux familles souche à l'universalité, valeur propre, selon Emmanuelle Todd, à la famille nucléaire égalitaire.

> Elle exerçait son métier avec l'intégrité de ces normaliens tirés du pays même, de la paysannerie auxquels on les rendait, quatre ans après, pour y faire germer et fleurir, avec les règles de la grammaire et du calcul, la notion du général, l'idée de l'universalité. (Bergounioux, 2012a, p. 43).

> Mais ce que cherche Octavie, ce sont des lumières, c'est la loi générale et des règles universelles. (Bergounioux, 2012a, p. 92).

Le géographe André Fel va s'appuyer sur ces témoignages parus dans les années soixante-dix pour consacrer un article, « Paysans français » (1992), à l'évolution du monde rural. Ce qui frappe alors l'auteur, déjà sensibilisé à ces problématiques par son travail précédent sur la Margeride, c'est l'importance accordée, dans chacun de ces récits de vie, à la famille paysanne, à la maisonnée. « *Et sur ces chemins* [relève-t-il] *nos narrateurs rencontrent, sans trop s'en rendre compte, des théoriciens et des penseurs. C'est Frédéric Le Play et ses types familiaux* » (Fel, 1992). Même si ces narrateurs cherchent à dépasser « l'*auto-portrait* paysan » et inscrire leurs propos dans une histoire plus large de la paysannerie, ils témoignent surtout d'un vécu et d'une expérience personnelle. « *Sans doute manquent-ils de références savantes. Mais c'est précisément parce que les auteurs s'ignorent les uns les autres et ignorent souvent les débats scientifiques qu'ils nous intéressent aussi, dans leur véracité* », précise André Fel (1992).

La démarche de Pierre Bergounioux est différente, qui mêle dans son récit une part de témoignage (informations factuelles) à la libre interprétation de l'écrivain, reposant sur son propre vécu (une enfance en Limousin) mais revisité au prisme de connaissances scientifiques certaines dans le domaine de la sociologie et de l'anthropologie (Bergounioux, 2014). Le point de départ de son roman, *Miette,* est la découverte, en 1993, d'une photographie de sa belle-famille prise en 1910 sur laquelle une paysanne austère pose avec ses enfants, Lucie, Baptiste, Octavie et Adrien. Dans ses *Carnets de Notes,* il mentionne :

> Je passe la moitié de la matinée à noter les impressions décousues, imprécises, décevantes que fait naître la photo de 1910 montrant Miette, souveraine, entourée de ses quatre enfants. L'oncle Adrien n'a pas un an. Il a dû bouger, son visage est flou. Il était le dernier de ce groupe obstiné, puissant. Leurs vies sont dignes qu'on s'en souvienne. Le peu que je sais d'elles suffirait, me semble-t-il, à faire un livre » (Bergounioux, 2012b, p. 327).

Dans *Miette*, Pierre Bergounioux met en scène, au cours du XXe siècle, les faits et gestes des membres de cette famille qui illustre de manière paradigmatique les principes et valeurs de la famille souche du Massif central. Le récit offre le prétexte à l'auteur d'explorer le caractère déterministe de l'existence, dans sa dimension anthropologique et, plus au-delà, ontologique. La photographie, écrit-il, « *les montre tels qu'ils auront été, déterminés, eux-mêmes, sans reste ni réserve, tels que l'heure et l'endroit l'exigeaient depuis trois mille ans* » (Bergounioux, 2012a, p. 27). Le déterminisme anthropologique – se marier pour l'une, devenir héritier pour l'autre – s'impose surtout aux aînés de la fratrie, Lucie et Baptiste,

> « Un destin classique emporte ceux qui ont vu le jour avant 1904 ; Lucie étant la première fille, fut la dernière à se marier dans un rayon d'une lieue. Elle entra comme bru, comme sa mère, dans une ferme dans laquelle elle fournit son lot d'enfants et sa part de peine. » (Bergounioux, 2012a, p. 52).

> « [Baptiste] fut comme Lucie, le dernier représentant du vieil âge. Il resta sur place tandis qu'elle entrait bru dans une ferme. » (Bergounioux, 2012a, p. 88).

Le devenir des aînés reste déterminé, assignés qu'ils sont à une place et une fonction dans la société traditionnelle, jusqu'à en perdre toute conscience de leur individualité, soumis « aux choses », selon l'expression de Pierre Bergounioux, cet esprit des lieux que l'on peut ici assimiler à la régionalité. La liberté narrative de l'écrivain permet alors de faire sentir combien le statut d'héritier conduit, certes à distinguer, mais plus encore à « dépersonnifier » celui qui le reçoit. Dans le système « à maison », il n'est finalement que le dépositaire temporel d'un patrimoine qu'il devra à son tour transmettre à un successeur. Il est bien, comme en rend compte l'écrivain à propos de Baptiste, « *l'esclave et le maître des choses* » (Bergounioux, 2012a, p. 87). Car le droit d'aînesse est moins un droit de propriété que le droit, ou plus précisément, le devoir, d'agir en propriétaire.

> Lui qui ne distinguait pas entre les choses et lui. Il avait été le fils de sa mère. Il appartenait à l'endroit. (Bergounioux, 2012a, p. 44).

> Il tenait de sa mère la résolution qui lui interdisait de jamais regarder à quoi que ce soit qui aurait été lui, d'écouter cette voix qui souhaite des ménagements, de l'indulgence, d'arrêter, cette faiblesse en quoi consiste, au fond, un soi […]. Il s'efforça d'épouser le grand mouvement afin de perpétuer ce que l'éternité qui avait précédé l'éveil du temps, sur les hauteurs, lui avait confié avec l'injonction de maintenir. (Bergounioux, 2012a, p. 101-102)

> Il aurait eu agréable que sa femme le regarde pour le maître des choses et les choses dont il était l'esclave pour les seules choses. Je doute qu'il ait jamais distingué en ce qui le concernait. Il ne paraît pas s'être attribué d'existence propre. Il s'est rapporté tout entier à ce qui n'était point lui. […]

Il recevait les directives des choses. Il accomplissait leur dessein. [...] Elle ne faisait pas du bien – c'est-à-dire de l'idée qu'il se faisait de sa personne – un très grand cas. [...] Pour comprendre, il lui aurait fallu se regarder un peu, du dehors comme un être distinct des choses auxquelles il s'assimilait et c'est ce que les choses ne permettaient pas. (Bergounioux, 2012a, p. 105-106).

Le modèle anthropologique de la famille souche conduit à établir des distinctions entre les enfants d'une même fratrie, selon leur rang de naissance. Cependant, alors qu'Emmanuel Todd interprète le résultat de ces pratiques comme un principe de hiérarchisation, donc d'inégalité, dans *Miette* Pierre Bergounioux insiste surtout sur l'idée de différenciation, des statuts et des trajectoires induites par la distinction initiale.

Les deux frères différaient sur ce point justement parce qu'ils étaient frères. Baptiste avait touché la propriété, c'est-à-dire la maison de 1830, la plus grande partie des terres et l'obligation de les représenter, ce dont Adrien, son cadet, s'était trouvé, par le fait, exempté [...] Les contributions des deux frères à la physionomie du lieu portent le sceau de leur condition respective. (Bergounioux, 2012a, p. 16-17).

Ajouté à cela que la première [Lucie] est devenue l'épouse d'un paysan des environs, la seconde [Octavie] professeur de mathématiques en restant célibataire et l'on aura du mal à les regarder pour ce qu'elles étaient : deux sœurs nées à quatre années de distance au même endroit. (Bergounioux, 2012a, p. 50).

La plume sensible – quoique éclairée – de l'écrivain permet de mieux saisir et donner à comprendre la dynamique propre de la famille souche qui articule en réalité deux types de valeurs ou d'assignations antagonistes. Le poids de la contrainte, du devoir, pèse sur les aînés, destinés à hériter et se marier, mais, en contrepartie, exonère les puînés de ces charges, et se faisant les libère. L'absence de détermination impose donc, *a contrario,* aux puînés une grande liberté, puisqu'ils peuvent, selon leur inclinaison personnelle, opter pour la sécurité en restant vivre dans la maison familiale (quitte à devenir autrefois cet « *oncle célibataire qui dort dans la grange* ») ou choisir de partir, tenter leur chance ailleurs, s'émanciper de la tutelle familiale.

Sa chance, si le mot convient, c'est que Lucie l'a précédée pour essuyer l'ombre portée sur le siècle naissant, des siècles passés et que Baptiste, depuis trois ans, se prépare à jouer activement le rôle qui lui incombe. [...] Elle s'est engouffrée dans l'échappatoire qu'on peut, rétrospectivement, déceler à la troisième place, entre une fille et un garçon devant, et encore un garçon derrière, et que les trois autres, en agissant conformément aux

prévisions, ont maintenue ouverte. [...] La chipie prend le large .
(Bergounioux, 2012a, p 59-62)

À une génération de distance [Adrien] serait devenu l'oncle célibataire qui
dort dans la grange et fournit, sans contrepartie, un obscur labeur. Mais
c'est maintenant. C'est 1910. [...] Il ne reste plus au cadet qu'à se
désintéresser du travail de la ferme, des labours, des fenaisons et des
moissons [...] Il s'absente, pilote une moto, se forme chez les serruriers [...
Miette] ne fit rien pour contraindre Adrien [...] Sans doute approuva-t-elle
son départ. (Bergounioux, 2012a, p. 135-137).

Adrien, étant homme et en dernière position, aurait pu suivre son
inclinaison singulière [...] s'embarquer. Nul n'y aurait trouvé rien à redire.
Il s'arrêta aux portes de Paris. (Bergounioux, 2012a, p. 141).

Sous cet angle, peu exploré dans les travaux des sociologues, la famille
souche, autoritaire, apparaît comme un oxymore puisque, au final, le
système impose à la fois la détermination et la non-détermination, la
soumission à un mode de vie et la liberté de s'auto-déterminer.

Adrien, avec le rang de benjamin et la liberté ou la privation ou la
dépossession – c'est pareil –, pouvait inspirer à sa sœur un sentiment pur,
visant sa personne et non, à travers elle, des étendues de bruyères et de
genêts [...] Il ne se souciait pas de tenir ensemble des choses comme son
frère aîné [...] Il était vraiment libre. Il agissait et parlait au gré des
circonstances, en cas de besoin. (Bergounioux, 2012a, p. 133).

Et pourtant, c'était comme Octavie et Miette et les autres, avant, pareil.
C'étaient les choses, leur détermination, mais négative, l'apparence de
liberté, l'indétermination malheureuse qu'elles assignaient aux cadets après
s'être annexé, aliéné l'aîné. [...] Elles s'étaient emparées de Baptiste mais
Adrien ne se trouvait pas pour autant délivré d'elles, rendu à lui-même
ouvert à quelque vie nouvelle, comme Octavie. (Bergounioux, 2012a,
p. 139-140).

Même si, sous la plume de Pierre Bergounioux, la liberté, conséquence
intrinsèque de la privation de propriété, apparaît comme une forme de
détermination, c'est cette apparente contradiction interne qui a permis aux
sociétés « à maison » de s'adapter à la modernité alors qu'on les pensait
condamnées dans les années soixante-dix. Il est du reste à noter que, bien
souvent, ce sont ceux qui possédaient le moins de biens – donc qui étaient
les moins soumis aux contraintes liées à leur statut – qui ont le plus tiré
leur épingle du jeu (Fournier, 2003), ainsi que l'illustrent les trajectoires
contraires des familles Santoire et Lavigne dans le roman de Marie-Hélène
Lafon, *Les derniers indiens* (2009).

Conclusion

Ces deux exemples avaient pour objectif de montrer la fécondité du croisement des regards entre la littérature et les sciences du territoire. L'intérêt des géographes pour l'œuvre de Georges Perec n'est plus à démontrer. La discipline s'est emparée d'*Espèces d'espaces* – ainsi que des productions suivantes –, chaque génération apportant sa relecture ou ses interrogations au vu des évolutions épistémologiques. De fait, dans les travaux de géographie, les références à Georges Perec sont aujourd'hui si nombreuses qu'elles sont devenues un lieu commun ; ici, c'est le titre d'un colloque ; là, l'expérimentation d'une méthode photographique pour observer les évolutions paysagères (*Le vieillissement des lieux*, Grison, 1998) ; ailleurs un clin d'œil (*Géographie mode d'emploi*, Simon, 2004) ; partout des citations et des références bibliographiques. L'œuvre de Pierre Bergounioux, écrivain discret, est moins connue (Coyault *et al.*, 2016). Par la narration, il n'en rend pas moins accessibles à la compréhension des mécanismes sociaux complexes que l'écriture scientifique peine tant à saisir qu'à faire partager. Cette capacité de la littérature à rendre compte des dimensions matérielles et immatérielles, individuelles et collectives, de l'existence, Pierre Bergounioux l'a lui-même longuement décortiquée (Bergounioux, 2014).

> La littérature est à la fois l'expression des fractions dominantes des sociétés successives et l'expression la plus rapprochée de l'expérience collective. Quant au style, il est indissociable d'une position dans l'espace social. Quand j'étais jeune, j'étais frappé par le décalage ou plutôt le fossé entre ce que je voyais et ce qu'on en disait autour de moi. Quand j'écris, je travaille sur cette incertitude entre l'expérience et l'expression, entre l'opacité et le discernement. (Thierry Clermont, entretien avec Pierre Bergounioux, 2014[2]).

Sa connaissance intime des territoires et des sociétés concernés lui permet ainsi de nuancer et préciser certaines mutations contemporaines. En ce sens, *Miette* constitue une source pour les anthropologues, les géographes et, plus largement, tous les spécialistes des sciences du territoire qui cherchent à saisir les changements qui affectent les sociétés rurales du Massif central. Ce faisant, il contribue à forger une nouvelle image de la « régionalité ».

---

[2] Thierry Clermont, entretien avec Pierre Bergounioux : « Je suis un crétin rural », *Le Figaro*, 23 octobre 2014, http://www.lefigaro.fr/livres/2014/10/23/03005-20141023ARTFIG00023-pierre-bergounioux-je-suis-un-cretin-rural.php

Sources primaires

Bergounioux, Pierre. 2012a [première édition 1996]. *Miette,* Paris, Gallimard, collection Folio, 167 p.

—. 2012b. *Carnets de Notes, 1991 – 2000,* tome 2, Éditions Verdier, 1260 p.

—. 2014. *Exister par deux fois,* collection Essais, Fayard, 295 p.

Carles, Émilie. 1977. *Une soupe aux herbes sauvages,* Simoen, 315 p.

Chaleil, Léonce. 1977. *La mémoire du village,* Paris, Stock, 363 p.

Chany, Alain. 1992. *Une sécheresse à Paris,* Paris, Éditions de l'Olivier, 118 pages.

Grenadou, Ephraïm et Prevost, Alain. 1966. *Grenadou paysan français,* Paris, le Seuil, 216 p.

Hélias, Pierre-Jakès. 1975. *Le cheval d'orgueil,* Terre humaine, Paris, Plon, 625 p.

Lafon, Marie-Hélène. 2011 [première édition 2009]. *Les derniers indiens,* Paris, Gallimard, collection Folio, 149 p.

Perec, Georges. 1974 [réédition 2000]. *Espèces d'espaces,* Paris, Éditions Galilée, 182 p.

Pinchemel, Philippe. 1978. Éditorial, *Espace géographique,* Volume 7, Numéro 7-2, p. 152.

Sources secondaires

Assier-Andrieu, Louis. 1981. *Coutume et rapports sociaux. Étude anthropologique des communautés paysannes du Capcir,* Paris, Éditions du CNRS, 215 p.

Augé, Marc. 1992. *Non-lieux, introduction à une anthropologie de la surmodernité,* Paris, Le Seuil, 160 p.

Augustins, Georges, Bonnain, Rolande, Peron, Yves et Sauter, Gilles. 1986. *Les Baronnies des Pyrénées. Tome II, Maisons. Espace. Famille,* Paris, EHESS, 215 p.

Bourdieu, Pierre. 1962. Célibat et condition paysanne, *Études rurales,* n° 5-6, p. 32-135 ; doi : 10.3406/rural.1962.1011

—. 1998 [première édition 1992]. *Les règles de l'art. Genèse et structure du champs littéraire,* Paris, Éditions du Seuil, collection Points Essai, 567 p.

Brunet, Roger. 1968. *Les phénomènes de discontinuité en géographie,* Paris, Éditions du Centre national de la recherche scientifique, 119 p.

Brunet, Roger, Ferras, Robert et Théry, Hervé. 1993. *Les Mots de la géographie, dictionnaire critique,* Reclus, La Documentation Française, 518 p.

Chamoux, Antoinette. 1987. Le fonctionnement de la famille-souche dans les Baronnies des Pyrénées avant 1914, *Annales de démographie historique*, p. 241-262 ; doi : 10.3406/adh.1988.1690

Claverie, Élisabeth et Lamaison, Pierre. 1982. *L'impossible mariage. Violence et parenté en Gévaudan, 17e-18e-19e siècles*, Paris, Hachette, 361 p.

Cortazar, Julio et Dunlop, Carol. 1983. *Les autonautes de la cosmoroute ou un voyage intemporel Paris-Marseille*, Paris, Gallimard, Collection Du monde entier, 280 p.

Coyault, Sylviane, Jacquet, Marie-Thérèse (dir). 2016. *Les chemins de Pierre Bergounioux*, Macerata, édition Quodlibet Studio.

Coyault, Sylviane. 2002. *La province en héritage. Pierre Michon, Pierre Bergounioux, Richard Millet*, Genève, Librairie Droz, coll. « Histoire des idées et critique littéraire », 289 p.

Fel, André et Gachon, Lucien (dir). 1983. *La Margeride : la montagne, les hommes,* Paris, INRA, 786 p.

Fel, André. 1992. Paysans français, *Géographie et cultures* [En ligne], 1 | 1992, mis en ligne le 8 janvier 2014 ; doi : 10.4000/gc.2555

Fournier, Mauricette. 2003. L'impossible projet de territoire : évolution agricole, révolution sociale, inertie politique au Pays de Saugues (Margeride), *Crises et mutations des agricultures de montagne*, Collection CERAMAC, Presses universitaires Blaise Pascal, Clermont-Ferrand, p. 583-602.

—. 2014. La liberté territorialisée ; montagnes idéalisées et critique sociale de Jules Vallès à Alain Chany, *in* Lionel Dupuy et Jean-Yves Puyo (dir), *L'imaginaire géographique. Entre géographie, langue et littérature*, Presses de l'Université de Pau et des Pays de l'Adour, Collection Spatialités, p. 349-360.

Hancock, Claire. 2003. *Paris et Londres au XIXe siècle : représentations dans les guides et récits de voyage*, Paris, Éditions du CNRS, collection Espaces et Milieux, 357 p.

Jablonka, Ivan. 2014. *L'histoire est une littérature contemporaine. Manifeste pour les sciences sociales*, Paris, Éditions du Seuil, La librairie du XXIe siècle, 352 p.

Langevin, Francis. 2010a. Un nouveau régionalisme ? De Sainte-Souffrance à Notre-Dame-du-Cachalot, en passant par Rivière-aux-Oies, *in* Sébastien Chabot, Éric Dupont et Christine Eddie (éd.), « Narrations contemporaines au Québec et en France : regards croisés », *Voix et Images*, vol. 36, n° 1, (106) 2010, p. 59-77.

Langevin, Francis. 2010b. La régionalité chez Hervé Bouchard, Éric Dupont et François Blais, *in* Zuzana Malinovská (dir.), *Cartographie du roman québécois contemporain*, Prešov (Slovaquie), Acta Facultatis

Philosophicae Universitatis Prešovensis, coll. Monographia (n° 112), p. 36-53.

Laslett, Peter. 1969. *Un monde que nous avons perdu : Famille, communauté et structure sociale dans l'Angleterre pré-industrielle*, Paris, Flammarion, 299 p.

Le Bras, Hervé et Todd, Emmanuel. 2012 [réédition revue de l'ouvrage de 1981]. *L'invention de la France, Atlas anthropologique et politique*, Paris, Gallimard, NRF Essais, 528 pages.

Le Bras, Hervé et Todd, Emmanuel. 2013. *Le mystère français*, Paris, Seuil, 308 p.

Le Play, Frédéric. 1871. *L'Organisation de la famille selon le vrai modèle signalé par l'histoire de toutes les races et de tous les temps*, Paris, Mâme.

—. 1877-1879. *Ouvriers européens. Études sur les travaux, la vie domestique et la condition morale des populations ouvrières de l'Europe*, Tours, Alfred Mame et fils, 6 vol.

Le Roy Ladurie, Emmanuel. 1972. Structures familiales et coutumes d'héritage en France au XVIe siècle : système de la coutume, *Annales. Économies, Sociétés, Civilisations*, Volume 27, n° 4, p. 825-846.

Lévy Jacques et Lussault Michel. 2003. Notice « Espace », *in* Lévy Jacques et Lussault Michel, *Dictionnaire de la géographie et de l'espace des sociétés*, Paris, Belin, p. 325-333.

Lussault Michel. 2003. Notice « Georges Perec », *in* Lévy Jacques et Lussault Michel, *Dictionnaire de la géographie et de l'espace des sociétés*, Paris, Belin, p. 702-704.

Mendras, Henri. 1967. *La fin des paysans*, Paris, SEDEIS, 1967, 364 p. ; réédition, Arles, Actes Sud, coll. « Babel », 1992.

Orain, Olivier et Sol, Marie-Pierre. 2007. Les géographes et le travail collectif, *La revue pour l'histoire du CNRS* [En ligne], 18 | 2007, mis en ligne le 3 octobre 2009, URL : http://histoire-cnrs.revues.org/4061

Reclus, Elysée. 2005. *Histoire d'une montagne*, Editions PyréMonde, 170 p.

Thiesse, Anne-Marie. 1991. *Écrire la France. Le mouvement littéraire régionaliste de langue française entre la Belle Epoque et la Libération*, Paris, Presses Universitaires de France, 320 p.

—. 1993. La littérature régionaliste en France (1900 1940), *Tangence*, n° 40, mai 1993, p. 49-64.

Todd, Emmanuel. 1983. *La Troisième Planète : structures familiales et systèmes idéologiques,* Paris, Éditions du Seuil, Empreintes, 251 p.

—. 1984. *L'Enfance du monde : structures familiales et développement,* Paris, Éditions du Seuil, Empreintes, 251 p.

Todd, Emmanuel et Le Bras, Hervé. 1986. *Les Trois France,* Éditions

Odile Jacob, Opus, 266 p.

Todd, Emmanuel. 1990. *L'invention de l'Europe*. Paris, Éditions du Seuil, Collection L'histoire immédiate, 537 p.

—. 1999. *La Diversité du monde : structures familiales et modernité,* Paris, Éditions du Seuil, Histoire immédiate, 435 p.

—. 2011. *L'origine des systèmes familiaux,* volume 1 : L'Eurasie, Paris, Gallimard, Nrf Essais, 756 p.

Wittmann, Jacques et Wittmann, René (dir). 1941. *Œuvres de F. Le Play. I – Principes de paix sociale : La famille*, Paris, Éditions d'histoire et d'art, Librairie Plon, Collection Les cahiers de l'unité française.

Wittmann, Jacques et Wittmann, René (dir). 1941. *Œuvres de F. Le Play. II – La Réforme de la société : Le travail*, Paris, Éditions d'histoire et d'art, Librairie Plon, Collection Les cahiers de l'unité française.

PART 2:

NEW EXPRESSION OF REGIONALITY IN THE FRENCH MASSIF CENTRAL: LITERARY REVIVAL IN SEARCH OF AUTHENTICITY

CHAPTER SIX

FROM *LA MONTAGNE* BY JEAN FERRAT TO THE WEBSITE OF THE REGIONAL NATURAL PARK OF THE MOUNTS OF ARDÈCHE (FRANCE): GEOGRAPHICAL IMAGINARY AND DEVELOPMENT OF A NEW TERRITORIALITY IN THE ARDÈCHE MOUNTAINS

ANTOINE MARTY AND MAURICETTE FOURNIER

Since the "cultural turn" of the 1970s, the study of representations associated with places and spatial categories has taken on an increasingly important place in geography. Geographic imaginary allows us to grasp spaces and their dynamics based on immaterial characteristics, their lived and perceived character. Projected on spaces, representations help to characterize and differentiate them. They make up the sensitive relationship between societies and spaces, and participate in the appropriation of territories by the social groups that practice them. The geographic imaginary (Bédard and *ali*, 2011; Dupuy and Puyo, 2014 and 2015), charged with positive or negative values, helps to make the spaces attractive or repulsive. It seems consubstantially determined by the dynamics driving the territories, and determining in these evolutions.

The physical characteristics of the rural mountain area contribute at first sight to singularize it. Relief, slope, altitude, climate, vegetation, adret / ubac exposure, are all physical elements that make up a specific spatial context for the societies that settle there. The appropriation of mountain space induces a specific socio-spatial organization, a physical and ideological geographical object, both the product of the organization of social groups and the support of their organization and activities (Debarbieux, 2001).

Figure 6.1 Homepages of the web site of the Monts d'Ardèche
Regional Natural Park
Translation of the main slogans of each page: Here the flavors are natural / Living
here is an opportunity / Here links are woven / Here biodiversity blossoms / Here a
generation "park" grows up.

From a diachronic perspective, the imaginary correlated to the mountain
has undergone significant recompositions and evolutions (Debarbieux and
Rudaz, 2010). Representations have evolved along with the socio-spatial
dynamics that have affected it. This article aims to highlight the
consubstantiality and reciprocal construction between the evolution of
representations and socio-spatial dynamics animating the Ardèche Mountains

from two documents: the song *La Montagne*, written by Jean Ferrat in 1964 and the website of the Monts d'Ardèche Regional Natural Park (PNR).

Directly inspired by Jean Ferrat's stay in Antraigues-sur-Volane, *La Montagne* evokes the rural exodus and the agricultural rejection that the territory experienced during the first half of the 20th century. The geographical imaginary that it translates is both socio-spatial representations that one can think is *a priori* shared by emigrants and representations peculiar to the singer. Moreover, the latter has in many respects an anachronistic dimension which prefigures the reconstruction of the imaginary associated with the mounts of Ardèche. The website (mainly its homepage) of the Monts d'Ardèche Regional Natural Park, a medium mountain area of the eastern foothills of the Massif Central, at the heart of which is the commune of Antraigues-sur-Volane, will constitute the contemporary "counterpoint" of this analysis. The result of a collective approach, the site conveys representations, which are certainly the result of a social consensus, but whose purposes are promotional.

The geographic imaginary "Territorialization operator": from representations to the territory's construction

Perceived space, lived space: towards the notion of territory

In geography, the study of spatial representations is at the origin of the concept of "perceived space". Constructed subjective or collective, it is the product of representations, affects, concrete experiences, images or even memories that are "projected" by an individual or a social group on space. The spatial representations then constitute a relational, sensitive and dynamic beam between a space and an individual or a social group. The degree of proximity which the author, who projects his representations, maintains with the space he represents, can constitute a new element of distinction. The concept of "lived space" refers to a space that is both perceived and practiced in a more or less intense way. This "lived space" corresponds to the superposition of the living space (i.e. a subjective construction generated by a concrete experience) and the perceived space, associated with the imaginary necessarily influenced by the practice of this space.

The representations projected by Jean Ferrat's song are those of the space experienced by the author. Indeed, the song was inspired during his stay in Antraigues-sur-Volane. This concrete experience helped to build his representation of the Monts d'Ardèche. Shortly afterwards, the singer finally settled in the commune.

Another parameter makes it possible to slide from the individual sphere to the collective sphere. The "occurrence" of socio-spatial representations within society, the way in which these are shared, from within or without in relation to the space considered, makes it possible to make the link with the notion of territory. Defined by Guy Di Méo (1994) as the appropriate portion of space by a social group, the territory corresponds to the superposition of a relative space organized by society, a living space composed of concrete experiences, and a lived space, fruit of representations and shared values. The representations conveyed by the website of the Monts d'Ardèche correspond to this collective and territorial prism. The selection of the elements visible on the site depicts an imaginary "common" to the local society. This imaginary, mobilized as a tool to promote the territory, thus has a collective dimension, identity and policy.

These two rural scripts (the song and the website) are thus positioned on different planes: two different eras, differentiated "positions" from the imagined object and a variable "occurrence" (an individual scale for the Song by Jean Ferrat, a collective scale for the Monts d'Ardèche website.

Symbolization of places and socio-spatial representations: operator of territorialization

The symbolization of places on the basis of spatial representations is at the origin of the process of territorial construction. According to Bernard Debarbieux (2009), two main dialectics contribute to territorialization from spatial representations. The dialectic "genericity / singularity" contributes to the creation of a symbolization of space, itself at the origin of the construction of a socio-spatial metaphor. Genericity is the symbolic game that leads to the apprehension of objects in a similar way. In this context, objects or places are apprehended in common, due to an assimilable form or function. Conversely, the process of singularity distinguishes objects or places which may have a sacred dimension for the social group at the origin of their specification. Selection operator, the process of singularity is a construction which isolates "objects" within their environment. In these objects symbolically common and shared values are inscribed.

The construction of the territory on the basis of this symbolization of space by socio-spatial representations is carried out according to a dialectic "differentiation / aggregation". Differentiation consists of a symbolic game that combines a form of spatial organization and a form of social organization, both specific. This game, which can be carried out endogenously or exogenously, singles out one space among others, in a comparative essence approach that distances it from otherness. The aggregation process also participates in territorialization by assembling and pooling spaces characterized by similar objects or systemic functioning.

The territory of the Monts d'Ardèche sung by Jean Ferrat

In Jean Ferrat's work, the symbolization of places on the basis of spatial representations makes it possible to construct a social metaphor of the traditional peasant and mountain society, threatened and deeply disrupted by the rural exodus. In terms of genericity, different elements can illuminate the analysis.

Avec les mains par dessus leurs têtes,
Ils avaient construit des murettes
Jusqu'au sommet de la colline

The lines refer to the presence of terraces, a generic form of adaptation of peasant agriculture to the constraints engendered by the slope, which has an important impact on the landscape. Their evocation is accompanied by social representations linked to the traditional agrarian system, to the harshness of the conditions of life implied by this mountain environment.

Les vignes, elles courent dans la forêt
Le vin ne sera plus tiré

The evocation of abandoned vineyards constitutes another element of genericity. Testimony of a traditional activity, their abandonment is symptomatic of the agricultural disavowal consubstantial to the rural exodus. These various elements compose the poetic and social metaphor of the peasant society woven by Ferrat. It emphasizes with tenderness the traditional and antiquated aspect of this society:

Les vieux, ce n'était pas original,
Quand ils s'essuyaient machinal,
D'un revers de manche les lèvres,
Mais ils savaient tous à propos,
Tuer la caille et le perdreau,
Et manger la tomme de chèvre

The territorialization modalities, to which the geographical imaginary of the song leads, correspond at the same time to processes of differentiation and aggregation. The various generic elements, symbolized by the imaginary, logically lead to a process of territorial differentiation. This singularization is based on common values (" *Qu'importent les jours les années, Ils avaient tous l'âme bien née*") and a form of socio-spatial organization perceived as singular. It should be noted that this process of distancing rests essentially on the opposition built with the city. Territorial aggregation, which pools different spaces within the same territory, is based first and foremost on the landscape coherence conveyed by various natural or artificial elements: relief, forest, terrace, grazing or "abandoned" vineyards. The title of the work, *La Montagne*, also illustrates perfectly the process of symbolic aggregation that the author operates. This aggregation is also based on a description of the peasant society, particularly its agrarian system, which emphasizes a similar functioning for the whole of this space. The description of the recomposition of local society, caused by the rural exodus, contributes greatly to the production of this process of generalization by amalgamating the similar negative dynamics that affect the Monts d'Ardèche. In particular, the author insists on the rupture of the relationship with the land, the meaning of which can easily be extended to "terroir" and "territory", suggesting a process of disintegration of territoriality and a form of identity dissolution of emigrants.

Ils quittent un à un le pays,
Pour s'en aller gagner leur vie,
Loin de la terre où ils sont nés

The territory of the Ardèche Mountains promoted by the Regional Natural Park

The information on the homepage of the website of the PNR of the mounts of Ardeche is particularly interesting because it constitutes the "showcase" of the territory. In a promotional way, it strives to convey an attractive imaginary. The result of a collective approach, it contributes to legitimizing the territorial dimension of the Monts d'Ardèche area and, beyond that, the very existence of the PNR. In terms of genericity, the first valued elements are, unsurprisingly, linked to nature and the environment preserved: use of green color, photographs of fauna and flora, slogan "*Ici la biodiversité s'épanouit*". The awarding of the UNESCO Geopark label in 2014 contributes to conveying these same representations of a unique and preserved natural space. The other generic elements (chestnut groves, terraces, vernacular architecture) carry the idea of tradition and authenticity.

Unlike Jean Ferrat's song, which does not mention any toponym, the site of the PNR highlights in its section "unmissable sites" some emblematic places in the Ardèche mountains. Among these special places, we can mention the Mont Gerbier de Jonc, source of the Loire River, to which are attached multiple symbolic dimensions ("original", "generous", "fertile" character) in which the local society is recognized. The Bridge of the Devil in Thueyts is also interesting because as a symbol of the idea of a link, it can suggest the importance accorded to territorial solidarity. Moreover, the aesthetics and the technique used during its construction enhance here traditional knowledge. The "chestnut trees celebrations" embody strong temporalities that are to be compared with these elements of exceptionality within their environment: paroxysmal moments of community life in the village, they are an opportunity to value a specific product of the territory and testify the importance of the seasons which induces a relation to the peasant society's own time.

As in Jean Ferrat's song, the different natural and landscape elements, "similar" within the Monts d'Ardèche, contribute to perceive it as a territory, by aggregation and differentiation in relation to external spaces. In this logic of territorial singularization, local quality products (blueberries, chestnuts, honey, water, wine, beef Fin-Gras of Mézenc) also suggest the existence of the territory. Products of the specificity of the terroir and local knowledge, participate in promoting authentic quality agriculture: they are therefore the products of the territorial specificity of the Monts d'Ardèche. It is suggested to visitors that the gastronomic quality of these products stems from the quality of the environment: "*Ici les saveurs sont naturelles*". On the other hand, socio-spatial representations emphasize the conviviality of local society. The text emphasizes the values of a model of a society of belonging: "*Ici des liens se tissent*". The local markets help to convey this representation of conviviality and authenticity. This common understanding of social organization and functioning builds territorial coherence based on shared values, the intensity of interrelations and societal solidarity. Distinguished spatial or social objects also participate in producing the territory. Thus, the Mont Gerbier de Jonc, the Mont Mézenc, the waterfalls, the emblematic buildings, are all symbolic materializations signifying the values shared by the social group: their spread constitutes for society so many catalysts of the socio-spatial specificity of the territory of the Monts d'Ardèche.

Through these two examples of the average mountain in the Ardèche region, it is clear that the spatial imaginary associated with spaces constitutes a powerful operator of territorialization. It contributes to the consciousness and appropriation of space by societies.

Socio-spatial representations and territorial dynamic: a reciprocal construction

Inversion of urban / rural value: a theoretical framework that illuminates the case of Ardèche

The purpose of this second part is to understand the dynamic link that exists between the evolution of the spatial imaginary and the dynamics and recompositions of the territories' objects of representations. The aim is to highlight the performative propensity of representations that partly determine territorial dynamics and, retroactively, to underline the impact of spatial recompositions on the production of representations. The diachronic comparative analysis of Jean Ferrat's song (1964) and the Monts d'Ardèche website (2016) are both of interest here.

The evolution of representations and the socio-spatial dynamics experienced by the Monts d'Ardèche are to a large extent similar to those that have characterized rural areas more generally (Hervieu and Viard, 1996). There is a reciprocal and concomitant play of construction between territorial recompositions and evolution of the geographical imaginary. The factors behind the recomposition of rural areas are important to emphasize, as they have, in part, contributed to overturning the image of rurality. Advances in mobility and the desire for ownership have led to a movement of urban loosening and periurbanization, supported by the possibility of accessing more space at a lower cost. In parallel with the modernization and marginalization of agriculture, the diversification of the uses of rural areas, in particular the development of residential and recreational functions has resulted in a recomposition of local societies (Cognard, 2010). Moreover, the deterritorialization of the "urban style life" was manifested by a form of convergence of urban and rural lifestyles. Thus, the growth of domestic comfort and the spread of mass consumption have contributed to the recomposition of rural spaces, to the emergence and spread of new imaginaries associated with the "urban" and "rural" spatial categories. Conversely, these new representations conveyed by rural areas, which reflect a reversal of values, have influenced their dynamics. The recomposition of the imaginary pertaining to each category thus appears simultaneously as a resultant and an operator of the territorial dynamics that these spaces are experiencing.

The reversal of values attributed to urban and rural spaces was gradually introduced in the 1970s in two ways. On the one hand, by "sliding" representations attributed to one spatial category towards the other. Thus, aesthetics and patrimonialization of nature have sanctioned the transfer of aesthetic representations (which is "beautiful"). The "pleasant" sociability, long associated with the urban life style as evidenced by the word "urbanity", has also migrated towards village sociability. Similarly, the spatial assignment of the imaginary linked to freedom has at least experienced a significant decompartmentalization (Debarbieux and Rudaz, 2010; Fournier, 2014). On the other hand, the inversion of values is also reflected in the revalorization of "permanent" representations, that is to say, always peddled by the same spatial category. Thus, for example, "tradition" or "calm", still attached to rurality but now valued, testify to a new idealization of the past. Conversely, the "progress" and the "speed", attached to the urban, seem to experience a form of devalorization reflecting a certain crisis of modernity. Trends in the socio-spatial representations of rural areas have contributed to the upgrading of their amenities, particularly in terms of quality and living environment. They thus contribute to define the degree of attractiveness of spaces, in a differentiated way.

In this perspective, the comparative analysis of the song and the website illustrates the evolution of representations and the reversal of values relating to the imaginary of urban spaces and rural spaces. The evolution of representations attached to the Ardèche mountains seems to correspond in a paradigmatic way to the evolution of the imaginary conveyed by rural spaces. The socio-spatial representations associated with the Monts d'Ardèche testify to the inversion of values and the symbolic shift of the socio-spatial recompositions animating the territory. Three major evolutions can be observed.

From a harsh environment to a living space rich in amenities

The Monts d'Ardèche were once perceived as a binding living environment, in order to take up the concepts of classical geography, a rough and difficult "way of life" for the traditional peasant society.

Avec leurs mains par dessus leurs têtes
[...]
Deux chèvres et puis quelques moutons
Une année bonne et l'autre non
Et sans vacances et sans sorties

From now on, their representations highlight the amenities of the living environment, first of all on a landscape level: the development of an imaginary associated with a preserved environment ("beautiful", "genuine", "abundant" and "generous") and the international recognition of the specificity of its relief (Geopark label). This inversion is also a consequence of the spreading, in the countryside, of the trend of mass consumption and domestic comfort. It has led to restoring a certain attractiveness to this space that was previously "repulsive", causing rural exodus as in Jean Ferrat's song. In a game of reciprocal construction and cyclic causality, this renewed attractiveness is reflected in the arrival of an allochthonous population which contributes to the development of representations, which in turn influences the attractiveness of the territory and thus contributes to territorial recompositions.

This "reversal" in the evolution of representations is especially evident in the ways of living attached to the space (the harshness of the old mountain life / recreational space today). It can be illustrated by the contrast between the text of Jean Ferrat's song ("*Et sans vacances et sans sorties)* and the Mont d'Ardèche slogan "*Vivre ici est une chance*". In *La Montagne*, it was the city that had the recreational offer:

Depuis longtemps ils en rêvaient
De la ville et de ses secrets
Du formica et du ciné

Les filles veulent aller au bal
Il n'y a rien de plus normal
Que de vouloir vivre sa vie.

Post-modern representations now apprehend mountainous space as a "pleasant living environment" and a "playground". This evolution was co-built with the development of tourism and leisure activities in the region. They mark a break with the traditional imaginary of a constraining mountainous area. It is interesting to note in this connection that at the beginning of the 20th century the Alpine high mountain was associated, in particular for a fringe of the English aristocracy, with a "playground" through the sport of mountaineering. The recreational potential of the mountain area thus seems to have simultaneously been democratized and generalized to all mountains.

From the "archaic" peasant society to the community of belonging

While Jean Ferrat sang about the traditional Ardèche peasant society with affection, his song nevertheless suggested an "archaic" and "conservative" dimension of the "vieux" evoked in *La Montagne*. The words of the song suggest a causal link between this static character and the departure of young people.

Qu'importent les jours les années
Ils avaient tous l'âme bien née
Noueuse comme un pied de vigne
[...]
Mais il faisait des centenaires
A ne plus que savoir en faire

These representations, which were negative at the time, contributed to the repulsive nature of the space and resulted in a massive emigration of young people to the cities, symbols of progress and modernity. In this respect, it is interesting to observe the distortion between the representations that Jean Ferrat lend to young people and his own almost anachronistic representations of a space which he fills with positive values, out of step with his contemporaries.

The imaginary attached to the contemporary local society, promoted by the website of the Park, presents a form of continuity with the past. But there has been a complete revaluation of the values attached to them. The community model based on inter-knowledge and the sharing of values of local society is now strongly valued: "*Ici des liens se tissent*" claims the website. As a filigree, the opposition is constructed with the negative representations conveyed by an urban sociability that is now considered contractual and superficial, even dangerous. The relation to time illustrates this inversion of values: the immobility of traditional society, once devalued in favor of modernity and mobility, is to a certain extent revalorized by the reassuring side of this "permanence" in a context where progress is worrying. It enables local cultural identities that embody shelters in a globalized and homogenized context to be preserved. With anticipation, Jean Ferrat illustrated this inversion.

Pourtant que la montagne est belle
Comment peut-on s'imaginer
En voyant un vol d'hirondelles
Que l'automne vient d'arriver

The lines express this indifference to the passing time. The rest of the text ("*Il faut savoir ce que l'on aime / Rentrer dans son HLM / Manger du poulet aux hormones* ") testifies to a certain mistrust of progress that finds a certain echo in today's society. It may be interesting to draw a parallel between the timeless character of the Monts d'Ardeche, which defines an "elsewhere" and the concept of heterotopia by Michel Foucault (1984), the concrete and social spatialization of utopia, which implies a form of breaking in real time. The evolution of the representations and territorial dynamics become clearer this time mutually: in a structural context of globalization, they tend to revalue the local identity and the territorial specificity of the Monts d'Ardèche, giving them a new attractiveness.

From the "outdated" to the patrimonialized

A last notable reversal highlights the deep evolutions of the spatial imaginary associated with the Ardèche Mountains. To a large extent, it derives from the elements mentioned above. This concerns the revalorization of traditions and know-how which is consubstantially associated with the infatuation of heritage (Gravaris-Barbas and Guichard-Anguis, 2003). The extension of the notion of heritage (from the extraordinary to the vernacular, from material to intangible) has led to a patrimonialization of rural territories, "nourished" by the feeling of disappearance, a threat to the specificities. In the globalized context, these specificities are henceforth like identity refuges. In this respect, patrimonialization is an instrument for promoting specificities, a tool for protection and a vector for the production of identity (Gravaris-Barbas, 2003 and 2005; Landel, 2007). The example of the Monts d'Ardèche illustrates these dynamics. Once their image was negative, outdated: " *Le vin ne sera plus tiré / C'était une horrible piquette*". It now has a heritage dimension.

This field is particularly mobilized by the Monts d'Ardèche website. Products resulting from the typicity of the terroir and peasant know-how, local gastronomy, folklore and traditional festivals, "picturesque villages", natural and landscaped heritage, all these elements that once referred to an obsolete image have now become patrimonial elements and territorial resources (Gumuchian and Pecqueur, 2007). Through them the local identity claims its historical and territorial anchorage. Territorial specificity is now being built on the basis of this material and this intangible, wanted authentic: "*Le Parc des Monts d'Ardèche est composé d'une mosaïque de paysages, sauvages ou façonnés en terrasses et fortement marqué par la culture de la châtaigne, des savoir-faire ancestraux, le volcanisme et un patrimoine architectural remarquable* ". The rise of tourist activity, which is the driving force behind territorial development oriented towards face-to-face economy, draws heavily on these elements that carry positive representations of authenticity and strong local identity. They must lead to the singularization and the rise of the attractiveness of the territory in a context of inter-territorial competition. The geographical imaginary, combined with the heritage richness of the Monts d'Ardèche, is thus mobilized by the site as a territorial promotional tool. The existence of a brand "product of the park" illustrates this commoditization of the heritage and highlights the evolution of representations. The imaginary conveyed by the village markets is particularly interesting because it is transversal to the three themes: interfaces producer / consumer and nature / culture, they represent idealized moments of social life in which territorial identity and community conviviality are expressed through the valorization of a terroir and patrimonialized knowledge.

Conclusion

Constructed subjective or collective, the geographic imaginary participates in the appropriation of space by an individual or a social group. It partly shapes the construction of the territory. Associated with spaces, charged with positive or negative values, representations confer on the different territories their attractiveness or repulsion. The socio-spatial representations are not fixed. The dynamics, subject to evolutions and even inversions, are social constructions that influence the evolution of spaces, and result reciprocally from the socio-spatial, organizational and functional recompositions that the territories experience. The case of the Monts d'Ardèche is a rich example.

The diachronic comparison between Jean Ferrat's song and the Monts d'Ardèche website illustrates the contribution of the geographical imaginary to the process of territorialization of space and the reciprocal co-construction between representations and dynamics that animate the territory. In this context, the Monts d'Ardèche territory proved in many aspects to correspond to an archetypal example of rural territory presenting a coherent territorial identity and having strong landscape amenity. The evolutions of the imaginary and the socio-spatial reorganizations of the territory simultaneously translate a new attractiveness that contrasts singularly with the repulsive character that Jean Ferrat described and regretted in 1964. The singer's representations were particularly original in that they demonstrate anticipation: against the current, Jean Ferrat idealized and already fantasized this mountain campaign, its tradition, its authenticity, its beauty. However, the author showed a certain empathy towards the young emigrants who left the "country": "if he explicitly regretted the rural exodus, the last verse expresses a "fatalistic" understanding ("*Il n'y a rien de plus normal / Que de vouloir vivre sa vie*"). He regretted, however, the disenchanted character of the urban lifestyle, and substituted for the freedom conveyed by the city a coercive vision of the urban:

Leurs vies, ils seront flics ou fonctionnaires
De quoi attendre sans s'en faire
Que l'heure de la retraite sonne
Il faut savoir ce que l'on aime
Et rentrer dans son HLM
Manger du poulet aux hormones.

The site of the Monts d'Ardèche PNR carries a consensual imaginary, built and shared by the local actors. The website's analysis is an opportunity to insist on the performative character of spatial representations, on their political and operational use in territorial marketing objectives and in support of public action. They help to legitimate the very existence of the territory, to strengthen the cohesion of local society and to justify the existence of an institutional structure.

A comparison of the geographical imaginary carried by the two writings of rurality makes it possible to emphasize the systemic evolution of this type of space: in half a century we have gone from the end of peasant society to the development of a model of a recreational society, which leans on the natural and cultural heritages; from a historical anchorage repulsive to an idealization of the past which, driven by the valorization of the heritage and the fantasized character of traditional sociability, to restore attractiveness to the territory and capitalize on a territorial identity perceived now as strong and rich; from a constraining environment that led to difficult peasant lives, to a life-style coveted by neo-rural people because of landscape amenity and quality of life.

Although the example of the Ardèche mountains illustrates the evolution of representations and the contemporary dynamics generalizable to a number of attractive rural spaces, it is nonetheless remarkable. Social metaphors constructed from spatial representations are based on the Ardèche case on social cohesion, solidarity in adversity, but also on the weight of the community.

Primary sources

Institut National de l'Audiovisuel (INA). 1966. Jean Ferrat, *Que la montagne est belle*: http://www.ina.fr/video/I08025042
Youtube, Jean Ferrat, *La Montagne:*
https://www.youtube.com/watch?v=tkI5wGVjfX8
Website of Parc Naturel Régional des Monts d'Ardèche (homepage):

http://www.parc-monts-ardeche.fr/
Geopark of Ardèche Mountains:
http://www.geopark-monts-ardeche.fr/accueil-geopark.html

Secondary Sources

Bédard, Mario, Augustin Jean-Pierre and Desnoilles Richard (ed). 2011. *L' imaginaire géographique, Perspectives, pratiques et devenirs*, Collection Géographie contemporaine, Québec, Presses de l'Université du Québec, 396 p.

Cognard, Françoise. 2010. *Migrations d'agrément " et nouveaux habitants dans les moyennes montagnes françaises : de la recomposition sociale au développement territorial. L'exemple du Diois, du Morvan et du Séronais,* thèse de géographie, Université Blaise Pascal - Clermont-Ferrand (France), 523 p.

Debarbieux, Bernard. 2001. « La montagne : un objet géographique ? », *Les montagnes : discours et enjeux géographiques*, edited by Yvette Veyret Paris, SEDES, p.6-27.

Debarbieux, Bernard. 2009. « Territoire – Territorialité - Territorialisation : aujourd'hui encore, et bien moins que demain... », in *Territoires, Territorialité, Territorialisation. Controverses et perspectives*, edited by Martin Vanier, Rennes, PUR, p.75-89.

Debarbieux, Bernard and Rudaz, Gilles. 2010. *Les faiseurs de montagne. Imaginaires politiques et territorialités (XVIIIe-XXIe siècle,* Paris, CNRS Éditions, 373 p.

Di Méo, Guy and Buléon, Pascal. 2005. *L'espace social. Lecture géographique des sociétés,* Paris, Armand Colin, 304 p.

Di Méo, Guy. 1994. « Patrimoine et Territoire : une parenté conceptuelle », *Espaces et sociétés,* n°78, ERES, p.15-34.

Dupuy, Lionel and Puyo, Jean-Yves (ed). 2014. *L'imaginaire géographique. Entre géographie, langue et littérature*, Presses de l'Université de Pau et des pays de l'Adour : coll. Spatialités, 427 p.

Dupuy, Lionel and Puyo, Jean-Yves (ed). 2015. *De l'imaginaire géographique aux géographies de l'imaginaire Écritures de l'espace*, Presses de l'Université de Pau et des pays de l'Adour, 175 p.

Foucault, Michel. 1984. « Dits et écrits, Des espaces autres » (conférence au Cercle d'études architecturales, 14 mars 1967), in *Architecture, Mouvement, Continuité,* n°5, octobre 1984, pp. 46-49.

Fournier, Mauricette. 2014. « La liberté territorialisée : montagnes idéalisées et critique sociale de Jules Vallès à Alain Chany ». In *L'imaginaire géographique. Entre géographie, langue et littérature,* edited by Lionel Dupuy et Jean-Yves Puyo, Presses de l'Université de Pau et des Pays de l'Adour, Collection Spatialités, p. 349-360.

Gravaris-Barbas, Maria. 2003. « Le patrimoine territorial. Construction patrimoniale, construction territoriale : vers une gouvernance ». in *La Mosaïque territoriale, enjeux identitaires de la décentralisation*, edited by J. Beauchard, La Tour d'Aigues, éditions de l'Aube, p. 51-66.

—. 2005. *Habiter le patrimoine. Enjeux, approches, vécu*, Rennes : Presses Universitaires de Rennes.

Gravaris-Barbas, Maria and Guichard-Anguis, Sylvie (dir.). 2003. *Regards croisés sur le parimoine à l'aube du XXIe siècle*. Paris : Presses universitaires de la Sorbonne.

Gumuchian, Hervé and Pecqueur, Bernard. 2007. *La ressource territoriale*, Paris, Economica, Anthropos.

Hervieu, Bertrand, and Viard, Jean. 1996. *Au bonheur des campagnes (et des provinces)*, La Tour d'Aigues, Éditions de l'Aube, 160 p.

Landel, Pierre-Antoine. 2007. « Invention de patrimoines et construction des territoires », in *La ressource territoriale*, edited by Gumuchian Hervé and Pecqueur Bernard, Paris : L'Harmattan, p. 149-157.

Lévy, Jacques and Lussault, Michel. 2003. *Dictionnaire de la géographie et de l'espace des sociétés*, Saint-Just-la Pendue, Belin, 1034 p.

CHAPTER SEVEN

PIERRE JOURDE'S *PAYS PERDU*: ELEGY OR BETRAYAL?

ANNIE JOUAN-WESTLUND

Pays perdu, a text written by Pierre Jourde in 2003 was inspired by Lussaud, a small rural village in Auvergne where the author's family was established for several generations. While Parisian literary circles praised the book for its reminiscence of Jean Giono and Julien Gracq's prose, a handful of farmers in Lussaud recognized themselves behind their literary identities. They felt that the fiction was an intrusion of their privacy and were outraged by the release of the small book. Hoping to appease the hostile farmers, the author who often spends time in the remote farming village located in the Cantal region at the threshold of the Plateau du Cézalier, decided to write a long letter to each of the five families featured in his fictional account of the village. In his letter meant to defuse the situation, Jourde asks for their forgiveness if he unintentionally hurt their feelings. He assures them that he meant well in writing about the village of his ancestors and retelling well-known stories of his childhood. A few months after the letter had arrived in Lussaud, Pierre Jourde came back to the village accompanied by his wife and three children for their annual summer vacation. As they were stepping out of their car to settle into their family house, the Jourdes were welcomed with threats, insults and stones. One farmer threatened Pierre Jourde with a hayfork and the author responded with his fists. The rest of the group chased the family away from the village with racial insults and threw stones at their car wounding the youngest child. The tragic turn of events proved that the letter of apology, meant as a peace offer, had not cleared the misunderstanding or mollified the infuriated villagers who continued to feel betrayed by Pierre Jourde.

To an ordinary reader, the main issue which is raised by this literary and news story is the following: How could a text originally conceived by the author as book of love ("un livre d'admiration", *La Littérature est un sport de combat*, 365) be so wrongly misjudged by its readers? This study investigates the multiple layers in a complex process that lead to the failed reception of a book considered unacceptable[1]. Its purpose is to explore both the textual and contextual aspects in the readers' and writer's misunderstanding generated by the book. The first level of misinterpretation lies in the genesis of a manuscript inspired by the author's unconscious intent to transcribe in writing his perception of a village built on a fiction that affected his family. The secondary level of misjudgment, which may have caused the villagers' violent rejection of the book, results from a conflict between the written text and the oral tradition of secrets imbedded in the small rural community. Finally, a stigmatized media representation of the events and villagers during the ensuing trial was an external factor that further promoted the farmer's anger and misunderstanding of Jourde's book.

Literature of Constraints

After the assault in Lussaud, Pierre Jourde gave a number of interviews in which he attempted to make sense of the failed reception of his homage to Lussaud[2].The fundamental paradox between the writer's intention and the reader's perception compelled the author to investigate the form and content of his work as well as the significance of Lussaud in his writing[3]. The remote village is not only the birthplace of his ancestors and his childhood memories, it is the origin of his fascination for the written word and the cradle of his calling as a writer:

> Je suis sans doute venu à la littérature par le monde paysan, parce que c'est un pays où l'on ne parle pas, très peu, en tout cas. J'ai très tôt eu le sentiment que la parole, en soi, était obscène. Si la littérature a une tâche, c'est d'aller au-delà de cette obscénité pour trouver des mots qu'il ne soit pas honteux de dire (*La littérature est un sport de combat*, 351).

One stereotypical perception of rural communities consists in characterizing farmers as taciturn people. The French qualification of "taiseux" is often used to refer to their legendary reluctance to

---

[1] Jérôme Cabot analyzed the reception of the book within a group of students studying cultural policy in a rural environment in "Réception d'un éloge paradoxal" (*Nouvelles Francographies* 6 forthcoming in spring 2018)
[2] These are available in *La littérature est un sport de combat* (Clermont-Ferrand: Page Centrale, 2015).
[3] His reflection inspired him to write *La première pierre* (2013) which was awarded the Jean Giono literary prize.

communicate their feelings. In the above quote Pierre Jourde does not mean that the villagers avoid speaking but rather that their exchange can carry a dangerous significance. In literature, Pierre Jourde found an escape from the unspoken rule practiced in the village. While most of his work is fictional, the author admitted his apprehension when he started to write *Pays perdu* and confided his unease about revealing to the public the existence of a village secured by silence and related to his intimate existence:

> Je n'ai jamais eu l'intention d'écrire quoi que ce soit sur ce village. Il me touche de trop près. Il a toujours été du côté du secret du repli, non de la parole (*Siècle 21*).

The first transgression committed by Jourde is therefore to himself and his commitment to never betray his tight relationship with a place that cherishes silence and secrets. Lussaud is the writer's placenta that molded his childhood emotions, deepest fears and memorable experiences.[4] It is also a necessary resource of silence ("une indispensable réserve de silence obtus" *La littérature est un sport de combat*, 351), which explains his fascination for the search of an authentic literary representation of life. In order to understand the genesis and reception of *Pays perdu*, one must not underestimate the role played by silence as the inspiration for his existence and his writing. Pierre Jourde's family history was founded on a secret kept in the Lussaud community. His father who was born of an adulterous relationship had to reach his fifties before he was officially recognized by both of his parents. After being raised by an old woman, he was hired as a driver and help by his mother who refused to recognize him as her son until much later. While his father lived a fictional life dominated by the secret of his origin, Pierre Jourde's mission as a writer is to search for the truth imbedded in a fictionalized existence: : "La tâche de la littérature, c'est de montrer la fictionnalisation de l'existence, la représenter et la combattre" (*Géographie Imaginaire*, 85).

A few critics have blamed Pierre Jourde for his carelessness, indiscretion and naivety in relation to his potential readers. They accused him of not having thought out all the aspects of the book's reception in the village. The criticism seems all the more paradoxical that it is addressed to a writer who has always expressed a great concern for the meaning and value of literature in general and his writing in particular. In *Littérature et*

---

[4] In another autobiographical text entitled *La Présence* (Les Allusifs, 2010), Pierre Jourde explores his deepest fears as a child while he was sleeping in the family home in Lussaud. The text presents the village and the home as a place where the living, the dead and the ghosts meet and haunt the young child.

authenticité (2001), Pierre Jourde dedicates several hundred pages to analyze the relationship between literature and life. He fully recognizes the danger in words that take on the color of authenticity (19) and the disconnection between what is visible and expressible. Fully aware of how words can betray a representation of reality, Pierre Jourde can hardly be accused of credulity. Despite this knowledge, *Pays perdu* was the outcome of an urgent need to write and restore the reality of Lussaud through literature:

> Alors, est-ce qu'il ne fallait pas parler, dire son fait à cette terre qui gardait en elle le père, réduit au silence? (*La première pierre*, 20)

The text originated from an impulse to break two forms of silence, the first related to his father's origins and the second specific to the village sociability. Conceived as a tombstone in memory of his father, the book is also a reflection of the author's view on literature destined to reveal the truth in a fictional existence:

> Le livre s'est écrit dans l'absolu, comme s'il ne devait jamais avoir de lecteur sinon toi. Tu te l'étais adressé, et à ton père. (*La première pierre*, 20)

This confession is essential to understand the initial misunderstanding that took place when the villagers read the book. Primarily meant to repair the insult and injustice inflicted on his father by a silent community and to bring him back from the dead, the written text referred to other deceased characters from a village stripped of its fiction ("déshabillé de ses fictions", *La première pierre*, 29)[5]. Unfortunately the process of digging up the dead and bringing to light some intimate family stories uncovered a prevailing fiction carried by several generations and threatened the social structure of the rural community. By revealing inherent secrets in the village in a written fiction, the author made himself guilty of forging reality and resorting to prostituted words which constitutes the major untruthfulness ("le mensonge du mensonge", *La littérature est un sport de combat*, 92)

Writing about a village against a personal tendency to keep secrecy is not the only ambivalence for the author who believes that reality can only be authentically recorded with unusual esthetic and ethical constraints. Jourde was blamed for offering his reader a derogatory depiction of the

---

[5] In *Pays perdu*, Jourde mentions another well-known incestuous relationship in the village. Unfortunately, he had not realized that the grandchildren were not aware of it.

village and its inhabitants. The pages focusing on the cow manure (*Pays perdu*, 135-140), dirt and lack of personal hygiene were perceived very negatively by the villagers who refused to identify with the dark and controversial description of their environment. The author's interest in the least glorious aspects of reality in the countryside has always been a characteristic of Pierre Jourde's writing who, in his defense, never ceased to pay close attention to shameful aspects of life in order to elevate them in literature. Favoring the transcription of worthless objects, dirty corners, ruins and broken tractors, the author wishes to shed a new light on what is typically perceived as crude:

> Les choses qui n'ont pas de valeur [...] recoins sales des vieilles maisons [...] murs lépreux et tracteurs en ruine ont plus d'épaisseur et de poids que les beaux objets que nous voyons en lumière (*Paradis Noirs*, 164).

The author's rather offensive depiction of Lussaud was interpreted as a critical view on rural life although it merely reflects his preference for humbling details usually left unnoticed or considered not worthy of attention. To him, the thickness and the weight of somber elements of reality provide precious objects of observation and sublimation in literature. Pierre Jourde's aesthetic approach to an authentic representation of life in literature is both unusual and demanding. The glorification of the prosaic is connected with a taste for gloom and blackness in all of his books. Some readers may appreciate the author's invitation to the heart of darkness in the isolated French rural village but those who live in it may have been shocked by the "voyage au bout de la campagne" offered in *Pays perdu*. The text's crude and dark metaphors need to be interpreted through the lenses of the author's childhood sensory memories. His perception of the place and its people was born out of his childhood fantasy, which explains the transformation of key village figures into gods and their behavior into heroic actions. The hero in *Paradis Noir* is an alter ego of the author, endlessly wandering in the Auvergne countryside, analyzing smells, colors and sounds to memorize and restore them with words in his books before they vanish. The author's taste for obscure and humbling details is also a strong statement against "littérature-terroir", a popular genre filled with folklore and positive qualities.[6] Favoring straightforward and crude words to nostalgic descriptions, Pierre Jourde aims to carry his impressionable childhood account of a rural way of life that is condemned to disappear. The book offers a dreamlike outlook on

---

[6] This form of literature commonly categorized as littérature-terroir, particularly popular among readers who live in the city has been referred to as "cash-registrer literature" ("littérature-tiroir") by Pierre Jourde.

dirty homes, alcoholism and intermarriages in a small community surrounded with cow manure. But far from degrading the village through its farm animal stench, the book aims to praise and elevate a primitive organic nature associated with freedom.

According to Umberto Eco, a text is a "lazy machine" that demands the reader's bold cooperation to fill in the gaps (*Lector in fabula*, 29). In some situations, the reader may elicit something in the text that the author may not have meant, and which the text nonetheless seems to evince in absolute clarity (*Lector in fabula*, 235).[7] In that case, the reader 's interpretation stands in complete opposition to the text's intention and the author's intent. The "empirical readers"[8] in Lussaud whose daily burden is to remove their cows' overbearing waste were not able to deal interpretively with *Pays perdu*'s in the same way as the author dealt with it in its genesis and therefore perceived the village description as an insult. Not surprisingly, a few of the farmers operated a semantic switch by misreading "a shitty country" ("un pays de merde") in the phrase "the country of shit" ("le pays de la merde"). The unconscious article substitution is at the origin of the main grudge against the author. When the fight started, Pierre Jourde did not realize what was at stake until one of the farmers confided that he should not have called Lussaud "un pays de merde."[9] Reflecting on this moment in *la première pierre*, Pierre Jourde realizes with a lot of lucidity the limits of his writing project. Even though he had written *Pays perdu* with no specific addressee in mind other than himself and his deceased father, it is eventually the readers of a text who convey its meaning. He accepted the fact that no grammar lesson could have ever changed the farmers' first impression or rectified the reception of the book in a village where some people were offended by a word choice, which could only be interpreted as derogatory, despising and patronizing. Convinced that a writer is only able to write freely if he considers his reader a non entity, Pierre Jourde had not anticipated that his *Pays perdu* would have reached the village in the middle of the Cantal mountains, where people are not avid readers and not particularly interested in his work. As he wrote the text and carefully changed the

---

[7] "Il arrive des situations où le lecteur met en lumière quelquechose que l'auteur ne pouvait pas vouloir dire et que pourtant le texte semble exhiber avec une absolue clarté" (*Lector in Fabula*, 1979)

[8] Eco makes the distinction between the "empirical reader" who reads the text pragmatically and the "model reader" who uses his "encyclopedia" (social baggage) to deal with the text interpretively in the same way as the author dealt with it during its conception.

[9] "T'aurais pas dû dire que c'était un pays de merde" (Pierre Laporte, *Le Monde*, 06/22/07)

names of his characters, Jourde had no reason to feel concerned about how it would be possibly perceived by the villagers of Lussaud. Because of specific particularities in each character's description provided in the book, the precaution proved to be ineffective. Everyone in the village could recognize themselves in their fictional characters and chose to interpret the descriptions of their harsh and crude way of life as a personal insult rather than a compliment.

Comments made by villagers and reproduced in *La première pierre* give ample evidence of the villagers' misinterpretation of *Pays perdu*, a reading process defined by Umberto Eco as the tendency to overestimate the importance of indices and traces in a text when the reader approaches the text with an intention of his own (*Lector in fabula*, 235). For instance, one farmer blames Pierre Jourde for insulting her in his description of the pile of cow dung located in front of her barn. Although the section does not identify any specific farm, she felt that the author was describing her own farmyard. By recognizing her cow manure, she concluded that the author had made a comment on the lack of hygiene in her household.[10] Favoring the trivial and prosaic, touchy villagers failed to see the poetic transformation of the village's unappealing reality into a mythological kingdom. The farmers' semiotic judgment and interpretive cooperation did not allow them to appreciate their literary representations as legendary animals and half -Gods. *Pays perdu* was conceived as a requiem to the immortals who inhabited the remote village condemned to extinction. Orpheus, the main inspiration for a book celebrating two dead people, a young girl and an old man, is also the key figure in a narrative meant to bring back the dead from a silenced dark inferno with words which would reveal and protect the village secrets. In *Pays perdu*, the author's quest and dilemma was to restore the unsaid within a dark unwelcoming environment:

> La langage littéraire, dans l'idéal, pourrait être celui qui, dans la révélation, préserve l'obscurité du secret. Ramène Eurydice au jour avec toute l'épaisseur de l'obscurité dont il la tire." (*La première pierre*, 144)

Literary Fiction *versus* Community Fiction

The poor reception of *Pays perdu* was partially caused by a compelling scrupulous writing project to unveil a real and imagined rural community.

---

[10] "Mais de la façon dont les phrases sont tournées on pourrait croire que c'est moi qui est sale. Mais je n'en suis pas sûr, je relirai le livre pour savoir se je dois porter plainte pour diffamation ou non." (*La première pierre*, 69)

In the process, the author's unconscious revelation or desecration of a consensus fastening the group social structure caused hostility among the farmers. Pierre Jourde's representation of the crude lifestyle in Lussaud could be compared to an archeological excavation of the collective memory of a remote hamlet where one can't say "I" ("Où ne sait pas dire le je", *La première pierre*, 115). An article entitled "Words uncalled for in Lussaud" ("Les mots de trop pour le hameau de Lussaud", *Libération*, 09/16/2005), supported the farmers and attempted to justify their violent physical response with the damage caused by words. The journalist rests his case on an assumption about life in the country characterized by intimate secrets and disclosures that should not be shared with outsiders in writing:

> En campagne, il y a des choses qu'il ne faut pas ressortir. Des rumeurs peuvent de dire entre quatre yeux mais personne ne peut accepter que ce soit écrit ou diffusé.

Accusing the author of transgressing the golden rule of secrecy, the article clearly supports the farmers in their condemnation of Pierre Jourde's indiscretion and deterioration of the reputation of the village. Much concerned with the "image" of his village tarnished by the book, Laurie's mayor declared that Jourde had wronged Lussaud by highlighting only the nasty aspects in the community: "ce qu'il y a de plus villain" (*Libération*).[11]

While the mayor's condemnation does not specify which particular aspects of the book he considers to be too sordid, the disclosure of intermarriages or the bleak description of the dirty hamlet, the article identifies the confrontation between the literary fiction and the community oral pact as the origin of the farmers' wrath against the author. *Pays perdu* not only revived deep old wounds, it revealed old resentments and broke the silent treatment experienced by Jourde and his relatives.[12] Pierre Jourde remains convinced that his book manifested his desire to make amend to his father who was wronged for many years in a village where

---

[11] Laurie is the larger village affiliated with Lussaud. Among other shops, Laurie has a restaurant called "La bonne auberge" and a grocery store that sells a few books. Rumor has it that some unknown individual regularly buys out all copies of *Pays perdu* making sure that the book is not available to tourists and the local population.

[12] In an interview, Pierre Jourde admitted that his family social status in the village and the fact that he lives in Paris probably contributed to the farmers' resentment. (Annie Jouan-Westlund, "Ecriture du territoire et territoire de l'écriture: entretien avec Pierre Jourde, *Nouvelles Francographies 6*, forthcoming in spring 2018)

his parents did not wish to officially and legally recognize his existence. Because his father was deprived of social recognition until he was fifty years old, the writer attempted to tell the lie surrounding his origins in the context of a village where people are deprived of privacy and prefer to pretend not to know community secrets. While paying a tribute to his father, Jourde was compelled to contextualize his father's adulterous origin as a common practice in a hamlet of eight households and five families, which are all blood related to a certain degree. By doing so, Pierre Jourde did not anticipate that mentioning a similar situation in another family in the village would be news to some people, who like him and his own father, had been kept in the dark about their ancestry. By bringing up the story of Jeanne and Henri in his book as a reminiscence of his grandparents, Pierre Jourde hit a blind spot in his book, which triggered some unexpected reactions.

The claim often made by journalists that farmers are taciturn by nature resonates as a cliché, which does not fully explain to what extent Lussaud's social fiction and its implication in the life of its inhabitants impacted the book's reception. The community self-representation is intrinsically linked to its paradoxical geographic situation, at the top of a vast territory isolated in a limited space, depriving the handful of farmers of any hope of privacy and drawing them to adultery. According to the author who spent most of his childhood in the village, the tendency to spread stories of infidelity is a characteristic generated by a space restraining movements, feelings and intimacy:

> Pas un moment, pas un lieu de liberté, aucun interstice par où échapper un instant à la communauté, ou presque […] L'épouse et la maîtresse, l'amant et le mari trompé se croisent plusieurs fois par jour. (*Pays perdu*, 61)

In Lussaud, houses made of thick and heavy walls built with dark volcanic stones of the Auvergne region consolidate and conceal all passions, rumors and legends which make up for an otherwise secluded and monotonous existence in the small hamlet. A lack of privacy in the village confined in a restricted space explains people's constantly watched intimacy and their tacit recognition of the social function played by secrets in the village. This paradoxical situation could explain why outsiders are not supposed to know what each and everyone already knows in the village: "Ce que chacun sait, il ne faut pas que tout le monde le sache.." (*La première pierre*, 126)

Transgressing a rule accepted by all farmers is less forgivable when the unveiled secret gets spread, written and shared with outsiders. By offering a written public disclosure of old family stories which were only meant to be whispered, unknowingly, Pierre Jourde did not merely betray the trust of some of his former village friends, he committed a worse crime by replacing an oral collective community fiction to a small group of people with a written personal literary fiction made public to all.

In his letters sent to each family who had shown some disapproval after the book release, the author reminisces about his friendly relationship with all the families in Lussaud. Not understanding why his book deserved such an unwelcoming reaction, he reminds them that the village is also his home. In his long letter, the author recalls the happy bonding moments he shared with the farmers. He also makes a point of reminding them the pleasure they all share in poking fun of each other:

> Nous avons tous plaisanté les uns sur les autres. Ca fait partie de l'amitié […] Nous nous sommes tous lancés des blagues. Je le fais de temps en temps dans le livre." (*La litérature est un sport de combat*, 365)

Referring specifically to an infamous New Year's Eve party during a power outage when he welcomed the entire village to his home full of cheer, jokes and happiness, Jourde infers to his established friendly relationship with the village inhabitants. In such circumstances, the author could not understand why he could poke fun at some of his friends in real life and not do the same in his book. Apparently, spoken words exchanged in a social village gathering do not bear the same significance as written words printed in a published book outside of the tight rural community. Secrets based on ancestral oral traditions were meant to stay in the privacy of the small hamlet.

The underlying ethical issue revealed by this conflict was raised by the author in his essay *La Première pierre*. In his profound introspection resulting from the failed reception of his book, Pierre Jourde does not question the legitimacy of his fictional use of information about people he knew from the village but recognizes the fallibility of language in doing so. In other words, Pierre Jourde is less self-critical of his personal use of secrets in his text than distrustful of the language ability to restore reality authentically. Full aware of the gap between the written and the spoken word, Jourde regrets the definite nature of the written text in which language tends to set and fasten a permanent representation of reality on the page. By giving the example of Tintin, one of the physically disabled characters depicted in the book with a hint of humor, Jourde understands that Tintin could perceive his fictional representation in the book as a mockery of his handicap limiting his self to his physical limitation: " Tintin se voyait dénoncé. Il n'imaginait pas d'autre motivation que la malignité. Il se voyait lié par les mots à son cadavre de handicapé" (131)

Paradoxically by offering Tintin a new fictional existence in his book, the author caused his death by using words that only conveyed his disability. Life and death are very much interconnected in Jourde's fictional project, which brings a small rural village back to life and calls its inhabitants back from the dead. Although not negatively connoted for the writer, figures of death and darkness were not well perceived by farmers who would have preferred to see a lighter, more candid representation of their village and their daily life in the book.

By revealing an adulterous relationship to the rest of the world, Pierre Jourde assures that he did not mean to do any harm. In fact, the mention of Jeanne and Henry's secret love[13] could be perceived as a way to dilute his own family drama into a rather common village practice. The section in the book where the author describes the time when his father confided to him his adulterous ancestry indicates the real stake in *Pays perdu*, which was breaking silence and paying homage to his father. Using a precious and rare opportunity to confide with his son, during a summer family tradition, "le jour des mûres", while they were picking berries in the mountains, the father decided to share his secret. Through an intimate conversation, the author discovered and transcribed the full extent of his father's condition as his own mother's farm hand while everyone else in the village knew he was her illegitimate child. This event addressed in the last part of *Pays perdu* is crucial to a narrative dealing with the unspoken, which damaged his father's life and turned him into a timid person who did not dare to speak. His father's unease with words haunted him to his death bed, another crucial moment in the conclusion of *Pays perdu* when the writer witnesses the agony and suffering of his dying father unable to utter his last words. In this respect, *Pays perdu* is a son's tribute to his father as well as a celebration of literature in its capacity to expose and transform dark secrets in poetic language. Unfortunately the written transposition included the revelation of a similar secret affecting people from another family who were not prepared to face a similar discovery in a published book.

Literary Fiction *versus* Media Fiction

The conflict between a collective oral fiction and a literary fiction provides a plausible explanation for the failed reception of *Pays perdu*. A further reason for the book's disapproval is directly connected to the

---

[13] Jeanne and Henry had a similar adulterous relationship to Jourde's grandparents. The difference is that Jeanne and Henry's respective children fell in love and married not knowing that their parents had had an affair. (*Pays perdu*, 61)

verbal and physical violence, which erupted during the confrontation between the author and a few farmers in 2005 and its judicial consequences.[14] During the scuffle, one of the farmers, who happened to be one of the elders, got seriously wounded by the author who hit him in self-defense, while the author's youngest child got injured during the stoning. The farmers involved in the fight immediately pressed charges against the author for inflicting bodily harm. The author filed similar charges for premeditated violence and racial insults against his biracial children. The resulting trial spurred national and international media interest, which drew enough attention to generate many articles in leading newspapers providing a story likely to intrigue readers.

Pierre Bourdieu investigated the invisible mechanisms of journalism and inherent exigencies of the profession that produce sensational and spectacular news. These aspects of the profession may account for the fact that most written accounts on the farmers attack reflected a polarized orientation based on fragmented pieces of information. Bourdieu suspects that "journalists, on the whole, are interested in the exception, which means whatever is exceptional for them" (*On Television*, 20) more likely to deem national and international media attention. Farmers from a remote village stoning a well-established Parisian literary critic would certainly fit in with journalists' search for extraordinary occurrences or "daily dose of the extra-daily" (*On Television*, 20). According to Bourdieu, journalists who are afraid of being boring to the reader prefer to opt for confrontations over debates, polemics over rigorous arguments and consequently encourage the promotion of conflicts. Through a close reading of the articles published on Lussaud, one notices the event presentation as a confrontation of individuals rather than arguments. Instead of calling the reader's attention to what was at stake with the publication and reception of *Pays perdu* in Lussaud, most papers treated the current event as an entertainment story reminiscent of a variety show. Some journalists went as far as characterizing the incriminated farmers as a pack of illiterate savages desecrating the freedom of expression ("Une meute de sauvages analphabètes ennemis de la liberté d'expression, *La literature est un sport de combat*, 94) while others who chose to side with the farmers, found their violent reactions both predictable and legitimate. Not only did most of the media representations of the attack produce a distortion of events, they contributed to the making a multi -layered cake of misinterpretations by substituting a societal confrontation between two distinctive groups of individuals for a serious discussion of the textual content and its reception.

---

[14] The trial took place in Aurillac on June 21, 2007. Six farmers were charged with inflicting grievous bodily arm with racial insults and condemned to pay a fine.

Pierre Bourdieu used the metaphor of eyeglasses to describe media perception and their transformation of actual events into stories:

> Journalists have special glasses through which they see certain things and not others, and through which they see the things they see in the special way they see them" (*On Television*, 19)

According to the sociologist, journalists inevitably project their own views onto the public. In their reports, they have a capacity to impose a perspective and have their readers wear the same glasses projecting a fragmented and divided vision of reality. Thus the media coverage of the human conflict in Lussaud illustrates rather well a way of thinking in clichés and preconceived conventional ideas usually considered as true. Journalists who covered the trial ensuing from the fight seized an opportunity to compare and contrast a representative of the Parisian intellectual elite to the farming community, country people to city people, a familiar dichotomy phrased by Prime Minister Pierre Raffarin in the late 1990s when he opposed "la France d'en-bas" to "la France d'en-haut".[15] Rather than investigating the events, most press articles offered their readers simplistic representations of key factors and characters in the conflict and projected a degrading stereotypical representation of the farmers and their rural life. One article compared them to Hugo's Thénardiers while others simply portrayed them as uneducated individuals who could barely express themselves. Trial reports referred to in *La première pierre* allude to the farmers' voluntary participation in what the author considers an appalling comedy of errors. The trial show largely scripted by the media resulted in an exercise of hypocrisy, which further patronized and disgraced the farmers. An article published in *Le Monde* provides a good example of this attitude. In her paper recounting the trial hearings, Pascale Robert-Diard chose to give the readers a phonetic transcription of the language used by one of the farmers and printed her grammatical errors and misspelling to better convey the inherent language deficiency and illiteracy in the countryside: "mais nous, on peut pas s'esspliquer comme lui, passe que lui, il est poète, alors…" This method participated in an elaboration of the main argument used by the farmers' lawyers and some journalists who supported them. The process consisted in defending the violent physical reaction of simple, taciturn, hardworking people to verbal insults made by an irresponsible intellectual gossiper on

---

[15] "Là-Haut" is the title of a short-film inspired by what happened in Lussaud in 2003 (*Là-Haut*, Réal. Bill Burluet, Maje Production, 2012, 24 min.)

the assumption that farmers could not compete with the author's superior language skills:

> De braves brutes des campagnes, blessées dans leur honneur, corrigent un bavasseur irresponsable, qui se vengent sur son terrain, celui des mots. (*La première pierre*, 80)

Written words initially held responsible for hurting the farmers' pride in *Pays perdu* were replaced by spoken words exchanged during the trial as exhibits by both parties. For instance, the farmers' defense lawyer consistently addressed the author as "Monsieur le professeur" to reinforce the cultural and social gap between the two parties. Likewise, the author's lawyer did not hesitate to underscore the farmers' deficient cultural background and denigrate his opponents with a warning: "Ce n'est pas des gens comme vous qui allez faire taire les écrivains." Contrary to journalists' wrong assumption that farmers possess limited language skills, Jourde admires his neighbors' verbal skills when they tell stories, bargain, hold debates or poke fun of each other in the village. In total contrast with the language creativity practiced in the village, the farmers' lack of communicative skills in the courthouse are represented as a disability evidencing their status as disadvantaged victims in the debate. A few journalists blamed Jourde for comparing the village to remote countries in Asia ("Une petite Mongolie inhabitée", *Pays perdu*, 24) and its villagers to some uncivilized tribes ("Une beauté tadjike ou kurde", 57) failing to see that the comparison was motivated by the farmers' pride and survival qualities. Ironically, in their articles, some journalists scripted a parody in which the farming community accepted to act as "good savages" who fall victim to the Parisian author.

The best illustration of this process can be found in the journalistic portrayal of Paul Anglade, the village's veteran who got seriously wounded by Jourde during the fight and was introduced as the main victim during the trial. Robert-Diart's description reads:

> borgne, son cou mince échappe à la raideur empesé du col de sa chemise neuve, à carreaux blanc et bleu. Sa nuque est hale, comme toute la moitié inférieure de son visage.
> Elle contraste avec la pâleur du front et du sommet du crane sur lequel il a plaqué le peu de ses cheveux lisses dont on devine qu'un demi siècle de beret les ont protégés de la lumière. (*Le Monde*)

The lyric representation of the good farmer is characterized by hard outdoor labor. His physical handicap and general grotesque appearance are connected with a beret, a traditional rural tradition supposed to fill the readers with a sense of nostalgia. In addition to a resemblance with Quasimodo, another fictional character taken from classic French literature, this passage underscores the gap between a stereotypical and humiliating representation of small farmers and Jourde's much more elaborate poetic literary depiction of farmers in *Pays perdu*:

> Avec son crane nu sous la casquette, son nez en bec de busard, sa peau rougeâtre parcourue de traînées noires et sa manche où pendait une poignée de plumes, il avait l'air d'un très vieil ange, cuit dans les fournaises et des beuveries, jusqu'à en perdre la mémoire du ciel (*Pays perdu*, 52).

Conclusion

Media accounts of the hearings produced a masquerade hiding the humanity and complexity of all individuals involved in the controversy. Their derogatory perceptions of the small rural community validated the farmers' reading of *Pays perdu* as an insult on their lifestyle rather than an imaginary literary homage to the village. They also underscored a lack of positive self-representation among the farmers in Lussaud. The publication of *Pays perdu* unearthed and revealed several competing fictions: a personal fiction poisoning the author's father's existence, an oral fiction cementing the village social structure and a journalistic fiction stereotyping the rural community. In the end, the third fiction proved to be far more detrimental to the village and its inhabitants than Jourde's epic account of a disappearing rural way of life. As a result, the silence broken by Pierre Jourde was inflicted on himself in a hamlet where a few farmers refuse to talk to him till this day. The title of his book proved to be premonitory and ironic. Lussaud, now partially "lost" to him and his family is accessible to readers throughout the world who can experience the uniqueness of the remote village thanks to *Pays perdu*. In *Géographie intérieure*, Pierre Jourde wrote "La réussite d'une écriture se mesure à sa justesse, au fait qu'elle ne triche pas" (210). The author's profound questioning of *Pays perdu*'s reception in his writing in *La première pierre* indicates that his misadventures made him fully aware of the brutality involved in the representation of reality with words. While running the risk of being misunderstood, the author has never ceased to pursue his quest to express his own truth in texts, which can sometimes be complex, demanding and problematic to some readers. *Pays perdu*'s publication and failed reception reminds us that if reality can inspire fiction, fiction can also tragically interfere with life, which is made of fiction. Pierre Jourde never intended to produce a realistic portrait of Lussaud in *Pays perdu* but rather the literary expression of his intimate impression of a village characterized by death and suffering. This analysis underscores the important role played by the reader who exercises his semiotic judgment to understand the meaning of a text. In the case of *Pays perdu*, the text conveyed some elements resulting in an interpretive cooperation, which produced an unhappy end. While the book's publication caused a conflict causing more suffering in the rural community, it enabled the author and the farmers to confront adverse but sincere perceptions of a rare and unique village bound to disappear from the French geographical and human landscape.

References

Blecher, Ludovic. 09/16/2005. "Les mots de trop pour le hameau de Lussaud." *Libération*. http://www.liberation.fr/actualite/societe

Bourdieu, Pierre. 1996. *On Television*. Translated by Priscilla Parkhurst Ferguson. New York: The New Press.

Eco, Umberto. 1979. *Lector in fabula: Le rôle du lecteur ou la cooperation interprétative dans les textes narratifs*. Paris : Grasset.

Jourde, Pierre. 1991. *Géographies imaginaires*. Paris : Corti.

—. 2001. *Littérature et authenticité : le réel, le neutre, la fiction*. Paris : l'Harmattan.

—. 2003. *Pays perdu*. Paris : L'Esprit des péninsules.

—. 2009. *Paradis noirs*. Paris : Gallimard.

—. 2010. *La Présence*. Paris : Les Allusifs.

—. 2013. *La première pierre*. Paris : Gallimard.

—. 2015. *Géographie intérieure*. Paris : Grasset.

—. 2015. *La littérature est un sport de combat*. Clermont-Ferrand : Page Centrale.

—. Summer 2008. "La fiction du secret." *Siècle 21*, n° 12.

Robert-Diard, Pascale. 06/22/2007. "Scènes de chasse dans le Cantal." *Le Monde*.

—. 07/05/2007. "Le village violé et l'écrivain." http://prdchroniques.blog.lemonde.fr/

Further Reading

De Almeida, Daniel. 06/26/2007. *Pierre Jourde prend la littérature dans l'estomac*. http://fluctuat.premiere.fr/livres

Assouline, Pierre. 07/05/2007. *L'affaire Jourde laisse un goût amer*. http://passouline.blog.lemonde.fr//

Burnat, Patrice. 06/21/2007. "Un écrivain lynché par ses personnages". *Le Figaro*.

Garcin, Jérôme. Sept 8-14, 2005. "Les raisons de la colère." *Le Nouvel Observateur*.

Guittard, Christian. 2007. *Saint Germani-des-Prés contre le haut Cantal*. http://www.cguittard.com/articles

Jouan-Westlund, Annie. Forthcoming in Winter 2017. "Écriture du territoire et territoire de l'écriture : entretien avec Pierre Jourde". *Nouvelles Francographies 6*.

Launet, Edouard. 06/21/2007. "Dialogue de sourds entre l'écrivain et ses personnages." *Libération*.

CHAPTER EIGHT

À PROPOS DE *PAYS PERDU* DE PIERRE JOURDE : QUESTIONS POUR L'ÉCRIVAIN, QUESTIONS POUR LES SCIENCES SOCIALES

PIERRE COUTURIER

En 2003, Pierre Jourde publie *Pays perdu*. Universitaire, auteur exigeant, Pierre Jourde est alors un auteur peu connu du grand public. Il faudra un an pour que le roman atteigne ses personnages. Car ceux-ci sont bien réels. Ce sont les habitants de Lussaud, petit village du Cézallier que la "route épuisée" atteint "au terme d'un amenuisement interminable" (Jourde, 2003). Pierre Jourde est l'un d'eux. "Á longues journées, au prix de milliers de kilomètres", il regagne régulièrement, depuis l'enfance, la maison de famille.

Le roman relate les funérailles de Lucie, une enfant d'une famille voisine des Jourde au village. On comprend que l'auteur a beaucoup en partage avec les parents, des paysans depuis longtemps fermiers des Jourde. La veillée funèbre est l'occasion de dérouler une fresque où défilent des personnages emblématiques d'un monde paysan qui achève de disparaître au moment où Pierre Jourde nous le rend palpable à travers une galerie de portraits réalistes et pénétrants. La description minutieuse des singularités physiques, des attitudes, des comportements, mène à une analyse psychologique et sociale ancrée dans l'ordonnancement des lieux. Les rapports des hommes à la matière brute, voire brutale, du lieu, des paysages, prennent sens dans une écriture sans fard, à la fois crue et sensible. Une écriture dont les habitants lecteurs (ou prétendant l'être) ne retiendront que la rudesse, la violence qui semble à première vue s'en dégager, pour la retourner contre son auteur. Les tentatives d'explication de l'écrivain n'y feront rien : moralement et physiquement agressé à coup de pierres jusqu'à la porte de la maison familiale par ses propres personnages redevenus de chair et d'os, craignant pour sa famille, il ne lui restait que le refuge d'une littérature cathartique, en l'occurrence un livre,

La première pierre, dans lequel il entreprend, une décennie après, d'analyser les événements.

C'est ainsi que *Pays perdu* défraya la chronique médiatique. Á ses frais, à ceux de la littérature et de la pensée. Certes, sans la puissance littéraire du texte le livre et son auteur n'auraient probablement pas été autant exposés. Mais l'intérêt des commentateurs s'est focalisé sur le décalage social censé expliquer l'accueil du roman, sans trop prêter attention à son objet fondamental. Il est vrai que l'intention cardinale ne se laisse pas saisir dans toute sa richesse sans effort de la part du lecteur et que plusieurs niveaux de lecture sont possibles. Le point de vue proposé ici n'est pas littéraire. Il ne prétend pas non plus épuiser les aspects d'une pensée exigeante qui fait corps avec une littérature sans complaisance. Il est celui d'un chercheur en sciences sociales. Car au cœur de ce roman sur la perte se trouve un questionnement qui entre en résonance avec des problèmes souvent débattus dans un champ scientifique, celui de l'anthropologie et des disciplines du monde social qui lui sont proches. Dans *Pays perdu*, le sentiment de la perte n'est pas séparé de son antidote, le mythe de l'authenticité. Or ce thème me semble pouvoir être rapporté au problème de la réception du texte par les habitants de Lussaud, lesquels sont aussi les protagonistes du récit. En somme, l'auteur se trouve dans la position de l'ethnographe confronté, généralement dans des temps différés, aux doutes sur la valeur opératoire de la catégorie "authenticité" et aux réactions de ses enquêtés. En ce sens, *La première pierre* peut être lu comme un essai réflexif qui, tout en restant un texte littéraire, est proche d'une démarche scientifique.

Voilà donc justifié le croisement des regards littéraire et scientifique. Reste à situer ce travail dans les rapports entre littérature et sciences sociales, du point de vue de celles-ci. En simplifiant beaucoup, et pour s'en tenir à la période contemporaine, on peut distinguer quelques champs de ces relations. Dans l'optique d'une sociologie de la culture, les textes littéraires et leur réception sont pris comme terrain en tant qu'ils informent sur la dimension culturelle des sociétés. Avec l'émergence des *cultural studies*, ce champ de recherche s'est élargi à l'interprétation socialement déterminée et aux modalités d'appropriation des œuvres littéraires (Moeschler, 2016). Par ailleurs, l'assignation d'une capacité heuristique à la littérature a pu légitimer des entreprises littéraires émanant du monde scientifique, notamment de la part d'anthropologues qui comptent parmi les plus célèbres. Enfin, dans les dernières décennies, les points de vue épistémologiques critiques réfèrent à la littérature pour questionner les modalités de production et d'énonciation de savoirs sur le monde social. Sans méconnaître les apports de ces diverses perspectives, ni les débats ouverts par leur confrontation, ce travail se situe sur un registre plus modeste[1]. Il s'agit d'esquisser un parallèle et d'interroger des points de convergence entre la pensée transmise par un texte littéraire et des aspects du débat scientifique portant sur l'authenticité d'une part, la réception des écrits ethnographiques d'autre part et de voir comment ces deux points se rencontrent.

Limitée, l'ambition n'en pose pas moins des problèmes méthodologiques. Á première vue, dans le cadre ainsi fixé, le rapprochement des sphères littéraire et scientifique se heurte à une différence irréductible concernant les façons que l'écrivain et le chercheur ont de produire du sens. Discordance qui, fondamentalement, met en jeu deux rapports au *je*. Comme tout artiste, l'écrivain à toute latitude pour dire *je*, pour engager délibérément et sans retenue la totalité de son être dans le processus créatif. Cet engagement est d'ailleurs perçu comme une marque d'authenticité. Le chercheur, quant à lui, s'efforce d'objectiver sa subjectivité, de la mettre à distance, non pas avec l'illusion de l'occulter mais, au contraire, dans le souci d'en mesurer et d'en maîtriser l'emprise. Le souci de distanciation vaut également pour le rapport à l'œuvre qui n'est pas lue ni perçue indépendamment d'un *habitus* du lecteur-chercheur. Lire un texte littéraire avec les lunettes des sciences sociales peut incidemment conduire, par transposition analogique, à détourner et travestir le contenu de l'œuvre sans pour autant enrichir l'outillage conceptuel du chercheur.

Dans le cas précis, le risque de contresens me semble toutefois réduit par les écrits de Pierre Jourde lui-même qui, parallèlement à la rédaction de *Pays perdu*, travaillait à un autre livre, *Littérature et authenticité* (Jourde, 2005), dans lequel il développe et prolonge la question abordée dans le *Pays perdu* par une critique explicite et précisément argumentée de "l'authentique" – critique qui débouche sur la construction d'une théorie de son opposé, "le neutre".

L'illusion de l'authentique

De son côté, l'anthropologie débat sur le contenu et le statut de la notion d'authenticité associée à celle de "tradition" depuis qu'elle s'est constituée en discipline "de plein air" (Laplantine, 2001), c'est-à-dire depuis qu'au début du XXe siècle, les anthropologues ont considéré l'enquête ethnographique comme une pratique inhérente à leur discipline. Une façon d'entrer dans l'actualité de ces débats est de les aborder dans le

---

[1] Pour un panorama des rapports entre ethnologie et littérature, voir *Ethnologie et littérature*. Cahiers de la Société des Etudes Euro-Asiatiques, 2005, n° 14-15. Paris : L'Harmattan.

champ de l'anthropologie du tourisme où l'authenticité est très habituellement convoquée. La question se pose alors de savoir s'il faut la cantonner à une catégorie à analyser (catégorie indigène) ou s'il faut en faire une catégorie d'analyse (Cravatte, 2009). Dans le premier cas, l'authenticité n'est pas une qualité intrinsèque d'un objet ou d'une situation. Elle est une construction sociale qui informe sur la façon dont les sociétés modernes se définissent en référence à des "traditions inventées" au sens que Hobsbawm (2006) donne à cette expression. Quant à la position qui consiste à faire de l'authenticité une catégorie analytique, elle soulève la question des critères d'objectivation de l'authentique et, par là, l'épineux problème de la légitimité du scientifique à dire la norme culturelle.

Dans la pratique, la démarcation entre catégories indigène et analytique, entre approches objectiviste et constructiviste, n'est pas toujours aisée. C. Cravatte (2009) évoque le brouillage des distinctions lorsque la marchandisation provoque des détournements de sens qui peuvent conduire à une perte d'authenticité mais aussi à l'émergence de nouvelles significations. C'est sans doute dans le champ de l'anthropologie océaniste que l'on perçoit le mieux l'ampleur des enjeux qui peuvent être liés à ces équivoques. Dans les années 1980-2000, des débats virulents opposent les anthropologues d'obédience constructiviste à leurs collègues inspirés par le post-modernisme, ces derniers accusant les premiers de s'instituer prescripteurs de normes culturelles dans le sillage des colonisateurs européens, alors que les premiers reprochent aux seconds un aveuglement qui aurait abouti à leur instrumentalisation par les mouvements politiques nationalistes (Babadzan, 2009). Alain Babadzan (2009) montre comment les élites politiques mélanésiennes ont cherché à asseoir leur pouvoir sur une "idéologie de la coutume" qui opère un renversement de valeurs : les traditions rurales longtemps stigmatisées par les élites urbaines au nom du Progrès et de la Civilisation se trouvent valorisées et réifiées dans une opposition symbolique à une "occidentalisation" aliénante réduite à sa dimension marchande. Les communautés rurales sont présentées "comme une sorte de conservatoire des valeurs et de l'authenticité ethniques" (Babadzan, 2009) parce qu'elles seraient moins impliquées dans l'économie moderne. Comme dans le cas du tourisme, l'authenticité promue par ces mouvements politiques est une mise en scène de l'autarcie.

Alain Babadzan (2009) parle de "critique occidentale de l'occidentalisation" à propos de la manière dont les élites politiques mélanésiennes construisent et donnent à voir l'antagonisme entre coutume et modernité. "Plus on est autarcique, plus on est authentique" écrit, quant à lui, Pierre Jourde dans *Littérature et authenticité*. Babadzan (2009) n'a aucun mal à montrer à propos des sociétés mélanésiennes que cette autarcie est un mythe qui occulte l'appropriation syncrétique des objets occidentaux depuis le XVIIIe siècle.

Qu'il s'agisse d'aller chercher ailleurs le pur et le vrai ou de répondre à l'injonction d'être soi-même, l'anthropologie montre que l'authenticité est un mythe. Luc Boltanski et Eve Chiapello (1998) ajoutent que le discours sur l'authenticité est gratifiant parce qu'il vient combler un manque, une perte ressentie par les membres des sociétés modernes. C'est pourquoi il satisfait ces deux êtres spécifiques de la modernité que sont le touriste et le consommateur (Boltanski, Chiapello, 1998). Pour Pierre Jourde (2005), "celui qui croit demeurer dans l'authentique est satisfait des choses et de lui-même". D'un point de vue fonctionnaliste, on pourrait dire que l'authenticité contribue à la cohésion de la société. Pierre Jourde (2005) nous éclaire et, éventuellement, nous dessille à cet égard :

> de tous les alcools spirituels, l'authentique est l'un des plus insidieux. Il créé une profonde accoutumance. Il nous aide à vivre parce qu'il nous permet de croire qu'il y a de la valeur dans ce qui en est le plus dépourvu en apparence. Il compense nos pertes.

Pierre Jourde entend préserver la littérature des vertus analgésiantes de l'authenticité. Dans Pays perdu la scène de l'enterrement révèle notre étrangeté à nous-mêmes. L'authenticité, écrit-il dans Littérature et authenticité, "est toujours celle de l'autre". A propos du paysage, il montre que "toute contemplation est une quête de la contemplation", une "expérience du vide" donc, Contre toute logique, c'est vers ce vide qu'il faut aller en refusant "le devoir de contemplation", en acceptant l'inutilité, l'injustifié, la gratuité, l'abandon, l'absence qui s'opposent à la présence artificielle de l'authentique. Car l'alternative c'est ce qui s'installe dans "la certitude glacée de l'être" : les bâtiments pimpants refaits à neuf, les promenades balisées, les lieux typiques, qui forment "l'inflexible quadrillage de l'authentique", où chaque chose est à sa place. "Le pays sera alors à notre portée, disponible, on croira l'avoir sauvé. Plus rien ne sera gratuit." Le titre du roman prend alors tout son sens :

> [...] nous ne gagnons le pays que pour voir à quel point nous le perdons, et pour tenter de le retenir un peu encore, de garder dans ce monde quelque chose dont nous ne savons même pas ce que c'est.

Le vide opposé à l'illusion d'une authenticité de l'émotion, à la revendication d'un objet auquel nous attribuons ce qui nous manque, Pierre Jourde le nomme "neutre" et s'attache, dans Littérature et authenticité, à en édifier une théorie fondée sur une idée par ailleurs constitutive des sciences sociales, la construction socio-cognitive du réel : "C'est l'apprentissage des distinctions qui nous fait apparaître le réel comme tel". Il informe alors sur la soif d'authenticité qui taraude les sociétés modernes : quand elle n'est pas réduite à une quête du "soi", l'authenticité est nécessairement recherchée dans un autre situé dans un ailleurs :

> Notre culture et notre attention (…) finissent par nous faire perdre les objets réels dont elles nous ont permis de délimiter les contours. D'un côté, la distinction n'a pas de raison de cesser, et l'on peut subdiviser à l'infini, raffiner sans cesse jusqu'à perdre tout objet réel. D'un autre côté, un objet de culture, ayant trouvé sa place, perd son étrangeté spécifique. Il se réduit à un emplacement dans un ordre.

La suite fait un sort à cette quête :

> Le rêve de l'authentique correspond précisément à une certaine forme prise par le désir de concilier réalité et culture : l'objet authentique serait à la fois parfaitement différencié, exactement délimité dans sa forme, mais cette forme fixe contiendrait une substance stable, nutritive, homogène. Le prêtre du culte de l'authentique est le *connaisseur*[2] , capable de discerner et d'apprécier de tels objets. Ce culte, qui consiste à croire que les objets existent, est un sommeil dogmatique.

C'est à nouveau le paysage, cet arrière-plan de l'âpreté sociale comme des moments de plénitude évoqués dans *Pays perdu*, qu'il convoque dans *Littérature et authenticité* pour éclairer le "neutre" :

> Le paysage nous laissera sur notre faim tant que nous lui demanderons d'alimenter notre appétit de réalité authentique. Peut-être ne faut-il chercher en lui que ce qui peut nous décharger de l'affirmation, nous soulager du désir d'être et en absorber les remous dans la réitération du neutre.

Refusant les gratifications de l'authenticité, s'attachant inlassablement à distinguer "réel et désir de réel" (Jourde, 2005), la littérature de Pierre Jourde ne fait aucune concession au pittoresque, au typique. Une littérature du dévoilement pourrait-on dire en reprenant une formule de la sociologie, dans la mesure où elle entend délester le lecteur de ce qui l'empêche d'être au monde et à lui-même. Mais ce dévoilement n'est pas ici le fait d'un écrivain autorisé, qui, investi de la légitimité conférée par une maîtrise du langage, se croirait en mesure de révéler un monde dissimulé sous les

---

[2] Souligné par l'auteur.

apparences. Comme les paysans qu'il décrit, Pierre Jourde se méfie des mots, de la parole qui "en fait toujours trop" (2013), qui n'est jamais ce qui est dit (2005). Il se défie du langage qui réduit les êtres et les objets à ce qu'ils sont : "La mort et le village perdu vont trop bien ensemble. Ils confèrent une valeur *a priori* aux mots qui les évoquent", écrit-il (2005) à propos de *Pays perdu*. Cette valeur n'est autre que l'authenticité dont Jourde nous dit qu'elle compromet toute possibilité de vérité. Il ajoute avoir pris toute la mesure de la difficulté en écrivant *Pays perdu* : "C'est justement dans la confrontation entre le langage et une expérience intense que la fausseté semblait la plus scandaleuse, que la bouche se blessait sur les mots". Il lui fallait donc préserver une forme de silence, ménager l'inconnu, le secret du "souffle" profond que cache en lui le pays. Ironie du sort, c'est par la révélation d'un de "ces pauvres vieux secrets autour desquels la famille se referme" (Jourde, 2013) que va se jouer la réception du roman.

La fiction du secret

À la lecture de Pierre Jourde, le secret au sens générique du substantif, l'irrévélé, apparaît lui aussi comme une illusion. Mais, à la différence de l'authenticité, il s'agit d'une illusion positive, paradoxalement conscientisée, voulue, construite et à laquelle on feint de croire. C'est pourquoi j'utilise le terme de fiction. Dans *La première pierre*, Jourde (2013) établit un parallèle entre l'écrivain et le scientifique, l'un et l'autre curieux de ce que cache le visible, avides d'un inconnu qui n'est jamais épuisé par la révélation. Alors que la poursuite de l'authentique est purement chimérique, la curiosité jamais assouvie qui nous pousse à la découverte de l'altérité, de ce que nous percevons comme le secret de l'autre, est au fondement de la vérité pour l'écrivain, de la connaissance pour le scientifique. La fiction du secret a donc des vertus à la fois littéraires et heuristiques. Dans *Pays perdu*, Jourde lui attribue aussi une vertu sociale.

Une lecture de *Pays perdu* au prisme du secret permet d'atteindre le sens que Pierre Jourde confère à l'écriture du roman et, au-delà, d'entrer dans une conception de la littérature. Le secret initial nous est dévoilé dans *La première pierre* quand Jourde révèle n'avoir jamais eu l'intention d'écrire sur Lussaud. Pour lui, le village "a toujours été du côté du secret, du repli, non de la parole". Mais, après tout, "un vrai roman est peut-être toujours un roman du secret. Il tourne autour de quelque chose d'obscur, profondément enfoui, et qui ne sera jamais tout à fait éclairci". C'est la mort de Lucie qui décide Jourde à parler du village. De fait, le récit opère un glissement analogique du pays vers la morte que *La première pierre* présente sous la figure d'Eurydice. Dans ce livre, Jourde, le narrateur, utilise la deuxième personne, comme s'il cherchait à rester étranger à ce qu'il décrit, notamment à la scène de l'enterrement. "Et c'est le pays tout entier, dont il te semblait qu'on l'enfouissait avec la jeune fille, que le livre a voulu remonter à la vie, avec son poids de secrets." Le mythe d'Eurydice est la métaphore d'une littérature qui restitue le réel tout en conservant une part de secret (l'usage de la deuxième personne semble en être l'indice), d'une écriture qui révèle sans jamais parvenir à tout mettre au jour sauf à tomber dans le piège de l'authentique.

Désormais, écrire sur le village est justifié sur un plan littéraire. Mais le sens de l'écriture n'est pas que littéraire et plusieurs niveaux de signification s'enchevêtrent dans *Pays perdu*. Au cœur du roman se trouve encore un secret profondément enfoui : le père de l'auteur est mort sans avoir pu révéler à son fils que le grand-père qui repose dans le caveau familial n'est pas le sien. Dans *Pays perdu*, il faut entendre *Défaut d'origine*, écrit Jourde (2013) par allusion au roman d'Oliver Rohe paru la même année et qu'une journaliste littéraire opposait à *Pays perdu*. Remonter la jeune Eurydice est, pour lui, une façon de donner une voie au père, d'exhumer le passé de ses propres origines. Un passé qui prend sens dans un tiraillement présent de l'auteur entre le "péquenot" en lui et l'intellectuel (Jourde, 2013), dans une nécessité de faire se rejoindre deux existences, l'une faite de souvenirs cachés, l'autre construite dans la lumière d'une destinée citadine.

Dès lors, Pierre Jourde s'emploie à montrer dans *Pays perdu* et dans *La première pierre* que, au sein des sociétés d'interconnaissance, on n'échappe pas aux lieux. Cette assignation symbolique à résidence doit beaucoup à l'omniprésence du secret qui "structure les imaginaires". Comment mieux en rendre compte qu'en évoquant l'un de ces secrets "su de chacun" mais pas pour autant "connu de tous" (Cabot, 2018) ? En l'occurrence, l'adultère commis jadis par Henri, chef d'un clan de Lussaud. "Autour d'Henri, chaque jour, il n'y avait que des gens qui savaient, et qui faisaient comme s'ils ne savaient pas." (Jourde 2013). Comme bien d'autres, ce secret est une fiction qui tient sa force d'une capacité à structurer le groupe, à mettre de l'huile dans les rouages grinçants des relations d'interconnaissance étroite. Or, la publication de *Pays perdu*, en portant le secret sur la place publique, vient rompre ce subtil équilibre.

Les décrits de l'écrit

Comme le remarque Jérôme Cabot (2018), il y a une certaine ironie à voir les habitants de Lussaud renvoyer à Pierre Jourde son origine "bâtarde" comme une révélation infamante en guise de représailles pour sa divulgation du secret d'Henri alors même que l'auteur de *Pays perdu* avait écrit pour exhumer ses propres origines. Les personnages du roman, devenus ses lecteurs, manifestaient ainsi leur ressentiment à l'égard du coupable de lèse-conventions sociales. Cela prend la forme d'une mise en scène décrite dans *La première pierre*. Prévenus de l'arrivée de Pierre Jourde, les habitants inscrivent sur un panneau planté à l'entrée du village "Bienvenue à Charletu le poète". La victime finira par comprendre que Charletu est le pseudonyme de celui qui serait son véritable père selon l'un de ces secrets partagés[3]. Il est tentant d'interpréter l'événement selon un point de vue fonctionnaliste dans la mesure où le texte littéraire en fournit l'argumentaire par ce qu'il dit du rôle social du secret. L'accueil fait au "poète" serait d'autant plus hostile qu'il aurait, par ses écrits, porté atteinte à la cohésion du groupe. Notons toutefois, sans que cela ne réduise la vertu heuristique du texte, que nous ne connaissons la réaction des habitants que par le récit que Pierre Jourde en fait et par les dépositions – en partie retranscrites dans *La première pierre* – dans le cadre des investigations judiciaires qui font suite aux agressions. En l'absence d'enquête socio-ethnographique, j'orienterai la réflexion sur l'accueil de *Pays perdu* vers un croisement du discours littéraire avec des questions que les chercheurs en sciences sociales, en particulier celles et ceux pratiquant l'enquête ethnographique sur des groupes restreints, se posent quant à la réception de leurs travaux.

Pour importante qu'elle soit, la publicisation du secret n'est qu'un aspect des griefs que les habitants de Lussaud adressent à Pierre Jourde. Jérôme Cabot (2018) montre que "l'éloge rugueux" qui dégage "le sublime de la crasse et de la déréliction" fait de *Pays perdu* un "écrit irrecevable". Pour Jourde (2013) cité par Cabot (2018), il fallait voir "De la royauté dans l'alcool, de la noblesse dans la solitude, de la grandeur dans la merde". Jérôme Cabot parle encore d'une "héroïsation" de la figure du paysan et d'une esthétisation de l'excrémentiel. À Lussaud, on restera insensible à la sublimation du "pays de la merde" et cette formule de l'écrivain lui sera retournée, déformée, par ses lecteurs l'accusant de les salir en parlant d'un "pays de merde".

Les sociologues et ethnologues qui pratiquent l'enquête ethnographique connaissent ce type de déboire en dépit de l'attention désormais portée par

---

[3] Alors que Pierre Jourde, lui, s'interrogeait sur son véritable grand-père.

l'anthropologie, états-unienne en particulier, à la question de la réception profane des travaux scientifiques[4]. Au gré de travaux réflexifs sur leurs pratiques de terrain, les socio-anthropologues ont érigé la restitution des résultats du travail ethnographique en problème éthique qui renvoie lui-même à des interrogations épistémologiques. Ce sont quelques aspects de ces travaux que je voudrais rapprocher du texte littéraire et réflexif que constitue *La première pierre* pour distinguer plusieurs niveaux d'analyse concernant la réception de *Pays perdu*.

Décalages culturels et décloisonnement des univers sociaux

Un premier niveau réfère au décalage culturel entre l'univers de production de savoirs universitaires et les collectifs sociaux constitués en objet de la connaissance scientifique. F. Weber (2008) remarque que pendant longtemps, ces deux mondes ont été nettement séparés. La question de la réception indigène des écrits scientifiques ne se posait, de façon accessoire, que dans les cas où les enquêtes portaient sur les milieux sociaux dominants. Cela n'empêchait pas des chercheurs travaillant sur des populations marginalisées et stigmatisées de se préoccuper des risques d'une exacerbation des représentations péjoratives qui pouvaient résulter de la publication de leurs travaux. Mais les populations observées n'avaient pas habituellement accès aux résultats des recherches les concernant.

La généralisation de l'internet a mis fin à ce cloisonnement, posant ainsi avec une nouvelle acuité la question de l'anonymat et de la confidentialité que les chercheurs se doivent de garantir aux enquêtés, et obligeant le monde académique à prendre au sérieux la réception indigène de ses travaux. On dispose désormais de publications abordant divers aspects de la question. Ainsi, ce qui a trait aux écarts de sens entre les registres discursifs scientifiques et profanes. F. Weber (2008) en donne une illustration en sociologie de la littérature, à propos de la protestation adressée à la revue *Genèse* par une femme écrivain s'estimant trahie dans un article dont l'auteure s'appuyait sur de longs entretiens qu'elle lui avait accordés. F. Weber montre que le malentendu porte principalement sur le statut des concepts utilisés par la sociologue. Ainsi le mot "stratégie" comme catégorie de l'analyse sociologique renvoie classiquement aux

---

[4] En témoignent les publications qui abordent de façon réflexive les dimensions tant épistémologiques qu'éthiques de la pratique ethnographique. Voir par exemple Cefaï (2003, 2010) et Fassin, Bensa (2008).

marges de manœuvre des acteurs dans un champs, alors que, pour l'écrivain, il a une portée morale et renvoie à des tentatives de manipulation portant sur la création littéraire et les relations personnelles. La réception de *Pays perdu* relève pour partie de ce niveau d'analyse. Elle tient à la fois du décalage entre deux registres de langage et du décloisonnement entre univers littéraire et populaire qui a permis au roman d'atteindre un public auquel il n'était pas destiné. On peut esquisser, ici, un rapprochement entre la démarche de certains ethnographes qui soumettent leurs écrits aux enquêtés avant la publication et la suggestion de certains habitants de Lussaud d'être associés au projet d'écriture sur le village. Pierre Jourde expédie l'éventualité dans *La première pierre* : illustrer et rassembler la communauté au prix d'un "produit décoratif" ? À l'évidence, pour Jourde, l'idée ne mérite pas quelques lignes alors que les débats font rage dans le monde scientifique autour de la possibilité d'une co-construction indigène et académique des savoirs. Pierre Jourde, quant à lui, préfère nous rappeler que les rapports de domination ne sont pas nécessairement univoques.

Ethnocentrisme de l'étranger

C'est par un étrange mépris, écrit-il dans *La première pierre*, que l'on méconnaît la capacité des paysans à se servir des mots, à user d'une "rhétorique d'autant plus fine qu'elle est habile à donner toutes les apparences de la franche rudesse". Et de dénoncer leur "numéro" à l'audience du tribunal où ils jouent "les pauvres paysans" qui n'ont pas les mots.

> Mais il est entendu qu'un paysan incarne le vrai, qu'il ne peut pas être autre chose que lui-même, que tout son être est dans son apparence. Le paysan du Cantal serait comme l'Indien d'Amazonie ou le Papou, cette substance naïve, exotique, à peine consciente d'elle-même.

Attitude factice mais éminemment recevable qui contraste avec l'irrecevable vérité du roman. En jouant à être ce qui est attendu d'eux, les paysans retournent à leur profit l'illusion de l'authentique. On pense ici à la phrase de Tchekov que Richard Hoggart met en exergue de son livre *Uses of litteracy* : "J'ai du sang paysan dans les veines : pas question de me faire le coup des *vertus paysannes*". Il y a d'ailleurs une analogie entre l'anthropologue britannique et Pierre Jourde : l'un et l'autre sont issus du milieu social qu'ils décrivent et s'en sont détachés pour devenir des intellectuels[5]. Et si la grande question qui parcourt l'ouvrage de Richard Hoggart est celle de l'ethnocentrisme de classe, n'est-ce pas cela, en fin de compte, que les paysans de Lussaud reprochent à Jourde lorsqu'ils lui font sentir sa position d'étranger ?

Cette position, les socio-anthropologues la vivent systématiquement dans l'expérience ethnographique. Pour Didier Fassin (2008), ce qui caractérise avant tout l'anthropologue sur son terrain, c'est "cette indépassable étrangeté de l'étranger qu'il est pour celles et ceux qu'il étudie". Il dit avoir appris à ses dépens que "le travail critique de l'anthropologue étranger donne lieu à des retours de bâton" et cite, à l'appui de son propre témoignage, celui de Nancy Scheper-Hughes (2000). L'anthropologue américaine avait publié, en 1979, un livre décrivant de façon précise et directe la détresse sociale en lien avec les troubles mentaux dans un village de l'Irlande rurale. Retournant sur le lieu de ses enquêtes, elle est expulsée du village par les mêmes qui lui avaient offert leur hospitalité vingt ans auparavant. Alors qu'elle voulait dénoncer une forme de domination culturelle, son travail avait été perçu comme ethnocentrique par ses enquêtés.

On voit que l'anthropologue n'en termine pas avec son terrain une fois qu'il l'a quitté physiquement. Pas plus que Jourde ne peut en finir avec Lussaud. C'est le constat que fait Natacha Gagné (2008) après avoir quitté la Nouvelle Zélande où son travail sur les Maaori l'a confronté aux enjeux politiques complexes de l'autochtonie. Les idées qu'elle développait dans sa thèse apparaissaient comme menaçantes pour ceux qui occupaient des positions les autorisant à se proclamer gardiens d'une authenticité culturelle maorie. Une fois encore, l'anthropologie océanienne nous ramène au mythe de l'authenticité, fondement symbolique des processus de réification des cultures et des identités en lien avec des projets politiques. Déconstruire le mythe expose l'anthropologue à l'accusation d'ethnocentrisme, le conforter rend certes son travail plus recevable mais au prix de ce que certains dénoncent comme un dévoiement des objectifs de la discipline.

Enjeux du *je*

Les écrits réflexifs sur la réception des travaux anthropologiques présentent donc de nombreuses correspondances avec ce que la littérature de Pierre Jourde nous dit de la position de l'écrivain au regard d'une pragmatique littéraire. Il en est une cependant qui me semble subsumer

---

[5] La famille Jourde est cependant embourgeoisée depuis plusieurs générations.

les autres : la difficulté, peut-être l'impossibilité pour le romancier, comme pour l'ethnographe, dans son travail d'interprétation, de faire une place au *je* de l'autre.

Marc Augé (2006), réagissant contre la prétention post-moderne de conférer à l'objet des études ethnographiques le statut de sujet, réaffirme la position d'auteur qui est celle de l'anthropologue. Sa signature est le signe de son autorité fondée sur une expérience, des hypothèses, des schèmes d'intelligibilité et, finalement, une interprétation du monde social qui va à l'encontre des formes de compréhension intuitives. Cette autorité ne se conçoit pas en dehors du *je* qui l'incarne au plan symbolique comme au plan des modalités concrètes de production et d'énonciation du savoir.

Pour Pierre Jourde (2013), "tout livre qui fixe la parole et la scelle d'un nom propre (…), quoi qu'il dise, dit *je*". Et "Le *je* qu'il est, même sans le dire (…), absorbe le monde". *Pays perdu*, dont le projet était de restituer leur histoire au père de l'écrivain et aux habitants du village, d'en faire des *je*, ne pouvait exister que "sur une contradiction" puisque personne d'autre que l'auteur ne peut être *je* dans un livre. Non seulement, dit Jourde dans *La première pierre*, le livre ne donne pas aux personnages la possibilité du *je,* mais il leur dérobe leur *je*, et avec lui, "cette ultime réserve" qu'est la conscience de chacun de n'être pas ce qu'il est. Il ne reste alors que deux solutions :

> Il faut prendre la parole, à son tour, pour montrer qu'on n'est pas ce qu'on est, qu'il subsiste en soi infiniment de richesses en dehors du livre.
> Ou bien, si l'on se sent si pauvre et si incertain qu'on se croit être entièrement dépossédé de soi, on va se battre, contre un livre, qui devient la figure visible et palpable de cette puissance aveugle, de cet ennemi qui vous vole secrètement et un jour vous prendra tout, la mort.

Ne doit-on pas considérer que l'appropriation du *je* de l'autre par l'écrivain est aussi le fait de l'anthropologue qui devient ainsi, quoi qu'il prétende, "l'écrivain ethnographe" dont parle J. Clifford (2003) ? La littérature de P. Jourde nous fait alors mesurer la portée de ce détournement du *je*. La réception indigène des écrits académiques est certes une question éthique qui se pose aux sciences sociales avec une acuité renouvelée depuis que les anthropologues écrivent sous le regard ce ceux qu'ils décrivent, pour reprendre une formule de Marc Augé (2006) qui a inspiré le titre de cette partie. Elle peut recevoir et, de fait, elle reçoit des réponses d'ordre technique (qui vont du "bricolage" empirique à la codification des pratiques ethnographiques) ou épistémologique (à qui s'adresse prioritairement la production de savoir scientifique ?). Au-delà des débats que ces réponses suscitent, la lecture de P. Jourde met en évidence la dimension métaphysique de la question.

Conclusion

Ce travail est né d'une rencontre du chercheur en sciences sociales que je suis avec *Pays perdu*. Rencontre qui n'avait rien de fortuit puisque le roman de Pierre Jourde recoupe mes objets et terrains de recherche. C'est ainsi que j'ai été amené à m'aventurer dans un territoire qui ne m'était pas familier, celui des rapports entre littérature et analyse du monde social. Ce manque de familiarité justifie une ambition théorique limitée partant de l'intuition plus que d'une hypothèse rigoureusement construite, qu'il y aurait un lien entre la question de l'authenticité et celle de la réception des écrits par ceux qui y sont décrits. J'ai essayé de montrer ce lien au plan empirique en m'appuyant sur les champs de recherche où il me semblait apparaître avec le plus de force. Surtout le texte littéraire de Pierre Jourde s'y prêtait (trop bien peut-être, pourrait dire son auteur) dans la mesure où on peut y voir des caractères d'une expérience ethnographique. La densité des écrits de Pierre Jourde rendrait dérisoire une prétention à épuiser les possibilités qu'ils ouvrent quant au rapprochement, au croisement, à la confrontation d'idées avec les sciences sociales dans une perspective pragmatique qui a été celle de ce travail. Parvenu à ce stade de mon exploration, l'articulation de deux *comment* me semble constituer les bases possibles d'un cadre théorique d'analyse et d'une collaboration entre les sphères littéraire et scientifique. Le premier est soulevé par Pierre Jourde (2005) : comment faire pour que la littérature soit autre chose qu'une "machine à langage authentique" qui "ne produit pas de sens" et qui "consomme du réel au bénéfice d'un *je* faussement neutralisé" ? Les réponses à ce *comment* littéraire pourraient alimenter le questionnement scientifique qui me semble résumer la réflexion proposée ici : comment penser une indexation de l'expérience ethnographique à son commentaire (Bensa, 2008) qui fasse droit au *je* de l'autre ?

Références

Augé, Marc. 2006. *Le métier d'anthropologue. Sens et liberté*. Paris : Éditions Galilée.

Babadzan, Alain. 2009. *Le spectacle de la culture : Globalisation et traditionalismes en Océanie*. Paris : L'Harmattan.

Bensa, Alban. 2008. "Conclusion : Remarques sur les politiques de l'intersubjectivité." *Les politiques de l'enquête : Épreuves ethnographiques*, edited by Didier Fassin and Albin Bensa, 323-328. Paris : La Découverte.

Boltanski, Luc and Eve Chiapello. 1998. *Le nouvel esprit du capitalisme*. Paris : Gallimard.

Cabot, Jérôme. 2018. "*Pays perdu* : De l'éloge paradoxale à la lecture offensée." in *Rural writing Geographical imaginary and expression of a new regionality*, edited by Mauricette Fournier, Cambridge Scholars Publishing.

Clifford, James. 2003. "De l'autorité en ethnographie : Le récit anthropologique comme texte littéraire." *L'enquête de terrain*, edited by Daniel Cefaï, 263-294. Paris : La Découverte.

Cravatte, Céline. 2009. "L'anthropologie du tourisme et l'authenticité : Catégorie analytique ou catégorie indigène ?" *Cahiers d'études africaines*, 2009/1 : 603-620.

Fassin, Didier. 2008. "Répondre de sa recherche : L'anthropologue face à ses *autres*." *Les politiques de l'enquête : Épreuves ethnographiques*, edited by Didier Fassin and Albin Bensa, 299-320. Paris : La Découverte.

Gagné, Natacha. 2008. "Le savoir comme enjeu de pouvoir : L'ethnologue critiqué par les autochtones." *Les politiques de l'enquête : Épreuves ethnographiques*, edited by Didier Fassin and Albin Bensa, 277-198. Paris : La Découverte.

Hobsbawm, Eric. 2006. *L'invention de la tradition*. Paris : Éditions Amsterdam.

Jourde, Pierre. 2003. *Pays perdu*. Paris : L'Esprit des Péninsules.

—. 2005. *Littérature et authenticité : Le réel, le neutre, la fiction*. Paris : L'Esprit des Péninsules.

—. 2013. *La première pierre*. Paris : Gallimard.

Laplantine, François. 2001. *L'anthropologie*. Paris : Éditions Payot et Rivages.

Moeschler, Olivier. 2016. "Allers-retours. Les usages des *cultural studies* par la sociologie." *SociologieS*, Dossiers, Sociétés en mouvement, sociologie en changement. Accessed April 11. http://sociologies.revues.org/5323

Scheper-Hughes, Nancy. 2000. "Ire in Ireland." *Ethnography*, 1/1 : 117-140.

Weber, Florence. 2008. "Publier des cas ethnographiques : Analyse sociologique, réputation et image de soi des enquêtés." *Genèses*, 2008/1 : 140-150.

Further reading

Cefaï, Daniel, ed. 2003. *L'enquête de terrain*. Paris : La Découverte.

Cefaï, Daniel. 2010. "L'expérience ethnographique, l'enquête et ses publics." *L'engagement ethnographique*, edited by Daniel Cefaï. Paris : Éditions de l'École des hautes études en sciences sociales.

Fassin, Didier and Albin Bensa, eds. 2008. *Les politiques de l'enquête : Épreuves ethnographiques*. Paris : La Découverte.

Wittersheim, Éric. 1999. "Les chemins de l'authenticité : Les anthropologues et la Renaissance mélanésienne." *L'Homme*, 1999/39 n° 151 : 181-205. DOI : 10.3406/hom.1999.453625.

CHAPTER NINE

PAYS PERDU :
DE L'ELOGE PARADOXAL
A LA LECTURE OFFENSEE

JEROME CABOT

Lussaud est un petit hameau d'Auvergne, perché à 1020 mètres d'altitude sur les marges orientales du massif volcanique du Cézallier, dans le département du Cantal. Après avoir été jadis une commune, Lussaud a été rattaché, en 1836, à celle de Laurie, distante de 5 km, laquelle a connu un déclin démographique notable : 670 habitants en 1836, 388 en 1921, 200 en 1968, 99 en 2011. Lussaud, quant à lui, est désormais habité par cinq familles d'agriculteurs, réparties en huit foyers, soit une vingtaine d'habitants, population vieillissante vivant modestement d'un élevage extensif et d'une agriculture d'autosubsistance voués à la disparition. Lussaud est à 21 km, soit trente-sept minutes, de Massiac (1826 habitants en 2011), chef-lieu de canton placé sur l'autoroute A75, la RN 122 allant vers Aurillac, et la ligne SNCF Figeac-Arvant en liaison ferroviaire avec Clermont-Ferrand, Aurillac et Béziers ; à 50 km, soit une heure de route, de la sous-préfecture, Saint-Flour ; à 93 km, soit près de deux heures, de la préfecture, Aurillac ; et à 89 km, soit une heure et demie, de la préfecture de région, Clermont-Ferrand.

Pierre Jourde a publié, en 2003, un texte d'inspiration autobiographique, présenté comme un roman : *Pays perdu*. Ce court récit se nourrit de sa connaissance de Lussaud, dont est originaire sa famille paternelle, propriétaire d'un important patrimoine foncier, et où son père est enterré. Depuis l'enfance, Pierre Jourde passe ses vacances dans la maison du Cantal, à laquelle est toujours attenante une exploitation, héritée de la grand-mère et louée en fermage ; il y participe à la vie sociale, aux fêtes et aux travaux agricoles. En février 1998 décède à Lussaud la jeune fille d'un couple d'amis paysans de Jourde, qui portera la bière de l'adolescente et la descendra dans le caveau. Le fil conducteur de *Pays perdu* est sa veillée funèbre, vers laquelle tous convergent : elle est l'occasion d'une série de portraits et, au-delà, d'anecdotes et de considérations sur la vie paysanne, sa rudesse et sa beauté. Contre le folklore idéalisant et les conventions de la littérature de terroir, la prose de Jourde développe un éloge paradoxal, dégageant l'héroïsme humble de cette paysannerie en voie d'extinction, puisant dans la mémoire orale les ingrédients d'une épopée.

Figure 9.1. Lussaud, août 2014 (crédit : Jérôme Cabot)

Ce hameau est un territoire d'une densité littéraire inégalée, également dépeint dans un autre livre de Jourde paru en 2010, *La Présence* et dans *Pays éperdu* de Bernard Jannin, également originaire de Lussaud, ce qui fait écrire à Jourde, dans la préface qu'il consacre à ce dernier ouvrage, le constat suivant :

> deux écrivains pour vingt habitants, soit dix pour cent de la population. Trois livres parlant de ces vingt habitants, évoquant ce petit coin de terre avec ses toponymes locaux, ses lieux-dits, ses maisons, ses secrets de l'espace et du temps. Cela fait de ce village l'endroit le plus littéraire du globe, loin devant Paris, New York ou Londres. (Jannin 2012, 8).

À ces trois titres s'est depuis, de surcroît, ajouté un quatrième, de Jourde encore : *La première pierre.*

Paru chez un éditeur confidentiel, *Pays perdu* parvient pourtant jusqu'à Lussaud en 2004. Bien que l'auteur ait modifié tous les noms de lieux et de personnes, et parfois changé les liens de parenté, les habitants s'y sont reconnus, n'ont pas tous perçu l'intention de célébration et d'hommage, et ont vu mépris et offense là où Jourde voulait mettre respect et lyrisme. Informé du malentendu, il adresse aux habitants une longue lettre d'explication, dont voici l'argument :

> Mon intention n'était pas du tout de commettre des indiscrétions ou de dire du mal, bien au contraire. (…) Ce livre est fait pour montrer que des villages comme le nôtre existent, qu'on y vit bien, et par certains côtés mieux qu'à la ville, en dépit des difficultés, qui ne manquent pas. Et je dis bien "notre village", parce que pour moi, je suis de Lussaud, et quand j'en parle, je parle de moi aussi, je m'inclus dans le livre. Je suis fier d'être de Lussaud et d'appartenir à cette communauté. (…) Ce qui me fait peur, c'est que le village disparaisse. Que cette manière de vivre n'existe plus. (…) Ce serait dommage de se vexer d'un texte qui rend plutôt admirable aux yeux des autres. Et cette admiration vient de ce que les habitants des grandes villes ont perdu force, endurance, hospitalité et gaieté qui se sont gardées là-haut. (…) Car pour moi, sans exagérer, Lussaud est un village d'exception.

Nonobstant, le 31 juillet 2005, des habitants de Lussaud ont accueilli Jourde et sa famille, de retour pour les vacances, par des insultes, des menaces et des coups. L'affaire s'est conclue le 21 juin 2007 au tribunal d'Aurillac par une condamnation de six villageois pour "coups et blessures volontaires en réunion, avec préméditation" et "injures raciales" (les enfants de Jourde sont métis), et a connu un traitement médiatique international (voir par exemple Blecher 2005 ; Burnat 2007 ; Robert-Diard 2007). Jourde ne reviendra pas à Lussaud avant juin 2009. L'affaire a donné lieu à un nouvel ouvrage, paru en 2013, *La première pierre* : Jourde (qui s'y parle à lui-même, en se tutoyant) y revient sur le fait divers et, au-delà, les raisons de la mauvaise réception de son texte et du malentendu tragi-comique auquel il a donné lieu ; on peut y lire son compte rendu de la rixe, de longues citations des dépositions, sa réponse au traitement journalistique et judiciaire de l'affaire, l'évocation de son retour au hameau.

Cet article a pour objet de relire le texte premier (y compris à la lumière de *La première pierre*) pour en dégager le projet esthétique, anthropologique et social, et d'examiner les raisons de sa réception ratée, à contresens, par les habitants qu'il dépeint. Sa grande qualité littéraire, l'originalité de son projet et la radicalité de ses conséquences en font un cas d'école hors du commun quant à la question de la réception, par ses habitants, de la mise en littérature d'un espace – avec sa construction d'images, son esthétisation des lieux, son articulation d'un discours – et de ses enjeux politiques, sociaux et identitaires.

Le brouillage des références spatio-temporelles

L'espace lisse contre le consensus homotopique

La sauvagerie, l'altitude, la désertification, l'enclavement font de Lussaud une matrice littéraire exceptionnelle. *Pays perdu* commence par de longues pages sinueuses comme l'itinéraire compliqué qu'elles dépeignent, jusqu'à l'arrivée dans le hameau. La référence géographique est d'emblée très loin de la littérature localiste :

> On est dans le loin. (…) la montagne passant la gueule entre tous les murs, ou l'horizon, plus grand qu'ailleurs, où se déversent et se vident les maisons, les chemins et les prés, rappelleront à chaque instant qu'on y est : loin. (2003, 13-14).

Le *loin* est, par définition, une notion relative. La destination ne célèbre pas l'esprit de chapelle ; tous les chemins semblent mener, non à Rome, mais à cet absolu négatif, fait d'effacement :

> nous allons quelque part, tout au bout de la route, comme si les voies multiples du monde devaient s'achever là, et nous arrivons dans ce qui n'est qu'à peine un lieu. (…) "C'est un pays perdu", dit-on : pas d'expression plus juste. On n'y arrive qu'en s'égarant. Rien à y faire, rien à y voir. (2003, 16-17).

L'un des effets paradoxaux de cette célébration du lieu conduit à sa dissolution référentielle. *Pays perdu* rompt le "consensus homotopique" propre à la littérature géographique, tel que le définit Bertrand Westphal :

> Lorsqu'une œuvre est nommément mise en relation avec un référent du monde "réel" elle est régie par ce que Samuel Kripke appelle un "désignateur rigide", qui est ici le nom du lieu (…). Dès lors que cette relation existe, on assiste non pas à une construction *ex nihilo*, mais à la reconfiguration d'un réalème [*i.e.* un élément de réalité]. (2007, 169).

Or, dans *Pays perdu*, Lussaud n'est nommé que par son initiale dans la dédicace liminaire, "Merci à tous les habitants de L*"* ; ce sont les conséquences judiciaires et médiatiques de la réception du texte qui, de l'extérieur, rétabliront le consensus homotopique que celui-ci avait rompu.

En outre, de nombreux autres toponymes brouillent la référence et introduisent l'espace monde dans ce coin reculé de l'Auvergne, à l'instar de "Une petite Mongolie inhabitée" (2003, 24), pléonasme le rendant plus mongol encore que la Mongolie référentielle, comme si cette dernière était caractérisée par une forte densité de population. Cette analogie avec l'archétype de l'espace plat, désertique, continental et inexploré, est récurrente dans le texte : le patois rappelle les langues altaïques ; les habitants, mal vus des villages voisins ou du curé, sont comparés aux brigands d'une zone tribale pashtoune ; telle figure locale est "une beauté tadjike ou kurde" (2003, 57), évoque un Sarrasin, un Tangoute, un Ouïgour, un Mongol d'Oulan-Bator, un sumotori ou un nomade kirghize. La rupture du consensus homotopique est accentuée par une multiplication de références géographiques contradictoires : villages tibétains, bourreaux chinois, *pueblos* indiens et dieux zapotèques, paysages de western. Il y a là l'expression d'un fort potentiel romanesque, d'un exotisme syncrétique des confins, de la Frontière et de la *terra incognita*. Dans *La première pierre*, on trouve une formule condensant efficacement ces références géographiquement contradictoires et symboliquement homogènes : Lussaud est "un compromis entre l'Asie centrale et le Far West : le Far Centre" (2013, 162).

Figure 9.2 Le Cézallier (crédit : Jérôme Cabot)

Mais le brigandage et le nomadisme introduisent autre chose : l'espace échappant, sinon à l'emprise de l'homme, du moins à celle de l'administration, de l'économie, de l'Etat et du droit. Lussaud est situé dans ce que Deleuze et Guattari, dans *Mille plateaux* (2013, 471-481 ; aussi Westphal 2007, 68-69), appellent un "espace lisse", par opposition à l'espace strié de la *polis*, la police, la politique et le policé : un espace nomade et non quadrillé, celui de la mer, du désert, et plus encore, de la *steppe*, mot aux occurrences innombrables dans *Pays perdu*. La résistance au remembrement est emblématique de cette population réfractaire aux espaces striés dont la cartographie, avec ses tracés et ses routes, ses latitudes et ses longitudes, est une représentation éloquente :

> Inutile d'aller visiter la Mongolie : c'est là qu'elle se trouve, en réduction, dans cette zone dont personne n'a jamais entendu parler, et qui figure toujours en blanc sur les cartes Michelin de la France, aux confins du Cantal et du Puy-de-Dôme, pour la bonne raison que là, il n'y a personne. (2013, 157).

Les voies de fait dont Jourde fut victime ne font qu'accentuer cette lecture du territoire dans *La première pierre* : "Nous ne sommes plus dans le Cantal, département de la République française, en 2005, mais dans des temps très anciens, ceux de la violence primitive, de la vendetta et du sacrifice" (2013, 56), une scène de bouc émissaire évoquant Ourartou, la Transoxiane ou les Kouchanes[1].

Anhistoricité pré-industrielle, mythologies et héroï-comique

Ce brouillage spatial a pour corollaire une intrication de périodes historiques lointaines. Les espaces lisses sont soustraits à l'Histoire, ou en tout cas à la modernité. Lussaud contient, sinon le monde, du moins ses espaces les plus vierges, et en même temps tout un pan de l'histoire primitive. Celle-ci remonte à l'aube de l'humanité (nombre d'éléments sont qualifiés de *préhistoriques*, la végétation colonisant un tas de fumier, un énorme pain massif, un vieux tracteur), et même avant les premiers hommes, le cimetière étant un "vieux saurien" (2003, 24), et le basalte la peau d'un animal antédiluvien. On trouve aussi, par petites touches, l'histoire des Aztèques, les potentats antiques et les juges médiévaux – "les dernières traces d'un monde disparu, comme si tu avais vu les derniers Mayas, les ultimes Babyloniens" (2013, 176).

Cette vision embrasse donc l'anhistoricité pré-industrielle, laquelle se fond avec le temps des légendes, entre mythologie et imaginaire médiéval. Les mythes, les contes, les fabliaux ou Rabelais sont des références explicitement convoquées. Tel habitant devient un fantôme, une sorcière,

---

[1] Ourartou : royaume du IXe siècle av. J.-C. sur le haut plateau arménien ; la Transoxiane : actuel Ouzbékistan et sud-ouest du Kazakhstan ; les Kouchanes : peuple indo-européen du Pakistan, de l'Afghanistan et de l'Inde du nord.

une vieille fée, un "roi qui aurait décidé de vivre une existence de paysan" (2003, 29), ou le fils légendaire de Mélusine, Geoffroy, né avec une défense de sanglier qui faisait saillie hors de sa bouche. Les sapinières après les tempêtes sont des charniers de monstres, et le volcan, un Léviathan. Deux époux à l'union interdite par des haines familiales sont continûment rebaptisés Roméo et Juliette. Jourde dépeint des bistrots légendaires aux menus pantagruéliques et leurs "agapes merveilleuses des légendes médiévales" (2003, 65).

Ce voyage dans le temps se nourrit d'éléments référentiels, à l'instar des gargouilles des édifices du bourg ; mais il a aussi pour effet d'irréaliser et d'ennoblir les éléments prosaïques des hameaux, tels ce sanglier domestiqué décrit comme un prince de légende, les bruits d'étable suggérant une gigantomachie[2], ou cette bouse métamorphosée en bauge de dragon par l'empreinte d'un pneu de tracteur. Même au plus fort de la rixe de 2005, telle que la narre *La première pierre*, cet imaginaire reste prégnant : "te reviennent, ce n'est pourtant pas le moment, des réminiscences littéraires, des fabliaux, des contes lestes avec poissardes fortes en gueule" (2013, 39).

Il en va de même avec le répertoire des références gréco-latines. Elles grandissent des éléments marqués par le prosaïque, le sale, voire le honteux. C'est ce que la tradition classique nommait l'héroï-comique, qui consiste dans une inadéquation entre un sujet vulgaire et normalement cantonné à la prose et la comédie, voire banni de la littérature, et le registre de langue, le style, les références que le texte lui associe, empruntés aux codes du sublime, du mythe, de l'épopée et de la tragédie. Les infirmités rappellent les cyclopes. Les bêtes à l'étable deviennent des sortes de Minotaure. La machine agricole est un dieu inexorable. Le fermier François a une "face d'imperator" (2003, 30). Les incartades expliquant une réputation sulfureuse proviennent de ce passé immémorial dont l'épique à petite échelle ne peut être restitué que par le lustre de la Grèce de Périclès : "cette renommée d'Aspasie villageoise" (2003, 60) – ou par celui de la langue latine : "*In illo tempore*, dans ce temps incertain des semi-légendes" (2013, 149). Dans *La première pierre*, les paysannes invectivant les Jourde en 2005 sont des Erinyes, et le prévisible lynchage revêt la fatalité d'une tragédie antique. Avec un brin d'autodérision, même le coup de poing qu'assène Jourde s'inscrit dans cet univers de référence : "Ce n'est pas du Homère, du Corneille, ni même du Rostand, mais c'est d'une belle simplicité épique. "Il dit, et frappe de sa lance." De fait, pour toute réponse, tu lui envoies un taquet (…)" (2013, 53).

---

[2] Gigantomachie : combat des géants contre les dieux.

L'alcoolisme donne lieu au développement le plus notable. Objet de stigmatisation et de honte, ou de gros comique, il ne se prête *a priori* guère à cet ennoblissement. Or, dans *Pays perdu*, les "beuveries aux épisodes héroïques" (2003, 70) transmutent les hommes en titans ou en dieux olympiens. Pour autant, le traitement est complexe, Jourde parle d'"une mauvaise plaisanterie mythologique, la parodie grinçante des puissances originelles" (2003,126). Il y a de la grandeur, mais sans nulle tragédie, le registre comique est maintenu par ce "démon facétieux (…), petit dieu rieur et familier" (2003, 127-128) qu'est l'alcool. Les lendemains de gueule de bois transforment les princes et les fées d'un soir en Cendrillons piteuses et sans magie. Mais "la légende vermeille du pinard" (2003, 130) a pour effet d'évacuer à la fois le misérabilisme et le comique superficiel.

Jourde, qui analyse finement les fonctions sociales que remplit l'alcool, voit dans ceux qui lui ont pleinement voué leur vie "l'abandon des grands mystiques" (2003, 129), le sacrifice poussé si loin qu'il va jusqu'au dérisoire, au manque de sérieux, jusqu'à ne plus rien avoir du sacrifice. Ce mélange de gravité et d'humour, sans pathos ni condescendance, caractérise également l'ivrogne qui, contre l'interdit frappant son chien à l'entrée du bal, s'écrie, "philosophe éméché du vivant, Diogène sublime : "Tu apprendras que le chien, c'est un être humain comme les autres""(2003, 84). Symétriquement à cet héroï-comique, les méfaits de l'alcool donnent lieu à une interrogation tragique et désespérée sur la vie éternelle, qui inflige au Christ le traitement inverse, relevant du burlesque, c'est-à-dire rabaissant une réalité consacrée par l'application de termes et de détails vulgaires, ici le rédempteur ayant les attributs et les pratiques d'un paysan de Lussaud.

Ce faisant, par son brouillage géographique, son anhistoricité, son syncrétisme de références littéraires et mythologiques, le texte se détourne du réalisme, registre sur lequel on attendrait la littérature de terroir. Jourde s'en explique dans *La première pierre* :

> Le livre ne se voulait pas réaliste, parce que la réalité n'est pas réaliste. Ou plutôt parce que le réalisme est impuissant à délivrer toute la charge d'imaginaire qui bonde le réel. Le livre était une élégie pour une jeune fille morte, une tragédie se déroulant en un même lieu en un seul jour, une épopée, un conte mythologique. (2013, 135).

Et cette charge imaginaire n'est de surcroît pas l'apanage de l'écrivain (abstraction faite des références lettrées qui lui sont propres), mais bien consubstantielle à la sociabilité de Lussaud et à son mode de vie :

François, qui touche juste, comme d'habitude, a glissé en passant, à toi qui es censé être le raconteur d'histoires, qu'il nous resterait les histoires, justement (…). Il sait d'instinct que l'expérience la plus drue, celle que nous vivons dans ces jours d'estive, si près semble-t-il des choses réelles, le froid, la terre, les bêtes, la sauvagerie, l'alcool et le gibier, est tout entière tissée d'imaginaire. (2013 : 167).

Donner des lettres de noblesse

Épopée, héroïsation et esthétisation

Au-delà de la restitution de cette charge d'imaginaire, qui est notamment celle de l'enfant émerveillé par Lussaud que fut Jourde, ces références aux espaces lisses et aux mythes ont pour effet de constituer une *épopée*. Le terme revient d'ailleurs fréquemment, à propos du bruit d'un tracteur ou de belotes aux "tricheries légendaires" (2003, 55). L'épopée a pour fonction idéologique, sociale et identitaire de doter une communauté d'un texte et d'un mythe fondateurs, la présentant dans son affirmation face à un ennemi, l'adversité, l'Autre (Madelénat 1986) : comme l'*Iliade* pour les Grecs, les chansons de geste pour l'Occident médiéval, le western pour les yankees… ici, *Pays perdu* se veut écrit pour donner ses lettres de noblesse à la paysannerie face aux forces de la nature et aux temps modernes. Il s'agit d'écrire pour les habitants de Lussaud, non certes comme lectorat, mais comme bénéficiaires symboliques. *Pays perdu* exalte un héroïsme modeste, humble, et opère par là un renouvellement de la notion de *héros*, le mot ou ses dérivés étant eux aussi récurrents.

L'héroïsation embrasse uniment, avec empathie et distance, la violence et le comique. Cet héroïsme qui s'ignore s'incarne dans des anecdotes où, précisément, hommes et femmes paient de leur chair : une page, ainsi, le magnifie à travers une description des mains paysannes. Les machines modernes œuvrent à une monstruosité archaïque, recréant des êtres antédiluviens, des monstres, tel cet accidenté énucléé qui se voit lui-même de son œil pendant au nerf optique. La litote, l'*understatement*, expriment une forme de flegme aristocratique face à ces avanies tragi-comiques, comme ce paysan scalpé par le passage en tracteur sous le linteau d'une grange, ou "l'homme en morceaux", victime de sa tronçonneuse, que les pompiers retrouvent "là-bas, au volant" (2003, 62).

Pays perdu élabore ainsi une esthétisation des corps meurtris par le travail, l'outil, les bêtes, le froid, le manque d'hygiène, l'alcool. La dent unique d'un personnage est vue comme l'expression d'un dandysme. Le texte, par conséquent, pousse cette logique jusqu'à exalter la fascination morbide exercée par la nécrose fétide des pieds de Germaine, le pus accumulé sous un fichu jamais ôté, les charognes de chiens morts entassées sous les draps du lit, l'odeur infecte des cadavres de cerfs putréfiés.

Pays perdu s'inscrit dans le registre de l'éloge paradoxal, dégageant le sublime de la crasse et de la déréliction. Les verres sertis de toiles d'araignées révèlent des "beautés fabuleuses" (2003, 54) ; la syllogomanie, accumulation compulsive de déchets, "édifie lentement le monument nauséabond de l'abandon" (2003, 53). Les fermes encombrées sont les "ultimes chapelles où se célèbre, dans une royale simplicité, le culte des dieux fangeux" (2003, 49), source d'une "jubilation dans l'effroi" quand "la saleté touche au grandiose". Il y a quelque chose, là, qui relève à la fois de l'esthétique incongrue et de la métaphysique : "cette sublime crasse (…) avait quelque chose de royal dans son dédain de toute hygiène et de toute propreté, comme un mépris des contingences" (2013, 136).

Métaphysique de la bouse

Les vaches, et plus particulièrement leur bouse, résument parfaitement la complexité de ce paradoxe. En décrivant les bovins comme des "bêtes aux yeux de déesse et au cul chocolaté de merde" (2003, 90), Jourde conjoint les connotations positives associées aux divinités grecques, et au chocolat, et les connotations négatives liées, ne fût-ce que par le niveau de langue, au prosaïsme du cul et de la merde, peu compatibles avec les dieux comme avec l'alimentaire. C'est que la bouse est, pour le meilleur et pour le pire, un marqueur identitaire du territoire : "on est au pays de la merde" (2003, 134).

Là encore, nulle plaisanterie scatologique. Pendant plusieurs pages, le texte célèbre "la matière sale, ce qu'on ne touche pas et dont on ne parle pas" (2003, 139), et déploie l'amplitude et la variété de sa présence, indice de l'activité économique principale de cette paysannerie d'éleveurs, trace du travail quotidien, à la fois encombrant déchet, signe de richesse et source d'engrais. Jourde déplie le paradigme dans toute sa richesse lexicale, écho de son "exaltation stercorale" et de la typologie très fine qu'il élabore, ennoblissant les tas de fumier par l'évocation de leur richesse ou leur "haute antiquité", personnifiant la bouse par un caractère funèbre ou sournois.

Au-delà de cette anthropomorphisation de la matière fécale, Jourde accentue ce traitement héroï-comique avec les mots, symboliquement prestigieux, de l'œnologie et la parfumerie, parlant de fragrances et de fumet : "c'est un parfum d'herbe, densifié et comme intériorisé, relevé d'épices, agrémenté de notes profondes" (2003, 135). La bouse est un concentré du lieu, sa quintessence. Son odeur est celle de l'herbe, du lait et du saint-Nectaire. L'éloge paradoxal n'est pas un exercice de style se plaisant à appliquer un traitement esthétisant à la matière tabou : il y a un enjeu initiatique dans ce "fumet acide et rongeant, qui empoigne, qui révolte, qui bouleverse l'âme" (2003, 136). L'odorat, le sens le plus animal, le moins cérébral, ouvre sur une portée métaphysique. En crevant, enfant, la croûte d'une bouse séchée,

> on éprouvait la sensation de l'intériorité, et c'était une expérience métaphysique et sale, comme lorsqu'on éventre un petit animal, et qu'on y trouve la matière première de l'univers, encore tiède, au lendemain de la création (2003, 139).

Jourde donne à la bouse une dimension organique et sacrée, en des termes quasiment panthéistes : "la grande idole des mouches, la déesse fiente, règne dans l'immanence. Ses avatars sont multiples, aux fragrances variées" (2003, 138). Aux "éclats du corps dispersé de la grande déesse" (2003, 140), tout finit par se mêler, cadavres, débris, déchets. La bouse, tout comme son émanation la mouche (2003, 146), est "l'esprit du lieu" – en tous les sens du terme, spiritisme et spiritueux – condensant le commencement et la fin de toutes choses. Jourde dégage le sacré caché à qui ne sait pas le voir – à commencer par les paysans eux-mêmes. Le prosaïque est la porte d'entrée vers une improbable spiritualité panthéiste.

La bouse, tout comme au-delà, Lussaud, permettent un élargissement du microcosme négligé, méconnu, en voie d'effacement, au macrocosme, avec ses grandes questions universelles, la vie, la mort, le Tout :

> Dans ces terres reculées, dans ces pays perdus, on vit toujours plus ou moins dans une légende (…). Les rois mages ne sont pas loin, ils arrivent, ils ont peiné dans la nuit étoilée, et traîné leurs brocarts dans la bouse. Jamais leur arrivée ne m'a paru aussi imminente que dans ces étables crasseuses. (…) Quelque chose va venir, du fond de ces paysages austères, où l'on attend depuis l'origine. Quoi ? Le monde. Le monde n'est pas encore arrivé. On l'attend. Il va naître. Oui, il y a, là-haut, pour qui sait écouter et sentir, au cœur de la matérialité la plus brutale, au cœur de ce qui paraît le plus éloigné de ce que nous sommes convenus d'appeler le beau, un noyau de spiritualité d'autant plus déchirante qu'elle est à la fois familière et hors d'atteinte. (2013 : 100-101).

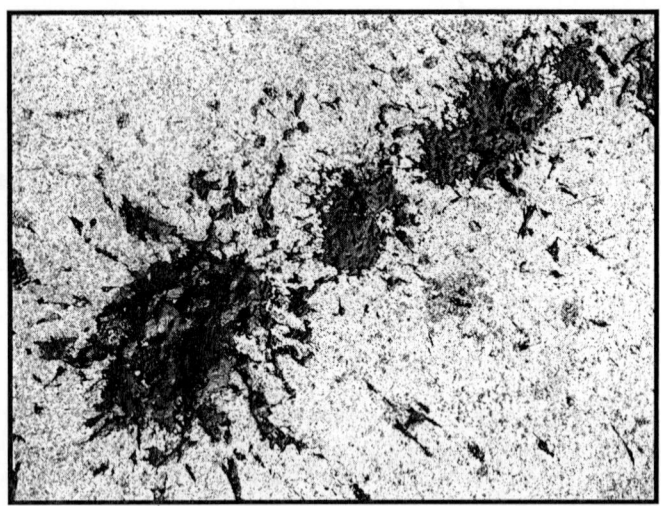

Figure 9.3 Entre Lussaud et la Coharde Basse (crédit : Jérôme Cabot)

L'ennoblissement, l'héroïsation disent aussi que, sur ces hauts plateaux volcaniques, on est plus près du ciel, du néant, des forces telluriques, et que les paysans sont la part métaphysique de l'humanité. On en a une illustration avec les propos phatiques[3] de Ritou sur la météo, dont l'apparente simplicité recèle une beauté humble et une profondeur modeste :

> Ritou savait faire vibrer les harmoniques de cette banalité, en tirer toute la richesse d'évidences pénétrantes, jusqu'à ce que le fond de l'air, dans ses variantes de fraîcheur et d'humidité, à force de splendide effacement, apparaisse comme le fond des choses. (2003 : 71).

Un écrit irrecevable

La beauté difficile et l'exhumation des morts

Il n'est pas surprenant que ce traitement de la bouse, incongru, transgressif, éminemment chargé de sens et de symboles, ait été déterminant dans la mauvaise réception de *Pays perdu* par les habitants de Lussaud, faisant fi des distinguos stylistiques, voyant une axiologie négative là où Jourde célébrait l'exceptionnalité d'un territoire : il lui fut

---

[3] Phatique : caractérise l'usage du langage utilisé uniquement pour établir la communication et maintenir le contact, sans apport d'information.

reproché d'avoir dit que c'était "un pays de merde" quand, parlant du *pays de la merde*, il désirait en faire l'éloge. L'un des agresseurs, dans sa déposition que cite Jourde, dit avoir voulu

> lui montrer que [son] tas de fumier n'est pas plus sale que le reste. (…) il parle de mon tas de fumier que j'entrepose à l'entrée du village et qui sali [sic] celui-ci. Mais de la façon dont les phrases sont tournées on pourrait croire que c'est moi qui est [sic] sale. (2013, 69).

La susceptibilité de cette lecture est riche d'enseignements, et Jourde revient dessus avec pertinence dans *La première pierre* : *Pays perdu* s'est écrit pour le compte d'un pays où il pense ne jamais devoir être lu, dans l'absolu, en faisant fi des lectures possibles. La démarche, en outre, était incommunicable, par pudeur non pas devant tel détail, mais devant le geste littéraire lui-même, devant l'existence même de ce livre d'admiration :

> ce dont on devrait avoir honte, il le revendiquait comme une fierté. Mais cette fierté, il en avait honte. Pas de ce que sont les choses, mais de les avoir tirées du silence pour se les attribuer à lui. C'était un livre qui avait honte d'être fier de ce qu'il décrivait. (2013, 138-139).

Dans *La première pierre*, Jourde anticipe la réception, se montre davantage précautionneux, conscient de l'éventualité d'être lu, y compris de façon malveillante : il fait preuve d'une forme d'autocensure, dit s'abstenir d'ajouter des anecdotes dramatiques ou savoureuses, désamorce toute offense dans l'allusion à une prothèse, formule une adresse amicale qui ne peut plus se dire de vive voix du fait du contrôle social pesant sur ses relations dans le hameau, mais aussi devance et interpelle une lecture hostile ou souhaite à demi-mot la mort de ses persécuteurs.

De ce pays, écrit-il dans *La première pierre*, il a voulu tout dire parce qu'il y aime tout : un hommage, ni éloge bucolique ni photo posée, pas plus qu'une attaque, mais le souci de dire aussi les petitesses, les faiblesses, les ridicules, "la beauté sans mièvrerie, la beauté difficile, qui vous rejette ou qui vous agresse" (2013, 19). Ce pays, se dit Jourde, "Tu voulais le rendre avec sa dureté et sa joie, sa beauté et sa violence. Sa puissance, quoi" (2013, 33). C'est la faute des lectures simplificatrices que d'avoir non seulement substitué, à la trilogie énoncée en quatrième de couverture – Alcool, Hiver et Solitude – la série plus racoleuse Alcool, Merde et Solitude, mais surtout, d'avoir retenu les thèmes au détriment de leur traitement littéraire, donc de l'intention esthétique et éthique : "De la royauté dans l'alcool, de la noblesse dans la solitude, de la grandeur dans la merde" (2013, 95).

Jourde, en outre, veut exprimer son attachement d'enfant à ce monde en voie d'effacement. Il exprime avec vigueur, sincérité et lucidité, à contre-courant de l'histoire du siècle et du monde tel qu'il va, sa nostalgie de l'enfance et du pays tel qu'il n'est plus peu à peu, gagné lui aussi par la modernité et l'industrialisation, les parpaings et le plastique, devenant progressivement un "espace strié" (Deleuze et Guattari). Son évocation, dans *La première pierre*, de la dernière estive à pied d'Auvergne, l'atteste : il regrette les travaux et les jours du passé, l'ère du "travail acharné, le travail comme foi" (2003 : 56), où le labeur était aussi une fête, un élan collectif, à la fois lutte et connivence avec le temps et l'espace – bref, l'époque, comme l'exprime si bien Ramuz, où être paysan était un état et non un métier.

Et il se trouve conforté dans la légitimité de ce regard par le fait que François, l'homme de la dernière estive, paysan de Lussaud, qui ne peut donc être suspecté de donner dans la nostalgie artificielle de l'urbain lettré, manifeste le même attachement à la beauté et l'authenticité des choses – autant que Jourde avec ses références culturelles et ses souvenirs d'enfance, qui décrit, en partie, le Lussaud des années 1960 plus que celui du début du XXIe siècle. Lussaud est perdu dans l'histoire autant que dans l'espace. La polysémie du titre embrasse à la fois l'enclavement, l'effacement, la perte et le deuil (à l'instar de celui de Lucie, dont la chute de *Pays perdu* évoque la perte irrémédiable) :

> Ainsi, depuis le début, à longues journées, au prix de milliers de kilomètres, nous ne gagnons le pays que pour voir à quel point nous le perdons, et pour tenter de le retenir un peu encore, de garder dans ce monde quelque chose dont nous ne savons même pas ce que c'est. (2003, 18).

Jourde a été accusé d'avoir exhumé les morts, ce que, pour le coup, il persiste à revendiquer comme étant l'essence même de son projet ; en témoigne la galerie de portraits des disparus qui ne viendront pas veiller le corps de Lucie, ou encore son hommage cru et violent à "la longue colonne des suppliciés", les estropiés, les accidentés, les suicidés (2003, 124-125). Mais son projet est, au-delà, de fixer une humanité qui s'éteint, la "mort lente" de ce pays (2013, 168), l'exode des femmes, le célibat des vieux garçons voués à enterrer seuls leurs parents. Au bourg, les aubergistes se succèdent, arrivés en avril, partis en février. Il n'y a plus de messe, sauf les enterrements. Il y a davantage de défunts que de vivants, comme l'atteste le monument aux morts dans un hameau d'un habitant. Dans le cimetière, les morts sont partout et nulle part à la fois, même les disparus continuent de disparaître, fondus dans un environnement minéral et dépeuplé. L'héroïsme humble commence avec ceci :

Y monter, c'est pénétrer sur le territoire d'une très vieille guerre qui s'achève, laissant ses blessés, ses invalides, ses vétérans et ses héros qui boivent un coup pour s'encourager à tenir le poste. (2013, 175).

Figure 9.4 Pâtures du Cézallier (crédit : Jérôme Cabot)

Mémoire orale vs Littérature écrite

Il y a, à l'origine de *Pays perdu*, une imprégnation de la transmission orale et une tentation ethnographique de la revivifier, la conserver et la transmettre. Même si Jourde se montre très nuancé sur son écoute du bavardage de sa vieille tante généalogiste, entre dévotion et distraction, *Pays perdu* restitue la tradition orale, consigne la mémoire, les veillées, les blagues, les racontars, l'identité collectivement construite de chacun, tout individu étant un "agrégat de récits plus ou moins pittoresques" (2013, 129). Jourde, par conséquent, embrasse tout, dit tout, sans jugement, avec empathie. Mais ce faisant, il rapporte ce qui se raconte mais ne s'écrit pas : les faillites et les combines, le vin rouge dans les biberons, une réputation sulfureuse, une hérédité alcoolique, une handicapée mentale obèse. Il est violemment transgressif, à Lussaud, de voir les secrets qui normalement ne se couchent pas sur le papier, passer d'une littérature orale qui s'ignore comme telle à la Littérature, figée dans l'écrit qui est chose rare là-haut, à l'exception du quotidien *La Montagne*, archétype de la presse quotidienne régionale dans tout son localisme.

De surcroît, Jourde réalisera trop tard que certaines histoires intimes notoires, qu'il pensait être des propos oraux anodins et connus, étaient restées ignorées des intéressés, notamment un adultère et un enfant illégitime. *Pays perdu* se présente d'ailleurs, entre autres choses, comme un tombeau du père de l'auteur, tué à petit feu par le secret de son origine adultérine : les deux grands-parents de Jourde étaient cousins germains, le grand-père n'a reconnu son fils que très tard, et la grand-mère l'a longtemps fait passer pour son chauffeur. La rupture du sceau enfermant les "secrets de polichinelle" (2013 : 149) est une revanche sur la mutité du père de Jourde. Il est, à ce titre, remarquable, à la fois triste et savoureux, de constater que la contre-attaque des habitants de Lussaud aura consisté dans la publication d'une autre rumeur infamante du même ordre, qui circulait manifestement depuis toujours à l'insu de Jourde sur sa propre bâtardise supposée, d'abord par la voie d'une pancarte à l'entrée du hameau lui souhaitant la bienvenue sous un autre nom que celui de son père, puis par une perfidie : "ton père n'est pas là où tu crois" (2013, 38). Lussaud ripostait par des fictions contre un livre qui dénudait ses fictions.

Dans *La première pierre*, Jourde continue à revendiquer d'écrire, pour l'humanité qu'elles révèlent, certaines choses qu'on préfère ne pas dire afin de maintenir une sociabilité possible. Il établit une nuance essentielle entre les futiles indiscrétions contemporaines du « people », et sa démarche anti-journalistique, attentive à l'épaisseur temporelle des destinées individuelles :

> Je ne suis pas de ceux qui pensent que la littérature justifie tout. L'éthique y est inséparable de l'esthétique. Si un roman viole l'intimité de personnes réelles par simple appétit de scandale, et par ce goût contemporain de l'exhibition qui constitue le degré zéro du réalisme, c'est à la fois une mauvaise action et un mauvais texte, parce qu'il ne produit pas d'autre sens que l'exhibition. J'ai tenté de faire en sorte que le peu que j'ai montré de la vie privée de certaines personnes soit toujours relié à une réflexion sur la possibilité de l'intimité dans une communauté paysanne, sur la place des handicapés, sur la mort, etc. (2007, 59).

Il montre dans cet article, et plus encore en 2013, la prise de recul et l'acuité qui lui ont fait défaut dix ans auparavant, en introduisant la nuance essentielle entre le secret su de chacun, et le secret connu de tous. L'indiscrétion peut circuler d'un individu à l'autre, être connue de toute la communauté. Faute de pouvoir conserver un secret dans une société restreinte, retirée, marquée par l'isolement et la promiscuité, la vie collective se maintient grâce à la fiction du secret, consistant à savoir et faire comme si on ne savait pas. Car sa publicité est taboue ; l'effraction est la même que celle qui consiste à franchir indûment le seuil d'une ferme. L'espace intime et le secret relèvent tous deux d'une forme de sacré, ne tolérant ni la transgression ni le trop de paroles ; et dans ce pays perdu, tout semble obscène, à commencer par la parole.

Le secret ne saurait être mis sur la place publique sans menacer le corps social ; or, par définition, le livre rend public, il publie, avec cette circonstance aggravante que les écrits restent. À la fonction phatique des paroles, maintenant le lien social et le vivre ensemble, meublant les silences, s'opposent la fixité et la densité de l'écrit. *Pays perdu* se heurte à une logique manichéenne et à une réception quasi magique, selon lesquelles il n'y a pas d'écrit innocent ni neutre, et écrire ce qui est mal, c'est le souhaiter.

Un texte voué à déplaire

Les difficultés d'un discours littéraire allogène

Jourde a écrit avec un fort sentiment d'appartenance à ce monde disparu. Dans *La première pierre*, il insiste sur le fait que *Pays perdu* n'oppose pas "eux" et "je"» mais articule un "nous", et le montre, lui, aussi concerné par les travaux, les beuveries, le purin dont il fut même baptisé en tombant dans la fosse. Bref, Jourde revendique une écriture endogène. Bertrand Westphal définit le point de vue endogène comme une vision autochtone de l'espace, par opposition à la vision onogène du voyageur, porteuse d'exotisme (2007 : 208-209) :

> C'était un livre qui revendiquait, comme lui appartenant en propre, à lui aussi, au-delà de tout jugement, la splendeur des horizons, l'horreur des blessures, la dureté des travaux, la mesquinerie des rivalités, l'héroïsme des vies ; la neige sur le volcan et les dents solitaires, la merde des vaches, les saouleries, l'ironie au coin d'un œil bleu. (2013, 138).

Mais cette revendication n'est acceptable que pour qui le considère fondé à la formuler, comme étant des leurs ; et ce n'est pas ce que lui renvoient les lecteurs ombrageux de Lussaud : *"Tu n'es pas chez toi ici !"* (2013, 51). La position de Jourde est donc plus ambiguë, comme il l'écrit dans sa présentation en ligne de *Pays perdu* :

> Le regard porté sur ce pays vient à la fois de l'intérieur et de l'extérieur. L'auteur, quoique originaire du village, est aussi un homme de la ville, un universitaire et un écrivain qui sait manier les mots. Toute représentation littéraire de l'autre est déjà, en soi, une violence, une prise de possession.

Cette violence est décuplée lorsque, comme c'est le cas dans *Pays perdu*, celui qui est représenté n'a pas une grande habitude de la chose littéraire, et peut se sentir, de surcroît, socialement dominé. Il n'y a guère de remède à cela. Même la familiarité que j'ai pu avoir avec la plupart des habitants de ce village, depuis ma petite enfance, n'a pas pu empêcher, avec la parution du livre, que ressorte de manière explosive la vieille méfiance du rural envers le citadin. Néanmoins, le livre n'est pas seulement celui d'un observateur extérieur, au regard ethnologique. Ma famille et moi-même y sommes des personnages, et nous n'y sommes pas mieux ni plus mal traités que les autres.

C'est-à-dire que, ni endogène ni exogène, il est allogène, ce qui est *"le propre de tous ceux et toutes celles qui se sont fixés dans un endroit sans que celui-ci leur soit encore familier, sans non plus qu'il demeure pour eux exotique"* (Westphal 2007, 209). Ce pays, dit Jourde, constitue sa *"texture mentale"* (2003,147) – mais, le font tout autant, ses lectures, ses références culturelles, dont on a vu le syncrétisme géographique, historique et mythologique appliqué à Lussaud. Et l'intérêt, et l'incommunicabilité, de ce ressenti métis, sont dans ce mélange, inaudible pour les Parisiens comme à Lussaud : "intellectuel chez les paysans, paysan chez les intellectuels, en exil de soi-même", dit-il dans *Pays retrouvé*. Or, à Lussaud, *Pays perdu* pâtit d'être non seulement un livre, mais de surcroît – triple domination – l'œuvre d'un propriétaire terrien (un "patron"), d'un citadin, et d'un intellectuel.

Il y a là une forme de tautologie. Le roman paysan est celui qui prend la paysannerie pour objet, jamais celui qui est écrit par des paysans. Depuis Gutenberg, le paysan est l'Autre de l'écrivain : celui qui est là pour amuser, faire-valoir des héros, ou raillé et dépeint dans sa noirceur, sa bassesse, sa convoitise (par Balzac dans *Les Paysans*, Zola dans *La Terre*), ou encore, à l'inverse, exalté, investi de valeurs d'intellectuels généralement urbains : l'idéalisation romantique, chez une George Sand, des sentiments purs et nobles ; le combat de la littérature régionale contre la IIIᵉ République, son jacobinisme, son centralisme linguistique et culturel, célébrant une paysannerie gardienne des valeurs traditionnelles (Thiesse, 1991) ; le nationalisme et l'idéologie réactionnaire, de Barrès à Vichy ; jusque, dans une version moins idéologique, au roman rustique de Henri Pourrat, l'exaltation de la nature et de la chasse chez Genevoix, ou le panthéisme mystique de Giono.

Écrire envers et contre tous les stéréotypes

Écrivant après ces quelques siècles d'histoire littéraire, Jourde, dont le projet allogène est précisément d'inverser l'échelle de valeurs, se heurte à ces représentations ancrées. Les comptes rendus journalistiques du fait divers et du procès, les plaidoiries, ne feront qu'ajouter, aux fictions du village, celles de la presse et du tribunal, comme le cliché opposant de braves brutes au bavasseur urbain : Jourde souligne combien ce topos erroné fait fi des joutes verbales et des répliques qui tuent émaillant la vie sociale de Lussaud, se laisse abuser par la comédie de la paysannerie jouée par les accusés, et manifeste finalement à la fois méconnaissance et condescendance. Il peut, à juste titre, déplorer que toutes les lectures de *Pays perdu*, dont il fait l'inventaire, se soient conformées à tel ou tel de ces stéréotypes – bucolique, misérabiliste, anti-intellectualiste, partisan de la liberté d'écrire, etc. (2013 : 91-92).

Plus particulièrement, pour le paysan, écrire sur son compte exprime forcément une intention maligne ; sa lecture du texte intègre nécessairement le regard stigmatisant, véhiculé par les normes sociales, et accessoirement par la littérature qui les légitime. Jourde évoque d'ailleurs, dans *La première pierre*, parmi les raisons expliquant la mauvaise réception de *Pays perdu*, le besoin de dignité de ces vies modestes et écrasées, un honneur d'autant plus hypertrophié que leur lot commun est fait de renoncement, et tout ce qui travaille les cœurs, la faim d'histoires, les disparitions, la soif de respect. Tout ce qui est écrit est donc pris en mauvaise part, Jourde se trouvant même accusé d'avoir dénigré les nombreux virages de la route menant à Lussaud, dans les sinueuses et amoureuses premières pages de *Pays perdu. A fortiori*, celles qu'il consacre à la merde sont emblématiques de cette lecture paranoïde :

> on est dans la mythologie, dans l'épopée, rien de petit dans ce pays, tout y est magnifié, jusqu'à l'humble merde de vache, et c'est bien pour cela que tu l'aimes. Mais tu l'aimes pour ce qu'ils n'aiment pas, pour cela même qu'ils pensent, ici, que quelqu'un d'extérieur les méprisera, les tas de fumier, le purin qui éclabousse les bottes et les mains, les bouses, alors ils ne lisent pas ce que tu as écrit, où se dit l'évidence de l'affection et du plaisir, ils superposent au texte leur fiction personnelle, ils n'y voient que la confirmation de cette fiction, comme le font tant de lecteurs, hélas. Aussi t'en veulent-ils, non pas de ce qu'ils croient que tu n'aimes pas, mais bien plutôt de ce qu'ils n'aiment pas en eux-mêmes. La merde, ils voient avant tout qu'ils y piétinent trop, et qu'il leur faut chaque jour s'en défaire, s'en nettoyer, alors comment admettre qu'on les renvoie à ce qu'ils se donnent tant de peine à évacuer ? (2013, 128).

Pierre Assouline a exprimé avec concision l'impossibilité d'une lecture correcte de la prose de Jourde, très littéraire, complexe, intertextuelle et paradoxale, par les paysans :

> on peut se sentir personnellement avili par un livre, surtout quand on n'en lit jamais et que l'on n'est pas préparé à considérer l'humour, le troisième degré, la talent dans l'indiscrétion impudique, l'exigence littéraire au détriment du tact élémentaire et l'amour vache d'un auteur pour ses personnages.[4]

Figure 9.5 Salers sur le Cézallier (crédit : Jérôme Cabot)

L'émergence d'une littérature écrite par les paysans est tardive : elle a dû attendre l'école obligatoire et l'extension de l'alphabétisation, sans que cela lève tous les obstacles sociaux, culturels et symboliques à son expression. *La Vie d'un simple*, d'Emile Guillaumin, paru en 1902, est considéré comme le premier titre du genre. Avec les Trente Glorieuses, l'exode rural et l'extinction progressive de la paysannerie traditionnelle, on assiste au traitement de la ruralité comme alternative à la modernité et à la société de consommation ; mais le phénomène produit majoritairement une version édulcorée, célébrant une vision nostalgique et lénifiante, emblématisée par la tétralogie de Claude Michelet, *Les Gens de Saint-Libéral*, et chaque terroir a désormais son écrivaillon. Entre folklore

---

[4] Le texte, publié en 2007 sur le blog de Pierre Assouline « La République des livres », n'est plus disponible en ligne.

gentillet et stigmatisation, la voie est donc étroite, et c'est de cela que se garde Jourde. Il y revient dans *Littérature contre journalisme* : "La paysannerie ne peut plus supporter, en termes d'image, que celle, insipide et désuète, que lui renvoie la littérature de terroir" (2007, 59). *Pays perdu* voulait faire œuvre d'écrivain public, écrivant pour le compte de héros méconnus, mais en solitaire. Le paradoxe est que tout livre dit Je, par son existence, affirme le Je de l'auteur même dans son effacement, par une opération de vampirisme de l'imaginaire. Il s'en explique dans la présentation de *Pays perdu* :

> je courais le risque de verser dans la complaisance, en transformant ces gens en figures folkloriques à l'usage des lecteurs de la ville. Je mesurais la difficulté d'éviter ce travers, lorsqu'on prend la parole au nom et à la place de ceux qui ne l'ont pas. Faire le malin avec la vie des autres, se couvrir des dépouilles de leur force ou de leur chagrin pour en devenir plus intéressant et plus vrai d'apparence, tel est le travers courant de l'écrivain.

Pour autant, l'éventualité de soumettre son manuscrit aux habitants est *a posteriori* écartée par Jourde, en tant qu'elle aurait promis un livre affadi et décoratif.

Au contraire, l'héroï-comique, l'exaltation brutale de la beauté dure, rude et sale annoncent autre chose, une voix inédite. Un tel projet se heurte aux élus et aux journalistes locaux, aspirant à "un pays clair, moderne, festif, un pays qui bouge. Ils veulent s'arracher aux âges sombres, à l'arriération, à l'enclavement, et surtout, surtout, ils veulent une bonne image" (2013, 100). L'entreprise littéraire de Jourde – en consonance avec des auteurs tels que les Limousins Michon, Bergounioux et Millet (Coyault-Dublanchet, 2002) – va à rebours du folklore, de la complaisance et du marketing territorial. Jourde – même si, parfois, il semble s'émerveiller de ce que la réalité soit si conforme aux clichés – écrit contre la carte postale, veut en dépasser les icônes. *Pays perdu* opère dans sa description de Lussaud un brouillage spatio-temporel qui, contre le consensus homotopique, célèbre un "espace lisse" enrichi de références géographiques contradictoires, d'une anhistoricité pré-industrielle, de légendes et de mythes. L'effet en est de donner ses lettres de noblesse au modeste hameau, dans une veine héroï-comique élevant le quotidien modeste au rang de l'épopée, produisant l'héroïsation des humbles et l'esthétisation du prosaïque, donnant une dimension métaphysique jusqu'à la bouse même. Cet éloge paradoxal d'une beauté difficile, dure et sale, produit un écrit irrecevable, en tant qu'il exhume les morts et fait passer la mémoire orale, ses secrets et ses tabous, dans la Littérature écrite. *Pays perdu* est, par essence, un texte voué à déplaire, empêtré dans les

difficultés inhérentes à tout discours littéraire allogène, et victime de son
projet fondamental d'écrire envers et contre tous les stéréotypes,
stigmatisants ou complaisants.

L'expérience métaphysique que Lussaud inflige à Jourde, et
l'expérience littéraire que Jourde inflige symétriquement à Lussaud, sont,
en dépit de l'inspiration prosaïque, organique et terrienne, à l'opposé de
l'ancrage identitaire et rassurant dans un terroir. À maintes reprises, *Pays
perdu* évoque un monde sans consistance ni résistance, marqué par une
fadeur paradoxalement intense, l'usure et l'effacement de la matière
comme de l'être individuel, la dépossession, l'exil, l'égarement, le
sentiment d'être de nulle part, dans un non-lieu au cœur même du pays. La
chute de *La première pierre* réunit cet effacement de l'être avec son
territoire en évoquant Jourde mort, diffus et présent, envers et contre tous,
en dépit de l'ostracisme – chez lui.

Primary sources

Jannin B. 2012. *Pays éperdu*. 103 p. Clermont-Ferrand : Page centrale.
Jourde P. 2003. *Pays perdu*. Paris : L'Esprit des Péninsules, 167 p. [rééd.
    Presse Pocket, même pagination].
—. 2007. "Littérature contre journalisme". *Le Magazine des livres*, n°6, p.
    57-59.
—. 2013. *La première pierre*. 191 p. Paris : Gallimard.
—. Sur *Pays perdu*. Consulté le 15 01 2018, URL :
    www.pierrejourde.fr/Romans/Pays%20perdu.pdf
—. Sur *La première pierre*. Consulté le 15 01 2018, URL :
    www.pierrejourde.fr/Romans/La%20premiere%20pierre.pdf

Secondary Sources

Blecher L. 2005. "Les mots de trop pour le hameau de Lussaud".
    Libération. Mis en ligne le 16 09 2005, consulté le 15 01 2018. URL :
    www.liberation.fr/societe/2005/09/16/les-mots-de-trop-pour-le-
    hameau-de-lussaud_532567
Burnat P. 2007. "Un écrivain lynché par ses personnages", *Le Figaro*. Mis
    en ligne le 21 06 2007, consulté le 15 01 2018. URL :
    www.pressreader.com/france/le-figaro/20070621/282016142910795
Coyault-Dublanchet S. 2002. *La province en héritage : Pierre Michon,
    Pierre Bergounioux, Richard Millet*. 289 p. Genève : Droz.
Deleuze G., F. Guattari. 2013 [1er éd.1980]. *Mille Plateaux. Capitalisme et
    schizophrénie* 2. 647 p. Paris : Editions de Minuit.

Madelénat D. 1986. *L'Epopée*. 264 p. Paris : PUF.
Robert-Diard P. 2007. "Scènes de chasse dans le Cantal". *Le Monde*. Mis en ligne le 21 06 2007, consulté le 15 01 2018. URL : www.lemonde.fr/livres/article/2007/06/21/scenes-de-chasse-dans-le-cantal_926470_3260.html
Thiesse A.-M. 1991. *Écrire la France : le mouvement littéraire régionaliste de langue française entre la Belle Epoque et la Libération*. 320 p. Paris : PUF.
Westphal B. 2007. *La Géocritique. Réel, fiction, espace*. 278 p. Paris : Éditions de Minuit.

PART 3:

NEW EXPRESSION OF REGIONALITY IN FRANCOPHONE AMERICA: TENSIONS BETWEEN MEMORY TO TRANSMIT AND VALUES TO SHARE

CHAPTER TEN

FILM ADAPTATION AND THE EMANCIPATION OF QUÉBEC COUNTRY NOVELS *THE WOMAN AND THE MISER* (CLAUDE-HENRI GRIGNON (1933); CHARLES BINAMÉ (2002)) AND *THE OUTLANDER* (GERMAINE GUÈVREMONT (1945); ÉRIC CANUEL (2005))[1]

MARIE PASCAL

During the last years of the Québec financial crisis of the 1930s, Québec's rural society, predominant since the wave of colonization of French-Canada during the 17th century, transforms progressively into an urban society. During this time, two genres of novel impose themselves: the *country novels* which put forward an idealized vision of traditional rural life, and the *novels of the industrialization* which, on the other hand, represent the darkness of an industrial world where class determinism is entrenched by the hardships of the two World Wars[2].

Of the first novels of this era, five were hailed as classics, and two would be adapted to the big screen: *The Woman and the Miser* (Claude-Henri Grignon (1933) and Charles Binamé (2002)) and *The Outlander* (Germaine Guèvremont (1945) and Éric Canuel (2005)). Written during

---

[1] I would like to thank my translator, Max Deller-Lestage, who has devoted time and energy in the translation of this article.
[2] We can highlight the fact that *The Woman and the Miser* was published in between the two wars, a period of reconstruction, while *The Outlander, G.* Guèvremont's first novel, wasn't published until a few months after Germany's surrender.

the darkest years of the crisis, these country novels are representative of the traditional French-Canadian spirit and place the archetypal family and the Catholic religion at the center of society. They also present the codes of this society, as well as the different pre-established orders, in a flowery language which opposes itself to that of France, previously considered as the only possible cultural and linguistic reference.

As represented in the stories, these different social orders become amplified by the presence and behavior of a character who transgresses them. In fact, these eponymous novels make explicit the intransigent aspect of a rural order which will finally be put into question and overthrown, by the avarice of Séraphin in Grignon's work and by Guèvremont's problematic descendant of the *coureurs des bois* – the Survenant who undermines the pre-established balance of the micro-society in Chenal du Moine. Emphasized by the transgression of the directors who adapt these two classics to the big screen, at the dawn of a new century and thus a new context, the transgression of these characters will see itself metamorphosed in a visual medium and will acquire a spectacular quality.

As such I propose to study the main aspects of the rural as presented by omniscient narrators in the hypotexts[3], to then show how Séraphin and the Survenant transgress this rural order by their mere presence. I will finally turn my attention towards the adaptations in order to study two important sequences, examples of the last form of transgression, that of the film, which makes the study of the rural even more complex due to the addition of a sequence which is not in the books, yet crucial in the movies.

Characteristics of rural Quebec

According to Michel Biron, François Dumont, and Elisabeth Nardout-Lafarge in *Histoire de la littérature québécoise,* the regional novel (also called « du terroir ») calls for a "return to the earth" (« un retour à la terre » (194)) and warns against the charm of the city. Furthermore, this genre permits a "return to the heroic figures of the past, as well as to the traditional way of life of an ethnic "we" defined mainly by French language and the Catholic religion". These aspects are well portrayed in the two novels and will be examined after a brief overview of a few key

---

[3] I am borrowing this term, "hypotexte", from Gérard Genette's work titled *Palimpsestes,* and am allowing myself to add to his concepts on transtextuality that of "hyperfilm", replacing the term "hypertexte" put forward by the critic.

sociological concepts concerning society and figures of "anomie" developed by Durkheim in *The Division of Labour in Society*.

A family-based society

As the final state of a long line of developments – from "hordes" (based on a complete resemblance among individuals), to "clans" (an organization of different hordes), the *society* is the ultimate step to human organization (Durkheim 1893, 150). These resemblances upon which all alliances between individuals are based, called "collective character" by Durkheim, are defined as the joining of all beliefs and feelings common among the average of all the members of a same society. As an inter-generational link, the collective character does not depend on the individuals' particular conditions: as the latter evolve, the former remains. In other words, the collective character is the main pillar of social cohesion and it engenders a positive type of social solidarity called "mechanical solidarity" – implying that not only are the individuals attracted to each other as they are alike, but also that they are attracted to their society of birth, their condition of existence. United by this principle, the individuals are interchangeable in terms of their function in the group, and uphold a maximum mechanical solidarity when their individual conscience is overlapped with the collective character, the collective thoughts and ideals. It is therefore interesting to define the degree of social cohesion in a given time and geographical era by using this accurate axis of mechanical solidarity.

In rural Quebecois society, the "*habitants*" (owners of the land) and "*cultivateurs*" (who work the land) are portrayed as extremely reticent to let any stranger disturb the fragility of the familiar, which they have struggled in preserving against cultural and physical colonization. Social rank is thus established by birth, inheritance of knowledge, and land is passed from father to son. From the second chapter of the *Outlander*, Père Didace is portrayed as concerned that his name will be passed down to one who is not worthy. With the death of his wife Mathilde, Didace loses hope that he will have a son other than Amable, who is fragile and not work oriented. On the eve of the Survenant's arrival, the thoughts of Père Didace, communicated through an omniscient heterodiegetic narrator, bring into focus the force of the collective character in relation to family heritage:

> When he was gone a man would be needed to carry on the Beauchemin name; Didace had been on the lookout for him for some time but had not

found him yet. A dull, vague uneasiness had long beset him, intermittent but difficult to repel, rather like a pain he had once had in the marrow of his bones, a pain that shifted up and down from his great toe to his knee and made him long to take down his gun an fire into his leg (10).

Through this diffuse yet insistent pain which takes hold of the entire character starting with the "marrow of his bones", an entire generational conflict is unveiled: the fear of losing the family land through an incompetent and sterile progeny. As such, we see this worry a few lines before the narrator's remarks: "it was on that evening, as they were sitting down to supper, that the Stranger knocked at the Beauchemin's door" (11). The passage operates as a prolepsis when one considers the role this character will have for Didace: that of a surrogate son.

Though this fear of an undeserving descendant torments the family patriarch, the arrival of the Outlander is an even greater threat to his faith in the collective character, a pattern that appears clearly as early as the incipit of the novel:

> One autumn evening, at Monk's Inlet, as the Beauchemin family were preparing for supper, they were startled by a knocking at the door. Outside stood a tall, stalwart young man, quite unknown [...] the stranger with quick, deft hands, bathed his face, sluiced his neck, scattered water over his hair while the eyes of everyone in the room followed his slightest movement. He seemed almost to have brought a fresh significance into an act that was indeed familiar to them all (11).

The members of the Beauchemin family represent a united entity, raising their heads at the same time, looking in the same direction as if they were a single person and sharing the same thoughts, as the pronouns "everyone" and "them all" demonstrate. This phenomenon of the exclusion of the Outlander by an undefined "everyone" can be analyzed throughout the novel, for instance during the many evening gatherings:

> And all the other neighbours dropped into the habit of coming in too. Curious to hear what the Stranger had to tell about the great world, the dwellers on the Inlet began to frequent the Beauchemin house. For them, with the exception of a few seafarers, the land they knew lay not only within the province of Quebec but entirely between Sorel, the two villages in the north, Yamachiche and Maskinongé, up to Lac Saint-Pierre, and Lavallière and Yamaska bays, at the furthest limit of their lands (25).

The strong feeling of belonging to the village and the ethnocentric vision of the individuals of this micro-society bluntly oppose the in-village to the outside where the Others – stigmatized as dangerous – might come from. Hence, the Outlander is the main target of these attacks, as we can see from Angelina's first thoughts upon their meeting[4], but so is the Acayenne, a bar-owner who enjoys a less than sunny reputation, as well as any kind of stranger[5].

But ultimately, in the country novel it is the woman's role to act as the mediator responsible for the passing of this collective character. At Phonsine's mercy – a young woman lacking strength and reticent to work – the Beauchemin family doesn't shine as bright as in Didace's late wife Mathilde's time:

> Didace was angry but he controlled himself, lest he might say too much. The women in the Beauchemin family, from their ancestress Julie down to his aunts, his mother, his sisters, his wife, and even his daughter Marie-Amanda, [...] had been fine, buxom women, all of them – square shouldered, always prompt to take their fair share of any burden. [...] And they bore a child almost every year. But now the daughter in law, a little Ladouceur girl from La Pinière, an orphan brought as a fine lady, makes a face like a fine lady at the prospect of hard work. Didace was furious: "A little chit of a girl like her! And not even a baby in her arms after three years of marriage!" (10-1).

Phonsine's lack of children is as reprehensible as her lack of enthusiasm regarding her daily chores. Furthermore, the fact that she is an orphan is almost explicitly correlated with her lack of natural strength, which opposes her to the long line of women of Didace's ancestry. This opposition between Phonsine and the women who have worn the name Beauchemin is often recalled, as in this passage detailing the preparations for New Year's celebrations:

---

[4] Although pious, she isn't quite objective when she first meets him even if she struggles against the effects of the collective character that has brainwashed her: "To Angelina's eyes the Stranger represented day and night; the man of the roads had shown himself a good worker, devoted to the soil... The heedless rover, without a family or aim in life, had proved himself a man skilled in five or six different crafts" (30). The oppositions and contradictions which appear in this passage expose Angélina's actual conflict between her slavish desire to belong to the collectivity and rejecting the foreigner, and her attraction to this man who is tenderly attached to the earth.

[5] The most accurate example is Amable crying out one day, in the presence of the Survenant, "these damned foreigners", to which the latter replies : "That's it, Amable, knock anybody who doesn't come from Monk's Inlet, or get your gun and shoot them" (96).

The very day after her arrival, Marie-Amanda undertook the great house cleaning which Alphonsine had always been putting off. For one whole day, the pulleys creaked under the weight of the rope from which they hung the various items of household linen. Toward evening the women carried armfuls of it into the kitchen; aching all over from their labors. A smell of cleanliness and comfort pervaded the whole house, and the men took unwonted care not to soil anything (48).

This description of Marie-Amanda's work lasts several pages and the narrator continually opposes Phonsine's fragility, her childlessness, to Marie-Amanda's force and courage, as well as the imminent birth of her third child.

Several scenes of daily life are thus represented, the place and rank of the protagonists are defined, and the details of the treatment outsiders receive are given recurrently, as in the case of the Outlander. However, rural French-Canadian society is not uniquely based on the principles of the family which orbits around a strong woman, but upholds within itself the importance of religion, pervasive in Claude-Henri Grignon's novel right from the title.

A society founded on religion

The French paratext of *The Woman and the Miser*[6] presents the importance of religion in a clearer way than the English title which nevertheless makes explicit the flaw of the woman's husband, that is, the "miser". Moreover, the name of the character itself, "Séraphin", is nowadays a common noun, explicit to the Québécois public as a reference to the sin of greed. From the paratext to the main character's name, the novel is thus steeped in religion and immediately offers the promise of reprisal, greed being one of the seven deadly sins for Catholics. Several times, the old man is in fact considered by the other characters to be a sinner, his behaviour with regards to his wife being interpreted by his young cousin as "a sin". The narrator, omniscient and extradiegetic, also takes him to be part of a long list of « damnés »:

---

[6] The French title – *Séraphin, un homme et son péché,* is indeed quite different from the English one, as it presents the protagonist's name right next to the fact he is the incarnation of a deadly sin, greed. The English title puts forward the role of the woman, which is an interesting perspective when one considers the role of women in the literary genre.

> The constant intensity of his passion had reached a level never to be known
> by those who mallow in laziness or pride or gluttony, not even by those
> who have an insatiable appetite for exhausting lust. Seraphin Poudrier
> topped them all by the pervasiveness of his sin that yielded more joy than
> any courtesan in the world could ever do (71).

Placed on an arbitrary scale, certain deadly sins are compared to
Séraphin Poudrier's greed, which trumps them all, as much because of the
pleasure procured as for the damnation incurred, the latter being the cause
of the miser's death. By this multitude of information, the protagonist is
stigmatized as a sinner throughout the novel, therefore engaging the
novelistic to cross-over to a religious discourse. But this portrayal of greed
goes much further in the novel since it appears as central in the
protagonist's life, destroys that of his wife as well as that of his many
creditors, and ultimately causes his downfall. Quite paradoxically though,
Séraphin channels God's Word when he explains to Donalda the vice of
gluttony.

In the same way, multiple religious rites are interspersed throughout
the novel, one such example being Donalda's wake. With regards to both
her agony and her burial, the characters enact clearly defined rites and
strictly follow Catholic procedures, explicitly showing the beliefs and
customs of the era. Thus, as the Priest arrives at the ill girl's bedside,
Bertine follows a protocol clearly detailed by Grignon: "She lit a blessed
candle, put holy water and a palm bough on a dish, then placed these ritual
objects on a small table near the sick woman, to whom she gave a white
towel" (43). The numerous prayers recited by the Priest are transposed, in
Latin and French, in the novel (47-50), but the two-page description of the
Priest's labour is truly noteworthy. Here, Grignon offers a brief look at
priests' lives and impact in French-Canadian colonial society:

> When he had helped someone make his spiritual peace with God, he
> tended to his physical needs. Following in the heroic footsteps of Curé
> Labelle, he assisted his flock materially. He shared with them the fruit of
> his labor, of his self-denial and of his poverty. He would have stripped the
> Christ for the love of Christ. One could knock at the door of his rectory at
> any hour of day or night. He would rise with a prayer on his lips and alms
> and humility in his hands. He gave himself body and soul, feeding himself
> worse than the poorest settler (45-6).

Spanning several pages, the priest's abnegation is portrayed in all its
grandeur when he finds himself at young Donalda's bedside. However,
even knowing the reasons behind this saint's death, he will forgive

Séraphin and ask for God's mercy. Such a fervour is notable throughout the novel and describes extremely positively this second pillar of French-Canadian society. Accentuating the role of the priest, Paul Gury – who puts forward the first big-screen transcreation of Grignon's novel (1949-1950), turns the priest into a powerful antagonist to Séraphin's ferocity.

Thus, Grignon's novel presents itself as a testimony of the lifestyle of this rural society as well as of the importance of religion, an importance which will actually be put aside in the second film adaptation. Séraphin is very typical of the Quebec country novel, and it was Grignon who invented the term "joual", as the only way of representing French-Canadians. As such, he defines the importance of this dialect in 1939, shortly after having published *Un Homme et son péché*, and contextualizes this term before putting it to use.

Intradiegetic transgression and transcreation

Given that rural life is clearly defined by its two pillars (family and religion), the presence or intrusion of a marginal character into this society, the outlander and the miser, will ultimately, after a brief period of questioning, reinforce the impression of mechanical solidarity. After having defined the intradiegetic transgressions of marginal characters in their relation to the dominant group, I will show how it is taken up and amplified, in an extradiegetic manner, by the adapters in two crucial scenes of the movie versions.

The Outlander: from the *coureur des bois* to the spectacular representation of modernism

Although the Outlander is constructed by Guèvremont as a disruptive element to the rural order, Biron *and al.* (2007) believe that the author displaces the main attitude of "earth novels":

> Instead of opposing rural and urban lives, the novels calls upon two more ancient mythologies: that of a rural life without a future – represented by the legitimate son – and that, at once more archaic and newer, of the instructed savage – portrayed by the Outsider[7].

---

[7] "La perspective de Claude-Henri Grignon déplace l'enjeu du roman de la terre. Au lieu de creuser le conflit entre la vie rurale et la vie urbaine, elle fait jouer l'une contre l'autre deux mythologies anciennes : celle d'un terroir sans avenir représenté

Outcast from society because of his endangering, occasionally unbeknownst to him, of several norms essential for social cohesion, the literary trope of the Outlander is found in many country novels, notably in the form of the *coureur des bois*, an ambiguous character because of his position between several cultures (that of the native Americans with whom he trades and that of the colonists who use him to deal with them) without belonging entirely to either one. Guèvremont's Outlander thus raises the issue of an ambiguous relationship, to the past on the one hand (as a relic of the historical *coureur des bois*), and to the future on the other (as a figure of openness to the world, one who travels between the rural world and modernity).

However, there are numerous characters who resemble him, even among the inhabitants of the Chenal. For instance, Père Didace is reminded by the Outlander of a common feature and he admits that his ancestors had a propensity for navigation:

> – Yes, just about as well the woodsmen ever can. [...] But, more to himself than his companion, the Stranger added, "Beauchemin, it sounds somehow as if the first of the name must have been fond of the roads."
> – You're right my boy. The first Beauchemin of our branch didn't stay put. They were two brothers, one tall one short. [...] They came from the old countries (98).

Here, the historical character of the *coureurs des bois* is compared to the Didace family who, as well as sharing certain qualities with him, comes from Europe, a land the Outlander is quite familiar with[8]. However, despite his complicity with the owner of a large piece of land and despite the respect of his peers, the Survenant is singled out for his language – mispronounced words and alien expressions – and his desire to travel. Even if he never transgresses the morality and order of the house which shelters him, since he steps aside to let Amable have the rank which is rightfully his, nor the order of the Chenal "clan", since he deprives himself of a loving marriage with Angélina, rich land owner who is coveted for her property, the Outlander, the "alienated hero", is deprived of the link to the mechanical solidarity the rest of the village benefits from. Even worse,

---

par le fils légitime et celle, plus archaïque et plus neuve à la fois, du sauvage instruit incarné par le Survenant" (250).

[8] The credits present several quotes and writings from the Outlander's travels, depictions of Europe, and navigation as his way of life, as if he had come from overseas. This feature isn't quite as emphasized in the novel even though some characters believe that the Outlander might not have been born in Canada.

his mere intrusion into the clan causes its members to worry, as is the case with Angélina who, despite her devotion to him, can't help picking out his faults during their first meeting.

More than once the Outlander will in fact deceive Angélina, preferring nights in Sorel's bar to her company. But it is more generally his lack of a family name, his thirst for discovery, his great knowledge of the wild world as well as his mastery of the colonizer's language[9], which depict the vast picture of his opposition to the rural society of French-Canadian farmers, his belonging to a modern world. Many of these oppositions are brought up by Peter Noble (2002):

> Deprived of their natural leaders and insecure in their confidence in their political and legal rights, French people in Canada clung to their land and their religion, changing gradually from a society dominated by the adventurous *coureurs des bois* and *voyageurs* to one dominated by the *habitants,* who remained in their communities and cultivated their lands. [...] Whereas the *coureurs des bois* needed space and freedom and chafed against the restrictions of living in a settled community, the *habitants* feared and avoided the idea of wilderness and clung to the familiar (13).

The ideals and values of Quebec's rural society at the beginning of the 20th century are therefore temporarily imperiled by the intrusion of this character who will nevertheless give way to the true owners and descendants of the Chenal du Moine. However, even if the marginal in *The Outlander* fails to root himself in this culture, in the sequel to this novel, *Marie Didace*, Guèvremont gives the Acayenne, a sailor's widow and owner of a Sorel bar, an important role to play. Following the Outsider's advice, the père Didace indeed marries the stranger, and causes a great commotion within the clan.

Spectacular force and modernity

The novel as a whole is reticent to let modernity, represented by the Outlander, have the last word, and his many transgressions lead to a rejection, and an eviction from the village. Canuel's film reinforces the spirit of modernity introduced in the novel, notably through a paraleptic sequence which lets the spectacular run free. According to Dominique

---

[9] E. Canuel's film makes abundantly clear that the Outlander passes on to the Père Didace this habit of speaking or interjecting in English. Though the latter is pro-French language, *"Neveurmagne"* is the last word he ever pronounces after the former's departure.

Chateau (1997), the movie is intrinsically *spectacular* since "disproportion and gigantism are necessary conditions of the spectacular [...] as well as panoramas, cinerama and omnimax" (115). However, if we question the content of the spectacular within the diegesis of the story itself, it is represented almost exclusively with the Outlander's larger stature, magnificent laughter, and his being often placed in the center of the shot. Indeed, Chateau argues that the spectacular is perhaps "too shiny, too magnificent" (115) and that it "grips the spirit by blinding the spectator" (116). Quite often, the Outlander is a source of strong female attention, as much for his virile force as for his disarming laugh, which is a constant feature in both the hypotext and the hyperfilm.

However, without a crucial sequence added by the director (1h47'52 – 1h49'29''), these features would be close enough to what Guèvremont describes in the novel, and wouldn't quite be analyzed as *spectacular*. In Canuel's film, as the first "metal horse" arrives in town, the villagers gather around this attraction, sequence which is magnified by a long vertical panoramic shot. As if on purpose, the cart suddenly makes a violent sound, scaring a hitched horse who gallops precipitously towards a young boy, Isidore, who is frozen with fear. Without the Outlander's intervention, the boy (as well as the hitch) would have been all but lost, edifying the marginal character as a true hero for the villagers watching the scene. Due to its content and its structure, this sequence is therefore intrinsically spectacular. As André Gardiès (1993) argues, to deserve this adjective a scene "must inscribe itself within a narrative moment", that is to say that the spectacular has to be announced: by music, by special cinematic effects or some kind of editing. Moreover, "an announcement strategy" (126) can prepare the spectator for this burst of emotion[10]. The panoramic shot, a cinematographic technique which is barely used in the whole film, and will thus not fail to have an impact on the spectator, can be thought of as this "announcement strategy". Moreover, the dramatic music, accompanied by the neighing of the horse which is echoed throughout the scene, enhances the spectator's anxiety for the fate of the child. Finally, the sequence is filmed in slow-motion, notably during the intervention of the Outlander, who stops the cart with his bare hands,

---

[10] "Pour atteindre sa plus grande efficacité, cet effet "spectaculaire" doit en outre s'inscrire dans un "moment" narratif. À ce titre, ce dernier devra être repérable et, au besoin, annoncé. Des marqueurs de début et de fin sont alors mobilisés, qu'ils soient diégétiques ou discursifs. [...] S'ajoutent des marques d'énonciation : changements d'angles de prise de vue et d'échelle, déploiement fastueux de la musique. De plus, une stratégie d'annonce prépare le spectateur à cet "événement" tant diégétique que discursif" (126).

emphasizing the tension of his muscles and the difficulty of the task. Proving that he has a superior knowledge of technology – he is the only one who knows what a "metal horse" is – the Outlander also shows how fast and efficient he and only he can be since, of all the villagers, he is the only one to intervene.

Highlighting the extraordinary character of the Outlander, this sequence shows his value in a way the hypotext never does. Isidore's mother and the hitch's owner thank him, and the latter then addresses the crowd to propose a reconciliation between the village and the foreigner. It is also possible to analyze the inclusion of this scene as part of Canuel's desire to represent the debate between modern and rural life, a vivid opposition during the writing of the hypotext, in the 1950s, for which the hyperfilm's Outlander (2005) offers a belated reconciliation.

Greed and the vanity of capitalism

The dialogue between the hypotext and the hyperfilm is just as important for *The Woman and the Miser*. Greed, troublesome from a religious standpoint, is placed at the center of the novel, and the writer shows its effect on the character's sanity, which was unprecedented for French-Canadian novels. Séraphin's exceptional qualities (his proficient calculations and his comprehension of human behaviour) are first and foremost put to use to amass as much wealth as possible. As such, there are several passages of the novel which focus on dubious transactions. Notably, a ten-page description of one such transaction ties the miser to a red-haired man seeking an abortion, with money borrowed from Séraphin, for a young woman whom he raped. After going into explicit details on the "unbearable silence" and the "anxiety-laden atmosphere, filtering everywhere like a stench" that is "beginning to surround and grip the red-headed man" (12), as well as Séraphin's dexterity, he who "would wait for his man" (12), the narrator turns little by little towards the reasons for the loan, causing the borrower to worry. The following pages explain the miser's chosen method for cornering his debtor: by convincing him that he doesn't have enough properties and that his debts are too important, he succeeds in obtaining the two best milk cows the man owns. After almost ten pages, the note is finally signed and transcribed by the omniscient narrator:

> 1980 this 17 July 1890,
>   If on the 17 October this year I haven't paid Seraphin Poudrier the farmer, the sum of a hundred bucks ($100), said Seraphin Poudrier will

keep for himself the two Jursy cows I promise to bring to his house on the
19 July 1890 (18).

Séraphin comes away doubly victorious: on the one hand, because he
benefits from the cows for the duration of the loan, cows which offer the
best milk in the region, but also because he knows in advance that the red-
haired man won't be able to pay him back in time, even though the sum is
merely 80 *piasses*, "premium for the favor I'm doing you. Good accounts
make good friends. Isn't it so?" (17).

Thus, it is the great intelligence of the miser who, not content with
simply knowing how to read, is apt to make rapid calculations, a fact
which is constantly referenced by the narrator. One such example is the
following passage where he greedily refuses to call on the doctor during
his wife's agony. He takes advantage of a quiet moment to calculate the
total of his belongings and revenues for the year:

> Endowed with a prodigious memory, he never wrote down the loans he
> made nor any other deal on the spot. [...] Seraphin could easily compute in
> his head the interest on $237 at twelve and a half percent for 92 days, for
> 101 days, or for 3 years and 3 days. With this kind of mental arithmetic, he
> never failed to impress a borrower and to force him into great admiration,
> not far removed from fear (26).

Through these calculations Séraphin arrives at a prodigious sum of
1903.03$ which, once added to the existing capital make 18,000$ (27).
The scene's juxtaposition of Donalda's suffering and the miser's
calculations emanate abjection, a theme which is recalled in a paraliptic
sequence (1h40'04'' – 1h41') in Charles Binamé's film (2002).

Vanitas and material possessions

Indeed, though Donalda dies in the hypotext after forgiving her
husband, certain that he is "poor as dirt", the most recent cinematographic
adaptation has her die right after she discovers that the miser is actually
incredibly rich. An added sequence, resembling the pictorial genre of
vanitas, uncovers Séraphin's treasure cove. According to the Oxford
Dictionary of Art (1996), *vanitas* is

> a type of painting concerned with the fragility of man and his world of
> desires and pleasures in the face of the inevitability and finality of death. It
> is essentially a biblical term, referring to the vanity of earthly possessions:
> the corresponding Hebrew term means « smoke » or « vapour ». The

vanitas tradition, which also appears in Western Literature and other representational arts, was particularly important element in painting in the Netherlands in the 17th century (880).

The importance and diversity of religious references is emphasized in this quote, drawing yet another parallel to our subject, but the *Oxford Dictionary* definition can also be analyzed as a proleptic reflection on Séraphin's downfall: the smoke in his barn (due to a fire which is, moreover, caused by the red-haired man). A multitude of codified details plainly represent *vanitas*, which put forward a direct opposition between death (represented by skulls, *memento mori*, or personifications of Death) and life. As Donalda enters the forbidden room, the camera angle – a subtle low-angle shot – amplifies the actual number of Séraphin's possessions, all related in one way or another to death and the passing of time (hanging beaver pelts, clock and lamp), to the futility of human life (painting and musical instrument), and, of course, to the vanity of material possessions (sacs of gold in the foreground). Additionally, the shot clearly places Donalda in the middle of the trophies, as if she were one of them. The discovery of these treasures allows Donalda to understand that she was bought and that her unfathomably greedy husband keeps them both in a state of suffering despite having the means live quite comfortably. Omnipresent in these codes, as well as in the musical choices which, from the beginning of the film, cast Séraphin as a deceitful character during his abject transactions (for instance when he robs a dead man and takes his measurements), death is casting a spell on Donalda in this scene as it is the last time the spectator sees her in good health.

Though Binamé's film is not particularly dense, it becomes more so with this pivotal sequence which ties together both the analepsis of Donalda's death, as well as Séraphin's (since it is during Donalda's burial that the red-haired man sets fire to the barn Séraphin throws himself into, attempting to save his treasure), while uncovering the extent of the miser's sin. The moral value is thus drastically different between the hypotext and the hyperfilm: in the former, Donalda dies peaceful and filled with pity for her husband while in the movie, her forgiveness speaks to a much larger sin since it is the direct cause of her death. Moreover, in the movie she refuses to be buried with her wedding ring, creating several other complications in the village and setting up her husband's downfall.

Given its multifaceted depiction, the rural life, as represented in these two pairs of works, takes on a new substance, in large part due to the multiple transgressions of the marginal figures as well as the work of the movie directors. Without these metamorphoses and transgressions, these portraits of rural ambiguities would certainly have been out of place at the dawn of the 21st century, century of the spectacular. The hyperfilms' critical eye on one of the qualities or faults of their main and eponymous characters thus deepens the spectators' understanding and lets them in on an endearing way of life long since passed, and a very powerful testimony.

Works studied

Binamé, Charles. 2003. *Séraphin*. Montréal: Atlantis.

Canuel, Éric. 2005. *Le Survenant*. Montréal: Les Films Vision 4.

Guèvremont, Germaine. 1945. *Le Survenant*. Montréal: Éditions Beauchemin. (for the English quotations: The Outlander. 1978. Translated by Eric Sutton. Toronto : McClelland and Stewart.)

Grignon, Claude-Henri. *Un Homme et son péché*. 1933. Montréal: Les Éditions du Vieux chêne. (for the English quotations: *The Woman and the Miser*. 1978. Translated by Yves Brunelle. Montréal: Havest House Ltd.).

References

Oxford Dictionary of Art. Ed. Jane Turner, n°31, Grove Oxford University Press. 1996.

Lavoie, Michel. 1970. « Du coureur des bois au survenant ; filiation ou aliénation ? ». *Voix et images du pays*, vol. 3, n°1: 11-25.

Biron, Michel and François Dumon, Élisabeth Nardout-Lafarge. 2007. *Histoire de la littérature québécoise*. Montréal: Boréal.

Durkheim, Émile. 1893. *La Division du travail social* (1st édition 1930). Annoted Edition : 2007. Paris: Quadrige/P.U.F.

Gaudreault, André. 1988. *Du littéraire au filmique – Systèmes du récit*. Paris : Méridien Klincksieck.

Genette, Gérard. 1982. *Palimpsestes – La Littérature au second degré*. Paris : Seuil.

Hamont-Sirejols, Christine, and André Gardiès (dirs.) 1997. *Le Spectaculaire*. Lyon: Aléas. (see "Pour une esthétique du spectaculaire", D. Chateau (109-118) ; "Le moment spectaculaire dans la narration cinématographique", A. Gardiès (119-127)).

Noble, Peter. 2002. *Beware the Stranger – The Survenant in the Québec Novel*. Amsterdam: Rodopi.

CHAPTER ELEVEN

LE PAYS RURAL RACONTE : UN CONTEUR A SAINT-ELIE DE CAXTON, AU QUEBEC

AURORE MIRLOUP AND PIERRE-MATHIEU LE BEL

Au Québec, la municipalité de Saint-Élie-de-Caxton a vu au début des années 2000 sa destinée modifiée suite au succès de l'œuvre de Fred Pellerin. Petite commune rurale d'à peine 2 000 habitants située en Mauricie, à deux heures de Montréal, entourée d'une trentaine de lacs et surplombée par un calvaire, Saint-Élie-de-Caxton semblait vouée à connaître le même sort que ses voisines en proie au déclin rural. C'était sans compter sur l'intervention d'un enfant du pays dont la portée fut telle qu'elle en sauva l'école et l'église tout en rendant célèbre un village jusque-là méconnu. Nous proposons ici de démêler la co-construction contemporaine de légendes et d'un lieu.

Fred Pellerin est né en 1976 à Saint-Élie-de-Caxton. Diplômé en littérature, il s'est fait connaître pour ses talents de conteur peu conventionnel à l'humour décalé, fantaisiste et empreint de poésie. Il a fait ses débuts dans les années 2000 comme guide touristique à Saint-Élie-de-Caxton. C'est là qu'il fait ses armes ; il décroche ensuite une chronique dans une radio montréalaise comme « correspondant étranger de Saint-Elie-de-Caxton ». Spectacle, cinéma, chanson, scènes nationales puis internationales, Fred Pellerin s'exporte de l'autre côté de l'Atlantique. Son dernier spectacle joué en France, *De peigne et de misère* est qualifié ainsi dans une page du *Monde* : « ... d'une virtuosité narrative peu commune et, qu'on ne s'y trompe pas, moderne » (Séry 2013, 12). Les œuvres de Pellerin sont d'abord des spectacles contés, elles ont été publiées sous forme de livre-CD dans un second temps. Son amour pour l'oralité, pour l'improvisation l'amène à faire évoluer ses personnages au gré des spectacles, de fait, il ne se définit pas comme un écrivain, ni ne considère ses écrits comme « littéraires ».

C'est donc la contemporanéité et l'impact en termes de développement et de planification locale de l'œuvre de Pellerin qui justifie à nos yeux de s'y attarder dans un champ de recherche qui table souvent sur les auteurs ayant certes connu le succès, mais perdu en ferveur populaire ou encore dont l'impact en termes d'aménagement n'a pas été aussi grand. Les œuvres de Balzac ou Zola, par exemple, ont attiré l'attention des géographes (Harvey, 2003) ou encore les œuvres de romans policier, plus contemporains (Schmid, 1995). On s'intéressera ici plutôt au processus de co-construction territoriale articulée entre les contes ruraux de Pellerin, leurs procédés narratifs et l'action collective. Pour ce faire, nous nous appuyons sur une série d'entretiens semi-dirigés avec des acteurs locaux, sur un questionnaire distribué auprès des visiteurs du village et sur l'analyse des livres d'or de l'auberge du village. Il importe cependant, dans un premier temps, de s'attarder à l'écriture de cet auteur. Quelle ruralité se dégage de ses procédés narratifs ? Ce regard sur les textes de Pellerin nous permettra ensuite de mieux faire ressortir leur réception à travers l'action des habitants et des planificateurs de même que son effet sur l'imaginaire des visiteurs. Nous verrons comment œuvre et lieu se sont mutuellement construits.

Des procédés narratifs entre réalisme et merveilleux

Quatre procédés narratifs nous semblent constituer une base sur laquelle s'établit le rapport de Pellerin au lieu, puis des visiteurs et des planificateurs au lieu. La première, et également la plus présente dans l'ensemble de son œuvre, est le recours au réalisme merveilleux. Ce genre littéraire est historiquement associé à la littérature latino-américaine où des auteurs, Gabriel Garcia Marquez en tête, ont dressé le portrait d'une région où le merveilleux fait partie de la vie quotidienne. Le "réel" et le "merveilleux" sont juxtaposés de manière à ce que le second semble faire partie du premier (Angulo, 1995 ; Esteban, 2000 ; Monet-Viera, 2004 ; Scheel, 2005 ; Schroeder, 2004) jusqu'à constituer une des caractéristiques fondamentales de l'espace concerné. Souvent définie par le terme de "réalisme magique", cette production culturelle introduit des éléments surnaturels dans une trame narrative par ailleurs réaliste, de façon à ce qu'ils semblent participer aux éléments les plus banals du quotidien, plutôt que de s'inscrire en faux contre eux. De cette manière, l'auteur met fin au conflit entre le naturel et le surnaturel et contraint le lecteur à suspendre son jugement sur la rationalité du monde fictif (Faris, 2004). Pour autant, la présence d'éléments magiques défiant l'explication empirique ne peut jamais tout à fait être réconciliée avec le côté réaliste de la trame narrative. Des éléments irréductibles tendent à chambouler les habitudes du lecteur, ce qui l'amène à douter lorsqu'il tente de situer les lieux ou les événements décrits sur l'échelle de ce qui est généralement conçu comme étant crédible. Plusieurs ressorts narratifs viennent renforcer ce réalisme merveilleux produit par l'auteur qui fait surgir des créatures légendaires chez des garagistes ou des coiffeurs. Tout d'abord, l'auteur a choisi le genre littéraire du conte et se définit lui-même comme « conteux ». Le conte se positionne à la rencontre du fait et de l'imaginaire et se distingue du roman, ou d'autres styles littéraires, par le degré d'acceptation de l'invraisemblance qu'en a le lecteur (Demers et Gauvin, 1976).

Ainsi, la galerie de personnages, pour fondée qu'elle soit sur l'existence confirmée d'habitants ayant réellement existé ou qui sont même parfois toujours en vie, est décrite d'une telle façon que le lecteur parvient péniblement à distinguer le réel de l'invention. En témoigne, par exemple, la figure de Méo Bellemare, le coiffeur :

> C'est le bon exemple de ces choses lues dans la fantaisie piétonnière. Méo, le barbier de Saint-Élie-de-Caxton. Comme on en trouvait dans chaque village […]. On le payait en liquide. Une once d'alcool par pouce taillé […] Méo pour sa part, se mit à boire à chaque crâne. De la coupe aux lèvres. Le seul imprévu étant qu'au fil des culs-secs, plus la journée avançait, plus les ciseaux louchaient ; À la messe, le dimanche, tout le monde prenait place dans son banc. De dos, on pouvait facilement déduire le moment de la journée pour chacun des rendez-vous. Selon le degré du dégradé (Pellerin, 2005, 54).

On trouve aussi le forgeron Riopel dont « l'invention la plus reconnue fut sans doute le fer à cheval à talon haut. Vint ensuite le grille-pain à une seule fente. Pour venir en aide aux familles au nombre d'enfants impair » (*Ibid.*, 103). On trouvera encore un éleveur de mouches, Toussaint Brodeur, la Belle Lurette qui pleure littéralement nuit et jour le départ de son amour ou encore Babine, le fou du village, qui échappe à la mort par les plus improbables façons.

Au personnage s'ajoute une description des aléas naturels qui soulignent à leur tour le merveilleux de la campagne québécoise. Si certains éléments sont campés clairement du côté du fantastique, d'autres laissent le lecteur indécis :

> Une sécheresse craquante plana sur le paysage. On accumula au total quinze années de sécheresse. Quinze ans. Condensés. En l'espace d'un été. C'est vous dire à quel point ça manquait d'eau. Des vies entières furent

bouleversées. Plus question de sourire. La peau croustillante menaçait de se déchirer de la joue aux oreilles. Des yeux gerçaient, à demi ouverts. Une poussière fine recouvrait tout, et pas une miette de vent pour la déplacer. Sec. La nappe phréatique chez le diable. L'eau bénite en grumeaux. Le niveau de la rivière qui descendait et qui chutait. Jusqu'à ce que les premiers poissons commencent à attraper des puces de chien et que les faunistes s'y mettent le nez. Des choses qu'on n'ose même pas imaginer. L'archiduchesse, par exemple. Elle-même en chair et en os. Au-delà de ses chemises et de ses beaux atouts. L'archiduchesse sèche ? Archi-sèche la bonne femme. Une archiduchesse qui se défaisait en poudre (*Ibid.*, 106).

Cette rudesse de la campagne éloignée s'ajoute à la galerie de personnages colorés pour créer une représentation de Saint-Élie-de-Caxton, puis de toute la ruralité québécoise comme constituant presque un univers parallèle. Sentiment renforcé par le flou temporel et la répétition des effets propre au conte ; chaque chapitre commence invariablement par la formule « ma grand-mère disait que… », par exemple « Ma grand-mère disait que l'histoire s'est passée dans le temps où c'est que du temps, il y en avait encore » (Pellerin, 2001, 11). C'est un passé d'autant plus difficile à situer chronologiquement que le lecteur s'aperçoit que plusieurs éléments physiographiques du Québec et du Canada sont attribués par Pellerin au passage de l'homme fort du village Ezimezac Gélinas.

De plus, l'auteur a recours aux néologismes ("translivide", "prémonitieuse", "mini-cipalité"), aux détournements d'expression populaire ("elle avait le don d'ambiguïté") et aux allitérations à foison. Enfin, cette tendance à conjuguer le premier nom commun qui passe ("bénévoler") pour en souligner l'intention mais aussi la fonction performative, sont autant de ressorts qui contribuent à créer, par le langage, un espace autre au milieu d'un espace réel et situé, à la manière d'une dimension parallèle repeuplée par l'auteur au gré de son inspiration mais avec de "vrais" habitants.

L'instance sur la réalité biographique d'habitant historique permet à la fois de rendre ardue la détection de la frontière de la fiction en même temps qu'elle permet de faire de ce petit village particulier ("c'est mon village") un village simultanément représentatif de tous les villages québécois, le village des représentations populaires. Dans *Il faut prendre le taureau par les contes*, chaque chapitre débute par une déclinaison toponymique de Saint-Elie-de-Caxton à la manière des paragraphes suivants :

Saint-Élie de Garnotte, sortie 166 de l'autoroute 40, à droite au T puis à gauche à la troisième lumière, toujours tout droit ensuite, malgré les

portions de terre battue, c'est mon village. Saint-Élie de Garnotte : quand
t'es perdu, t'es rendu ! When you're lost, you're là (Pellerin, 2003, 18).
Saint Elie de Carbone, copie conforme de lui-même, c'est mon village.
Comme un miroir poli qui réfléchit franchement, sans se prendre pour une
fenêtre. Saint-Elie de Carbone : égal à lui-même. (*Ibid.*, 107).

Saint Elie de Canon, qui se défendit de l'invasion par la bouche de ses
refrains, c'est mon village (*Ibid.*, 94)

Saint-Élie de Castor, ni pour le cinq cennes, ni pour les dents longues, ni
pour la queue plate, c'est mon village. Saint-Elie de Castor : qui vous
ronge quand il vous manque. D'ailleurs, un des gros problèmes en ce qui a
trait au manque, c'est la lacune. Ça ne laisse pas de trace, mais ça fait
défaut. Comme dans tous les milieux ruraux (*Ibid.,* 47).

En faisant varier les toponymes, le conteur établit une parenté implicite
entre les villages du Québec[1] et Saint-Élie. Un village qui se définit par
son isolement, son caractère ordinaire, sa résistance tranquille et le
manque qui s'installe chez celui qui le quitte. L'universalité ne tiendrait
donc pas tant aux paysages, mais aux sentiments éprouvés, qui rappellent
la nostalgie de la maison d'enfance. Plus qu'une continuité entre le réel et
l'imaginaire, c'est l'intégration langagière qui confère un statut équivalent
aux anecdotes, quelle que soit leur provenance. Recourir au merveilleux
pour prouver son existence topographique et sociale abrite une forme
d'engagement dans une résistance rurale positive. "De notre côté, on
préfère encore vivre à l'ecart plutôt que de vivre à l'équerre" (Pellerin,
2005, 11). En atteste la digression sur le point qu'occupe le village sur la carte.

Saint-Élie-de-Caxton est un village qui n'a toujours pas de point sur la
carte du pays. Encore moins sur celle du monde. Et ce n'est pas parce
qu'on n'en a pas voulu. Pendant longtemps, on a attendu le formulaire à
remplir du ministère topographique. Jamais reçu. Il était donc devenu
nécessaire d'agir et d'imposer notre libellation. Sans condition. Les
habitants du village ont fait front commun, du tour et de la tête, et demandé
reconnaissance de leur existence. Avec traçage de notre petit point localisé
en guise de bonne foi. En réponse aux pressions, les autorités tracèrent un
piton noir dans l'agrandissement qu'on trouve au coin inférieur droit de la
carte du Québec (*Ibid.*).

Au final, la tâche du conteur est cohérente avec cet acte de
reconnaissance cartographique : il s'agit de faire exister davantage le

---

[1] Comme les noms de villages commencent très souvent par "Saint" ou "Sainte" le
rapprochement n'en est que plus aisé.

village par l'intermédiaire de ses contes : "Plus les histoires circulent, plus le monde existe" (Pellerin, 2013, 88). Non seulement cela, mais la mise en conte devient une ressource, un savoir-faire partagé par ses personnages-habitants. Ainsi "[l]es gens de mon pays démontrent des capacités étonnantes dans l'art de la parlure. Le village étant situé à la rencontre des placottes tectoniques qui font des secousses parlantes au moindre frottement, on ne se surprendra pas que ça jase autant" (*Ibid.*, 153). Ailleurs, Pellerin ajoute :

> Il aura fallu déterrer les mots parce que chez nous, comme dans tous les villages, il existe des milliers d'histoires tenues au silence. Un monde entier dans les souvenirs que les morts emportent souvent avec eux. Des anecdotes en cachette, des souvenirs à retrouver pour en goûter l'ampleur légendaire. Des secrets qui n'attendent que le grand jour pour germer en jasures (Pellerin, 2009, quatrième de couverture).

C'est cette ressource immatérielle que constitue le conte, ressource que les habitants et élus de Saint-Élie ont mobilisée afin de valoriser leur municipalité.

Un aménagement touristique qui s'appuie sur le conte

Une reconnaissance, Saint-Élie en a certainement une aujourd'hui, après plus d'une décennie de rayonnement de l'œuvre de Pellerin. Dès 1997, Fred Pellerin, alors étudiant, fait visiter les rues de son village et, pour renouveler le genre de la visite guidée, se prend à inventer des légendes, en s'appuyant sur des personnages hauts en couleur. Certains personnages sont des résidents actuels du village, tandis que d'autres l'ont été. Plus tard, forte du succès du son jeune citoyen, la municipalité cherche à développer le concept pour rendre le village attractif, car, en dehors des trente-huit lacs à proximité et de la montagne du Calvaire, il se distingue peu des autres villages du Québec, dont plusieurs partagent avec Saint-Élie une destinée démographique déclinante, au point de menacer de fermeture son école primaire.

En 2004, élus, acteurs du développement local et Fred Pellerin se réunissent et retiennent l'idée d'un audio-guide afin d'attirer davantage de visiteurs. Dès lors, un circuit touristique audio est construit à la manière d'un musée. Les visiteurs peuvent arpenter le village et des affiches numérotées leur indiquent les éléments construits ou naturels qui font partie du commentaire audio. La réalisation du projet est assurée par un atelier de création visuelle et multimédia pour un coût total de 200 000 $CAN, financés par le gouvernement du Québec et le programme Pacte

Rural au niveau de la Municipalité Régionale de Comté (MRC,
l'équivalent approximatif d'une Communauté de communes en France) de
Maskinongé et la municipalité de Saint-Élie. À l'époque, Fred Pellerin
écrit et enregistre les textes gracieusement. Les commentaires audio
s'articulent entre des anecdotes farfelues inventées de toutes pièces et des
précisions historiques authentiques relatives au passé de la municipalité.

> J'aime beaucoup l'approche du faux documentaire, explique Fred Pellerin.
> Ce qui m'intéresse, c'est l'équilibre entre le merveilleux et le réel, entre le
> vrai et le faux. Les gens viennent chercher chez nous du délire ; l'important
> n'est pas de créer de la vérité

déclare-t-il dans une entrevue (Larochelle, 2012), fidèle à la philosophie
de ses contes. L'audioguide devient ainsi un maillon supplémentaire entre
cette mémoire orale et les visiteurs. L'un d'eux explique que "l'audioguide
amène à faire un lien entre la légende et la réalité" (questionnaires papier).

Une carte de Saint-Élie, dessinée par l'artiste, complète la panoplie du
visiteur qui se fait remettre l'audioguide ; les sites évoqués sont
scrupuleusement reproduits et numérotés, chaque numéro renvoyant à une
plage de l'audio-guide.

Trois types de sites bien différents sont reproduits sur cette carte où le
respect de l'échelle est visiblement interprété très librement : des sites
patrimoniaux, des sites "domestiques" et des sites imaginaires. On y voit
aussi des êtres humains aux proportions de géants. Quel est le point
commun entre la montagne du Calvaire et la Traverse de Lutins, l'église et
l'arbre à paparmanes, ou encore la maison de chez Meo le Coiffeur ? Les
mots de Fred Pellerin, bien réels eux. Mis au service d'une certaine idée de
la ruralité, dynamique et créative, ils servent de fil conducteur pour le
visiteur.

Si l'expérience de ce dernier est guidée par le conteur, les choix
esthétiques de l'aménagement municipal sont en cohérence avec l'univers
de l'artiste. Un peu comme un pastiche de son œuvre. Si le slogan choisi
par la commune "Saint-Élie-de-Caxton, ça existe vraiment", est bien signé
de Fred Pellerin, on voit aussi fleurir des inventions langagières un peu
partout, émanant tantôt d'une très sérieuse concertation du conseil
municipal pour trouver "l'aide-fureteur" (pour le panneau d'affichage) ou
bien "l'endormitoire" (pour l'hôtel), tantôt par la contagion langagière qui
gagne les commerçants ou les hébergeurs (par exemple les gîtes baptisés :
L'Adèle au bois dormant).

La fantaisie langagière s'accompagne de fantaisie tout court, dont se
parent les aménagements touristiques : l'ancien garage Léo Déziel, lieu de
"jasage" est reconverti en Garage de la culture, où le visiteur peut

retrouver, par exemple, des accessoires utilisés dans les films *Babine* et *Ésimésac*, tirés de l'œuvre de Pellerin. La signalétique urbaine (plaques de rue) est à l'effigie des lutins (figure 11.1) présents dans l'œuvre du conteur mais faisant partie depuis longtemps des blagues entre les villageois.

Figure 11.1 Exemples d'aménagements urbains à Saint-Élie-de-Caxton : slogan qui orne la maison du citoyen (mairie), plaque de rue, traverse de lutins, enseigne à l'entrée du presbytère-restaurant, ancien garage Léo Déziel reconverti en espace culturel, le « garage de la culture », avec des peintures ornementales regorgeant de farfadets

Et ça fonctionne. Trente mille touristes en moyenne viennent chaque été depuis 2007, cinquante mille en 2014. Pour les plus jeunes, la balade peut se faire à pied avec l'audioguide loué au bureau d'accueil touristique. Pour un public plus âgé ou familial, des visites guidées à bord d'une carriole tirée par un tracteur permettent de faire le parcours de manière plus succincte mais moins exigeante (45 minutes au lieu des 2 heures de marche requises afin de bien voir tous les lieux de l'audioguide). Cette journée à Saint-Élie coûte 15 $ en 2014, balades et accès aux lieux compris.

Les conséquences de ce succès ne se font pas attendre, des commerces s'installent, des restaurants ouvrent, des activités alternatives voient le jour (yourtes "Le Rond-Coin"), ateliers d'artistes, scènes de débats et de concerts intimistes, qui concourent à rendre cette commune attractive pour des néo-ruraux inspirés par l'atmosphère et la dynamique qui en émane. Le cas du presbytère, que l'on retrouve souvent dans les contes de Pellerin, est intéressant ; sur le point d'être vendu, comme beaucoup d'autres au Québec, faute de moyens pour l'entretenir, décision a été prise d'en transformer une partie en restaurant et chambres d'hôtes loués à un gérant. L'autre partie a été maintenue comme logement pour les membres de l'église. Cette double fonction du lieu pouvant paraître antinomique, permet à la Fabrique de préserver à la fois le bâtiment et une partie de sa fonction traditionnelle. Le passage de touristes permet, en outre, d'y recueillir des dons plus importants. La gérante du Lutin Marmiton, confie qu'elle est tout à fait consciente de l'importance de Pellerin pour le développement de son entreprise : "C'est lui le ministre du tourisme", dira-t-elle.

C'est non seulement le secteur marchand qui bénéficie de cette manne, mais également le secteur public. En 2005, l'école était menacée de fermeture parce que trop peu d'enfants, 58 à l'époque, y étaient scolarisés. Aujourd'hui, 120 enfants sont accueillis. Alors même que les communes alentour continuent à perdre de la population, Saint-Élie voit passer la sienne de 1 350 habitants en 2005 à 1 972 habitants en 2014.

On le voit, l'aménagement urbain use (et abuse ?) du genre féérique. Le succès du site peut parfois tendre vers une marchandisation, voire une disneylandisation qui pourrait nuire à son authenticité : muni de son bracelet événementiel le touriste paye son entrée à Saint-Élie qui lui donne droit d'accès aux attractions du village pour la journée. L'anecdote des cailloux en référence à l'histoire des habitants de Saint-Elie, surnommés les "tireux d'roche", en est révélatrice : les visiteurs ont été invités à signer des cailloux lors de leur passage dans le sentier botanique. Devant l'amoncèlement rapide des pierres et afin de satisfaire certains touristes qui voulaient repartir avec un souvenir, les cailloux ont finalement été mis en vente, 1 $ pièce, devant des élus qui n'en reviennent toujours pas lorsqu'ils voient arriver des camions remplis de pierres afin de répondre à la demande.

Pour spectaculaire que soit cet exemple de vente de pierres, ce village, où les soirées sont réputées calmes, réussit néanmoins à préserver sa tranquillité et à éviter une marchandisation complète : une réglementation dissuasive avec une taxe journalière prohibitive a été mise en place à destination des commerces itinérants afin de leur limiter l'accès au village et de privilégier les commerces permanents.

C'est parce que c'est la revitalisation plutôt que la croissance qui constitue l'objectif que la population locale est impliquée depuis le début dans le projet, croit le maire de l'époque. Les premières réunions publiques attiraient pas moins de 300 personnes et le soutien des habitants a, depuis, été constant. Ils prennent plaisir à discuter avec les touristes et il n'est pas rare que ceux-là soient invités à s'asseoir un instant sur les chaises ou les bancs disposés sur les perrons des maisons. Certains locaux s'approprient et adaptent librement l'image du lutin (figure 11.2), et si toutes les manifestations ne sont pas toujours du meilleur goût, la dérision est aussi un signe qui atteste de l'appropriation de ce patrimoine par les habitants.

Figure 11.2 Un exemple de dérision populaire à l'encontre de l'effigie du lutin

En plus de diffuser les représentations fantaisistes de Saint-Élie, l'artiste a insisté pour que les avant-premières de ses films aient lieu dans son village et que les figurants en soient des habitants. La présence de personnalités et de journalistes venus de Montréal couvrir l'événement chez eux, de même que leur participation aux films sont autant d'éléments qui suscitent la reconnaissance et l'adhésion des habitants.

Les élus et les agents de développement participent activement à ce processus de mise en légende du village. Ainsi, le coordonnateur du tourisme, recruté en 2009, a été sélectionné pour ses casquettes multiples : journaliste et professeur de français et enfant du pays. Choisi pour ses qualités de communicant mais aussi pour sa connaissance des lieux et des mots. Cette position intermédiaire entre univers fictif et réel, entre réalisme et merveilleux, est également pleinement assumée par les discours des politiques locaux. Le maire, rapportant ses propos d'une conférence de presse :

> La première question qu'on m'a posé c'est si j'avais déjà vu les lutins. Très honnêtement, je les ai pas vus, mais je les ai sentis. […] Un jour, on s'en allait chez nous, j'arrive à la Traverse des lutins, y'avait un monsieur couché sur l'asphalte, je pensais qu'il était malade, je m'arrête, je descends de l'auto, il se retourne, il avait un appareil photo, il m'a fait…. Chhhht. J'ai compris qu'il avait peut-être vu le lutin.

L'échange se poursuit entre ceux qui créent la légende du lieu et ceux qui la reçoivent, entre ceux qui racontent et ceux qui viennent se faire raconter des histoires ; à ceci près que, pour le touriste, venir sur les lieux donne en plus l'illusion de pouvoir évoluer au sein d'un monde imaginaire, de prendre part à la légende à la manière des enfants qui désirent entrer dans le livre d'histoires.

L'imaginaire des visiteurs

Les questionnaires distribués révèlent que les premiers motifs d'une visite à Saint-Élie-de-Caxton ont à voir avec l'univers de Fred Pellerin, soit la fascination pour ses contes et légendes soit le désir de mieux connaître l'auteur. Si les attentes des visiteurs intègrent aussi l'attrait patrimonial, pour la nature, l'intérêt pour retrouver des modes de vie d'antan, ou encore une sensibilité aux lieux de mémoire, ce ne sont pas les motifs les plus cités. La fantaisie est de mise, puisque quinze répondants sur vingt et un ont fait une réponse relative à l'imaginaire créé par les contes de l'artiste : "je n'ai aperçu que les pas des lutins mais entendu leurs rires" (questionnaire papier).

Pour traiter de la place de cet imaginaire, nous avons choisi d'explorer leurs traces dans les livres d'or de l'auberge du village. L'endroit garde un registre entre 2009 et 2014 où chacun est invité à inscrire ses commentaires, positifs ou non, au sujet de son passage. Nous y voyons plusieurs sources d'intérêt : ce sont des écrits libres et spontanés, des instantanés de l'état d'esprit du visiteur à l'issue de sa visite. Ils expriment une réaction à chaud, et relèvent du registre de l'impression ou de l'opinion (Le Marec, Topalian, 2003). Le scripteur n'écrit d'ailleurs pas toujours pour être lu, toutefois nombreux sont ceux qui signent leur propos. Leurs premiers lecteurs sont bien souvent les visiteurs suivants, qui feuillettent ces pages pour prolonger leur visite, s'inspirer ou réagir aux réactions précédentes. Le destinataire du livre d'or n'est pas identifié clairement, ce qui donne la liberté au visiteur de choisir à qui il s'adresse : au gestionnaire du lieu, à la Nation, à l'auteur ou encore à lui-même. Pour Le Marec et Topalian (2003), si cette expression est écrite, elle reste cependant "liée au registre éphémère de la prise de parole oralisée, conjoncturelle et éphémère". Ces écrits, à la fois privés et publics, ne procèdent pas toujours d'une intentionnalité explicite : jugements sur la visite le plus souvent, témoignages, aspirations, tribune adressée à nos dirigeants, rêveries, c'est en cela qu'ils suscitent notre intérêt : parmi des écrits très éclectiques, on peut voir surgir une inspiration, une créativité issue de l'imaginaire du visiteur.

Pour étudier la rencontre entre un imaginaire produit par la littérature et l'imaginaire du visiteur, ces livres d'or s'avèrent extrêmement enrichissants, offrant la dimension spontanée, créative, affective et sensorielle qui fait défaut dans les questionnaires. Très peu de contributeurs se sont penché sur l'analyse des livres d'or, si ce n'est en sciences du langage (Krylyschin, 2014), en sciences de gestion et muséologie en lien avec des problématiques de fidélisation des publics de musées d'art (Passebois-Ducros, 2003 ; Le Marec et Topalian, 2003 ; Allaine et Candito, 2009).

À la lecture des livres d'or, plusieurs dimensions apparaissent. Nous référons aux dates des entrées lorsqu'elles existent, car tous les visiteurs ne fournissent pas toujours les informations relatives à leur identité ou leur moment de passage. Tout d'abord, les visiteurs évoquent l'auteur qui par ses spectacles a guidé leurs pas vers ce village. Ils tutoient souvent directement l'auteur : "Quelle belle découverte dans ce merveilleux village. Merci à Fred Pellerin de nous avoir donné envie de le visiter et même de nous accompagner dans la visite ! Magique !" (Livre d'or, 4 juillet 2010) ; "Merci Fred de nous faire découvrir ton village par ta poésie" (Livre d'or, 16 juillet 2010).

L'esprit des lieux, et même la magie des lieux est un élément fort qui imprègne de nombreux commentaires : "À chaque fois que nous venons à Saint-Élie, il se passe quelque chose de magique. C'est sans doute à cause des lutins et de l'arbre à "paparmanes" ! " (Livre d'or, 5 août 2013).

L'univers de conte est perçu par les visiteurs qui voient revivre la légende, ils entrent dans le conte à leur façon en assimilant les codes comme les invraisemblances temporelles dans cette citation :

> Votre coin d'pays prend des airs de conte imaginaire. Trop souvent on tasse les histoires mais ici tout vit et tout revit. Votre folklore est et restera ! Merci pour ces beaux moments d'imaginaire et qui sait peut-être reviendrons-nous dans 100 ans (Livre d'or, août 2009).

Ensuite, les références à l'œuvre sont multiples, entre autres à travers les lieux investis par sa galerie de personnages :

> Les légendes de Fred Pellerin sont captivantes. La visite se cristallise chez Léo Déziel pour les initiés. Ce garage avait été décrit par lui d'une telle façon que quand je l'ai aperçu, sur le coin, il était comme je l'avais imaginé, ça prouve qu'il est un bon conteux (8 juin 2011).

Enfin, l'élément intéressant est la contagion langagière du style de Pellerin dans les propos des visiteurs en une sorte de créativité mimétique :

> Comme l'endormitoire nous gagnait, madame a bifurqué vers Saint-Elie de Caxton. Pendant quelques jours, nous avons dû surveiller les panneaux pour les traverses d'orignaux… J'avoue qu'une traverse de lutins… Ça déstabilise un motocycliste… (21 juin 2013)

> Une "pellerinade" bienfaisante pour le corps et l'esprit (Livre d'or, juin 2012).

En outre, la dimension patrimoniale est présente, un patrimoine qu'il convient pour les uns de conserver car il est associé à des valeurs positives : solidarité, altruisme que l'on prête à la ruralité du temps jadis. Lorsqu'ils évoquent le patrimoine, les visiteurs glissent tantôt sur des aspects historiques, relatifs à la mémoire collective de leur nation, tantôt sur des souvenirs beaucoup plus personnels associés à leur enfance : "Merci pour la conservation du patrimoine et merci à Fred de ressasser nos souvenirs d'enfance avec nos grands-parents" (Livre d'or, juillet 2009) ; "...connaître son histoire, le patrimoine si important aux Québecois qu'on oublie malheureusement si souvent" (Livre d'or, juin 2010).

> Merci de m'avoir permis un retour aux sources... Continuez de faire vivre ce beau voyage ! Cela nous permet de voir qu'il est encore possible de vivre en communauté et en se souciant de son prochain ! (Livre d'or, 30 août 2009).

Ainsi, ces commentaires attestent des multiples niveaux de réception d'un artiste et de son œuvre ; à Saint-Élie, ils se cristallisent autour de l'idée d'une quête dont l'objet varie, la première se situe dans le réel-actuel (l'écrivain), la seconde confronte la dimension imaginaire de l'écrit au réel, la troisième se joue dans le registre du merveilleux situé dans un lieu réel. Un triptyque qu'on peut exemplifier comme autant d'objets de recherches pour les visiteurs :

1   – Trouver Fred, sa maison, les traces de son passage, etc. dans l'espoir de le rencontrer en chair et en os : « belle visite, hier, dans votre village, accompagnée de Fred. J'aurais tellement aimé rencontrer ce Fred... en personne. Une cassette c'est mieux que rien » (Livre d'or, août 2012).

2   – Trouver les personnages issus de la mythologie de l'auteur, que ce soit par les maisons, ou en rencontrant leurs descendants. "Meo le coiffeur, il a des enfants qui peuvent témoigner. En fin de compte, c'est des contes, mais c'est des vrais personnages", nous dira le coordonnateur du tourisme et des communications de Saint-Elie-de-Caxton. Ou encore, plus troublant, en découvrant leur tombe dans le cimetière. Outre l'émotion, repérer des stèles aux noms de personnages fabuleux, affublés de qualités surnaturelles, apparaît comme une mise à l'épreuve de l'intellect des plus cartésiens.

3 – Trouver les lutines, ou toute autre créature fantastique, ou assister à un événement magique : des vidéos circulent sur internet où l'on voit des visiteurs se mettre en scène alors qu'ils surprennent des lutins.

> Je crois que j'ai aperçu un lutin. J'ai croisé sa route. J'étais à vélo et en passant j'ai vu un bout de capine à travers les branches. Elle est passée vite, mais je suis certaine que c'en était un ! (Livre d'or, juillet 2007).

Cette quête de l'illustre et de l'extraordinaire dans un décor ordinaire montre les différents registres d'attraits développés par le village à partir des inventions de Fred Pellerin. La patrimonialisation de l'auteur et de ses contes est singulière aussi dans le sens où elle ne construit pas un village de légende *ex nihilo* mais qu'elle intègre le patrimoine rural existant.

Figure 11.3 Saint-Élie-de-Caxton et Fred Pellerin, ou l'"heureux mariage" entre patrimoine matériel et immatériel, entre l'Histoire et la légende

Saint-Élie-de-Caxton et Fred Pellerin, c'est l'histoire d'un mariage improbable entre deux patrimoines : patrimoine matériel (église) et immatériel (la légende orale, le folklore revisité), cultuel et culturel, l'histoire et la légende, l'ancien et le contemporain, la tradition et l'imagination (figure 11.3). L'authenticité de la démarche artistique "localisée" en amont du succès et l'universalité du propos de son auteur sont sans doute à l'origine de la réussite de la démarche de développement touristique de ce territoire. Selon le coordonnateur du tourisme et des communications, c'est un heureux mariage, d'une municipalité avec un conteux. Le travail de l'une et l'autre sont indissociables.

Conclusion

Fred Pellerin se définit modestement comme le maillon entre une mémoire orale ancestrale qui se passait « d'une bouche à l'oreille, qui se transmettait sans manquer de maillon » et un spectateur urbain contemporain. "Alors moi, je raconte. J'ai l'oreille en forme de vieux. J'ai beaucoup côtoyé les ancêtres, notamment ma grand-mère. Une femme contante. Comme le verbe. Au participe présent" (Pellerin, 2005, 15). Il s'en va "déterrer les mots" (*Ibid.*) de telle sorte que ses contes deviennent médiateurs entre les lieux. Les procédés narratifs qu'il mobilise créent une géographie spécifique. Flou temporel, néologismes et flottements à la limite du plausible et de l'imaginaire mettent en branle les ressorts qu'on retrouve dans le réalisme merveilleux. Ils dépeignent un espace qui se distingue par cet aspect fantastique, mais qui se pose en représentant d'une ruralité fière commune à l'ensemble du Québec.

Localement, ce sont non seulement les lieux réels de l'œuvre, mais aussi les procédés narratifs et l'esprit des lieux insufflé par le conteur qui sont instrumentalisés par des acteurs territoriaux pour valoriser un espace rural isolé. Inversement, en offrant, il y a dix-neuf ans, un travail de guide à l'auteur et en lui offrant un matériau mémoriel et légendaire riche, le village a permis à l'auteur de construire son univers narratif. Par ailleurs, les visiteurs se saisissent différemment de ces représentations socio-spatiales et participent à leur tour à la co-construction du lieu, en lui insufflant un renouvellement économique et démographique, en orientant certaines des décisions esthétiques, notamment. Comme certains l'ont fait remarquer dans le cas de la littérature du réalisme magique latino-américain, le fait que les visiteurs comme les politiques reprennent à leur compte ce passage entre les éléments réalistes et magiques constitue une caution au moins implicite de la présence du merveilleux dans l'espace concerné (Esteban, 2000). L'étude des livres d'or permet de faire ressortir une adhésion de l'imaginaire du visiteur au monde porté par le discours de Pellerin et des acteurs économiques et politiques de son village. Ce qui est le plus marquant dans cette étude de cas, c'est l'intrication, de tous, auteur, acteurs du territoire, population locale et visiteurs dans la construction de la légende rurale, légende qui semble constitutive de l'identité territoriale. Comme l'écrit Pellerin « La vérité, loin de l'arrivage, sert plus souvent de point de départ sur laquelle bâtir tous les possibles » (Pellerin, 2013, 73).

Sources primaires

Pellerin, Fred. 2001. *Dans mon village, il y a belle Lurette*. Montréal : Planète rebelle.

—. 2003. *Il faut prendre le taureau par les contes !* Montréal : Planète rebelle.

—. 2005. *Comme une odeur de muscles*. Montréal : Planère rebelle.

—. 2009. *L'Arracheuse de temps*. Montréal : Planète rebelle.

—. 2013. *De peigne et de misère*. Montréal : Planète rebelle.

Références

Allaine, C. et N. Candidato. 2009. "Les traces des visiteurs au musée : entre implication et considération". *Les Cahiers du Musée des Confluences*, 4, 121-134.

Angulo, Maria-El. 1995. *Magical Realism. Social Context and Discourse*. New York: Garland.

Demers, Jeanne et Lise Gauvin. 1976. "Autour de la notion de conte écrit : quelques définitions". *Études françaises*, 12, 1, 157-177.

Esteban, Angel. 2000. *Introduction à la littérature hispano-américaine*. Paris : Ellipses.

Faris, Wendy B. 2004. *Ordinary Enchantments: Magical Realism and the Remystification of Narrative*. Nashville: Vanderbilt University Press.

Harvey, David. 2003. "City Future Contained in City Past: Balzac in Paris". *After-Images of the City*, edited by J. Ramon, 23-48. Ithaca, NY: Cornell University Press.

Krylyschin, Marina. 2014. *Propositions pour une analyse de discours en situation de réception : textes d'exposition et livres d'or*. Paris : Université de Paris 5.

Larochelle, Renée. 2013. "La magie de l'arbre à "paparmanes"". *Le Fil*, 49, 9.

Le Marec Joëlle, Roland Topalian.2003. "Énonciation plurielle et publication de la parole du public en contexte muséal : le cas de "la tribune des visiteurs"". *Communication et langages*. 135, 12-24.

Monet-Viera, Molly. 2004. "Post-boom Magical Realism: Appropriations and Transformation of a Genre." *Revista de Estudios Hispánicos*, 38, 1, 95-117.

Passebois-Ducros, J. 2003. *Modes de valorisation des expériences esthétiques et processus de fidélisation des visiteurs de musées d'art : une application à la réception de l'art moderne et contemporain*. Montpellier 2 : Université des Sciences et Techniques du Languedoc.

Scheel, Charles W. 2005. *Réalisme magique et réalisme merveilleux : Des théories aux poétiques*. Paris : L'Harmattan.

Schmid, David. 1995. "Imagining Safe Urban Space: the Contribution of Detective Fiction to Radical Geography." *Antipode*, 27, 3, 242-269.

Schroeder, Shannin. 2004. *Rediscovering Magical Realism in the Americas*. Westport: Praeger.

Séry, Sacha. 2013. "Avec Fred Pellerin, ça jase et ça jacte !" *Le Monde*, 4 juin, 12.

Chapter Twelve

"Ast'heur qu'on est là" [1]: An Attempt to Map Contemporary Acadie through its Songs

Marie-Laure Boudreau

As is the case for Zaire, Haute-Volta, or the Union of Soviet Socialist Republics (U.S.S.R.), one would find it difficult to find Acadie on a globe today if searching by place-name. Even with the help of Internet-based mapping tools, the results are puzzling. For instance, when the "Google Maps" search engine detects an IP address in Louisiana, the first result that appears for the search term "Acadie" is a motel in Eunice, a small town northwest of Lafayette, Louisiana. From les Iles-de-la-Madeleine, Quebec, the first result is apparently the website of the company that operates the ferry between Iles-de-la-Madeleine and Prince Edward Island (PEI). From Quebec City, it has been reported that the search leads to an Acadian credit union, whereas from Caraquet, New Brunswick (NB), the first result is "Acadieville," a village located southwest of Miramichi[2]. None of these results are on a country scale… Where, then, is the geopolitical location of Acadie? Acadie has a flag[3], but it does not have an official capital, nor does it have well-defined borders. Nevertheless, Acadie must exist, because Acadian identity is proudly proclaimed by a group of people. While some members of that group see determining an exact location to be named Acadie a necessity for the future of their identity, the majority of

---

[1] In reference to the title of a song by Edith Butler. Literally: "Now that we're here."

[2] These results have been collected in the months of May and June 2014, through web communications with an informant in each region, whom I asked to report their results on the web search for "Acadie."

[3] There are even two: one for "Northern Acadie" (Canada, Maine (USA)) and another in "Tropical Acadie" (Louisiana).

them do not seem to care. They are Acadians, but also, by imposed necessity, Canadians, New Brunswickers, Nova Scotians, Quebecers, Americans... Indeed, attempting to attribute a precise location to Acadie becomes complex as we realize how much its parcels of land are geographically scattered, and mostly rural. Is Acadie somewhere today? If so, where?

I suggest that a possible answer to that last question can be found in the mentions of geographic locations in contemporary Acadian songs[4]. Acadie would be the spaces that musicians who identify as Acadians refer to in their song lyrics. This process of mapping through songs shares similarities with the literary constructions of space studied in "geocriticism," a branch of literary criticism developed by Bertrand Westphal in France, and Robert T. Tally Jr. in the Unites States. The first notes:

> Less clearly on the margins of reality than it was in the prewar era, fictional discourse has gained the force of persuasion. And if credibility in fiction has always been measured in terms of the reference to the "real" world, in the post-modern era one can no longer say that the world of cement, concrete, or steel is more real than the world of paper and ink (Westphal 2011, 3).

In a similar fashion, can we say that a world of invisible man-made borders is more real than the world of soundwaves? I argue that Acadian singers create their world through singing, while evoking a mental imagery of landscapes for the listener. One also names a place to attribute a meaning to it. If naming is not a physical appropriation of territory, it represents at least a conceptual one, and this, even though Acadians did not "assign" the place-name. Indeed, "to name" does not necessarily mean "to give name." As Reuben Rose-Redwood, Derek Alderman, and Maoz Azaryahu discuss in their article about toponymic inscription, there are often political implications in assigning place-names. However, when it is the case that:

> a commemorative name is given to a place, it increasingly becomes associated with its geographic location: history becomes geography. [...] As a result of the conversion of historical names into place-names, the geographic denotation takes over while the existence of a historical referent becomes increasingly obscure to most users (2010, 459).

---

[4] Written from 1960 to today; still sung today.

There is indeed a political reason why Acadie does not exist on the map anymore: the original territory named as such was renamed "Nova Scotia" by the English in 1621 (Daigle 1993, 5), although the name Acadie was restored in 1632 (Daigle 1993, 5), and later oscillated between the two as the French and English disputed the land until the deportation of the Acadians began in 1755 (Daigle 1993, 38). However, some of them eventually returned, although not on the exact same land; they resettled in neighboring areas (Vernex 1979, 39-40). From this new "home," more recent exiles will later occur, in the 20th century, mostly due to socio-economic factors: "L'attraction urbaine est subie, non souhaitée. On va vers la ville parce qu'il y a du travail non par désir d'un cadre de vie différent" (Vernex 1979, 96) [Urban attraction is suffered, not desired. One goes toward the city because there is work, not because of the desire to live a different life][5]. In exile, singing about familiar places can suggest nostalgia, as the "[exile's] sadness can never be surmounted" (Said 2002, 173). However, melancholy is not always the conveyed mood, as the Acadians are known to enjoy festivities and playing music together. A partly common musical repertoire is shared across different areas of Acadie, and within this repertoire, a plurality of places mentioned in song exists. The song "Vivre à la Baie"[6] can be sung on the shore of the *Baie de Plaisance* as well as "À Moncton" can be sung in Baie-Sainte-Marie: linking the diaspora through a toponymy of Acadian places made out of soundwaves.

A place steeped in history

Acadie has not always been a "virtual" place. The first political divisions, during the Nouvelle-France era, were well-defined, at least by the cartographic standards of the time. While the ownership of its territory alternated between France and England, the agricultural settlement of Acadie nevertheless occupied a rather precise location on the map. Unfortunately, as History has shown, it would not survive in that geographic dimension. Around 1755, Governor Lawrence undertook the deportation of Acadians to various points down the American East Coast and in other cases, to France (Vernex 1979, 39; Leblanc 1983, 143-166). Acadie was then annexed to the English colonies once and for all, and its name was erased from the map. Some Acadians were able to escape

---

[5] Translation by author.
[6] Short for Baie-Saint-Marie, Nova Scotia.

deportation by fleeing "into the woods,"[7] while others returned from deportation after 1763, but could not reintegrate their former lands, because they had been redistributed to the Anglophone colonizers. As a result, they re-settled along the coasts, as in Baie-Sainte-Marie, Nova Scotia (NS), where the Acadians moved from a traditionally agricultural livelihood to one based on fisheries and forestry. Today, Acadians are found along a fragmented territory dispersed through the Canadian Maritime provinces, Northern Maine and Coastal Quebec. Other Acadians are established in the southern United States of America, in Louisiana (known as "Acadie tropicale"), where inhabitants are called "*Cadiens*," "Cajuns," or "*Cadjins*."[8] Another part of the diaspora can be found in France, but for the purpose of the present study, the focus will be kept on North America, and in particular on "Northern Acadie," where the Acadian "national sentiment" (Thériault 1993, 66-67; Bourque and Richard 2014) was first officially revived at the end of the 19th century.

National sentiment

Despite the dispersal, Acadian identity continued to exist, along with a desire to reunite with long lost kin. Elites and clergy sought to reinforce this identity into a "national sentiment," to preserve both the French language and the Catholic religion among the Acadians. These efforts led the Acadian National Conventions[9]. The first took place in Memramcook, N.B., in 1881, and three years later, a flag and a national anthem were chosen at the second Convention, in Miscouche, P.E.I., in 1884.

The avoided topic of geographic territory

According to Benedict Anderson, the elements required for the establishment of a national identity are "the census, the map and the museum" (1991, 163). Reviewing the case of Acadie, we find that there are quite a few museums, and that the question of the map is as

---

[7] Reference to the title *Cent ans dans les bois* [A hundred years into the woods], a novel by Antonine Maillet recalling the time after the Deportation, when the Acadians had to hide to avoid trouble.

[8] There are different spellings across the literature, although, as Sara Le Ménestrel explains in her introduction to *La voie des Cadiens*, a linguistic committee formed in Lafayette in 1991 favored the orthography "Cadien" (1999, 29).

[9] See Bourque, Denis and Chantal Richard. 2014. *Les Conventions Nationales – Tome 1*. Moncton : Institut d'études Acadiennes.

problematic as the question of the census. Or, as Antonine Maillet's famous theatrical character "la Sagouine" explains:

> Pour l'amour de Djeu, où c'est que je vivons, nous autres !... En Acadie, qu'ils nous avont dit, et je sons des Acadjens. Ça fait que j'avons entrepris de répondre à leu question de natiounalité coume ça : des Acadjens, que je leur avons dit. Ça, je sons sûrs d'une chouse, c'est que je sons les seuls à porter ce nom-là. Ben, ils avont point voulu écrire ce mot-là dans leu liste, les encenseux. Parce qu'ils avont eu pour leu dire que l'Acadie, c'est point un pays, ça, pis un Acadjen c'est point une natiounalité, par rapport que c'est pas écrit dans les livres de Jos Graphie (1974, 192).
>
> [For God's sake, where do we live, us! In Acadia, they told us, and we are Acadians. So, I took upon myself to answer to their nationality question like that: Acadians, I told them. The one thing I am sure of, is that we are the only one to bear that name. Well, they did not want to write that word on their list, the *censer* officials. Because of the fact that they had for their say that Acadia, that's not a country, and then Acadian is not a nationality because of the fact that it is not written in Jos Graphy's books.][10]

Maillet, through the voice of La Sagouine, reflects with humor on the fact that Acadian "national" identity does not rely on geographical or territorial claims. Thus, for the government, they do not constitute a legitimate group choice of nationality or ethnicity in the census. Jean-Claude Vernex addresses the discussion of territorial questions held at the first National Convention:

> Marked by a profound social and political conservatism, the ideology underlying the sense of belonging that was propagated by the patriotic discourse of the leadership of the day avoided any implicit reference to territorial demands. Acadia became a concept of history, a reference point in time. Obviously emotionally charged, the concept of Acadia was free of any spatial expression insofar as that final step would have implied the mapping of precise geographical boundaries. But what exactly were the relations experienced between the Acadian and his space? (1993, 197-98).

It could be argued that the church and the elites did not want to lose their positions in creating a revolutionary climate in the population, as there had been in Quebec with the patriots a few decades earlier, in which the French-Canadians were defeated (Aquin 1988, 69-70). Indeed, seeking to avoid conflict with Anglophone authorities, which controlled the territory on which they inhabited, Acadian elites refused to address any

---

[10] Translation by author.

clear territorial claims or any regional definition of a place that would overlap geopolitical territory, even at a conceptual level[11].

Desire to "re-politicize" a territory: mixed feelings

Long after the National Conventions of the 19th century, the 1960s brought important changes in the Acadian society, among them: the creation of a Francophone university in N.B. in 1963; N.B. was officially declared a bilingual province in 1969; and the creation of various Francophone political and social associations (Thériault 1993, 84-85). The issue of delineating a precise territory on the map that could be officially called "Acadie" started to be raised, though one inevitable and major problem arose: where? The historical Grand-Pré, where no Acadians live anymore? While some considered the "Acadian peninsula" in N.B., others stressed a need for a "metropolitain center": Moncton? "Montréal pour le Québec; Moncton pour l'Acadie," as Quebec filmmaker André Gladu implies in his documentary "Tintamarre: La piste Acadie en Amérique" (2005). Nonetheless, the fact that Moncton is shared with Anglophones could be problematic, and not without historical tensions (Vernex 1979, 56-57)[12]. Michel Roy, in *L'Acadie perdue,* comments: "si l'Acadie c'est Moncton et Moncton l'Acadie, je préfère pour ma part tous les ailleurs du monde" (1978, 67) [If Acadie is Moncton, and Moncton is Acadie, I personally prefer all "the elsewheres" in the world][13]. It is reasonable to think that his statement would be echoed by many others. In addition, what would happen to the Acadians living elsewhere? Why one place over another?

---

[11] On the other hand, they avoided any disturbance, propagating the images of a submissive and resigned people, with the help of myths such as "Evangeline" (Longfellow's "heroin"). Nonetheless, Henry Wadsworth Longfellow is an American who never set foot in "Acadie." As a matter of fact, his landscapes descriptions ("This is the forest primeval. The murmuring pines and the hemlocks, Bearded with moss..." (1916, 27) do not correspond to the landscape of Grand Pré... But Longfellow never identified as an Acadian author. Therefore I will not mention him any further.

[12] Michel Brault and Pierre Perrault's documentary film *L'Acadie, l'Acadie ?!?* offers many historical examples about these tensions.

[13] Translation by author.

Conceptual appropriation of place

Let us reexamine the question addressed by Vernex about the "the relation experienced between the Acadian and his space" (1993, 198), through the connection (and distinction at the same time) made by Michel de Certeau between "place" and "space": "On this view, in relation to place, space is like the word when it is spoken" (1984, 117). Also reflecting upon the notions of construction and appropriation of place, Yi-Fu Tuan, scholar in the discipline of human geography, considers that naming a place is more significant than materially transforming it:

> Insiders see "homeplace" – an environment that is familiar to them, not because they have materially transformed it but because they have named it. It is their place – their world – through the casting of a linguistic net (1991, 686).

However, as was stressed earlier, "to name" has a twofold meaning; it can mean to give a name, while it can also mean utilizing the name. In the case of Acadian "homeplaces," many have names given in another language: Native (mostly Mi'kmaq) or English. "As a particular geography of public memory, a city text represents not only a version of history but also commemorative priorities and hegemonic discourses of former periods" (Rose-Redwood, Alderman and Azaryahu 2010, 460). On the one hand, English place-names most often represent large territories, such as province names or cities (Nova Scotia, New Brunswick, Prince Edward Island, Moncton, Fredericton, Halifax, Charlottetown, etc.). On the other, smaller cities and rural areas often bear Native names or French names describing the landscape of the area (Scoudouc, Miramichi, Bouctouche; Cap-Pelé, Petit-Rocher, Cap-aux-Meules, Etang-des-Caps, etc.). As Tuan develops further: "The meaning of a real place is constructed [...] through accretional layers of gossip and song, oral history, written history, essays and poems" (1991, 692). "Gossip and song" are therefore opportunities to redefine a place already "named". Whether it be placing small communities "on the map," or appropriating "foreign" names, it seems as though the Acadians try to construct meanings of place in songs.

Contemporary songs as a form of oral poetry

Despite the development of an Acadian literature in the 20th century, it is primarily through "oral poetry," in the sense that Paul Zumthor describes it[14], that cultural expression happens within Acadie, whether it be song, poetry or theatrical performance, even if it uses the written medium beforehand, or audio-visual media for its dissemination. The preeminence of oral poetry over literature is not only due to the fact that being in the "New World," Acadie is relatively "young," but also because education was only accessible to a minority before the 20th century[15]. Oral expression is still very much the means of cultural dissemination today. At the same time, as Zumthor notes, oral expression is not only a way to create bonds inside a group of people, but also for that group of people to be heard and recognized by others:

> La communication orale remplit, dans le groupe social, une fonction en grande partie d'extériorisation. Elle fait entendre, collectivement et globalement, le discours que cette société tient sur elle-même. Elle assure ainsi la perpétuation du groupe en question et de sa culture (2008, 169).
>
> [Oral communication, in a social group, largely fills a function of exteriorization. It reverberates, collectively and globally, the discourse which that society holds on itself. It thus insures the perpetuation of that said group and its culture.][16]

Beyond cultural continuation, the sentiment of belonging to a territory can also exist through cultural objects. It appears that contemporary songs would be located at the intersection between media and oral poetry, being at the same time a creation destined to be performed and, when captured on a medium, transformed into "mediatized orality" (Zumthor 1990, 18). "[Les] media modernes [...] donnent à lire ou à voir des images de l'espace qui conditionnent les perceptions et façonnent par retour de

---

[14] "On peut parler de poésie orale lorsque transmission et réception s'opèrent par la voix et l'ouïe, et donc coïncident en une seule et même action. Cette action est la *performance* (dans le cas d'improvisation, la phase de production se fond, elle aussi, dans la performance). L'existence d'une performance est le seul élément définitoire de l'oralité ; même si la production et la conservation de l'œuvre requièrent l'usage de l'écriture, le fait de la performance suffit à en faire pleinement une oeuvre orale." (*Oralité*, 182). [One can speak of oral poetry when transmission and reception occur through the voice and the ear, thus coincide in one and the same action. This action is *performance* (in the case of improvisation, the production phase merges in the performance). The existence of performance is the only defining element of orality; even if production and conservation of the work require the use of writing, the fact of the performance is sufficient to fully make it an oral work.] (Translation by author).

[15] Even so, in 1922, more than 90% quit school before the 9th grade (Lafreniere 1971, 16).

[16] Translation by author.

nouvelles réalités" (Frémont 1999, 128). [Modern media allow us to read
or to see images of space, which affect perceptions and shape in return
new realities.][17] While images of space can also be suggested in songs,
they could potentially provide answers, or at least avenues towards the
geographic localization of "Acadie."

A tour

When trying to come up with a song that would take the listener on an
Acadian journey through place-names, "La Vieille brosse en Acadie,"
would be number one. The song was written by George Langford, a singer
songwriter from Iles-de-la-Madeleine. Legend has it that he wrote this
song about his college years in Bathurst, where he allegedly told the
principal that his father was sick and dying, and used this lie to go "bar
hopping" ("sur la brosse") with the most beautiful girl of the region ("avec
la plus belle fille du pays"). Even if the story is true, Langford
nevertheless reassures us in the song that his father is alive and well,
waiting for him in his kitchen with forty ounces of gin ("Mon père
m'attend dans la cuisine/ avec un quarante onces de gin"). Throughout the
three verses, Langford names the places of his pilgrimage: Caraquet,
Pigeonhill, Pokemouche, Tracadie, Shippagan, Bathurst, Néguac,
Bouctouche, Moncton, Les Îles[18]. One should not believe that he thus
attempts to delineate Acadie in its whole entity through this trip's account,
but it is nonetheless a helpful overview of various places where Acadians
can be found. As an example, Iles-de-la-Madeleine is part of Quebec
province, while the other places are located in the province of New
Brunswick. Langford is elaborating a "tour" rather than a "map" (Certeau
1984, 119), and a short anecdote is associated with each stop along the
tour.

> From the folktale to descriptions of residences, an exacerbation of
> "practice" ("faire") (and thus of enunciation), actuates the stories narrating
> tours in places that, from the ancient cosmos to contemporary public
> housing developments, are all forms of an imposed order. In a pre-
> established geography, [...] everyday stories tell us what one can do in it
> and make out of it. They are treatments of space (Certeau 1984, 121-22).

Since Acadie is overlaid with "imposed geopolitical order," telling the
everyday stories work towards the fabrication of an Acadian-owned

---

[17] Translation by author.
[18] In reference to "Iles-de-la-Madeleine."

geography. In relation to "imposed order" geopolitics, Langford winks at us when he mentions in the song a family of rich English-speaking industrials, known for its monopoly over the region: "À Bouctouche on va faire la table ronde/ Ayoù c'qu' Irving est venu au monde/ Si l'monde était pas venu à lui/ Il serait jamais né par ici." Furthermore, Langford gives a mention to an Acadian dialect specific to South-east New Brunswick, "le chiac": "Schooner, Moosehead[19]/ On continue la *run*/ On va aboutir à Moncton/ J'vas pratiquer mon chiac avant/ Pour pas avoir d'l'air ignorant."

As mentioned earlier, place-names are often derived from another language than French: many come from Native languages, others from English. The case of "Moncton" is very specific, because the town was named in honor of Robert Monckton, a colonial administrator of the British Empire who played a key role in the Acadian deportation (Jobb 2005, 120-25). However, the spelling of the town is slightly different... mistake or disguised insult? It is up to each individual to interpret.

Depicting the everyday

In his attempt to appropriate the place named for the English enemy, the poet Gérald Leblanc depicts everyday Moncton in "Rue Dufferin," a song by the band 1755, for which Leblanc wrote the lyrics.

> Dans la ville y a beaucoup de monde / Toutes sortes de faces à toutes sortes de places / ... / Y a beaucoup d'arbres même si les rues sont sales / J'su' pas loin du campus pis j'su' pas loin d'chez *Duanes*...

Leblanc draws an impressionist painting through words, evoking the city in a manner of building a bridge between what defines a city in general and what is specific to Moncton.

> Chacun sait de quoi il retourne quand on parle d'une "pièce" dans un appartement, du "coin" de la rue, de la "place" du marché, du "centre" commercial ou culturel, d'un "lieu" public, etc. Ces mots du discours quotidien discernent, sans les isoler, des espaces et décrivent un espace social. Ils correspondent à un usage de cet espace, donc à une pratique spatiale qu'ils disent et composent. (Lefebvre 1974, 25-26).
> [Everyone knows what it means when one talks about a "room" in an apartment, the "corner" of the street, the market "square," the commercial or cultural "center," a public "place," etc. These words of everyday

---

[19] Local brands of beer.

discourse discern spaces, without isolating them, and describe a social space. They correspond to a usage of that space, thus to a spatial practice they tell about and form.]

While establishing things that Moncton may have in parallel with other cities in the world (a lot of people, a lot of trees, dirty streets, suggesting being close to all contrasts) highlights the urbanity of this "Acadian city," it is also distinguished from other cities by its specificities: the name of the street, the name of the coffee shop where Leblanc went. "Everydayness" in Moncton is also highlighted by the sometimes-sour relationships between Anglophones and Francophones. The bridge of "Rue Dufferin" exemplifies this last aspect with a sense of humor: "Les vieilles anglaises l'autre bord de la rue/ N'aiment pas mon chien mais ça fait rien/ Il les aime pas lui non plus."

But while everydayness is underlined in Moncton, Acadian rural places have sometimes been described in a similar fashion, for example in Bertrand Déraspe's song (first recorded with Suroît) "Pointe-aux-loups": "On a une belle église pis un *post office*/ Un gros magasin pis ben du terrain/ On a d'l'asphalte pis une belle jetée *J.W.J Delaney*." In this example, which happens to be the chorus of the song, Déraspe enumerates the landmarks of the smallest village on Iles-de-la-Madeleine's "mainland."[20] In doing so, he attempts a similar enterprise as Gérald Leblanc, in that he tries to legitimate the status of Pointe-aux-loups; in this case, not by appropriating the place named for an "enemy" (as in the case discussed above with Moncton and Robert Monckton), but simply in highlighting the presence of the village on the map.

Cri de terre[21]

Inspired by free verse poetry, certain song lyrics may be more hermetic than others to the listener, such as "Petitcodiac" by Zéro Degré Celsius. Here, place-names are sung as calls, almost incantations: "Petitcodiac/ Micmac/ Kouchibouguac/.../ Kejimkujik.../ Beaumont/ Néguac/... / Cap Maringouin/ Cap Enragé/ Kouchibouguac/..." These are names of Nature Reserves in New Brunswick and Nova Scotia, interspersed with river names. The song also exemplifies that landscape description is often used in Native and French place-names (while the "commemorative" (Rose-Redwood, Alderman and Azaryahu 2010, 460) place-names occur in

---

[20] In reference to the islands joined by road.
[21] In reference to the poem by Raymond-Guy Leblanc.

English)[22]. Beyond geography, there are also implications of another order; Kouchibouguac, acting as a refrain, is not only a National Park, it is also the place of a "second deportation" (Rudin 2011, 217). In 1969, the creation of the park forced the expropriation of over 250 families, most of them of Acadian descent. Some resisted. Among them Jackie Vautour, the spokesman for the expropriates refusing to leave his property, came to symbolize this resistance (Rudin 2011). In the song, Zéro Degré Celsius claims this land as Acadian, inspired by other revolutionaries: "Crazy Horse/ Beausoleil / Louis Riel/ Jackie Vautour/ À c't'heure c'est notre tour."

A second exile

While Acadian people have experienced forced migrations through deportation, the more recent exiles are caused by socio-economic factors. Unemployment is high; particularly among Francophones (Beaudin and Leclerc 1993, 260)[23]. The majority of Acadians live in rural areas. Due to the scarcity of employment opportunities outside seasonal occupations in fisheries and tourism, and adding to the sometimes-difficult conditions for small agricultural farms, many are tempted to move to urban centers, such as Montreal, Toronto or Vancouver. Others find work in the oilfield industry, in the Canadian Plains. For exiles, nostalgia for Acadie persists and surfaces in songs:

> Qu est-ce qu'un gars de Mont-Carmel fait dans la ville de Montréal/ À *watcher* les *cars* passer tous l'après-midi ? / S'ennuie assez, pourrait brailler/ Trop *stuck-up* pour s'en aller/ Qu'est-ce qu'un gars ferait pas pour gagner sa vie ? (Babin "Un Gars de Mont-Carmel").

In "Mourning and Creativity," María Cristina Melgar paraphrases Sigmund Freud on "Mourning and Melancholia": "remembrance and memories – sources of knowledge, elaboration, and inspiration—play a fundamental role in working through mourning" (2009, 111). The song also makes allusions about community practices, for instance the singer sings about waking up without much to do on a Sunday morning in Montreal, and going to church not because he "is a Saint," but because he

---

[22] There may be English place-names describing landscape also, but not the reverse (French "commemorative" place-names).

[23] There has been some improvement since the 1990s. For the most recent statistics on employment in the Maritime provinces of Canada:
<http://www.statcan.gc.ca/tables-tableaux/sum-som/l02/cst01/lfss01a-fra.htm>

remembers that there was "such a thing" as going to church back home. Singing about being away from home may help relieve from the distance "between a human being and a native place, between the self and its true home" (Said 2002, 177), a process which can be compared to a form of mourning. In the case of "le gars de Mont-Carmel," the exile may also be momentary, a transition caused by unemployment at home. Many other Acadians may find relief in the song because they are experiencing a similar feeling; they may identify with the singer even if they are not from Mont-Carmel, but rather come from another rural community.

Acadians may inhabit the city, but as Vernex observes:

> The mental imagery of every Acadian is of water, forests, and infinite pitchings of a boat upon the sea. It is a landscape filled with space and in rhythm with the muffled and regular shaping of waves and the rustling of forests…It is a landscape that lies deep in the heart of every Acadian exiled to the towns or metropolises of the continent and that, associated with a profound desire for tranquility, for authenticity in social relations, and for simplicity in life-style, makes understandable the emotional reaction of young Acadians to urbanization and the difficulties they have in adapting to this type of environment (1993, 202).

While the urge to depart may be present for some – who become expatriates rather than "exiles" – the reason that motivates departure is oftentimes necessity, not willingness, as Daniel Léger sings in "Le dernier bateau" : "Je respire à pleins poumons le vent du suroît/ Qui glace les moissons et le souffle des chevaux/ Je descends de la montagne prendre le dernier bateau/ C'est contre mon gré si l'hiver m'éloigne/ De l'Île d'Entrée." Here again, the place-name "L'Île d'Entrée" (Entry Island), part of the Iles-de-la-Madeleine archipelago, ties the cultural identification to a space. Yet, surprisingly, most inhabitants of Île d'Entrée are descendants of Scottish rather than French descent (Caldwell and Waddell 1982, 200). As a native from Iles-de-la-Madeleine myself, I can affirm that the island is nevertheless an iconic referent in Madelinot[24] consciousness, partly because it is the first island around which the ferry from P.E.I. navigates. Its remoteness (it is the only inhabited island that is not reachable by land) and its wild character (few houses) also makes it very present in Madelinot collective consciousness, and beyond, as a more general Acadian referent, since Daniel Léger is not from Iles-de-la-Madeleine, but from New Brunswick, where similar situations of "forced" departure occur. For exiles, but even for expatriates, who chose to live somewhere else, there is

---

[24] Common identifier for Iles-de-la-Madeleine inhabitants.

often a form of nostalgia for home. In either situation, singing about a place perpetuates it in people's cultural memory. As Yi-Fu Tuan states:

> A material building, if not properly maintained, will soon fall apart. To continue to exist, places must be kept in good repair… Much the same is true of places created by language, oral and written. "Mount Misery" will fade from consciousness if it is not kept alive by social support – if the name is not passed on by word of mouth or written on a map that is periodically consulted. "Mount Misery" will continue to exist in people's minds and even, in the course of time, seem more real if not only the name is used but stories, continuingly elaborated, are told. What was a mere marker on the horizon can be transformed, by imaginative narration, into a vivid presence (1991, 689).

In this regard, there are sometimes lesser known, rural place-names that are mentioned in songs, as demonstrated with the aforementioned example of "Pointe-aux-loups." As a Madelinot myself, I know of a song named after pretty much every community (the communities in question are smaller than municipalities[25], so they are not always on official maps). Some of these songs have been composed by people who were not necessarily professional musicians, but they became widespread in oral tradition and local choirs[26].

Leaving home

> Nous n'avons aucune raison de penser que nos parents, notre famille ou notre pays constituent des racines naturelles. Nous avons autant de raisons de penser que c'est en partant de tout ce qui est donné et naturel que nous pouvons découvrir du nouveau, que nous pouvons changer. D'une certaine façon, une vie humaine […] n'est faite que de nouveaux départs (Nancy 2011, 23).
>
> [We have no reason to think that our parents, our family, or our country constitute natural roots. We have as many reasons to think that it is in leaving everything that is given and natural that we can discover new things,that we can change. In a way, a human life […] is made of nothing but new beginnings.][27]

---

[25] Smaller than the former municipalities before 2002, year of the fusion into one municipality: Iles-de-la-Madeleine (Falkert 2010, 21).

[26] Some of these songs were recorded on an album entitled *Le tour des îles,* vol. 1 produced by Arrimage, in 1993.

[27] Translation by author.

While exiles leave because of exterior factors, expatriates are often young people who are curious "to see the world". Both types of departure exist in the Acadian communities, although there may be economic motivations attached to "seeing the world." Nonetheless, departure can sometimes be seen as a positive thing by the one who leaves, while not as such by the ones who are left behind. "Tu me dis que tu t'en vas à Montréal/ Ben, prends ton bagage pis crisse ton camp," sings Cayouche ("La chaîne de mon tracteur"). In the song, where Cayouche plays the role of a father talking to his son, moving away is seen as a form of abandonment of the community and its identity values. Similarly, in "Pourquoi s'en aller," the singer asks the artists who pursue their careers "in the city" why they have to leave, while suggesting that they in fact miss their home even though they pretend to like the city life. For Cayouche, who is quite popular in rural communities, it is much easier to criticize the ones who move away:

> Y'a des artistes acadiens qu'avont perdu leur chemin / Ils s'en avont allé pour s'exiler / Montréal ou Toronto / Y'avont dit qu'y faisait beau / À c't'heure ils commencent à s'ennuyer / Pourquoi, pourquoi s'en aller / Rien que pour travailler ? / On est si ben chez nous à s'promener partout / Pourquoi, pourquoi s'en aller ?

But not everyone can afford to perform only at home. In fact, the majority of artists have to tour outside of their region to earn a living. Lisa Leblanc, for instance, sees herself as a bohemian:

> Un moment donné, j'déciderai d'enfouir mes robes de gipsy / Au fond de mon garde-robe / De mes vieilles valises, j'sortirai c'que j'ai vécu / Pour les exposer sur des murs que j'pourrai appeler les miens / … / Je remarquerai plus les cabines de téléphone su'l'bord de la rue / Quand j'aurai d'autres fils avec la réalité / Que les grandes lignes d'Hydro qui me suivent partout.

The electric lines she sings about tie the Acadian landscapes together across the American continent, the thread linking the pieces of Acadie, virtually.

Acadiana or "Tropical Acadie"

Acadians from the North are well aware of their Southern cousins who live in Louisiana. Thus George Langford sings, in "Acadiana" : "Le *highway* mène au Mardi Gras, chez les Cajuns de la Louisiane, mais la route qui mène aux États, a' traverse un grand' embarras". Not only does the border (between Canada and the United States) complicate exchanges between Acadians of the North and the South (a phenomenon that happens to Acadians who live in Northern Maine, directly across the Saint-John River)[28], but also does the great distance between the border and the Southern state of Louisiana. Waylon Thibodeaux describes the paradox of distance in a song written for the 1999 Congrès Mondial Acadien:

> Chère Acadie, je pense souvent à toi / Mais je n'peux pas me détacher du pays où je suis né / Ceux qui n'sont pas Acadiens, ne peuvent pas comprendre / Qu'est-ce que c'est d'avoir le cœur en Acadie et les pieds en la Louisiane.

Thibodeaux exemplifies the fact that the Acadian has an organic tie to his environment. This may be true of other peoples, but somehow, the fact that Acadians had to adapt to their new place, to show resilience, may explain the relation to the inhabited land. Home is where the Acadian is, and where he is is a little bit of Acadie, whether in Louisiana, New Brunswick, Quebec, China, etc. Where in the world is this dear "Acadie"?

"Acadie in the day and age of planes" [29]

While already uprooted once and again, it is somehow utopian to believe that Acadian communities would move once again to a precise region because it would be labelled "Acadie." In an example illustrating the ties to one's region, Kenneth Saulnier, a native of Baie Sainte-Marie, sings about going back and living there for the rest of his life: "J'veux m'en aller vivre à la Baie / ... / J'y resterai le restant de ma vie / Y' où c'qui fait beau / À la Baie Sainte-Marie" (1755 "Vivre à la Baie"). It seems very unlikely that the singer would change his mind and move to a self-described new "Acadie". Besides, would the delineation of an official territory modify Acadian identity? Meanwhile, what prevents blurred "virtual frontiers" in today's world ?

> a world where electronic media are transforming the relationships between information and mediation, and where nation-states are struggling to retain control over their populations in the face of a host of subnational and transnational movements and organizations (Appadurai 1996, 188-89).

---

[28] Barry Jean Ancelet did a presentation at Congrès Mondial Acadien in 2014, in Edmunston, highlighting the border issue.

[29] Citing an expression used by Barry Jean Ancelet ("L'Acadie à l'heure des avions") (Personal communication)

While humans inhabit a physical space, transportation is very much eased, physically and virtually. Why would we not be able to conceive of an "Acadie in the day and age of planes?" Jacobus et Maléco, a duo of Acadian rappers now known as Radio Radio, express their identity in these contemporary factors in mind. The stylistic change in their music also reflects an idea of transnationalism, through the esthetic of rap. They nevertheless attach a local meaning to it, singing in the French dialect typical of Baie-Sainte-Marie. In reference to "Vivre à la Baie" mentioned earlier on, here are excerpts from "Back à la Baie":

> J'veux point m'en aller vivre à la Baie / même si l'monde croyont que j'l'ai chanté / Parsonne vient d'nulle part, à c't'heure qu'y a des *planes* / mo j'veux embarquer dans y'une, en jouant la *train* / sur mon violon / ... / Chu un "amaritchain" mais d'une Acadie, *mind you* /... / Quoi-ce la Baie représente pour toi? / Quoi-ce la Baie représente pour moi ? / Si tu penses/ point trop/ y fera beau/ faisons-la une autre fois."

The young rappers are "inhabited" by their native region, "la Baie" (Sainte-Marie), and the place remains an anchor for them. If they leave, to sail other shores, it is not to find a "lost" Acadie. They are "amaritchain" (Americans) but "d'une Acadie," suggesting that there is more than "one"[30].

In our current world, where the notion of culture is not necessarily linked as much to the territory as it once was (Appadurai 1996, 48-50), and where means of communication are manifold, the question of an Acadian geography is of a contingent nature. Indeed, the Acadians may be an example of the fact that identities do not need to be linked to the land, and correspondingly, that different identities can coexist inside a same nation-state; put another way, that the nation-state and its geographic territory alone should not be the only factor in the identity of a group. Their example may be one that could inspire multicultural nations across the world. Also, among Acadians, if their cultural consciousness has survived to this day through this ambiguity, are there no other concerns to address regarding Acadie's future?

If we are able to see through song lyrics a type of conceptual appropriation of a flexible territory, it also reflects the geographic adaptation that the Acadians lived through, from the coasts of Atlantic Canada to the Louisiana Swamps. Echoing Louder and Wadell's

---

[30] In a similar fashion, the original French title of the book edited by Dean Louder and Eric Waddell about Francophone North America *Du Continent perdu à L'archipel retrouvé* [From lost continent to recovered archipelago]' (1983) expresses a related idea of geographic representation.

"archipelago" while keeping in mind the symbolic Acadian star, Acadie seems rather like a constellation: one that is constituted of Acadian communities linked together by virtual lines. And, not unlike the stars, it may be difficult to make a total assessment.

Discography

1755. "Rue Dufferin." Les Retrouvailles de la Famille / Live au Colisée de Moncton. ISBA. 1994. 2 CD.

—. "Vivre à la Baie." Les Retrouvailles de la Famille / Live au Colisée de Moncton. ISBA. 1994. 2 CD.

Babin, Albert. "Un Gars de Mont-Carmel." Tu As Quitté Sans Saluer. R.P.M. 1995. CD

Butler, Edith. "Asteur qu'on est là." Asteur qu'on est là. SPPS. 1979. LP.

Cayouche. "La Chaîne de mon tracteur." Un Vieux Hippy. Ind. 1994.CD

—. "Pourquoi s'en aller." Roule, roule. Ind. 1999. CD.

Jacobus et Maléco. "Back à la Baie." Walla Walla. Ind. 2005. CD

Langford, George. "Acadiana." Collection Souvenir- Les grands succès de Georges Langford. Gamma. 2003. CD.

—. "La Vieille brosse en Acadie." Collection Souvenir- Les grands succès de Georges Langford. Gamma. 2003. CD.

Leblanc, Lisa. "Lignes d'Hydro." Lisa Leblanc. Bonsound. 2012. CD.

Léger, Daniel. "Le dernier bateau de l'île d'Entrée." La Route M'appelle. l'lages. 2000. CD

Suroît. "M'en allant par Saulnierville Station." Suroît. Select. 1993. CD

—. "Pointe-aux-loups." Suroît[31]. Biplan.1977. LP

Thibodeaux, Waylon. "Si longtemps séparé." Tu me fais crier. Rockin' River. 1999. CD

Zéro Celsius. "Petitcodiac." Contes du coude/Tales from the bend. SOPREF Local Distribution. 2002. CD

Other references

Anderson, Benedict. 1991. *Imagined Communities: Reflections on the Origin and Spread of Nationalism*. New York: Verso.

Appadurai, Arjun. 1996. *Modernity at Large: Cultural Dimensions of Globalization*. Minneapolis: University of Minnesota Press.

---

[31] This band has more than one eponym album.

Aquin, Hubert. 1988. "The Art of Defeat." *Writing Quebec: Selected Essays by Hubert Aquin*. Ed. by Anthony Purdy. Edmonton: University of Alberta Press. 67-76.

Beaudin, Maurice and André Leclerc. 1993. "Economie acadienne contemporaine." *L'Acadie des Maritimes*. Ed. by Jean Daigle. Moncton : Chaire d'études acadiennes Université de Moncton. 251-298.

Bourque, Denis and Chantal Richard. 2014. *Les Conventions Nationales – Tome 1*. Moncton : Institut d'études Acadiennes.

Brault, Michel and Pierre Perrault. *L'Acadie, l'Acadie ?!?* (Ottawa : Office National du Film du Canada, 1971). DVD.

Caldwell, Gary and Eric Waddell. *Les Anglophones du Québec : de majoritaires à minoritaires*. Québec : Institut québécois de recherche sur la culture.

Certeau, Michel de. 1984. *The Practise of Everyday Life*. Trans. By Steven Rendall. Berkeley: University of California Press.

Couturier-LeBlanc, Gilberte, Alcide Godin and Aldéo Renaud. 1993. "L'enseignement français dans les Maritimes, 1604-1992". *L'Acadie des Maritimes*. Ed. by Jean Daigle. Moncton : Chaire d'études acadiennes Université de Moncton. 543-586.

Daigle, Jean. 1993. "L'Acadie de 1604 à 1763, synthèse historique". *L'Acadie des Maritimes*. Ed. by Jean Daigle. Moncton : Chaire d'études acadiennes Université de Moncton. 1-43.

Falkert, Anika. 2010. *Le français acadien des Iles-de-la-Madeleine : étude de la variation phonétique*. Paris : L'Harmattan.

Frémont, Armand. 1999. *La Région : Espace vécu*. 2nd édition. Paris : Flammarion.

Gladu, André. *Tintamarre : la piste Acadie en Amérique* (Ottawa: Office National du Film du Canada, 2005). DVD.

Jobb, Dean. 2005. *The Cajuns: A People's Story of Exile and Triumph*. Hoboken, NY: Wiley.

Lafreniere, Alphonse. 1971. *La Commission de planification académique de l'Université de Moncton*. Vol.1. Moncton.

LeBlanc, Raymond-Guy. 1992. *Cri de Terre : poèmes*. 3rd edition. Moncton : Editions d'Acadie.

Leblanc, Robert A. 1983. "Les migrations acadiennes". *Du Continent perdu à l'archipel retrouvé : Le Québec et l'Amérique française*. Ed. by Dean R. Louder and Eric Waddell. Québec : Presses de l'Université Laval. 137-162.

Lefebvre, Henri. 1974. "La production de l'espace". *L'Homme et la société* 31, no. 31-32 : 15-32.

Le Ménestrel, Sara. 1999. *La voie des Cadiens*. Paris : Belin.

Longfellow, Henry Wadsworth. 1916. *Evangeline, a Tale of Acadie.* Boston: Houghton Mifflin.

Louder, Dean R. and Eric Waddell, Ed. 1983. *Du Continent perdu à l'archipel retrouvé : Le Québec et l'Amérique française.* Québec : Presses de l'Université Laval.

Maillet, Antonine. 1974. *La Sagouine : Pièce pour une femme seule.* Montréal : Léméac.

Melgar, María Cristina. 2009. "Mourning and Creativity." Ed. by Leticia Glocer Fiorini, Thierry Bokanowski, and Sergio Lewkowicz. *On Freud's "Mourning and Melancholia."* London: Karnac.

Nancy, Jean-Luc. 2011. *Partir, le départ : petite conférence.* Paris : Bayard.

Rose-Redwood, Reuben, Derek Alderman and Moaz Azaryahu. 2010. "Geographies of toponymic inscription: new directions in critical place-name studies." *Progress in Human Geography.* 34, no 4: 453-470.

Roy, Michel. 1978. *L'Acadie perdue.* Montréal : Editions Québec-Amérique.

Rudin, Ronald. 2011. "Kouchibouguac: Representations of a Park in Acadian Popular Culture ". *A Century of Parks Canada 1911-2011.* Ed. by Claire Elizabeth Campbell. Calgary: University of Calgary Press. 205-233.

Said, Edward W. 2002. *Reflections on Exile and Other Essays.* Cambridge, Mass: Harvard Uinversity Press.

Thériault, Léon. 1993. "L'Acadie de 1763 à 1990, synthèse historique". *L'Acadie des Maritimes.* Ed. by Jean Daigle. Moncton : Chaire d'études acadiennes Université de Moncton. 45-92.

Tuan, Yi-Fu. 1991. "Language and the Making of Place: A Narrative-Descriptive Approach." *Annals of the Association of American Geographers.* 81, no 4: 684-696.

Vernex, Jean-Claude. 1979. *Les Acadiens.* Paris : Editions Entente.

—. 1993. "Space and Sense of Place: The Example of the Acadians in New Brunswick". *French America: Mobility, Identity, and Minority Experience Across the Continent.* Ed. by Dean R. Louder and Eric Waddell. Trans.by Franklin Philip. Baton Rouge: Louisiana University Press. 191-211.

Westphal, Bertrand. 2011. *Geocriticism: Real and Fictional Spaces.* Trans. by Robert T. Tally Jr. London: Palgrave-Macmillan.

Zumthor, Paul. 1990. *Oral poetry: An Introduction.* Trans. By Kathryn Murphy-Judy. Minneapolis : University of Minnesota Press.

—. 2008 . "Oralité." *Intermédialités.*12 : 169-199.

CHAPTER THIRTEEN

UTILISATION DE LA PERIPHRASE DANS LES TOPONYMES NON OFFICIELS DU QUEBEC

EKATERINA ISAEVA

Aujourd'hui, les médias, publicités, enseignes des rues, guides et sites touristiques abondent en périphrase de noms de lieux. Ce phénomène linguistique et culturel s'explique par le fait que, avec le temps, l'informativité d'un nom de lieu se fait incomplète ou s'efface. Les Toponymes Périphrastiques (TP) recèlent non seulement la situation géographique, des caractéristiques réelles ou anciennes, la spécialisation économique d'une région, mais également d'autres spécificités ou une information complémentaire d'un lieu par rapport aux toponymes officiels qui les désignent avec moins de précision. Il est de notoriété courante que la ville de Saint-Pétersbourg, en Russie, possède différents surnoms tels que la Palmyra du Nord, la Venise du Nord, la Ville sur la Néva, Deuxième capitale ou Capitale culturelle, tandis que, en période soviétique, on la nommait encore Ville de Lénine, Berceau de la Révolution, Ville des deux révolutions. À son tour, la France est riche de la nomination non officielle de ses objets géographiques : Lyon – Capitale des Gaules, Toulouse – Ville rose, Paris – Ville-lumière, Toulon – Port du Levant.

Le Québec, province francophone du Canada, n'a pas évité ce phénomène de langue et de culture. La recherche de l'identité nationale après la Révolution Tranquille des années 1960-1970 incite les Québécois à restituer leur mémoire historique se traduisant par l'apparition des nominations parallèles, des surnoms ou périphrases des noms de lieux du Québec (Dorion & Lahoud, 2013). Ainsi, la ville de Montréal possède plus de trente-cinq surnoms, tandis que la capitale québécoise, la ville de Québec, a reçu trente nouvelles nominations périphrastiques et la province elle-même sept : la Belle Province, Frogland, la Presqu'Amérique, la Terre de Caïn, le Tibet catholique des neiges… Les exemples cités expliquent le fait que les surnoms ou les toponymes périphrastiques n'ont pas subi l'usure du temps parce qu'ils sont de consommation populaire (Dorion & Lahoud, 2013).

Les surnoms de lieux ou les toponymes non officiels, ou encore les toponymes périphrastiques restent peu étudiés. Néanmoins, il existe des banques de données des surnoms des noms de lieux constitués par Kane et Alexander (Kane & Alexander, 1979), Dorion et Lahoud (Dorion & Lahoud, 2013) ou même le *Dictionnaire des noms de lieux non officiels de la Russie* (Ahmetova, 2015). Une large variété de toponymes périphrastiques présents dans le français du Québec m'a incitée à les analyser et à en faire une classification dans une approche de langue et de culture, ce qui présente l'objectif principal de cet article. Le matériel de ma recherche a été recueilli avant tout dans la banque de données et le *corpus* des surnoms du Québec, constitué par le chercheur québécois Henri Dorion et publié dans son livre *Le Québec autrement dit* (Dorion & Lahoud, 2013), la base de données de la Commission de toponymie du Québec, ainsi que grâce aux réponses reçues auprès des étudiants québécois de l'Université Laval, située dans la ville du Québec, qui font leur stage linguistique à l'Université d'État des Sciences Humaines de Russie.

Mais avant de présenter les résultats de l'analyse verbo-culturelle des toponymes périphrastiques du Québec, je considère important de m'arrêter brièvement sur la périphrase qui est une unité stable relevant du domaine de la phraséologie. Les dictionnaires linguistiques (DEL, 1990) donnent les définitions suivantes :

> La périphrase (du grec περίφρασις, signifiant expression descriptive ou même allégorie) est une figure de style qui permet de désigner, d'une manière indirecte et descriptive, des objets ou des phénomènes réels principalement de l'ordre émotionnel, expressif ou évaluatif.

À titre d'exemple, l'expression "un ami vert" se veut désigner la forêt, alors que l'expression "le second pain" renvoie aux pommes de terre. Dans la périphrase, au premier plan, sont avancés une qualité ou un trait qui se présentent comme essentiels dans un contexte et une situation socioculturels concrets. Ainsi, l'objectif principal de la périphrase sert à "accentuer l'expression du texte, l'efficacité d'un énoncé" (DEL, 1990). Une des particularités foncières de la langue étant celle de transmettre le même sens par différents procédés y compris par la nomination secondaire (Telia, 1977), les expressions périphrastiques détiennent une information complémentaire qui permet de présenter une nouvelle image de l'objet.

En tant que figure stylistique, la périphrase est utilisée dans des noms de lieux en les remplaçant par une expression imagée contenant plusieurs mots et ainsi plus d'information. La raison de la création d'un toponyme périphrastique se retrouve, à notre égard, dans le désir des individus, s'identifiant à la même langue et à la même culture, de présenter une qualité ou une valeur importante d'un lieu, partagée de tous et qui reste gravée dans la mémoire collective d'un peuple (Isaeva, 2007). Il est à noter, également, que les toponymes périphrastiques, tout en fonctionnant comme des unités de discours relevant de la nomination secondaire, sont non seulement riches d'expression, mais contiennent du jugement du monde et de soi-même (Dorjieva, 2011). Donc, il serait possible de proposer la définition suivante d'un toponyme périphrastique : "nom substitué à un nom de lieu officiel contenant de l'information complémentaire relevant de la valeur collective partagée".

La toponymie du Québec, dont la formation a commencé avant la pénétration des Européens en Amérique du Nord, reflète aussi bien les particularités géographiques que celles de la culture autochtone ou francophone du Québec (Dorjieva, 1910). Dans ce contexte, les noms de lieux périphrastiques du Québec représentent un intérêt incontestable à l'étude dans une approche verbo-culturelle, c'est-à-dire, d'une part, à l'analyse des topolexèmes comme des unités de langue et, d'autre part, à l'étude de leur composante culturelle.

Ainsi, j'ai étudié, en premier lieu, la structure des TP qui se présente sous forme constituée de deux parties, dont la première est souvent composée des mots suivants : capitale ; village ; pays ; région ; forêt ; bassin ; île ; porte, porte d'entrée ; perle ; berceau ; reine ; royaume ; paradis ; jardin ; œil ; cœur ; carrefour ; grenier.

L'analyse quantitative effectuée démontre que le plus grand nombre de TP (135)[1] inclut le mot "capitale" souvent avec la précision "mondiale" : la capitale des Bois-Francs (Arthabaska)[2] ; la capitale mondiale du bleuet (Dolbeau-Mistassini). Selon Henri Dorion (Dorion & Lahoud, 2013), il ne s'agit pas ici de la notion politique ou territoriale du terme, mais surtout des caractéristiques supérieures (industrielles, culturelles et autres) que ce lieu comporte. L'adjectif "mondial" ajouté au terme de "capitale" est employé souvent affectueusement ou ironiquement.

Le lexique comportant les noms des pays et des régions du monde (53) est largement représenté par les TP dans lesquels la comparaison de la province du Québec se fait par rapport aux autres lieux (un autre pays, une autre région du monde), qui servent de prototype ou de modèle de référence. Le Québec et ses régions sont comparés le plus souvent à la Sibérie par association au froid qu'il fait : la Sibérie du Québec (Abitibi) ;

---

[1] Le chiffre indique le nombre d'exemples relevés dans le *corpus* analysé.
[2] Entre parenthèses est donné le toponyme officiel.

à la Suisse pour son caractère montagneux : la Petite Suisse du Québec (Bois-Franc), la Mini-Suisse québécoise (Kinnear's Mills, région de) ; à la Russie : la Petite Russie (Guyenne) ; à la Belgique : la Nouvelle-Belgique (Namur). Bien souvent, la précision "petite" ou "nouvelle" est relative à l'ethnicité.

Ensuite, ont été analysés vingt-trois TP avec la composante "pays" : le Pays des chutes (Côté-de-Beaupré) ; le Doux pays (Kamouraska) ; vingt-trois topolexèmes avec la composante "Porte/Porte d'entrée", se rapportant aussi bien à une région qu'aux lieux plus petits situés à l'orée d'une région connue : la Grande porte de l'Amérique (Saint-Laurent, fleuve) ; la Porte orientale du Canada (Québec) ; la Porte des Cantons-de-l'Est (Saint-Alphonse-de-Granby) ; la Porte d'entrée du parc de la Gaspésie (Sainte-Anne-des-Monts). Cette liste de TP est suivie de quinze topolexèmes avec la composante "le berceau" qui désigne l'origine d'un phénomène ou d'un événement géohistorique, industriel, socio-culturel, scientifique ou ludique tels que le Berceau de la Nouvelle-France (Québec) ou le Berceau de l'industrie chimique (Shawinigan). Les mots "perle, joyau", comme une partie composante d'une métaphore, donnent treize TP imagés : la Perle de l'Estrie (Coaticook) ; la Perle du lac Saint-Jean (Roberval) ; la Perle du fjord (Sainte-Rose-du-Nord). Ensuite ont été analysés douze TP avec les mots « reine ou princesse » et cinq TP avec le mot "royaume" qui représentent, dans la plupart des cas, la haute qualité d'un lieu ou d'une industrie, mais également qui donnent des qualifications ironiques : la Reine de la Côte-Nord (Baie-Comeau) ; la Princesse de l'Estrie (Granby) ; la Reine du papier (Kénogami). Le *corpus* analysé inclut onze TP avec l'insulonyme (nomination d'une île) dans lesquels une caractéristique ironique d'un lieu n'est pas rare : la Plus grande île privée du monde (Anticosti, île d') ; l'Ile des débrouillards (Canuel, île). L'oïkonyme "village" a été révélé dans dix TP, comportant l'image de la riche faune et flore du Québec : le Village de l'oie blanche (Baie-du-Febvre) ; le Village des lilas (Cap-à-l'Aigle). Les métaphores "paradis" et "jardin" entrent dans quatre TP chacune : le Paradis des artistes (Baie-Saint-Paul) ; le Jardin du Nord (Arundel). Il faut également porter attention aux TP, peu nombreux, avec les composantes "carrefour" (2) : le Carrefour du Nord (Chibougamau) ; "forêt" (2) : la Forêt enchantée (Fort-Témiscamingue, parc du) ; "bassin" (2) : le Bassin laitier du Québec (Coaticook, région de) ; "grenier" (2) : le Grenier du Canada (Hébertville, région d'). Les TP ayant les composantes antroponymiques "l'œil" (2) : l'Œil du Québec (Babel, mont), "le cœur" (2) : le Cœur forestier du Québec (Dolbeau), représentent souvent le centre de la région, en plus de traits spécifiques d'un lieu.

Les toponymes périphrastiques, qui possèdent, dans la première partie, les mots susmentionnés, se rapportent le plus souvent à la province du Québec, à ses régions et à ses sources hydrauliques. À cet égard, la catégorie "Les régions du Québec" est la plus nombreuse.

Analysons maintenant la deuxième composante du TP qui attribue de l'information complémentaire ou une valeur ajoutée à un lieu, parce qu'il est souvent lié non seulement à l'image pittoresque incontestable du Québec, mais également à l'importance historique ou culturelle que ce lieu évoque pour les Québécois et qui, comme je viens de le mentionner, représente la raison pour laquelle ce TP a été créé.

En premier lieu, l'image du Québec représentée par les TP est liée à ses traits paramétriques ou physiques ainsi qu'aux différentes couleurs, qui ont trait, souvent, au relief, à la flore et au climat de la province.

Dans le premier groupe sont inclus les TP avec les mots désignant la forme, la couleur et l'apparence d'un lieu :

- L'Île qui penche (Anticosti, île d'). Référence[3] : L'ensemble de l'île ressemble à une immense plate-forme qui s'est inclinée vers le sud. Ainsi on retrouve beaucoup de falaises sur la rive nord et surtout une pente douce du côté sud.
- Les Îles percées (Boucherville, îles de). Référence : Le fleuve, en cet endroit, est parsemé d'îles, si près les unes des autres qu'elles semblent entrecoupées par plusieurs ruisseaux.
- La Ville du rocher (Grand-Mère). Référence : Grand-Mère est ainsi dénommée à cause d'une légende amérindienne née de la forme d'un rocher qui se situait dans le Saint-Maurice. En effet, un énorme rocher ressemblant à la silhouette d'une vieille dame séparait les chutes de Grand-Mère en deux.
- Le Pays des chutes (Côte-de-Beaupré). Référence : La Côte-de-Beaupré se distingue par ses nombreuses chutes et gorges offrant des panoramas impressionnants.
- Le Village blanc (Saint-Michel-de-Bellechasse). Référence : Le cœur du village constitue un ensemble de maisons de bois peintes en blanc.
- Le Pays bleu (Lac-Saint-Jean, région du). Référence : C'est la région du plus grand lac du Québec dont la couleur lui a conféré ce nom.

---

[3] La grande majorité des références présentées dans cet article proviennent d'une source dont la qualité est incontestable. Il s'agit de l'ouvrage *Voyage à travers le Québec, Villes et villages du Québec* (référence complète de cet ouvrage dans la section référence en fin d'article).

- La Région verte (Lanaudière). Référence : La région offre un cadre propice aux randonnées nature et aux découvertes culturelles.

Le groupe suivant est composé des TP qui représentent le climat du Québec et notamment son hiver rigoureux et son été chaud. Ainsi, les notions de vent, nordicité, neige, été indien, saisons sont les parties intégrantes de ces TP :

- La Capitale de la neige, la Capitale de la nordicité, la Capitale des vents (Québec). Références : Les sports d'hiver et le Carnaval de Québec ainsi que la neige abondante et toutes ses variations procurent ces surnoms à la ville de Québec, sans compter le relief élevé et montagneux où le vent souffle fort, en hiver comme en été.
- La Ville aux quatre vents (Montréal). Référence : Les vents du nord-est provoqués par l'effet de vallée ne sont jamais chauds. Les régions près du fleuve, qui subissent ce vent au printemps, vent qui passe par-dessus les eaux encore froides, reçoivent donc de l'air froid.
- La Ville aux deux saisons (Québec). Référence : Bien qu'ayant un climat continental avec quatre saisons définies, Québec, tout comme sa région, se distingue surtout par un hiver long et froid et un été chaud.

Parallèlement à l'image du Québec, la valeur concrète ou utilitaire liée à la flore, à la faune, aux ressources naturelles, à la puissance économique ou industrielle de la province, au tourisme, à la science et à l'éducation est un trait caractéristique de la province et constitue des TP.

Au temps des premières colonies de la Nouvelle-France, les relations et les rapports des administrations, des missions religieuses ainsi que les journaux de voyage des premiers explorateurs de l'Amérique de Nord abondent en description de la flore et de la faune de cette région (Isaeva, 2006). Le *corpus* des TP analysés comprend, en premier lieu, les noms du monde végétal :

- Bleuet : le Pays des bleuets (Lac-Saint-Jean, région du). Référence : La région du Lac-Jean est bien connue, entre autres, pour ses bleuets et les paysages ceinturant le lac sont dominés par les bleuetières.
- Canneberge : la Capitale de la canneberge (Baie-du-Febvre). Référence : La région des Bois-Francs développe l'industrie de la

canneberge qui est devenue la plus importante culture fruitière au Québec.

- Lilas : le Village des lilas (Cap-à-l'Aigle). Référence : Selon une longue tradition, les passionnés d'horticulture se côtoient ici au grand plaisir des résidents et des visiteurs. Solidairement, les résidents de la rue Saint-Raphaël ont planté des lilas sur les parterres autour de leur maison ou autour des nombreux gîtes et auberges pour visiteurs. En marchant sur la rue principale de Cap-à-l'Aigle, les visiteurs peuvent admirer les aménagements paysagers authentiques de ce village.
- Érable : le Paradis de l'érable (Beauce). Référence : 98 % du sirop d'érable produit au Québec provient de la Beauce.

Des toponymes périphrastiques du Québec sont composés, également, d'autres noms d'arbres, de végétaux, de fruits et légumes comme pommier, lin, fruits de forêt, haricots, pommes de terre.

Après les TP représentant le monde végétal du Québec, analysons maintenant ceux qui contiennent les noms d'oiseaux, de poissons et d'animaux :

- Oiseaux : le Village de l'oie blanche (Baie-du-Febvre). Référence : Chaque année, de mars à mai, Baie-du-Febvre accueille près de 500 000 oies blanches en migration vers leur lieu de nidification ; le Pays de l'oie blanche (Nicolet, région du). Référence : Nicolet est sans contredit la ville la plus peuplée de ce secteur du pays de l'oie blanche.
- Poissons : le Village des petits poissons de chenaux (La Pérade). Référence : Depuis plus de soixante-dix ans, le Centre de pêche Marchand de Sainte-Anne-de-la-Pérade est l'endroit par excellence de la pêche aux petits poissons des chenaux, une activité hivernale unique en son genre ; le Royaume de la ouananiche (Lac-Saint-Jean, région du). Référence : Ce saumon atlantique fait la fierté et est l'emblème de la région depuis 1988.
- Animaux marins : la Capitale du crabe des neiges (Sainte-Thérèse-de-Gaspé). Référence : Le surnom est donné à ce lieu grâce à l'industrie de la pêche et son havre de pêche animé par les morutiers, les crabiers et les homardiers.

Si le monde végétal et animal a été bien examiné et décrit dans leurs relations et journaux de voyage par les premiers découvreurs du Canada à partir du XVIe siècle, ses ressources naturelles, et surtout les minéraux, ne sont explorés qu'au XXIe siècle. Les noms de minéraux et de métaux figurent dans les TP du Québec, c'est pourquoi il semble évident de les mettre dans une catégorie spéciale :

- Minéraux : le Pays de l'amiante (Thetford, région de). Référence : L'exploitation de l'amiante pendant plus d'un siècle a laissé des cicatrices à la grandeur du territoire, sous la forme d'immenses mines à ciel ouvert.
- Métaux : la Capitale du cuivre (Saint-Tite). Référence : Bien que l'exploitation minière ait pris fin en 1999 en raison de l'épuisement des réserves de minerai de cuivre, le surnom est resté ; la Capitale du fer (Sept-Îles). Référence : La région a connu une croissance économique significative dans les années 1950 grâce à l'essor de l'industrie minière.

Les ressources naturelles sont la base du développement de l'économie en général et c'est pourquoi ont également été analysés les TP désignant des industries et les domaines de l'économie :

- La Capitale de l'acier (Tracy). Référence : La ville est située en plein cœur de la vallée sidérurgique et métallurgique de Sorel.
- La Capitale agroalimentaire du Québec (Saint-Hyacinthe). Référence : La richesse de son sol et la clémence relative de son climat ont placé Saint-Hyacinthe à l'avant garde du développement agroalimentaire.
- Le Berceau de l'industrie chimique (Shawinigan). Référence : L'économie de cette région est fondée sur la minéralurgie et sur l'industrie pétrochimique.
- Le Bassin laitier du Québec (Coaticook, région de). Référence : La laiterie, spécialisée dans les produits "À l'ancienne", s'approvisionne dans les nombreuses fermes laitières de sa région.
- La Reine du papier (Kénogami). Référence : Une des premières usines de production de papier a été construite dans cette agglomération.

Les toponymes périphrastiques, dont la deuxième composante se rapporte aux domaines du tourisme, de la science et du savoir, ont été analysés tout de suite après la catégorie susmentionnée étant donné que ces domaines sont proches de l'économie :

- L'Île de Bacchus (Orléans, île d'). Référence : C'est Jacques Cartier qui, en 1535, à la vue de cette île verdoyante, la surnomme "île de Bacchus", en raison des vignes sauvages qui y poussent.
- La capitale de l'hébergement et de la restauration (Rivière-du-Loup). Référence : L'industrie touristique constitue un apport économique considérable pour la région. Des emplois permanents et saisonniers dépendent uniquement du secteur de l'hébergement et de la restauration.
- La Ville de la haute technologie (Bromont). Référence : En 2012, l'Université de Sherbrooke, IBM et Teledyne-Dalsa y inaugurent un centre de recherche et développement en microélectronique.

L'histoire, la culture, le sport et les distractions (plaisirs gastronomiques inclus) occupent une place importante et sont des valeurs partagées par les Québécoises et les Québécois et ce fait se reflète également dans les noms de lieux non officiels.

Il existe également des TP dont les références historiques sont liées aux premiers explorateurs du continent nord-américain, à la colonie de la Nouvelle-France et à l'histoire du Québec :

- La Cité des pionniers (Lachine). Référence : L'ancienneté des lieux dont les origines remontent au début de la colonie de la Nouvelle-France a sans doute inspiré ce surnom.
- Le Village des Patriotes (Saint-Denis). Référence : Est situé ici un musée appelé la Maison nationale des Patriotes qui présente l'histoire du mouvement patriote qui fut dirigé par le plus illustre des résidents du village, Wolfred Nelson.
- Le Berceau de la Nouvelle-France, le Berceau de l'Amérique française (Québec). Référence : La capitale de la province est considérée comme un des plus anciens lieux de peuplement de la Nouvelle-France.

Dans cette même catégorie, sont entrés des TP mémoriaux avec les noms des personnalités historiques, politiques, culturelles aussi bien que ceux des personnages littéraires :

- Le Pays de Papineau (Lièvre, vallée de la). Référence : Louis-Joseph Papineau (1786-1871), politicien québécois.
- Le Pays de Maria Chapdelaine (Mistassine, région de). Référence : Maria Chapdelaine est un personnage d'un roman rédigé en 1913 par l'écrivain français Louis Hémon.

- Le Pays de Gilles Vigneault (Natashquan). Référence : Gilles Vigneault (1928-…), poète, auteur-compositeur-interprète québécois.

Les TP comportant des composantes architecturales, folkloriques et artistiques se retrouvent dans la catégorie que nous pourrions nommer "Patrimoine culturel". De multiples églises, clochers, moulins représentent une image formée d'éléments du paysage architectural et artistique du Québec :

- Le Village des cinq églises (Inverness). Référence : Aujourd'hui, il y a ici plusieurs églises rappelant la diversité confessionnelle et culturelle du village.
- Le Village aux moulins (Mansonville). Référence : Selon la carte Walling de 1864, il y avait, dans Mansonville, cinq moulins (un à tisser, deux à scie, un à tanner et un à grain).
- Le Paradis des artistes (Baie-Saint-Paul). Référence : Peintres, sculpteurs, musiciens viennent régulièrement ici pour décrire les beaux paysages de la région.
- La Capitale de la sculpture de bois (Saint-Jean-Port-Joli). Référence : La Biennale de la sculpture, un événement artistique unique, se déroule dans cette région.

Le folklore, et notamment les contes fantastiques du Québec, a engendré de nombreux TP dont les suivants :

- La Forêt enchantée (Fort-Témiscamingue, parc du). Référence : Des légendes sur de nombreuses cérémonies spirituelles qui avaient lieu dans ce site sont à l'origine de ce surnom.
- L'Île des sorciers (Orléans, île d'). Référence : Les insulaires ont été effrayés, jadis, par des feux follets qu'ils considéraient comme la manifestation de sorciers.

Il est notoire que le sport, et surtout le hockey sur glace, joue un rôle important dans la vie des Québécois. Néanmoins, les TP de cette catégorie comprennent également d'autres sports tels que la voile, le ski de fond, la motoneige, l'escalade, le vélo, la randonnée pédestre et la plongée sous-marine :

- La Capitale de la voile (Berthier-sur-Mer). Référence : C'est en été que le lieu prend tout son sens grâce à des accès publics au fleuve

comme la marina avec emplacement pour 80 bateaux et services
pour plaisanciers.
- La Capitale du ski de fond (Morin Heights). Référence : Tout le
  village est un gros centre de ski de fond.
- La Capitale de la motoneige (Saint-Zénon). Référence : Des
  aménagements faits pour développer le sport d'hiver.
- Le Berceau de l'escalade au Québec (Val-David). Référence :
  L'école Passe-Montagne y forme des grimpeurs depuis une
  trentaine d'années.
- Le Carrefour du vélo (Haut-Richelieu). Référence : C'est une piste
  cyclable séparée des routes sur pratiquement toute sa longueur
  (presque 50 km).

Un groupe assez important de TP se retrouve dans la catégorie que
nous dénommerons "distraction, loisirs et vacances". Au Québec,
annuellement, ont lieu différents festivals locaux et internationaux dans le
domaine de la littérature, de la musique, de l'art et autres, ce qui se reflète
dans la nomination non officielle des noms de lieux :

- La Capitale des loisirs de l'Outaouais (Aylmer). Référence : C'est
  un véritable paradis des golfeurs et c'est encore le site de
  l'hippodrome Connaught.
- La Capitale des parcs et du bien-être (Granby). Référence : La
  Montérégie offre des paysages spectaculaires ou les vergers et
  vignobles tiennent la vedette ; la région regorge de produits du
  terroir.
- La Capitale mondiale des casinos en ligne (Kahnawake). Référence
  : Malgré la vive opposition de la population à l'expansion des jeux
  d'argent dans leur communauté, ce territoire a été transformé en
  capitale mondiale des casinos virtuels.
- La Capitale de la chanson (Petite-Vallée). Référence : Le Festival
  de la chanson est un concours musical annuel qui a lieu à Petite-
  Vallée, en Gaspésie, depuis 1983.
- La Capitale du polar, la Capitale du roman policier (Saint-Pacôme).
  Référence : La Société du roman policier de Saint-Pacôme, fondée
  en mars 2001, récompense chaque année l'auteur du meilleur
  roman policier québécois francophone publié.
- Le Berceau de la villégiature au Canada (La Malbaie). Référence :
  Riche de plus de deux siècles de villégiature, cet immense territoire
  a su attirer très tôt les bourgeois bien nantis de la grande société
  nord-américaine, à la recherche de calme, d'air pur et de beauté.

Les distractions gastronomiques ou "les plaisirs du palais" sont très appréciés chez les Québécoises et les Québécois dont la cuisine est composée de différents mets nationaux et internationaux. Les noms de plats entrent souvent dans les TP de la catégorie gastronomique :

- Le Berceau de la poutine (Warwick). Référence : La poutine est un mets d'origine québécoise constitué de frites et de fromage en grains (cheddar frais) que l'on recouvre généralement d'une sauce brune.
- La Capitale des fromages fins du Québec (Warwick). Référence : Les fromages Du Village 1860 témoignent du savoir-faire des maîtres fromagers de cette région.
- La Capitale de la poutine (Victoriaville). Référence : Depuis plus de vingt-cinq ans, le restaurant Max Poutine, dans la région de Victoriaville, a su réinventer la poutine avec plus de cent variétés au menu.
- La Capitale de l'omelette géante, la Capitale gastronomique de l'Estrie (Granby). Référence : Depuis 1988, des chefs se réunissent ici pour faire une omelette de 15 000 œufs.
- La Capitale des plaisirs du palais (Saint-Prime). Référence : Cette région est connue pour le fromage réputé qu'on y fabrique.

Et, enfin, un autre groupe très important de TP représente les traits distinctifs de la société québécoise qui sont décrits avec ironie et humour, souvent par les habitants eux-mêmes. Les TP qualitatifs de cette catégorie caractérisent aussi bien la province du Québec que ses habitants :

- La Ville la plus drôle du Québec (Drummondville). Référence : dans les années 1980, la revue humoristique *CROC* avait élu Drummondville "Ville la plus drôle du Québec".
- La Capitale du bout du monde (La Reine). Référence : L'autodéfinition ironique de la Capitale mondiale du bout du monde caractérise assez bien ses résidents.
- La Plus grande île privée du monde (Anticosti, île d'). Référence : C'est la plus grande île du Québec.
- L'Ile des débrouillards (Canuel, île). Référence : L'autodéfinition de cette petite île, entre le rivage et la pointe ouest de l'Île Saint-Barnabé, à Rimouski.
- Frogland (Québec, province de). Référence : Le mot anglais *frog*, dont les anglophones ont qualifié les Français, a donné ce surnom pour désigner et la France et le Québec.

Si les noms de lieux officiels créés pendant la période de la Nouvelle-France comportaient la composante relevant de "la richesse matérielle" (Isaeva 2006), les toponymes périphrastiques n'en contiennent pas beaucoup :

- Le Pays du ventre en or (Abitibi). Référence : "Moi, j'viens d'un pays qui a l'ventre en or" chantait avec entrain Raoul Duguay au sujet de sa région.
- La Cité de l'or (Bourlamaque). Référence : Ici se trouve la plus profonde mine d'or du Canada accessible aux touristes.
- Le Village du mille dollars (L'Anse-Saint-Jean). Référence : De récents travaux d'exploration en profondeur ont dévoilé que les entrailles de la région regorgent, sur le plan minier, d'un potentiel notable.
- L'Île aux trésors (Orléans, île d'). Référence : Le monde végétal de cette île québécoise est un vrai trésor !

L'analyse effectuée permet de tirer une première conclusion en ce qui concerne l'information complémentaire véhiculée par les toponymes périphrastiques du Québec. Ceux-ci sont liés aux valeurs partagées et jugées importantes par les Québécois et insistent sur leur importance respective. La conscience interprétante des Québécois contribue à la création de multiples nominations secondaires ou périphrastiques des lieux qui reflètent l'histoire, la culture, la nature, l'économie et également des valeurs inhérentes à la société québécoise. Les TP des lieux du Québec révèlent des traits importants de l'identité des Québécois. Le plus grand nombre de toponymes périphrastiques comportant de l'information complémentaire par rapport aux noms de lieux officiels se rapporte à l'économie, au tourisme, à la science et aux loisirs. D'autres TP, assez nombreux, dans un ordre décroissant, concernent les domaines du monde végétal, du sport, du monde animal, des ressources naturelles, de l'histoire et de la mémoire collective, de la gastronomie, de l'humour, de l'architecture, du folklore et de l'art.

La recherche ultérieure de noms de lieux non officiels pourrait se finaliser en la constitution d'un dictionnaire des toponymes périphrastiques du Québec.

Références

Ahmetova, M.V. 2015. *De A-Aty à Yarsk. Dictionary of the Names of Non-Official Places* [Slovar' neoficial'nyh nazvanij naselennyh punktov]. Moscow: «Forum» Press.

Dorion, Henri & Pierre Lahoud. 2013. *Le Québec autrement dit et un tout du monde en surnoms.* Montréal, Québec : Les Éditions de l'Homme. 272 p. ISBN 978-2-7619-3251-6.

Dorjieva G.S. 2011a. *French Toponymies of Quebec (ethnolinguistic aspect)* [Frankofonnye toponimy Kvebeka (ètnolingvističeskij aspekt)]. Ulan-Ude. Bouriatie University Press. 352 p. ISBN 978-5-9793-0431

—. 2010b. *Natives' Toponymies of Quebec* / Ed. by L.V. Shulunova [Aborigennye toponimy Kvebeka: nauč. red. L.V. Šulunova]. Ulan-Ude. Bouriatie University Press. 204 p. ISBN 978-5-9793-0325-3

Isaeva E.V. 2008a. *Toponymical Processes of Verbalization of the Concept "Land of New France".* Nom. Socium. Culture. Material of the second Baikal international conference of onomastic (September 4-6 2008) [Toponimičeskie sredstva verbalizacii koncepta «Zemlja Novoj Francii» Imja. Socium." Kul'tura. Materialy II Bajkal'skoj meždunarodnoj onomastičeskoj konferencii (4-6 sentjabrja 2008g.)]. Ulan-Ude: Bouriatie University Press. P.78-82. 300p.

—. 2008b. Image Content as Part of the Concept of the "Land of New France" [Soderžanie obraznoj sostavljajušej koncepta «Zemlja «Novoj Francii»]. *Philological problems*, N°6: P.8-12. ISSN 1562-1391

Kane, Joseph N, and Gerald Alexander. 1979. *Nicknames and Sobriquets of U.S. Cities, States, and Countries.* Metuchen: Scarecrow Press.

Telia V.N. 1977. *Secondary Nomination and its Types. "Verbal Appointment: Types of Names":* under the writing of B.A. Serebrennikov [Vtoričnaja nominacija i ee vidy. Jazykovaja nominacija: Vidy naimenovanij / Ed. by B.A. Serebrennikov]. Moscow : Sciences [Nauka]. p. 84-112.

Commission de toponymie de Québec. 2016. *Montréal, valeur traditionnelle autochtone.* 10 janvier 2016. http://www.toponymie.gouv.qc.ca/ct/toposweb/fiche.aspx?no_seq=421 64

Moscow. 1990. *Soviet Encyclopedia : Encyclopedic Dictionary linguistic* / Ed. by V.N. Yartseva [«Sovetskaja ènciklopedija». "Lingvističeskij ènciklopedičeskij slovar' (LÈS)" pod redakciej V. N. Jarcevoj]. http://tapemark.narod.ru/les/#17

Voyage à travers le Québec. 2016. *Villes et villages du Québec.* 12-15 janvier 2016. http://grandquebec.com/villes-quebec

PART 4:

NOIR IN THE COUNTRYSIDE:
RURAL AREAS IN THE DETECTIVE NOVELS AND CRIME FILMS

CHAPTER FOURTEEN

THE STAGING OF THE MONTALBANO LANDSCAPE

ALESSANDRA BONAZZI

*Visitors are well advised, and are finally
prepared to enter the magic theatre on whose
stage the absent is made present, the present
made absent.*
—Gunnar Olsson

Andrea Camilleri's Geography lesson

In 1999 Andrea Camilleri intervened in *The construction of the Sicilian landscape: a debate between geographers and writers*. He, of course, was on the side of the writers and stated that, as "one who tells stories he invents," the only viable way for him is invention. Indeed, in the words of Ruben Monterosso, he defines himself as a novelist and therefore a man of great faith:

> And faith, as we know, in moving mountains, was the bane of cartographers, who couldn't draw any fixed map; with loss of caravans, hindrance of commerce, and disappearance of entire civilizations. Only the weakening of faith [...] made it possible to draw reliable maps (Camilleri, 1999, 191).

If novelists are thus the only ones still able to move mountains and object to the cartographic disenchantment of the world, then, Camilleri goes on to say, the problem becomes how to do it (Camilleri, 1999, 193). The strategy is usually to construct for their characters a land made up of different parts, shaping and structuring it from material reality. For Camilleri the construction of such a land means technically drafting a "literary geography" that remodulates and structures from scratch the pre-existing "real geography." And writers who design or erect an "ideal habitat for their characters" can be sorted into three categories: geographers, topographers and topologist-toponomasts. Geographers write about utopias or travels – Thomas More, Jonathan Swift, Jules Verne, and some examples of topographers are William Faulkner and Gabriel Garcia Marquez. On the contrary, the last category of topologist-toponomasts includes "Italian (especially Sicilian) writers" who prefer real locations, "allowing themselves to make what I would call slight shifts or rearrangements of a cityscape or a rural locale. But these shifts are slight, often hardly noticeable" (Camilleri, 1999, 194).

In his lesson Camilleri thus established an exquisitely Sicilian tendency (Luigi Pirandello, Vitaliano Brancati, Elio Vittorini) and admitted his propensity, as a Sicilian, to build a literary topology that *rearranges* the places of Sicily's real geography. Sicily functions as a geographical predicate of the topological and topographic character of its insular writers, and also offers itself as privileged narrative material. Camilleri's world is the Agrigento area and Porto Empedocle, which become, with *slight shifts*, the province of Montelusa and Vigàta. Both are home to Camilleri's historical novels as well as the latest adventures of Inspector Salvo Montalbano. But the matter is not limited to the remodeling of different bits of land to build an imaginary geography, made up of landscapes and places that evoke real ones. Anticipating Ogborne's remarks (Ogborne 2005-2006), Camilleri's narrative claims a near coincidence between words and space, between literary territory and geographical territory. And it is precisely in the "almost," i e in the *shift and the toponomastics*, that the road of invention is made visible. If "the problem of all science is to match the South Seas, their immense, jagged blue, with the blue map of the South Seas" (Magris, 2009, 25), we can say that Camilleri's problem goes in the opposite direction, that of reconstructing the immense, jagged blue of the South Seas starting with the blue geographical map. Camilleri's map is of western Sicily and a precise portion of its space (Porto Empedocle and the Agrigento area), and the problem gets solved by translating the measurements into vital topological deformations that give creative form to the tale (Vigàta, Montelusa, Marinella). This is as much as can be said of the relationship between geography and literature, as Camilleri said in 1999, even if, a few years later, Camilleri would come to grips with the practical effect of his theoretical geography lesson. Looking carefully at maps on the Agrigento and Porto Empedocle area, Camilleri would notice with surprise that distances, places and spatial relationships that form the geographic warp of the literary woof of the Montalbano detective novels, find their exact correspondence in the map space. The architects who submit this cartographic counterpoint to Camilleri's attention then edit a guide with twelve itineraries, accompanied by the systematic compilation of a geography of Montalbano's locales (Clausi and *al.*, 2006). Here is how the authors in the introduction comment on the surprise:

> the honesty and literary consistency that Camilleri has repeatedly spoken of concerning the construction of his "thrillers" also corresponded to a spatial, "physical" consistency if compared to the fishing village of Porto Empedocle. To a "cage," which, although not consciously structured a priori, had, however, to be present in the writer's head in order to make his stories work. (Clausi and *al.*, 2006, 16)

The topological structure then takes as its implicit narrative model the structure of the geographic dictation, and Camilleri's road of invention occupies the space that separates topography from topology. In other words, while it is always possible to place on the plane of reality "the immense, jagged blue" of the narrative, the threshold that separates the geography from his imagination is constantly blurred. A blurring that, from Edward Said onwards, we have learned to understand from the material scope of its semantic effects. The rhetoric that supports the geographic imagination in which Salvo Montalbano acts is a map with place names and boundaries that are at times *rearranged* (topology), a process that makes the totality of its discursive facts – urban landscapes, rural landscapes and seascapes – more complex, livelier and richer by virtue of the maps that draw them (topography).

A brief geography of Salvo Montalbano

From 1994 to 2016, there have been about thirty detective novels (crime fiction) whose hero is Salvo Montalbano. One thing must be immediately noted. The Inspector travels very little but is constantly on the move in the vicinity of Vigàta, spinning a dense web of literary and real locations.[1] Following Gianfranco Marrone's indications (2003), we can establish a habitual spatial behavior by which to outline a geographical hierarchy of the space from Marinella – where Montalbano lives and from which every narrative commences. A hierarchy that reverses the usual value rapport between center and periphery, by assigning to it the degree of greater value. The geographically peripheral island and Agrigento

---

[1] Montalbano's literary places, none of them far from Vigàta, are: Brancato (Racalmuto), Calapiano (Gagliano Castelferrato), Comisini (Comitini) Gallotta/Giardina (Giardina Gallotti), Montechiaro (Palma di Montechiaro) and Montereale (Realmonte).

province thus become semantically the central place against which to measure the value of everything that lies outside (Catania, Palermo, Rome, Milan, Genoa, Italy, Germany, Tunisia, South Africa). Beyond that, the Sicily of the Montalbano thrillers forgoes the literary tradition of the closed isolated place of the detective plot (Pezzotti, 2012), giving strategic weight instead to a Mediterranean Sea setting, whose geographic flows signal, first of all in literature, the fluid nature of the lines that organize contemporary space. Thus, peripheral Vigàta intercepts the global flows of international arms trafficking, goods and men, grafting them onto the crime plots of its local geography (Chu, 2011). In this way the periphery, or the island, takes on the threshold function of a space that connects proximity and distance.

To this first observation of scale and location must be added that of the critical function and identity of landscape. Marrone (2003, 221) explains its function by the so-called anthropic areas that charge the narrative locales with "deeper categories that provide its meaning" and contribute to the construction of identity of the hero and the other characters. And this reciprocal construction of identity and membership, this close relationship between the outer and inner landscape actively sustains the unfolding of the narrative. It suffices to recall that each novel opens with the description of the stretch of beach, sea and sky visible from the window of his house in Marinella, or how Montalbano uncovers the truth from his deep knowledge of the area, which he investigates by interpreting the codes of conduct rooted in the environment and place where the act of violence has occurred.

The shapes of the landscape are those of western Sicily and Porto Empedocle. As one literary critic has written, "Vigàta is the most invented center of the most typical Sicily" and its borders get stretched and deformed to the point of encompassing all of Sicily (Pezzotti, 2009). Nevertheless, the typicality of the landscapes in and around Vigàta is not traditional or, as Marrone says, of the picture postcard type, but also reveals its environmental decay, urban and suburban landscapes of never finished buildings, water tanks, anodized aluminum frames of houses, suburban condominiums, animal pens, illegally built seaside towns and the just as illegally built hotel next door to a Greek Temple. Beyond the urban blight sanctioned by crooked zoning laws and the political impotence of the authorities, there are also landscapes of extraordinary beauty: the Sicilian hinterland, the shorelines near Vigàta and the Scala dei Turchi. In short, the panorama is broad enough to encompass the gamut of contemporary Sicily. As for the rural areas, Camilleri says:

My Sicily is first of all the western part [...] cube homes amid the scorched earth. [...] Mine is the Sicily of Agrigento, Mazzara, that area there, that is Vigàta. (Scarpetti, Strano, 2004, 129)

Somewhere I've written, maybe in *The Terracotta Dog*, that Montalbano likes to cross the landscape of the harsh, arid, barren Sicily with its scrawny houses teetering on the hills, almost on the verge of collapsing. This is the Sicily that Montalbano likes, and whenever he can he leaves the main roads to take alternative paths and get a better view of those parched places. (Ferlita and *al.*, 2003, 14)

When the cultural landscape deteriorates, Montalbano veers toward political criticism. In the same year Camilleri gave his lesson on literary geography, his Montalbano detective novels were turned into a television series. While an average book publication sells more than 500,000 copies in a year, a television broadcast of the same work reaches 10 million viewers.[2] So Montalbano became a "hit" and the geography of his literary places was staged in TV media terms and transposed in the forms of TV drama, which in Italian is called by an improper use of the English term *fiction* – a term which, as we know, comes from the Latin *fingere*, in its threefold sense of model, imagine and simulate. With a sweep of the hand the TV transposition reversed the relationship between geographical imagination and reality, flattening the topology into a set of landscapes, and redefining the position of Montalbano's geography.

Let us dwell a moment on the triple effect of this move. The first is the change of direction in the relationship between topography and topology. On the one hand, Montalbano's literary geography establishes a precise relationship between topology and pre-existing material reality, the Porto Empedocle out of which Camilleri builds Vigàta. On the other hand, the geographical imagination of Vigàta concretely modifies the real world that precedes it: Porto Empedocle. It happens that the latter, in the wake of the literary and television success linked to Montalbano, decided to change its name to Porto Empedocle-Vigàta. And when Italian readers were outnumbered

---

[2] These figures only relate to Italy. The latest Inspector Montalbano survey, *The Pyramid of Mud*, aired in 2016. In all, 28 episodes have been aired from 1999 to the present. Among the TV drama spectators we must take into account those who later have become readers of the Montalbano novels. On the size of the Camilleri/Montalbano literary event, see the www.vigata.org website. In addition, the television rights have been sold in the United States, Canada, Latin America, Australia, France, Spain, Finland, Norway, Denmark, Sweden, Belgium, the Netherlands and Luxemburg. And further, in Hungary, Slovakia, the former Yugoslavia, Albania, Georgia, Bulgaria, Germany, England (BBC), Wales, Scotland, Romania and even in Iran.

by Italian viewers, this change had a really incisive effect on the tourist trade (Lo Piccolo, 2009). However, it was the international scale of the Montalbano "hit" (Rinaldi, 2012) which was the decisive factor of the renaming, which confirmed the original Montalbano geographic location and tried to attract all the tourists that the TV drama lures away from Ragusa. What Marrone calls "product of imagination" is the process that geographers simply call landscape. The second effect is the loss of the special dimension of each literary text. In (tele)vision language the referent, i.e. the object, performs the function of signifier. Thus, in the visual sign, the semiotic triangle is reduced to a line, or the segment that joins the referent-signifier with the signified. And all referents lie before us already organized in landscape form. By contrast, the literary text obliges us to interpret and imagine the landscapes assigned to the linear dimension of the written text, thus turning that line into a multi-dimensional structure (Socco, 1996). The final effect is immediately visible: the move from western Sicily to eastern Sicily. And then the transition from the literary geography in the staging of the landscape with its concrete action on reality.

The landscape goes on stage

As we read on the RAI (*Radiotelevisione Italiana*) website, "transposing Andrea Camilleri's novels into TV dramas" means "bringing onto television, one might say in real time, a literary phenomenon that is without equal: almost two million books sold in Italy, a publishing epidemic without end (www.montalbano.rai.it/HPprogramma). Here, in relation to this epidemic, we will deal exclusively with how the landscapes work, those places that are not part of the text but intrinsic to the visual terms of TV drama, those responsible for the spread of the Montalbano epidemic in a geographic area stretching from Norway to Japan, via Turkey.

The shift from the written landscape to its stage version requires first and foremost a radical restructuring and dislocation of the material of reality. As anticipated, the setting of the drama shifts to eastern Sicily, less compromised and decayed than the coast and the rugged hinterland of the Agrigento area. An excellent summary of the location is found in Sironi's thirteen bird's-eye shots that make up the opening theme: Scicli, Modica, Ragusa (World Heritage towns of UNESCO) and the Punta Secca lighthouse at Santa Croce Camerina , where Montalbano's house stands. As Sironi himself says:

> The triangle of the extreme south of Sicily, Porto Palo, Ragusa, Pozzallo, was just what we were looking for, and there we found Montalbano's

famous seaside home, which is the home of a Sicilian nobleman who in
1930 was issued a special government permit to build a house right on the
beach. But beyond that we wanted to find something that would allow us to
have images of the great Sicilian baroque, and there stood Scicli, Ragusa
and Modica. (Scarpetti, Strano, 2004, 139)

From here Vigàta and Montelusa, like every geographical landscape,
are assembled from an abstract synthesis of concrete landscapes: the
baroque Cathedral of Ragusa is the background of the Piazza of Vigàta,
while the police station is the Municipal building of Scicli. And a few
steps away are the police headquarters of Montelusa. The restaurant where
Montalbano dines is in Ragusa, while the flat rock of the walk to the dock
after lunch is located in Punta Secca. Lastly, to have a coffee in the central
square of Vigàta Montalbano must go to the Piazza Duomo in Ragusa Ibla.
As Clausi observes (2006, 357), "the choice of locations has privileged the
visual charm of place rather than the spatial-temporal coherence present in
the stories." The first observation tends toward a general aestheticization
of the landscapes. However Camilleri writes:

> So there is a novel Vigàta [...] and a television Vigàta, which is the
> gorgeous one of Scicli, Modica, etcetera. Now what happens to me is that
> when I write a new Montalbano I risk being influenced not so much by the
> television landscape, but rather by the *landscape* (Scarpetti, Strano, 2004,
> 139)

Here Camilleri senses that the issue cannot be reduced merely to the
aesthetic requalification of the landscape, i.e. the writing of an aesthetic
landscape text, but rather refers to the capacity of the landscape as such to
affect the topology of his literary invention. The TV drama does not just
build a series of spectacularly beautiful scenery, but assembles an
"*effective geography*, the same that affects the actual reality, transforming
its meaning and value" (Marrone, 2009, 223). The visual transposition also
affects the look of the characters, who inevitably are made more youthful.
The literary Montalbano is a bit shorter, with a mustache, not immediately
handsome, who chooses to live in one of the numerous illegally built
houses made up of three railroad rooms. His TV version is much younger
and more good-looking, and lives in a lavish aristocratic villa. In short, the
projection of the written word onto the TV screen requires, like any
translation, the betrayal of at least *one dimension* to guarantee a sense of
verisimilitude with respect to the image suggested by the linear structure
of the literary page.

But what happens during the TV drama's ten seasons, from 1999 to
2016, is the progressive depletion and systematic cleansing of the

geographical locations where the television plots of Montalbano are set. In other words, the world crowded with people, modern suburbs, dusty countryside, the walls overlaid with funeral notices, advertising and the attrition of time in the form of peeling plaster, and the hanging clothes and the plants on balconies, the all-too-human summation of an invented land, is gradually transformed into an empty, clean, quiet, rural movie set. Sometimes there remains some distant extra in the background and a monumental presence of the landscape itself. A landscape whose skyline deviates little from the urban one photographed by the Alinari brothers and, still earlier, from the layout of ideal Renaissance cities. Mitchell offers the best explanation of this process. In his analysis of English landscape painting, he draws attention to the meaning of the presence and placing of the local population in the picturesque scenes of Turner, Prout and Fielding:

> The ostensible picturesque subjects [...] are depicted with Turner's usual grandeur and poetry, but his foregrounds are unusually full of human activity that exceeds its nominal function as frame or complement to the view. The landscape, Turner's drawings seem to insist, is never empty; the tourists will discover it is already occupied. Other picturesque artists like Prout or Fielding typically make use of foreground figures, in carefully studied local costumes (Prout) or engaged in characteristic local activities (Fielding). But these place – and time – bound figures [...] are always subordinated to the scenes they frame. The juxtaposition enhances the power of the cultural and natural monuments, a power that belongs implicitly, not to the local figures who ignore them, but to the viewer of educated sensibilities who can appreciate them (Mitchell, 1994, 110).

With a kind of semantic hyperbole, screenwriters eliminate anything that may distract or disturb the process of their viewers' visual appropriation. So the television medium absolutizes the landscape, which acquires a strong predominance over the story, betraying its narrative mechanism while it heightens the value of a universally available landscape. By these means the border landscapes of the heterogeneous, crowded, compromised literary topology (the coast, Porto Empedocle, the scorched terrain) give way to the impeccable baroque of the urban centers (UNESCO Heritage Sites), and to the lovely rural villas and an appealing, embracing countryside. Emptied of people and machines, cleaned, sorted, suspended in time, the topological imagination has become both the set for the Montalbano stories and the pre-eminent semantic content. As such, it also establishes the best possible position from which to control the material production of the landscape and from which to see the landscape itself. In fact, in the last season increasing use has been made of camera movements that emphasize Montalbano's raised position and control, with him gazing downward, until the panning shot reaches the action taking place on the lower level (*The Pyramid of Mud, A Delicate Matter*). Thus, what has always been before our eyes becomes something new, obtained by means of a geographical montage that obeys the effective terms of what is called the geographical landscape, organized and represented by the gaze of the viewer who starts from a point of command (Cosgrove, 1985). But the landscape is also given as a dynamic relationship between the temporal and spatial dimensions, capable of anticipating and orienting the future. Alessandra Vietina, speaking of the Montalbano thrillers (Vietina, 2010), emphasizes that the new technologies lead to a territorial uprooting of the "crime" and become problematic for an inspector who is accustomed to finding the solution and the guilty parties by his knowledge of the mechanisms and logic that regulate the characters' territory and social space. Salvo Montalbano was born in 1950 and began his literary existence in 1994. Over the years he has grown old, his father has died, and the G8 summit in Genoa, the attack on the Twin Towers, the "refugee emergency," terrorism and the "Arab spring" have all taken place. The space of the world has changed, and he has felt its changes. As Camilleri himself says, Montalbano is "in crisis because of the globalization of information, which deprives the police investigation of that sense of "territory" which is so important to his character" (Lodato, 2002). The hyperbole reported for the TV drama's landscape goes exactly in this direction, radicalizing and anticipating Montalbano's inner discomfort on a visual level. The landscape that the TV series articulates denies the basic topological structure, its variable geometry, its function of keeping characters under control, prefiguring, as an *active verb* already recognized by Camilleri himself, the loosening of that linear rapport between signified, signifier and referent precisely of the geographic plot of the novels.

On the side of the geographical imagination of Sicily we see in real time on (tele)vision what produces the (tele)vised landscape when its *projection* circulates in a decidedly global space. On the side of Sicilian reality we observe instead the effects of the landscape's very concrete topographic material impact. In the promotional role which the TV drama plays for the territory of Ragusa we again recall the series of impressive aerial shots of the Ragusa landscape, whose striking beauty imposes itself on the viewers' imagination: the initial shots, in fact, focus on Mazara del Vallo, a modern port town, the territory's only atypical element, followed by a bird's-eye view of Ragusa Ibla, nestled between the curtains of the Hyblaean Mountains, while the montage juxtaposes a shot from the sea of

Montalbano's cottage, located on Punta Secca, with the landscapes of Modica and Scicli, they too with their baroque monuments nestled in the Hyblaean landscape. From this summary, each episode depicts other dislocated places spread over a fairly broad spatial context. Without mentioning them all, it suffices to recall: the Castle of Donnafugata, the Donnalucata beach, the Eremo della Giubiliana hotel, Villa Criscione, the Fornace Penna, Favignana, the island of Levanzo, the Villa of the Monsters in Bagheria, Tindari[3]. The result is the flowering of a Montalbano's Sicily tour produced by the now global "Montalbano effect." Ragusa is the chief tourist spot (Department of Tourism Region of Sicily, 2014, "Sicily. Its myth and image as a world-class tourist destination"). Traditionally neglected since the days of the 18th-century Grand Tour and the subsequent tourism of the Romantic era, it is only since of the second half of the 20th century that Ragusa has begun to be visited by artists and intellectuals. Now it has become a landscape for material consumption, produced by the staging of the TV drama, which actively works at bolstering its "re-branding strategy" (Ponton, Azero, 2015). On the side of the geographical imagination, Mitchell's first four "Theses on Landscape" (1994, 5) help us understand how the strategy of "landscape effect" transforms Vigàta into all of Sicily, and all of Sicily into "Montalbano's Sicily." To conclude, I make mine the words of Gunnar Olsson, who was also present at Andrea Camilleri's geography lesson:

> there are close parallels between landscape and Karl Marx's conception of commodity, for in both cases there is a braiding of reification and deification, fetishism and alienation. (Olsson, 1999, 136)

References

Camilleri Andrea. 1999. "I luoghi letterari tra realtà e finzione". In *La costruzione del paesaggio siciliano: geografi e scrittori a confronto*, edited by Girolamo Cusimano, 191-196. Palermo: Università degli Studi.

Chu Mark. 2011. "Crime and the South". In *Italian Crime Fiction in Modern Italy*, edited by Giuliana Pieri, 89-114. Cardiff: University of Wales Press.

---

[3] For a detailed list of places I refer to: Clausi and *al.*, 2006.

Clausi Maurizio, Davide Leone, Giuseppe Lo Bocchiaro, Alice Pancucci Amarù, Daniela Ragusa, eds. 2007. *I luoghi di Montalbano: Una guida.* Palermo: Sellerio.

Cosgrove Denis. 1985. "Prospect, Perspective and the Evolution of the Landscape Idea", *Institute of British Geographers*, Volume Number: 10. 45-62.

Ferlita Salvatore, ed. 2003. *La Sicilia di Andrea Camileri: Tra Vigata e Montelusa.* Palermo: Kalós.

Lo Piccolo Francesco, ed. 2009. *Progettare le identità del territorio.* Firenze: Alinea Editrice.

Lodato Saverio. 2002. *La linea della palma: Lodato Saverio fa raccontare Andrea Camilleri.* Milano: Rizzoli.

Magris Claudio. 2009. *Danubio.* Milano: Garzanti.

Marrone Gianfranco. 2003. *Montalbano: Affermazione e trasformazione di un eroe mediatico.* Roma: Rai.

Mitchell William, John, Thomas, ed. 1994. *Landscape and Power.* Chicago: University of Chicago Press.

Ogborn Miles. 2005-2006. "Mapping words". *New Formations*, Volume Number: 57. 145-149.

Olsson Gunnar. 1999. "Landscape-border station between stonescape and mindscape". In *La costruzione del paesaggio siciliano: geografi e scrittori a confronto,* edited by Girolamo Cusimano, 135-145. Palermo: Università degli Studi.

Pezzotti Barbara. 2009. "Conversation on a New Sicily: Interview with Andrea Camilleri", *Storytelling: A Critical Journal of Popular Narrative*, Volume Number: 9.1. 37-52.

Pezzotti Barbara. 2012. *The Importance of Place in Contemporary Italian Crime Fiction: A Bloody Journey.* Plymouth: Fairleigh Dickinson University Press.

Ponton Douglas Mark, Vincenzo Azero. 2015. "The Montalbano Effect: re-branding Sicily as a tourist destination?" *On the Horizon*, Volume number: 23. 342-351.

Rinaldi Lucia. 2012. *Andrea Camilleri: A Companion to the Mystery Fiction.* Jefferson and London: McFarlan & Company.

Scarpetti Roberto, Annalisa Strano. 2004. Commissario Montalbano: Indagine su un successo. Firenze: Zona.

Socco Carlo. 1996. "Lo spazio come paesaggio", *Versus. Quaderni di studi semiotici*, Volume Number: 73/74. 193-215.

Vietina Alessandra. 2010. *Montalbano, Maigret & Co: Storia del giallo in televisione.* Alessandria: Edizioni Falsopiano.

CHAPTER FIFTEEN

THE OUTER HEBRIDES, LOST ISLANDS…
REFOUND BY PETER MAY

FRANCK CHIGNIER-RIBOULON

The Outer Hebrides are a type of Far-West, like Connemara (Ireland) or other isolated regions (North Cantal in France…). The image of isolation is not only linked to distance or density but these islands were considered, until now, as a backward country. Peter May writes "the islands are unique and kilometers are not enough to measure how far they are from London" (2013, 7). I was inspired by the idea of "lost and re-found" by Louder, Morissonneau and Waddell (1979), when geographers from Quebec re-discovered small French speaking minorities all over North America. Thanks to them, Quebecers re-found French speaking minorities, while they were very nationalist, claiming independence, fearing a slow extinction of the French language in North America.

A parallel can be made for the Outer Hebrides, with the work of Peter May. He is a Scottish novelist and a former screenwriter for television. Now living in France, he writes detective stories. Among them, he has edited a Scottish trilogy that takes place in the Outer Hebrides. The three books are "the Blackhouse"[1], "The Lewisman" and "The chessmen". First published in France, they became best-sellers and won literary awards. A few years later, he edited a book, with David Wilson, a photographer, presenting the archipelago with attractive pictures of landscapes, expressing his feelings and using his books' success to give a better image of the islands.

Fin MacLeod, the hero of the trilogy, is a police inspector, working at the present time but he grew up in Lewis Island and remembers the 1960s, when he was young. Therefore, the stories enable comparison between the two periods, showing evolutions and contrasts. The success of the books has helped in a rediscovery of the specific culture of the archipelago.

---

[1] For this paper, "The Blackhouse" is mainly used. It is the first book of the trilogy and the islands are presented.

Tourism stakeholders and services have integrated this field in their strategy of growth.

A world away

Located in the North-Western part of Scotland, the Outer Hebrides are an archipelago stretched along approximately 200 kilometers between the Atlantic Ocean and the Minch, a very dangerous strait "see Figure 15.1". The sea is often agitated by storms and the strait is a difficult journey from Mainland Scotland to the islands ("the rising swell from the Minch", May 2009, 394). An "icy water" (2009, 23) with "drownings each month" (26). Indeed, in the past, relations with the Mainland were rare and difficult, and the Outer Hebrides "were commonly regarded as the most 'outlying' inhabited lands of the British isles" (Geddes 1955, 3). They are the true "Far-West" but a large part of Western and Northern Scotland has very low human densities also, the Scottish population being concentrated in the Lowlands, overall in the Glasgow and Edinburgh urban conurbations. In 2013, the total population of the Outer Hebrides isles was about 27,400 inhabitants (Comhairle nan Eilean Siar 2015), for 3,000 square kilometers; the average density is about 9 inhabitants per km². In a geographical perspective, even strong, territorial exclusion is relative. This archipelago is long "see Figure 15.2" and isolation cannot be considered to be the same everywhere. According to the Outer Hebrides project for European Leader program 2014-2020, almost 22,000 people live on the main isle of Lewis and Harris; around 80% of the total population. Furthermore, the urban agglomeration of Stornoway, with suburbanized areas, counts approximately 13,600 inhabitants, according to my own calculations[2]. Therefore, about 50% of the islanders live in or close to the main town. Consequently, services (ferries for instance), food prices are different, and isolation is stronger in peripheral villages or islands, and daily life is often harder.

Although the landscape is so nice, and well described by Peter May (2009, 256, for example) and beautifully photographed by David Wilson, (in Peter May 2013), life on the isles was and remains arduous. Throughout the book, Peter May (2009) talks about the violence of nature, especially the wind: "Fin had forgotten this wind, this incessant push that leads here after traveling 3,000 miles over the Atlantic" (23), "The

---

[2] With the 2011 census data and zones, maps of the Ordnance Survey and Google Earth.

inexhaustible Atlantic anger" (67), "The wind. Never tired of blowing" (43), "Stooping to fight against Westerly winds" (43).

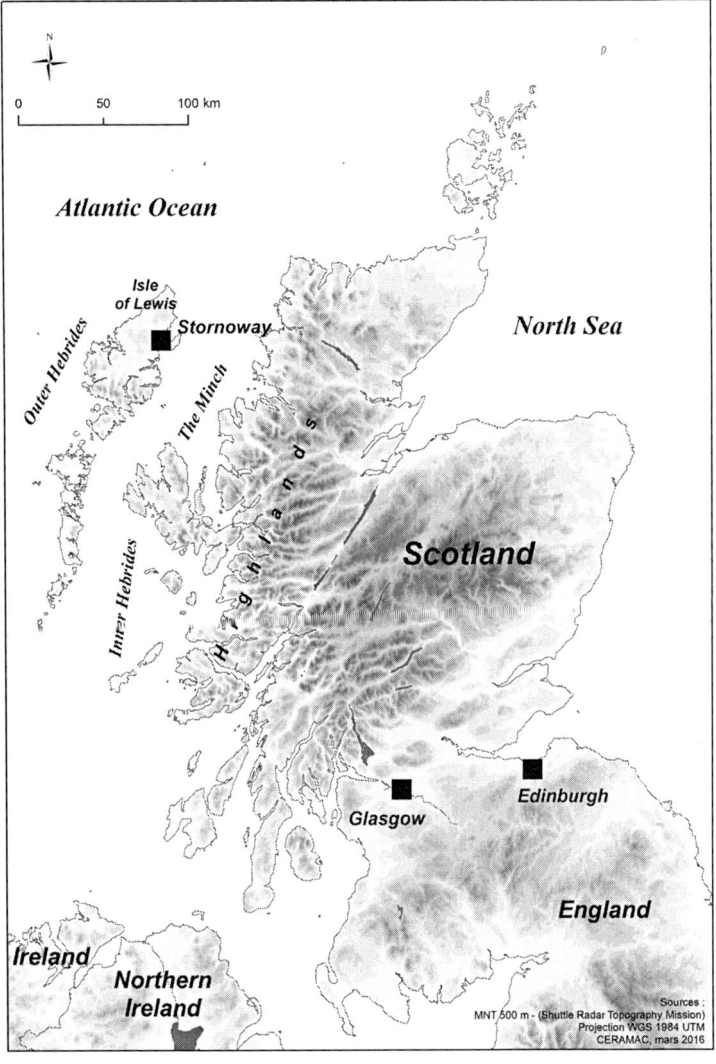

Figure 15.1 The location of the Outer Hebrides in Scotland

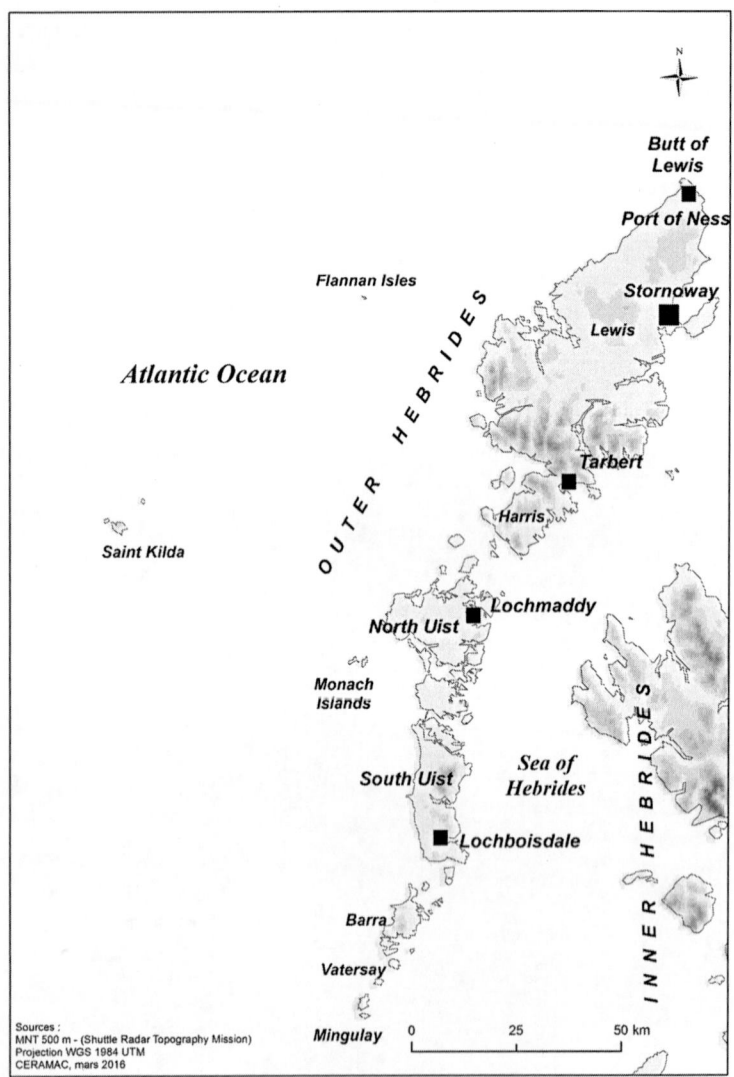

Figure 15.2 The archipelago of the Outer Hebrides

And rains, common, cold, and in relation to the wind: "the rain began to fall heavily. To the horizontal" (108). Weather and sky change continuously: "the blackest of the Northern skies" (67), "Harris Mountains stood before them. They pierced the layer of low and dark clouds, creating huge holes that revealed the sparkling streaks of blue and white" (256). More widely, temperatures are low and summer often too short for good crops, autumn rains coming too soon, like the cold wind. In the same way, a large part of the land is poor, especially inland. Peatlands, moorlands and swamps are everywhere "see Figure 15.3", lakes also (the "lochs"). Nevertheless, some better land exists, the 'machair' in Gaelic. Machair is a "gently sloping coastal dune-plain formed by wind-blown calcareous shell-sand" (Hansom & Angus 2005, 401). This soil was improved by farmers, adding seaweed or sheep droppings.

Figure 15.3 The peatland

The Outer Hebrides seem to be the end of the earth, a far-away country between violence of nature, poverty of land, and, for people of the Lowlands, closer to hell than human societies. Therefore, people were considered, and still are, as peasants ("a 'teuchter', a North-Western slob", May 2009, 371) or, worse, mentally retarded... or Barbarians.

From exclusion to marginality

Geographical isolation has led to marginality, understood as self-exclusion (Chignier-Riboulon 2014), sometimes in relation to past policies (Clearances, for instance). Local societies tended to close into themselves. Exclusion was shown also by geographical fragmentation and dependence on the British mainland, concretely relations were not South to North of the archipelago, but to the East (Hache 1982, 751). Contrasts were even religious, as Peter May writes (2011).

For centuries, the isles were extremely poor, not only because of physical conditions. Most of the population lived on crofts: farmers operated on land for which they paid a rent (Caird 1964). Farms were small-scale food producers, primarily potatoes, turnips and rye. However, production on the farms was poor and crofters had another activity to survive: fishing, depending on types of fish and seasons (Geddes 1955, 71; de Planhol 1966, 122) or they made tweed, "working for a pittance in cramped and ice-cold shelters and garages" (May 2013, 84), or they worked in a kelp factory, to produce fertilizers. The second problem was the size of the tenure. Peter May gives us the example of MacLeod's parents: "We only had 3 hectares of land, which span in a long narrow strip from the house to the coast" (2009, 27). The aim is to get different quality of land, and especially a piece of 'machair' "see Figure 15.4". Families lived in 'blackhouses', which were very primitive stone made dwellings, still common in 1947, in Lewis, where they represented "about 40 per cent of the homesteads" (Geddes 1955, 79), and the last was only abandoned in the 1960s (May 2013, 115). In the 1920s, 'white houses' were built as replacements and, often, the former dwelling was close by as in May's novel (2009, 25).

Figure 15.4 The form of the parcel on the 'machair'

The authors emphasize the strength of religion on local life, and Peter May shows the evolution between the 1960s and 2000s. Protestantism was hard until the last decades and even taking children to the swings was a sin (2009, 46). On Catholic Southern islands, Peter May specifies life was, relatively, more good humored (2011). In the same way, everything was closed on Sunday and it was impossible to buy a newspaper; when May arrived on the islands, as a screenwriter, he was very surprised (2013, 58-60), because change was slower than on the Mainland.   Otherwise, religion brought hope for people, especially when the believers sang the praises of the Lord: "They expressed their gratitude to have found a sense in their life so rough" (2009, 101). Nevertheless, behind the strength of faith and social control, there existed a long standing competition between churches, each one defending the "truth" in a perspective of social grouping: "each one was a place of rallying where the hatred and the distrust of another one converged" (68).

In this context of isolation, poverty and salience, young people were bored, as in other very isolated places (Chignier-Riboulon, 2009), and "the drink question" (Thompson 1968, 150) remained a continuing problem. "The morose existence of kids. Nothing to do, or not much" (May 2009, 52). Indeed, leaving the island to go to Glasgow provided "the prospect of endless opportunities" (181). These parameters and unemployment had contributed to a long tradition of emigration to the Mainland or overseas territories. In "The Blackhouse", inspector Fin MacLeod grew up at the end of the 1960s and in the early 1970s; at this time unemployment was high, according to Thompson (1968, 130).

Contemporary transformations of society: towards new issues?

One of the aims of Peter May is to present changes in the Outer Hebrides between 1960/70s and 2000s. He underlines improvements, for example about connections to the Mainland, by ferry or plane. In the same perspective, local authorities try to develop the islands economically, to maintain the population and counter ageing.

As in other countries (like Margeride, in France, until the 1970s), the Outer Hebrides entered late into contemporary modernity. Isolation through insularity and climate, self-exclusion of every church, townships working as "'sociable hamlets' and 'little commonwealths'" (Thompson 1968, 133), the strength of "one of the oldest forms of communal life in Britain" (133) had limited the influence of the British Isles and foreign countries (by television). Poverty and Gaelic were common in late modernization. Conversely, collective representations on people of the islands, considered as "backward and narrow-minded peasants" (Hache 1982, 749) had also contributed. In The Blackhouse, the chief inspector arriving from Inverness (a small sized town in Europe) is contemptuous when he speaks to MacLeod: ""The locals are not very evolved." He had a disdainful grin. "Doggone, you will know."" (May 2009, 50). This type of attitude is classic in a situation of cultural and social domination or towards minorities (French speaking minorities in Canada, regional minorities in France, Kurds in Turkey...). Minoration and minorization behaviors both work (Chignier-Riboulon, Garrait-Bourrier 2013).

On the one hand, the idea of 'minoration' is inspired by Deleuze (1993). It tends to indicate that a strategy is pursued to decrease the value or the importance of a group. As such, underestimation places the subject in a situation of minor. Outer Hebridean people, like other minorities, have undergone a long history of minoration. Gilles Deleuze chose the word "minoration" (1993) as a key concept; it defines the process in which we are interested. By opposing the dominant to the dominated, Deleuze established a reflection about norms developing into three stages: an ontology of vital energy and becoming an epistemology of culture based on a logic of variation and a political thought built on the theory of domination and of "becoming-revolutionary" (or how experimentation can modify history to find answers to what is intolerable).

On the other hand, minorization indicates a more psychological subjection, by which the majority intends to limit the general impact of the group by denying it, by real, physical or psychological violence. In this way, the process of reduction joins that of humiliation, rejection, contempt (Mounier 1947).

Nevertheless, this general attitude is tending to disappear. Archipelago Authorities consider there is a "growing interest from Scotland" (LUC 2014, 6), and from the European Union. The objective is to improve integration, cohesion and equality, on different scales. The islands benefit from these policies in relation to additional costs for transports and disruption of transportation services in case of "storms or high winds" (LUC 2014, 6). This interest has assisted the acceleration of change. This expanding context takes place in line with sustainable development, by preserving the natural environment, developing renewable energies, helping local food production or maintaining rural services (Outer Hebrides Leader 2015). For instance, within the evaluation report of the Leader 2007-2013 program (LUC 2014), it is specified "crofting contributes to the social structure, biodiversity, sense of place and cultural heritage of the islands." (6). Indeed, crofting is a cross-thematic. 82 projects were supported by the European Union program Leader, worth 3.11 millions of pounds.

The tourism sector is considered as a key tool for the economic growth of the islands; each authority tries to help tourism initiatives, in part with

European funds. In this way, the success of Peter May's books contributes to the policy to attract tourist flow. On the website of the agency for Outer Hebrides tourism (www.visitouterhebrides.co.uk), the Peter May trail is mentioned (www.petermaytrail.com). The trail is also proposed in visitors' information centers, with leaflets. On one side of the leaflet are pictures of places cited in the trilogy. On the other side is a short biography of the author, with photographs, and a few elements from each book. The front shows covers of the books and a map for locating each place. The leaflet even suggests scanning the QR code, for those who have the application to access the Outer Hebrides website. This type of strategy is now relatively common, linked to the success of the books. It is the case for Carlos Ruiz Zafon for Barcelona or for Dan Brown for Paris or Florence, for example[3]. Of course, these documents are also useful for all people in the tourist sector: the author (his books are sold in the tourist centers), shopkeepers, craftsmen, accommodations, restaurants. Moreover, sites presented in the books providing tourist visits are distributed all over the islands (except the Southern ones).

Finally, the Outer Hebrides are becoming a changing society. Local authorities support traditional economic sectors in a sustainable way, but these provide fewer direct jobs. According to the Leader project (2014-2020) proposed by Comhairle nan Eilean Siar, less than 3% of the active population work in fisheries (19) and about 100 active people are employed in Harris Tweed industry, in 20 units (The Scottish government 2015, 97). Although the tweed sector is currently creating some jobs, the fishing sector lost 43% of its jobs between 2001 and 2012 (Leader 2015, 65). Furthermore, a proportion of these people work part-time. In the same way, local administration considers:

> Crofting is the predominant form of land use in the Western Isles and is the foundation of the way of life, the language and the culture. About 77% of the land area is held in crofting tenure and is therefore subject to crofting legislation. There are some 6,000 crofts distributed among 280 townships. Of these, 94% provide less than 2 days' work per week for their occupiers and typically average 3 hectares in size.
>
> The quality of land and sizes of crofts and grazings vary considerably throughout the area but generally, the smallest crofts are to be found on the poorest land and most of the large full-time crofts are in Uist (Comhairle nan Eilean Siar website, page economic development).

---

[3] Jack Kerouac in a literary road trip, crossing New-York, Chicago..., Donna Leon with her Chief inspector Brunetti in Venice, Stieg Larsson in Stockholm... Sometimes, publishers propose tourist guides, with walks.

Therefore, Peter May specifies 40% of the active population work in the public sector (2013, 32). And the public sector is traditionally important on the islands (Outer Hebrides Leader 2015). More specifically, Gaelic services in the Outer Hebrides are one of the most important economic sectors with about 1,000 jobs (Faragher 2014).

Landscape versus cultural heritage?

During the last centuries, the Outer Hebrideans were isolated and, consequently, as elsewhere, culture was better preserved (Hache 1982, 747). Geddes thought the Outer Hebrides were the heart of the North and West of Britain (1955, 3). Today, they are the last territory where the Gaelic language is still spoken by a majority, but it is endangered, with about 57,000 speakers in 2011. In the past, discourses contributed to reinforce negative representations of culture and people. Times have changed, but maybe too late. Image and discrimination are not the only factors explaining the strong decrease of the local culture. The "wild and grandiose nature" described by Xavier de Planhol (1966, 224) now attracts new people and, in part, weakens local identity.

Peter May loves these islands and their culture and writes favorable phrases in his foreword: "Music is primitive and typically Celtic – Gaelic psalms sang *a capella* giving you the creeps to Karen Matheson's, Capercaillie's, Runrig's or Julie Fowlis' masterful melodies" (2013, 7). However, for the last centuries, Gaelic culture was defined as a peasant's culture as other dominated cultures (see Rohou, for the Briton case). Fin MacLeod remembers his 1960s (2009), from page 29 to 40 he narrates his first day at school. He didn't speak English, and pupils laughed at him. Then, the schoolteacher chose a pupil to translate for him and, finally, she asked Fin's parents to speak English at home. At this moment, there was a strong link between learning the language of the majority and social success, here and everywhere. Even if, like in Canada for French speaking minorities, research has shown, already after the Second World War, "that the bilingual child tends to assimilate knowledge at a greater rate and to a greater depth" (Thompson 1968, 138). Nevertheless, maybe, this book was written in a period of change.

The Second World War and its racism, claims to independence against colonization had progressively disqualified policies of assimilation (Schnapper 2007, 14). The goal was to assimilate cultural minorities and immigrants, for building the nation, or continuing to do so. In the former British dominions, immigration policies were restrictive and the cultural majority dominated: in Australia, the labor Party demanded a "white

Australia" until 1965 (Pons 1996) and, in Canada, the "speak white" sentence was common during the 1960s. Cultural monolithism was the rule. Monolinguism was the norm in the school education system to help everyone rise in the social hierarchy. From about the mid-1960s to the end of the 1970s, this dominant collective representation had changed, at least in North America, Western Europe and former dominions in the Pacific Ocean. In the United Kingdom, in 1972, the government built an "integration policy defined as an equal opportunity strategy and no more a flattening process for assimilating" (Schnapper 2007, 22).

Minorization and minoration processes cannot explain alone the decline of traditional culture. The high unemployment rate and emigration, poverty and long term problems in the crofting system can also explain changes. Comparison with French-speaking villages in Manitoba (Canada) enables us to view another example (Chignier-Riboulon, forthcoming). At the end of the 19th century, the Catholic Church worked to settle French-speaking Catholic people in the Prairies, in its competition with Protestant expansion. The strategy was to implement villages; each village being an autonomous entity, with its lands, church and priest. These communities, strong but oriented to themselves, disappeared over the 1960s, in relation to the modernization of agriculture, the desire for freedom and the demand for social progress. People looked for a better state of well-being. And to achieve a better life it was necessary to live in an English and urban environment, like in May's novels. Currently, the strength of the geographical and social environment is a daily pressure. Assimilation is the easy way. In this context, French-Manitobans say "se faire avaler" (to be ingested). Finally, geographical, social and economic evolutions express "la fin d'un monde", the end of a world or a dying world, as Peter May says (2013, 56). In the Outer Hebrides, townships are less and less self-centered, and, it is still difficult to be proud to have a Celtic culture, and not so useful in modern daily life, except in Gaelic services.

The strong relation between Peter May and the islands are not only linked to landscapes. Several times in his books, he describes the beauty of the language. In his transversal book, written after his crime novels, he speaks about "these islands staying in your skin and blood" (2013, 9).

The Outer Hebrides are the last place in Scotland where the Gaelic language continues to be spoken by a majority of the inhabitants. However, their number is decreasing constantly, even if decline between 2001 and 2011 was much lower, and in spite of measures to encourage learning or speaking it[4]. Of course, the Gaelic language Act is recent

---

[4] I never hear Gaelic in Stornoway stores, especially in the supermarket in spite of many customers.

(2005) and the current Gaelic language plan for 2015-2020 is a stage in an (expected) perspective of renewal: the percentage of Gaelic speakers who are under 18 years old is increasing but, currently, cannot counterbalance the ageing and death of the oldest groups (Gaelic Language plan 2015, 11). Attractiveness for landscape is both an opportunity and a risk for a long-lasting renewal.

Works studied

May, P. and David Wilson. 2013. *L'Ecosse de Peter May* [Hebrides]. Arles: Editions du Rouergue.

May, P. 2011. *L'homme de Lewis* [The Lewisman]. Arles: Actes sud.

—. 2009. *L'île des chasseurs d'oiseaux* [The Blackhouse]. Arles: Actes sud.

Other references

Caird, J.B., 1964. The making of the Scottish rural landscape. *Scottish Geographical Magazine*, 80(2): 72-80.

—. 1951. L'île de Harris, Outer Hebrides (Ecosse). *Annales de Bretagne*, 58(1): 119-131. Doi: 10.3406/abpo.1951.4421

Chignier-Riboulon, F. Forthcoming (paper accepted). Résistance séculaire et fragilité du Manitoba francophone, *Cultures et résistances*. Montpellier: Presses universitaires de la Méditerranée.

—. 2014. Les ressorts psycho-sociaux du changement, des éléments fondamentaux difficiles à actionner, *La mutation des systèmes productifs français*, edited by Gabriel Wackermann. 178-187. Paris: Ellipses.

Chignier-Riboulon, F. and A. Garrait-Bourrier. 2013. Introduction. *Les minorités isolées en Amérique du Nord, résistances et résiliences culturelles*, edited by Franck Chignier-Riboulon and Anne Garrait-Bourrier, 7-17. Clermont-Ferrand: Presses Universitaires Blaise Pascal.

Chignier-Riboulon, F. 2009. *Les quartiers entre espoir et enfermement*. Paris: Ellipses.

De Planhol, X. 1966. Paysages agraires et vie régionale des Hébrides externes. *Annales de géographie*, 75(408): 224-231.

Deleuze, G. 1993. *Critique et Clinique*. Paris: Editions de Minuit.

Geddes, A. 1955. *The isle of Lewis and Harris*. Edinburgh: University press.

Hache, J.-D. 1982. Insularité et institutionnalisation dans les Hébrides-extérieures d'Ecosse. *Revue Française de Science Politique*, 32(4-5): 743-767. Doi 10.3406/rfsp.1982.394035

Hansom, J.D. and S. Angus. 2005. Machair of the Western Isles. *Scottish Geographical Journal*, 121(4): 401-412.

Louder, D., C. Morissonneau and E. Waddell, eds. 1979. Du continent perdu à l'archipel retrouvé : le Québec et l'Amérique française. *Cahier de Géographie du Québec*, 13(58) : 5-13.

Mounier, E. 1947. *Traité du caractère*. Paris: Editions du Seuil.

Pons, X. 1996. *Le multiculturalisme en Australie, au-delà de Babel*. Paris: L'Harmattan.

Rohou, J. 2011. *Fils de ploucs*. Rennes : Éditions Ouest-France.

Schnapper, D. 2007. *Qu'est-ce que l'intégration ?* Paris: Gallimard/Folio.

Thompson, F. 1968. *Harris and Lewis: Outer Hebrides*. Newton Abbot: David & Charles.

Websites

Comhairle nan Eilean Siar. 2015. *Socio-economic* Update n°30. Accessed 9-13-15. www.cne-siar.gov.uk

Comhairle nan Eilean Siar. 2016. *Economic Development and Business support*. Accessed 2-22-16. www.cne-siar.gov.uk

Faragher, Rick. 2014. *Isle of Lewis: language and life inside the Outer Hebrides*. BBC News, 9-16-14. Accessed 8-8-15. www.bbc.com

LUC (Land Use Consultants). 2014. *Outer Hebrides Leader Program 2007-2013, Evaluation, Final report*. Accessed 12-8-2015. www.landuse.co.uk

Outer Hebrides Leader and European Maritimes and Fisheries fund. 2015. *Local development strategy 2014-2020*. Accessed 12-8-2015. www.outerhebridesleader.co.uk

The Scottish government. 2015. *Gaelic language plan 2015-2020, draft for consultation*. www.gov.scot

The Scottish government. 2015. *Scottish annual business statistics 2013*. www.gov.scot

CHAPTER SIXTEEN

AESTHETICS, REPRESENTATION AND COMMUNICATION OF RURAL IN RUSSIAN MAFIA CINEMA (1988-2010)

OKSANA DOGNON

Introduction

The criminal romance or disclosure of the criminal aesthetic, also known, as the "coherent deviant aesthetic" (Ferrell, 1995), became largely popular with the Russian population in its greatest parts through mafia movies, which were intended to seduce this type of spectator. There is the cinema and *the cinema*. Despite their identical writing and consonance (pronunciation), they are not the same. There is the cinema of filmmakers produced with the main goal of communicating a purely artistic message, therefore their principal reason is to facilitate the perception of the mafia's aesthetic represented in these films. And there is the realistic cinema the main purpose of which is to convey the producers' realism of the events that took place during a defined period of Russian history. For our research, this period is the Russian great criminal revolution of the 1990s.

This division within the mafia cinema genre is perfectly applicable to the theory of André Bazin (1981), wherein the author considered two types of filmmakers: The ones who believe in an image and those who believe in reality. In other words, those

> who can bring themselves the representation to the (artistic, expressive) end and those who produce the films where the essence of the real is the most accurate representation possible of the supposed truth.

Consequently, Bazin continues to assert that the recording of reality and development of real effects enables the film to emerge from the deepest truth of reality. This theory fits perfectly according to the purpose sought by the mafia cinematography: to reproduce reality. Russian mafia movies' filmmakers can be classified, despite the very short time of this genre's existence, as "producers" of reality. But, especially mafia movies are the kind that not only transform the mafia reality in fiction, but at most, reproduce, or "recycle" some of these cases' reality in "small details"[1]. Consequently, there was a transformation or the reproduction of the aesthetics of the fictional mafia into the reality. The cinema, thus constructed a real circuit of the interdependent between the real and the fictional. That's why we can affirm without fail the existence of the "multiple reproductions" theory and the theory of "re-use", in case of the Russian mafia phenomenon. The key element remains, however, the point that this real organization has been inspired by fictional crime, and reincarnated favorite movies in their own reality.

Figure 16.1 Image of the teaser of the film Bimmer, 2003, Director: Buslov Piotr, Producers: Sergei Chliants.
Source: http://kinokong.net/5779-bumer-2003.html

---

[1] Bazin, André, 1981, French cinema of the occupation and resistance: The birth of a critical esthetic (François Truffaut, Ed., Stanley Hochman, Trans.). New York: F. Ungar Pub. Co.

The representation of the real in the fictional

One of the principal goals of this article is to understand the relationship between the "real" and the "fiction" of the Russian mafia phenomenon and their structuring in mafia aesthetic, based on the cinema of the mafia type in Russia and worldwide, as well as its various representations and communication aspects. The relationship between the "image" media and Russian and Soviet political bodies have taken different forms throughout the twentieth century. These relationships have had their happy days and their darkest hours, according to the different stages of the development of cinema, economic health, and timeliness of the country's involvement in various conflicts during the restructuring of the state/during the break of the USSR. So, this breakdown of the USSR brought essential changes (Luneev, 2000) in all areas of the country, for instance, as economical as cinema.

Russian mafia as a myth

From the beginning of the era of the breakdown of the USSR, the reality of new Russian cinema was "classified." (Gurov, 1990) This new era in the history of Russia has produced its own myths, editions, and "documented" its own history. At this time, there also appeared a need for new products and a fresh type of a cinema genre of this "new wave of cinema"[2] coming from Russia. Actually, Russia is caused to be criminal in the eyes of Westerner viewers. Thus, began the trend of the "inaccessible" criminal characters. Concerning the viewers, they had fully accepted "the criminal protagonist" and swiftly took the habit of seeing him. In the meantime, they also stopped seeing the bad and dangerous sides of the criminal protagonist. Regarding the producers of the "criminal type" of films, they made an effort to erase the negative view of the criminal protagonist by the viewers, taking away all the negative aspects and replacing them by extraordinary acts and by the dynamics of the characters of the criminals protagonists in general. Those protagonists are afraid of nothing and move forward by all means, without stopping for a second, to achieve their goals. Obviously, the Russian viewers "got the message" and

---

[2] New wave of cinema, also known as *Nouvelle Vague*; originally created by the non-traditional French filmmakers originally referred to a group of individualistic, innovative, and non-traditional French filmmakers, directors and producers in the late 1950s and early 1960s. French New Wave Film (Nouvelle Vague), http://www.newwavefilm.com/new-wave-cinema-guide/nouvelle-vague-where-to-start.shtml

turned their passive fascination into an active reaction. So they "played" their films and the leading role in their own lives. They performed their roles under the same conditions and the same rules as their favorite cinema's heroes did. The rules, they learned them through their "teacher", the cinema of the mafia genre. So the "mafia"'s principal goal was not only to be appreciated by the public, but also to adapt the cinema to the reality, and to become "a vertical value", which was spread over time and has been lasting for already more than twenty years. It was the era of the Great Criminal Revolution. This period could also be called an adaptation of mafia movies in our reality (Sergeev, 2002). The population enhances "criminal affairs"[3], giving reason to felony; reflecting a criminal lifestyle as an attractive adventure and not as a dangerous profession. The spectators amplify the attraction with danger in their own eyes by their imagination. In such a case, the director of the film plays the role of the producer of the images that the viewer wants to see. The director does not bear the responsibility for these images. The only trick that the right director should know is to make the choice of the images that the viewer will want to see at some point in the future.[4] The main goal of this work is to, therefore, distinguish the development of the commonalities between the two phenomena: the real mafia and the mafia from the screen and the films of the same genre, in Russia and in the world, which will indeed structure a single phenomenon of mafia aesthetics through its various communications aspects. The question is obvious, whether the process of the propaganda and the promotion of the Mafia through the mafia cinema genre, especially dedicated to it, has had managed to reach its primer objective and to influence the public unconscious.

Furthermore, we wish to show, through this article, that the Russian mafia cinema plays an important role in the "communicational policy" of the real mafia itself. Subsequently, we need to define what is the modernization of the Russian Mafia phenomenon in this development and what was the "tempo" given for the development of the movie genre called "criminal", or the Russian mafia genre. Regarding the mafia communication, it's interesting that the fictional mafia copied the reality of the bona fide mafia. The genuine one had their business partially running in big cities, but also in rural areas. This last point had our particular attention, as there exists very little to no information at all, on the Russian mafia phenomenon correlation with the rural areas, unlike the Sicilian Mafia,

---

[3] Nikolai Modestov, 2007, Criminal Moscow: A Documentary Chronicle of the Lawlessness of the '80's and '90's, Criminal Moscow
[4] Sydorov A., the co-director of the film Brigade:
http://ru.wikipedia.org/wiki/Бригада_(телесериал)

which has a great part of its business run in rural zones. "Organized crime is especially likely to be more prevalent in cities and countries with advanced levels of economic development, the history of the Mafia in rural Sicily to the contrary notwithstanding." (Finckenauer and Voronin 2001) Nevertheless, Russian mafia, the authentic but also the fictional ones, had a part of their business happening in rural areas. However, as the spectrum of mafia activities in rural areas was limited, one of the principal domain of their activities was concentrated on business with cars.

Figure 16.2 Image of the teaser of the film Brigade, 2003,
Director: Alexei Sidorov. Producers: Alexander Akopov, Alexander Inshakov,
Anatoly Sivushov, Valeri Todorovski
Source: http://fanparty.ru/fanclubs/club-of-fans-of-a-film-brigada/pictures/167521

Russian Mafia in the Rural

The role of the car and its representation was very important, due to the fact that in the reality of Russian criminals, cars became a genuine business card of their owner. In real life, the vehicle portrays the image and reputation of its possessor, while in the criminal genre movies, it plays a very special role. For instance, sometimes, the vehicle also participates in a crime scene description, where the life of the film in general depends on the director's wish. Already at the time of the Great Criminal Revolution, the high value and demand of cars became the new ways of business for bandits. Thereby, the attacks against vehicles' owners have become a lucrative and widespread ways of a legal business. Often, the criminals were hiding under police inspectors' uniforms. Officially, they were placed to monitor traffic at the exit of highways. In reality, they were seeking to steal cars, hoping to sell them later. In this period of history, almost everyone could be robbed or killed. Every single driver was in danger. There were established categories of risk: first, the owners of a vehicle and secondly, at a greater risk, although they occupied a less important positions, were people who were not owners of the used car, but who did driving as their business; their job was to be a driver-carrier. This type of control was performed outside of the city, mainly in rural areas, generally not far away from Moscow, or others cities. By the way, the selection of territories by criminals did not, as the researcher didn't tend to explain it, depend on their primary wish to occupy a designated territory. However, during this period of Russian history, criminals could occupy any territory legally, mostly after this territory was attributed to their criminal organization, after the division of territories by the bosses of different criminal groups (Matskevitch, 2009). Indeed, Russia's rural areas are more spaced out and therefore sparsely populated. Generally these types of "policemen" were placed near highways' exits. Their work consisted of the use of "their own selection" (Matskevitch, 2009) of cars by brand. They were far more, depending on the price of the car, capable of making immediate calculations of their possible gain. As it was already emphasized on, some of the officers were specialized in larceny of new or used cars, while others only stole goods, which were periodically located in the containers of transporting cars. Moreover, there were groups specialized in the monetary claims for offences linked to drivers' misconducts. They stopped each potential perpetrator, and the driver, even if they perfectly knew that they hadn't done anything, was obliged to pay to the "militsiya" in order to be freed. Everyone knew that at the time of the 90s, almost every criminal group was partly composed with former militsiya's[5] employees. In most of the cases, in their arsenal, they had weapons of all types (firearms, air weapons, and non-lethal weapons), police uniforms and many vehicles. And finally, there were organizations specialized in extortion of new cars in large numbers. These cars were transported inside of Russia, from one city to another in order to be sold elsewhere in the country or abroad. Criminal organizations were doing their hunting, similar to businesses of cars transportation, for the commercialization of new cars abroad. In general, this type of organizations, of which Vitaly Demochka[6] was the boss, belonged to the type of criminal organizations with a strict and punitive discipline, having a hierarchy and respect toward others criminal groups. Nothing could happen without the consent of the chief.

---

[5] Currently renamed in a police
[6] http://en.wikipedia.org/wiki/Vitali_Dyomochka

The communication of the criminal aesthetics

Figure 16.3 Image from the shooting of the film "Spets", 2004,
Director: Vitaly Demochka Producers: Vitaly Demochka
Source: https://vk.com/wall-35761247?offset=60&own=1&z=photo-
35761247_303494839%2Fwall-35761247_268

Transformation of the criminal authority into the movie director

We defined the character particularly interesting and important for our research: his name is Vitaly Demochka, former criminal tycoon and criminal chef, originally from the city of Ussuriysk, turned director, producer, actor and writer. He started his profession in the audiovisual production in order to communicate his own criminal reality in small details. As Demochka told himself, it is phenomenal in its own sense that Hollywood producers have managed, without knowing and planing it, to inspire Russian criminal leaders and some members from criminal groups giving them the ideas for their future expansion and development. Here is his story: He started the production of his first TV show "*Spets*"[7] in 2004. Already after one year, in 2005, his film was broadcast on the local channel UHF, consisting of seven parts of 50-80 minutes, each. The

---

[7] Film Spets, 2004, Diomochka. V, http://serial-spec.ru/vitalij-demochka.html

special feature of this film was that it was shot by local "gangsters" and was drawn from their own criminal lives in the Russian Far East. The spokesman of the channel said the film caused a split in the audience: "The representatives of one camp had thought that the film is immoral. They complained: 'Where will go the world, if the Mafia is authorized to make the film about themselves?'. Others viewers saw them as heroes." The spokesman affirmed, "[i]n general, the reaction was significantly positive for two reasons. First, the film was shot here. It's our film and secondly, the originality of the idea that most of the roles were played by real criminals." The criminal authority (Demochka)[8] produced the action film from "A" to "Z" 'made by criminals', in which he and his criminal 'brothers' were respectively the director and actors of leading roles. Thanks to this film, former criminals have become local television stars. Vitaly Demochka, who is known by his nickname Bondar (Cooper) believes that the images of a gangster life, represented in the current Russian films or about the Russians criminals in Hollywood productions have nothing to do with reality. Consequently, he decided to produce and direct his own TV Show. For information, Cooper had not lied about his own "professional experience" at age of 33 (at the time of shooting his film in 2004), he gave a lasting impression. He already made four trips to jail and stayed there for six years. Demochka's last clash with the law was the most spectacular of his acts: he killed an opponent during a meeting with other criminals, while they discussed their business. As he acknowledged himself, "I had a reputation as someone who can get a gun and shoot someone of gender was this man. [...] But the guy had deserved it. My hands will never hurt any honest and decent man." (Parfitt, 2004). Demochka was also the author of the script, producer, director and the main protagonist of his own film "Spets". An article about this performance, written by the producer Demochka was published in the "The Daily Telegraph" newspaper (Parfitt, 2004). The main story of the TV show is based on real events that took place over 10-15 years ago. The film speaks about the extortions and blackmail that were used by the film protagonist and his criminal group against businessmen, making the stopover in Vladivostok on the way to their transfer of new Japanese cars for sale in Siberia and Moscow. A particularly important point for our research is that the criminal extortion of those vehicles almost always happened in the rural zones of the Vladivostok or Ussuriysk. As it was explained previously, the reality of rural extortions had moved to the cinema. According to series producer of "Spets"[9], his colleagues producers from Moscow tried to criticize the film,

---

[8] http://en.wikipedia.org/wiki/Vitali_Dyomochka
[9] Demochka Vitaly, director of the TV show "Spets", Demochka Vitaly,

in regard to the small budget and the unprofessional shooting.[10] However, Vitaly considers that his role was more important. Actually, it is related to the originality of the idea and that Demochka, like the author of the film, respected all the details following reality. Subsequently, more than 200 people were implicated in the production. Not being able to pay for "fake blood" and expensive accessories necessary in the production of such films, Vitaly decided to approach reality at the maximum. Even the wife and the mother of the protagonist played their own roles in the film.

Since the end of the film in 2005, ten "actors" of the TV show ended up in jail with charges for various crimes. Meanwhile, another "actor" was killed during the production of the film, and another died in a car accident. But it happened outside of the shooting. "It turns out that the guys are no longer with us, and the film is likely to remain the most significant memory of them," the film director reflected sadly. The shooting lasted 14 months. According to Demochka, the production took additional time because his colleagues had to continue their "business" in parallel with the memorization of their roles. There was also another reason: the local police, while denying having taken part of the production, opposed the film in sum. Subsequently, they refused to grant their permission for the shooting taking place in their city and its circumferences. Although Demochka had a reputation and was popular, it was impossible to find an agreement between them. He decided to continue shooting the film by any means (McGraw-Hill, 2002) and consequently, he was forced to endure the situation and hide with his production group in rural zones, situated within a short distance of Usuriysk. One day, the police discovered the "working place of Vitaly and his group but were already too late as the film production has been almost finished". Finally, the director of film "Spets" found that the obligation to be out of the city for the shooting brought them luck, as he considered that the scenes shot in the rural area were the best and most successful parts of the film[11]. Regarding the choice of actors he replied, [w]e know this life from the inside out, we just transferred our life to the screen." There was no script, as such. Only Vitaly knew the scenario of the film. Before each episode of the shooting, he told the "actors" what they needed to do, to say, how to act and move. Then Demochka did the montage of the film himself. Moreover, the TV show is named after the main character, "Spets," who is also the film's director. It tells the story of a brutal fight between his gang with other groups for control of rackets in Ussuriysk, a small town near Vladivostok. The

http://serial-spec.ru/vitalij-demochka.html
[10] http://www.novayagazeta.ru/arts/58058.html, 10.05.2013
[11] Demochka Vitaly, 2010, "Special", *Book on demand,* p.400

bandits themselves did all the dangerous *stunts and tricks*, including the fights and the car accidents. During filming, a nightclub and a casino were partially destroyed, and one of the operators by chance escaped injury when the driver lost control of the car. During the production of the film, about twenty cars were destroyed, including six that could not be repaired. But the producer did not seem concerned by the expenses linked to the production of his "first" baby.[12]

Almost all the scenes were filmed in one shot with multiple cameras, because it was more expensive to restore cars or the decor. Immediately after the film came out, the critics accused the director of attempting to profit from his dark reputation. Demochka, however, says he has not earned a dime from the film. His objective was different; he wanted to tell the truth to the public about the criminal world and how it functions. The filmmaker really used to "wear many hats" simultaneously, as he financed the entire film production himself. Furthermore, he refused to calculate how much it cost him, saying only that the budget was far from being a Hollywood's one. Vitaly Demochka is also a writer and published books like: "The beginning of the end", "Indistinctly", "Old", "The gas crisis", "Gas crisis-2", "Special", "Baton", "Kill Bill" and of course, he's also the author of the book "Special"[13] inspired by his own film "Spets". Today Vitaly Demochka asks that people call him a former bandit, seeing as he put a stop to his criminal affairs, leading a new life following the law in Moscow. He recalled that once in the capital, his first taxi driver stole a thousand of rubles from him, while his first real estate agent took all of the money he dedicated for the purchase of his first apartment in Moscow. After these events, Vitaly Demochka decided to sleep in his new car in order to at least save that from a thief. Currently, he is quite respected among the Moscow authorities, as he has managed to keep identical objects to those he used in his film, a black Mitsubishi Pajero. And like in his film, his driver is also a "man-terminator", called Tumak. He wears a long black leather coat and crocodile skin boots with pointed toes. We chose this example of Vitaly seeing that the inspiration by criminal romance has not seen his injunction only by criminal networks. Its use was more extensive by producers and other representatives of the arts community. In our case, it was the circle of the Russian cinema that was inspired by criminal reality for the creation of many works intended, in some way, to pay tribute to crime and the Russian Mafia. In our case, Vitaly's story and its cinema adaptation, are particularly interesting for its rural representation. Rural areas are somehow represented poorly in the

---

[12] Demochka called his first production in this way.
[13] Demochka Vitaly, 2010 "Special", *Book on demand,* P.400

audiovisual production, and almost not present in the mafia genre cinema. The principal reason for such an absence is the fact that classical mafias (Italian, American, and several others) do not have many activities outside of the big cities. Their businesses are concentrated mostly in huge places, with big populations and important money circulation. However, Vitaly had his criminal activities based in rural zones and interpreted the reality in his film. The case of Vitaly is a really complete communicational system and can be seen with references like: newspapers, articles, books, reviews of different origins, TV programs and shows, and of course, the film itself. In Vitaly's case, "[t]he film producers have managed to engage a symbolic relationship between the film and the viewer."*14*

Figure 16.4 Image from the film Bimmer 2, Director: Buslov Piotr, Producers: Sergei Sel'ianov, Sergei Chliants, Vladimir Ignat'ev.
Source: http://izhevsk.ru/forums/icons/forum_pictures/004590/4590674.jpg

The Mafia's objects represented in the form of a weapon in the Russian cinema, using propaganda

Thus, a more important part of our work is focused on the study of "Russian mafia's communicating objects," which have become representative of "attractiveness", the identification of the mafia film genre, as well as the mythic "weapon" of the mafia's propaganda. There is a close parallel between their use in real life and cinema, which can be explained by their appreciation and popularity among the Russian viewer. The aesthetics of mafia's contemporary identity in cinema through its

---

14 This critic has been written into the French version of Rolling Stone magazine following the release of the movie "V for Vendetta" by James Mc Teigue in 2006.

objects are represented in each work of the "Mafia" genre: in music, language, preferences in lifestyle: cars, dress code, tattoos, money, behaviour and 'codes' in the criminal underworld, as well as tombstones and graves of criminal brothers. It operates a public communication and therefore a changing social representation of spectators.

The phenomenon of the Russian mafia despite it being fairly new in the world of classical mafia, has already won a high position in the international society. Here, it is necessary to distinguish the opposition of rural areas opposed to the big city in the Russian Mafia cinema and its influence on the viewer. In the case where the criminal hero finds himself in the countryside, in exile, or if he fled there voluntarily, rural zones represent tranquility and peace, often misleading because shortly after, the criminal is found. The influence of rural areas is a benefactor on the Russian Criminal protagonist.

Rural zones often turn the hard personality of a criminal into that of an actual human being. An example of this are the films *"Bimmer"* and *"Bimmer 2"*, which are crucial in the representation of rural areas and their influence on the evolution of the four criminal friends. The special feature of this film, a BMW car, is the main hero and is shown in the final scene, abandoned, founding its "death" in the forest, without its owners...

The cars representation in the mafia cinema

Like everything else, the cars of the mafia are distributed according to their degree of fame. For instance, during the 1990s, the latest car models and higher class brands like BMW, Mercedes 600 and only some 4 * 4 were used by criminal leaders and thieves in law with awareness, while later, at the end of the 1990s and in the beginning of the 2000s, they were used by "new Russians" - rich people. Unlike BMW cars, Mercedes vehicles were not selected for their operational functions, but for their aesthetic qualities, design and due to the popularity of the brand in Russia at this historical period. They were heavily used by "serious" people, who has influence in Russian politics or finance. Whereas BMW cars were a cliche of Russian organized crime. It was also translated into Russian language as the fighting cars of the criminal brothers.

One of the historical moments of the mafia in rural areas represented in cinema, was actually connected to a BMW car, such an example can be found in "Bimmer"[15] and "Bimmer 2". Bimmer is a 484 BMW, a vehicle that, in the end of the 1990s and the beginning of the 2000s, was just

---

[15] Bimmer, 2003, film of Pyotr Buslov

considered to be a miracle. Four friends and Bimmer's owners were stopped by police after a burglary, and a fight took place. One of the four friends was able to escape, leaving the other three in battle with the police. He ran away on Bimmer, betraying his friends, leaving without any concern as where he'll go, which is why he found himself in the countryside, in a sparsely populated rural area. Once he was far away, he realized that it was impossible for him to remain "head to head" with Bimmer because he felt guilty for his treason, and Bimmer would always just remind him of that. The importance of Bimmer's role is even more significant in the final scene, which we can also see as the "key stage". This scene is represented from an exterior point of view, having the camera pan out toward the abandoned Bimmer, left with a working battery, alone in a deserted rural area... This scene is highly significant and signifies that the end of the film is the death of Bimmer, abandonned, without its owners. It also represents that the four protagonists' friendship

Figure 16.5 Image from the film Bimmer 2, Director: Buslov Piotr, Producers: Sergei Sel'ianov, Sergei Chliants, Vladimir Ignat'ev.
Source: http://e38.ru/node/2972 ; http://e38.ru/files/kotcar.jpg

is broken. Two of the four friends end up being killed by the police, while the third was arrested. Only the fourth is the one who betrayed his friends and was left alive and free. It is a wonderful representation of rural areas in a criminal film. Bimmer decayed without the presence of its owners, and this idea is the main element. However, the representation of rural zones and their role have an extremely important influence as well. This film represents rural places as peacefully quiet; they come with silence, balance and unity with nature, which do not exist in the big city. Often, the criminal hero escapes from the big city to seek tranquillity and balance. The best example of that are the aforementioned movies. In fact, the director of Bimmer and Bimmer 2 gave primary importance to bimmer's life first, while the lives of the main characters only were on the second stage. Despite the fact that the four friends were still gravitating in the central field of the film, their importance came only after Bimmer's. The principal finding of the film is that the mafia's aesthetical object became a main character in itself. Bimmer stays an excellent example of a film where an object takes the protagonist's place. Seeing the popularity of the first film, a sequel, Bimmer 2, has been issued. In the second part, the story again revolves around the car of the main hero. This car-protagonist, although still manufactured by BMW, is a different model. Also, despite the fact that the film is a sequel, there are more differences between both movies than common points, maybe due to the fact that the second film is made by another director. The story of the second film has nothing in common with the original movie's subject. The sequel seems to be less original, as it treats a dull love story rather than the expected theme of the famous mafia. Concerning the technical points of the two films' musical representation, the background music was perfectly selected, even though it would be preferable to understand the language to get the words, as most of the songs in both films have been composed specifically for Bimmer and Bimmer 2. Firstly, the original soundtrack of Bimmer, was composed by a band, which had the same name as the film; the release of the music had immediately won respect and a good reputation within the network of organized crime. Thus, it was the initiation of such a success for more than the "mafia" film genre. The first film gave a real boost for this genre, which was already popular among Russian spectators; it mostly brought something new to the genre, through the aesthetic representation of its accessories, which took a front row seat, as the contributors to the development of the new "Robin Hood" criminal revolution style. The principal role of this film corresponding to our field is related to the importance the producer of the film gave to an accessory, the BMW vehicle. An object has been treated in an innovative way and thus, without antecedence. Hence, the aesthetic of mafia in the film is shown via the four friends from the criminal world. Throughout the film, they are looking for financial resources without any other occupation than "running" in the black Bimmer. Another question a viewer can ask themselves is why is the car's name "Bimmer"? Actually, bandits named their cars like that (from the BMW class). At the time of the Great Russian Revolution, this kind of car was the main choice of transportation for criminals. Representatives of criminal groups always preferred dark-coloured cars, black in general. In what concerns the BMW, the main hero in the film "Bimmer", there is a special feature. The car in the film is treated not as an accessory facilitating the circulation of its criminals owners, but was described above all as an "inhuman" principal character of the film.

Conclusion: The role of mafia movies

The arrival of mafia movies as a special genre was propelled by events in the Russian history. It is important to notice here that Soviet cinematography was always built on real events and the every day life of its citizens. The era of Mafia movies arrived during the post Soviet Union split. The Russian mafia had no analogue or any historical example to get inspired from the cinema of its own country. That is also the reason why organized crime in Russia has developed only after the Soviet Union breach. As the Soviet system had absolutely no crime in the country, or at least the population strongly believed in that, cinema had no inspiration to invent the criminal genre. Hence, once the Soviet system has been destroyed, and international video production could finally come to Russia, local organized crime developed very quickly and was principally interposed on Hollywood production (Karishev, 2007 and 2008). In this paper, we did not speak about the Russian mafia in Hollywood movies, but about local productions. First, even before the break of the USSR, Soviet films still had an incredible influence of the wind of liberation (Ogurechnikov, 2008), which has been brought to Gorbachev's glasnost era. Russian censorship had brutally replaced glasnost of Gorbachev's policy. Regarding the Russian spectator, they were not at all prepared for this cinematic release. To give an example of cinema of the Gorbachev's era, there were films that have been called thcernukcha or black cinema. However, these films were not necessarily black films. There have also been other movies that ended up being not developed, because, for instance, they were denied a broadcast because of their quality. Then there were the films that were previously banned during the Soviet system. These movies were able to relay a message very openly, a part of them even shocking the public, who was not yet ready to see that kind of portrayal on screen. Once they were broadcast, the public's reaction was not necessarily the expected one by the produced of this Russian cinema genre. On the other hand, these films were often full of vulgarity, hard and so "impossible" by their "truth". The public shared a slight degree of shock, but also experienced some form of seduction. It was the time of fashion in the 1990s, talking about the Russian mafia and the Russian organized crime, as an interdependent parts. The changes made by the break of the USSR had fully contributed to the mafia's involvement in cinematography. These dirty investments of all kinds in the cinema field and the weak state support forced filmmakers, who were in financial difficulty, to accept all kinds of financing. Therefore, these new sources produced new genres of films, which have quickly become popular and loved by the audience. Among them, there is the mafia criminal genre. The arrival of the Russian mafia in film financing circuits is also a mediating communication between the life of organized crime, mafia and the general public. It is expressed in particular by the introduction of what we might call the aesthetic of the mafia,

> high degree of sophistication and ruthlessness has attracted the world's attention and concern to what has become known as a global Russian Mafia (Finckenauer and Voronin, 2001).

The Russians "do not fit" in the media landscape and international film scene because they still think and act according to 'post-Soviet" rules in the economy, the arts, the symbolic and intercultural communications. It is the domination of Soviet artistic and economic know-how that mixes with new values, as they are present in the phenomenon of "mafia aesthetics" and opposed to being applied internationally. In most cases, when it comes to criminal organizations and groups, their "being" as it was during the period of the Great Criminal Revolution is undoubtedly the domination of the American cinema.

References

Bazin, A. 1967–71. *What is cinema?* Vol. 1 & 2. Berkeley: University of California Press. Edition Cerf (french version). 372 p.

Ferrell, J. 1995. Culture, Crime, and Cultural Criminology. *Journal of Criminal Justice and Popular Culture*, 3/2: 25-42

Ferro, M. 1993. *Cinema and history*. Paris : Gallimard.

Finckenauer, J. O. and Yuri A. Voronin. 2001. The Threat of Russian Organized Crime. Issues in International Crime. U.S. Department of Justice. Office of Justice Programs. National Institute of Justice.

Gurov, A. 1990. *Professional Crime Past and Present*. Moscow: Iuridicheskaia Literatura.

Karishev, V. 2007. *The Russian Mafia (1988-2007)*. Moscow: Eksmo.

Karishev, V. 2008. *Great Criminal Revolution (1988-1994)*. Moscow: Eksmo.

Lotman, J., R. Grigoriev and M. Lotman. 1998. O*b iskusstve : struktura chudožestvennogo teksta : semiotika kino i problemy kinoėstetiki : stat'i, zametki, vystuplenija (1962-1993)*. Sankt-Peterburg: Iskusstvo-SPB.

Luneev, V. 2000. Study of Russian organized crime in Russia during the period of the new criminal law (1997-1999). *The organized crime and corruption*. N.1

Matskevitch, M. 2009. La mafia russe en Europe : mythe ou réalité ? (Aspects criminologiques). *Revue internationale de droit comparé*, 61-3 : 621.

McGraw-Hill. 2002. *Dictionary of American Idioms and Phrasal Verbs*. The McGraw-Hill Companies Inc.

Modestov, N.S. 2001. C*riminal Moscow* 1-2. Documentary chronicle of criminal lawlessness 80-90es of XX century. Moscow: Tsentrpoligraf.

Ogurechnikov, P. 2008. *The culture of the screen, like the new myth: on the cinema example*. PhD. Himki. Russia.

Parfitt, T. 2004. Mobster turns from gunning down rivals to shooting TV series. *The Telegraph*. Moscow. : http://www.telegraph.co.uk/news/worldnews/europe/russia/1469963/Mobster-turns-from-gunning-down-rivals-to-shooting-TV-series.html

Razinkin, V. and Alexey Tarabrin. 1998. *Tsvetnaya mast: Elite of criminal world*. Moscow. p. 180.

Romm, M. 2003. *Kak v kino*. Moscow. Dekom. p.104-112

Sergeev Y., 2002, *This is not a Brigade this is "brotherhood"*, Komsomolskaya Pravda, n/a

Smorodinskaya, T., Karen Evans-Romaine and Helena Goscilo. 2007. *Encyclopedia of contemporary Russian culture*. London. New York: Routledge.

Filmography

Bimmer. Directed by Buslov, Pyotr. 2003. Bimmer Film series. Russia.

Bimmer. Directed by Buslov, Pyotr. 2006. Bummer Film series. Russia.

Brigade. Directed by Sidorov, Alexey. 2002. Beta Film GmbH. Russia. http://www.avatarfilm.ru/brigada_about.html

Brother. Directed by Balabanov, Alexey. 1997. Kino International Corp. Russia.

Brother 2. Directed by Balabanov, Alexey. 2000. CTB Film Company. Russia.

Godfather. film series:
- *Godfather I.* Directed by Coppola, Francis Ford. 1972. USA. Paramount Pictures.
- *Godfather II.* Directed by Coppola, Francis Ford. 1974. USA. Paramount Pictures.
- *Godfather III.* Directed by Coppola, Francis Ford. 1990. USA. Paramount Pictures.

Liubit po russki. Directed by Matveyev, Eugeni. 1996. Mosfilm. Russia
Mama Don't Cry. Directed by Pegemskiy, Maxim. 1998. STB. Russia.
Outskirts. Directed by Lutsik, Petr. 2004. Goskino.
Scarface. Directed by De Palma, Brian. 1983. Universal Pictures. USA.
Scarface. Directed by Hawks, Howard. 1932. *The Caddo Company.* USA.
Spets. Directed by Demochka, Vitaly. 2003. Vitali Demochka Video Channel on YouTube. Russia
Upir. Directed by Vinokurov, Sergei. 1997. Film Studio Gorky. Russia
Vremya pechali yeshchyo ne prishlo. Directed by Selyanov Sergey. 1995 . STB. Russia.
8 ½$. Directed by Konstantinopolsky, Grigori. 1999. Film Studio Gorky.
V for Vendetta. Directed by Teigue, James Mc. 2006. Warner Bros. Pictures. United States

Further Reading

- Beumers, Brigit. 1999. *Russia On Reels: The Russian Idea in Post-Soviet Cinema.* IB Tauris. PY

  This is the first book to deal exclusively with Russian cinema of the 1990s. It introduces readers to the currents and common interests of contemporary Russian cinema, offers close studies of the work of filmmakers like Sokurov, Muratova and Astrakhan, reviews the Russian film industry in a period of massive economic transformation, and assesses cinema's function as a definer of Russia's new identity.

- Galeotti, Mark. 1998. The Mafia and the New Russia, *Australian Journal of Politics and History* 44. no. 3: 415-429. First published online: 18 DEC 2002. DOI: 10.1111/1467-8497.00029

  The rise of the Russian mafiya, a distinctive form of organised crime, reflects more than just the temporary dislocations and uncertainties of the country's transition from a Soviet state to a free market democracy. Rooted in Russian tradition and Soviet practice, it is also a formidable obstacle to this evolution. This has serious implications for the new Russian polity: weakening central authority, diluting the state's monopoly of coercion, discrediting the market economy and ultimately usurping and distorting the very functions of the state. Any solution will have to come not from tougher policing (which itself would threaten a return to authoritarianism) but from a wider political and cultural response.

- Fikenauer, J.O. and Elin J. Waring. 1998. *Russian Mafia in America: Immigration Culture and Crime*. Boston: Northeastern University Press.
  Does a "Russian Mafia" really exist? This book seeks to answer that question by investigating in detail such topics as the characteristics of the Russian criminal tradition of Vory v Zakone ("thieves professing the code"), contemporary Russian mobs, criminal activity among Russian immigrants, claims of KGB involvement in American crime, and connections between crime bosses and gangsters in both countries.
- French New Wave Film. New wave of cinema, also known as a Nouvelle Vague; originally created by the non-traditional French filmmakers and referred to a group of individualistic, innovative, and non-traditional French filmmakers, directors and producers in the late 1950s and early 1960s. French New Wave Film (Nouvelle Vague), http://www.newwavefilm.com/new-wave-cinema-guide/nouvelle-vague-where-to-start.shtml
- Friedman R. 2000. *Red Mafiya*: *How the Russian Mob Has Invaded America*. Boston: Little Brown and Co.; 296 p.
  In the past decade, from Brighton Beach to Moscow, Toronto to Hong Kong, the Russian mob has become the world's fastest-growing criminal superpower. Trafficking in prostitutes, heroin, and missiles, the mafiya poses an enormous threat to global stability and safety. Today, the mafiya controls over 80 percent of Russia's banks and has siphoned off billions of dollars in Western loans and aid, almost certainly derailing the chance for a stable democracy there. But that is just the beginning, for the mafiya is now in every corner of the United States and has infiltrated some of the banks and brokerage firms that handle your money. And American law enforcement is just waking up to this staggering problem.
- Kabakov, A. 1995. *Last Hero*. Dep. Ed.: M- Saint-Petersbourg "Vagrius".
  Kabakov, Alexander is a journalist, fiction writer, and playwright who became well-known in 1989 for No Return, a short dystopian novel first published in the journal The Art of Cinema. No Return has been translated into several languages, including English, and adapted into a film. Kabakov has worked at the newspaper Kommersant since 1997

after long stints at Moscow News and Gudok, a railroad industry newspaper.

- Kryshtanovskaya O. 1995. *New russians elite, working hard, include on themself, Izvestiya (jornal)*. Author is in the opposition to the Putin's politic.
- Varese, F. 2001. *The Russian Mafia: Private Protection in a New Market Economy*. Oxford.
Unique insight into the history and organization of the Russian Mafia. Challenges widely held views of the Russian Mafia. Based on in depth interviews with the Mafia, criminals and officials, archival documents, and reports from undercover police operations. Comparative study making references to other Mafias (the Japanese Yakuza, the Sicilian Cosa Nostra, American-Italian Mafia and the Hong Kong Triads). https://global.oup.com/academic/product/the-russian-mafia-9780198297369?cc=us&lang=en&

CHAPTER SEVENTEEN

SOUS LES VENTS DE NEPTUNE (2004) DE FRED VARGAS - L'INVENTION D'UN AILLEURS ?

CHRISTOPHE GELLY

Pour qui connaît l'œuvre de Fred Vargas, l'idée de convoquer l'auteur à propos de l'imaginaire canadien peut sembler étrange. En effet, les romans policiers qu'elle écrit depuis 1986 (celui dont il sera question est le onzième) semblent plutôt centrés sur la redéfinition et "l'acclimatation" de stéréotypes génériques abordés dans une perspective et selon des références très françaises. Ainsi, le commissaire Jean-Baptiste Adamsberg, son personnage récurrent, est un enquêteur ancré dans un paysage très parisien et doté de racines françaises qui sont très souvent mentionnées dans les romans – il est originaire des Pyrénées et ce roman, tout comme la plupart des récits policiers de Vargas, fait grand cas de cet ancrage puisqu'il motive l'un des fils essentiels de l'intrigue, centré sur la recherche par Adambsberg de son frère en fuite depuis son accusation infondée pour meurtre. Le caractère même du commissaire, surnommé "le pelleteur de nuages", personnage lunaire agissant sans méthode apparente, préférant s'inspirer de l'atmosphère des lieux et des personnes pour guider son travail et se ressourçant à travers de grandes marches solitaires plutôt que dans la pratique d'une investigation scientifique, fait penser à un autre grand intuitif, le commissaire Maigret, que Simenon avait surnommé "l'accoucheur de destinées". Cette autre référence francophone, sinon française, suggère bien que l'écriture de Vargas s'inspire d'un modèle "continental" du genre policier, qui fait prévaloir sur l'action du polar ou la réflexion du *whodunit* classique un modèle à la fois poétique et presque théâtral, fondé sur une galerie de personnages et de lieux qu'il s'agit d'explorer avant tout, quitte à reléguer au second plan l'intrigue criminelle proprement dite. Ainsi, le commissariat dans lequel officie Adamsberg est peuplé de policiers tous plus excentriques – et attachants – les uns que les autres, d'Adrien Danglard, inspecteur méthodique et érudit mais ayant un fort penchant pour la boisson, père célibataire de cinq marmots à qui il raconte parfois ses aventures à la brigade, à Violette Retancourt, corpulente lieutenante qui sous un air maussade permet souvent à Adamsberg de se tirer des mauvais pas où le mène son habitude de la flânerie. Le but de cette étude du roman sera ici d'interroger la manière dont Fred Vargas négocie cette "sortie du territoire" de son héros pour le mener à Ottawa, dans le parc fédéral de la Gatineau, pour une formation de deux semaines sur le traitement des empreintes génétiques dans le cadre d'une collaboration entre les polices des deux Etats. Cette étude tentera de montrer comment le Canada est reconstruit comme un lieu très largement imaginaire – notamment sur le plan linguistique – ce qui permet à l'auteur de mettre en scène, assez différemment de ce qu'elle pratique dans ses autres romans, la méthode d'analyse – l'herméneutique – de son enquêteur. Dans cette optique, le réalisme de la représentation romanesque dans cette œuvre sera abordé en premier lieu, avant de questionner le rapport au langage comme symbole de l'altérité. Nous verrons que ces différents sujets prennent un sens particulier dans la pratique du genre policier de Fred Vargas.

Le Canada imaginaire

Dans cet *opus*, Adamsberg et plusieurs membres de sa brigade sont donc invités au Canada pour une formation de police scientifique, mais le récit insiste d'abord sur les rapports du commissaire avec son adjoint Danglard, qui lui semble inexplicablement hostile. Avant le départ pour le Canada, Adamsberg est en proie à plusieurs malaises et évanouissements dont il ne peut s'expliquer la cause. Avec l'aide de Danglard, il parvient à comprendre que ces malaises sont causés par une réaction psychique à la lecture d'un article de presse qui relate l'assassinat d'une jeune fille de trois coups de couteau, qui vient de se dérouler en Alsace. Cet article fait ressurgir en lui le souvenir de son frère en fuite, inculpé quelque trente ans auparavant pour le meurtre de sa fiancée, et à qui il a pu épargner la prison en falsifiant le dossier à charge, mais qu'il n'a jamais réussi à innocenter, malgré son identification certaine de l'assassin. Cet assassin serait le juge Fulgence, personnage influent et protégé par ses relations, auteur de crimes en série qu'Adamsberg a traqué durant une partie de sa carrière jusqu'à son décès il y a quatorze ans – le nouveau crime serait donc l'œuvre d'un "fantôme"… Lors de son séjour au Canada, Adamsberg a une aventure sans lendemain avec Noëlla, une jeune Française expatriée qui est retrouvée morte après son départ, dans une scène de crime où

précisément sont retrouvées les empreintes génétiques du commissaire.
L'enquêteur prend ainsi la place du suspect traqué, et devra prouver que ce
crime a été en réalité commis par le juge Fulgence désirant se débarrasser
de son ennemi qui le recherche depuis si longtemps.

La trame de l'intrigue elle-même est, comme souvent chez Vargas, peu
vraisemblable puisque l'on y croise un tueur en série quasi-octogénaire, un
motif criminel peu commun (il s'agit pour le juge de tuer pour reconstituer
avec ses victimes un puzzle onomastique inspiré du jeu de Mah-Jong) et
des scènes pour le moins aussi cocasses qu'inquiétantes. Ainsi,
Adamsberg se voit contraint pour échapper à la police canadienne de
"faire corps" avec sa collègue Violette Retancourt : lors d'une fouille de la
chambre de celle-ci, il se dissimule sous le peignoir de Retancourt dont la
corpulence lui permet de cacher le fluet commissaire aux yeux des
policiers canadiens. Plus généralement, le Canada ne joue en réalité qu'un
rôle secondaire dans l'intrigue elle-même puisqu'il est en quelque sorte le
théâtre où se déplace l'affrontement entre Adamsberg et le juge Fulgence ;
le nœud du récit reste bien cette confrontation qui prend racine et se
déroule essentiellement en France. Cependant, la reconstitution du Canada
est bien en quelque sorte l'un des buts majeurs de l'œuvre, mais selon des
objectifs qui n'ont rien de réaliste. Le premier but est de mettre en
évidence un décalage linguistique très – peut-être trop – appuyé, qui vise à
exprimer le sentiment de confusion qui touche Adamsberg dans un texte
qui fait remonter à la surface un passé douloureux. Adamsberg semble
ainsi en proie à un syndrome d'étrangeté du réel, comme si le *jet lag*
culturel et linguistique qu'il subit persistait et venait troubler sa vision de
la réalité déjà de coutume fort approximative et peu orthodoxe. Fred
Vargas s'ingénie ainsi à faire du décalage linguistique le signe d'une
déliaison d'avec le réel qui exprime la rupture des statuts usuels[1] – le flic
devient la bête traquée, le passé revient hanter le présent. Cette étrangeté
de la langue est comme omniprésente, sur-accentuée dans le texte pour
incarner la perte des repères. Voici par exemple la manière dont se
déroulent les présentations des binômes français et canadiens censés
travailler ensemble pendant leur séjour :

> – Chacun de vous s'amanchera avec l'un des membres de la Brigade de
> Paris, et on changera les paires tous les deux ou trois jours. Allez-y de tout
> cœur mais menez-les pas tambour battant pour vous faire péter les
> bretelles, ils ne sont pas infirmes des deux bras. Ils sont en période
> d'entraînement, ils s'initient. Alors formez-les au pas de grise pour

---

[1] Ce phénomène courant dans les processus mentaux du détective de fiction a déjà
été relevé par Roger Dadoun.

commencer. Et faites pas de l'esprit de bottine s'ils ne vous comprennent pas ou s'ils parlent autrement que nous. Ils sont pas plus branleux que vous autres sous prétexte qu'ils sont Français. Je compte sur vous.

En somme, à peu près le même discours que celui qu'Adamsberg avait tenu à son équipe, quelques jours plus tôt. (pp. 132-133)

Il ne s'agit pas ici, bien sûr, pour Vargas, de pratiquer un "documentarisme" linguistique, de tenter le réalisme de la représentation – même s'il l'on ne peut exclure totalement la tentation du pittoresque – mais plutôt de forcer le trait pour communiquer à son lecteur cette impression de distance avec le réel qui est celle que ressent Adamsberg dans cette épreuve où son passé resurgit et le déstabilise. Bien sûr, cette manière de forcer le trait n'a pas été toujours lue comme pertinente, dans la mesure où elle ne correspond pas à une vision très réaliste de la distance culturelle et linguistique. C'est ainsi que certains commentaires[2] furent assassins quant au pittoresque linguistique employé ici et jugé peu réaliste.

> Je le mentionne d'emblée, j'ai dû lire la section québécoise du récit avec un dictionnaire des québécismes et des expressions québécoises parce que je n'y comprenais strictement rien! Oui, nous utilisons des expressions assez imagées et différentes (vous en avez un bon exemple quand j'écris d'ailleurs)... mais pas à TOUTES les phrases !!! C'était une vraie énumération, et pas nécessairement des expressions les plus fréquentes !!! Et ce n'est pas tout le monde qui sacre aux deux mots et qui parle de la façon décrite dans le livre.   Nous sommes polis, parfois, aussi !! Autre chose, le fameux "tu" utilisé – souvent en double – pour poser une question... oui, c'est vrai, nous le faisons. Mais pas à chaque maudite question que nous posons. Et surtout pas quand la question est négative ou qu'elle comporte un interrogatif !! Et ce ne sont que quelques exemples... mais disons que bon, c'est loin d'être représentatif du parlé québécois. De plus, certains mots très "Québec" mélangés à des structures de phrase ou d'autres mots très "France", ça fait bizarre... bref, pas évident ! En plus que certaines expressions sont réutilisées genre... souvent !! J'en ai été assez irritée, après un moment !! http://moncoinlecture.over-blog.com/article-28648003.html

Cependant il est possible de considérer cette stratégie dans une autre perspective que celle du réalisme. Fred Vargas recrée un Canada imaginaire jusque dans ses expressions pour mettre en avant une caractéristique générale de son enquêteur, dont nous suivons la perspective pendant la majeure partie du récit : son rapport problématique au réel. C'est une qualité qui est également une manière de relire une tradition

---

[2] Voir aussi à ce sujet l'article de Nadine Vincent.

précédente du genre, dans la mesure où la littérature policière compte nombre d'excentriques du type d'Adamsberg, de l'individualiste Maigret au lieutenant Columbo en passant par Sherlock Holmes qui, comme on sait, rangeait son tabac dans une babouche et s'entraînait au tir dans le confort de son appartement. Cette excentricité a d'ailleurs pour fondement un élément qui est repris dans l'écriture de Vargas à travers les rêveries d'Adamsberg, à savoir le besoin de cacher le déficit identitaire de l'enquêteur, qui parce qu'il doit attribuer les rôles actantiels dans l'intrigue (en d'autres termes dévoiler la culpabilité d'un personnage) se voit contraint, lui, à abandonner toute identité saillante, ce que le texte dissimule par cette excentricité. Autre lecture de cette identité problématique : Jacques Dubois explique l'excentricité de la plupart des enquêteurs dans le genre policier par une réaction névrotique à la tension créée par des exigences contradictoires, par "l'impossible conciliation romanesque entre le régime herméneutique et le régime proprement narratif" (p. 79). En d'autres termes, l'enquêteur manifeste sa position inconfortable au carrefour du récit littéraire et de l'enquête criminelle – censément purement rationnelle et logique – par cette propension à l'excentricité. L'étrangeté linguistique à laquelle est confronté Adamsberg, son inadéquation à son environnement, est une manifestation particulière de son rapport problématique au réel déterminé par le genre.

On voit donc que la pratique du genre policier par Fred Vargas ne rompt pas totalement, même si elle l'adapte, avec une référence sous-jacente à certains mécanismes "canoniques" du genre. Cette référence se retrouve également dans la manière dont Adamsberg, avec son adjoint Danglard, organise une relecture du réel afin de sortir de la confusion. Il s'agit ici de parvenir à une explication englobante d'un réel dont la cohérence est présupposée de façon "totale". Chaque élément doit donc être signifiant, voire sur-signifiant pour satisfaire à une vision pansémiotique du monde. C'est pourquoi les éléments les plus "canadiens" de l'intrigue, au-delà des caractéristiques linguistiques, doivent finalement reparaître dans la lecture finale, mais intégrés dans celle-ci. Un exemple qui ne concerne pas la représentation du Canada se trouve dans l'épisode où Adamsberg comprend enfin l'origine des malaises qui le touchent depuis plusieurs jours et qui sont dus chaque fois à la réapparition du tueur en série Fulgence et aux images et objets croisés par Adamsberg évoquant l'arme employée par le tueur – un trident.

> Adamsberg se redressa dans son fauteuil. Les trois punaises rouges
> alignées au mur de son bureau, les trois trous sanglants. La longue
> fourchette à trois dents que maniait Enid, le reflet des pointes du Trident.
> Et Neptune, levant son sceptre. Les images qui lui avaient fait si mal,

déclenchant les tornades, faisant affluer le chagrin, libérant en une coulée de boue son angoisse revenue. (p. 31)

Cet établissement de connexions imaginaires dans un univers sursignifiant va finalement "envahir" l'univers canadien représenté dans le roman, lui insufflant une cohérence et une hostilité qu'il n'avait pas au départ. Ainsi de la mention du poisson particulier qui vit dans le lac Pink et qu'Adamsberg s'imagine sous un jour des plus significatifs :

> Le lac Pink atteignait une profondeur de vingt mètres et son fond était recouvert de trois mètres de boue. Jusqu'ici tout allait bien. Mais en raison même de cette profondeur, les eaux de sa surface ne se mêlaient pas aux eaux du fond. A partir de quinze mètres, celles-ci ne bougeaient plus, jamais remuées, jamais oxygénées, non plus que les vases qui renfermaient ses dix mille six cents ans d'histoire. Un lac d'apparence normale tout compte fait, se résuma Adamsberg, et même carrément rose et bleu, mais recouvrant un second lac perpétuellement stagnant, sans air, mort, fossile de l'histoire. Le pire étant qu'un poisson marin y vivait encore, issu du temps où la mer était encore là. Adamsberg examina le dessin du poisson, qui évoquait un hybride entre carpe et truite, portant des barbelures. Il eut beau relire le panneau, le poisson inconnu ne portait pas de nom.
> Un lac vivant posé sur un lac mort. Abritant une créature innommée dont on possédait un croquis, une image. Adamsberg se pencha par-dessus la barrière de bois pour tenter d'apercevoir sous l'eau rose ces inerties cachées. Pourquoi fallait-il que toutes ses pensées le ramènent au Trident ? Comme ces griffures des ours sur les troncs ? Comme ce lac décédé qui vivait sans un bruit, tapi sous une surface de vie, boueux, grisâtre, où se mouvait un hôte hérité d'un âge mort ? (p. 154-155)

Ce poisson n'est pas seulement l'un des fils de la trame policière qui ramèneraient l'enquêteur sur la piste du criminel, il joue plusieurs rôles distincts qui, tous, signalent la nature de la réalité canadienne comme reconstruction imaginaire dans l'univers de Vargas. C'est d'abord un signe de la résurgence du passé et de l'impossibilité de l'oubli, donc un "corrélat objectif" (selon la formule de T.S. Eliot), une expression des sentiments mêlés de crainte et d'hostilité éprouvés par Adamsberg. C'est aussi le signe de la lecture "projective", et donc relativement problématique, qu'Adamsberg fait d'un réel qu'il sur-interprète. C'est enfin le symptôme d'un manque – là où Adamsberg est confronté à la réalité, il voit une autre réalité, inspirée par son histoire.

On voit donc ici que la représentation "pittoresque" du décalage culturel n'est certes pas le dernier mot de Fred Vargas, mais aussi qu'elle n'hésite pas à se "servir" du Canada comme représentation pour nourrir l'intrigue de son roman, parfois de façon peu vraisemblable. Est-ce une faiblesse de cette écriture ou peut-on reconsidérer et justifier cette pratique dans un cadre générique ? Ce cadre peut-il contribuer à expliquer les rapports entre les différentes variétés de français dans le roman ?

L'altérité, le genre, le langage

Cette seconde partie de présentation du roman sera développée autour de trois questions qui découlent de cette figuration d'un Canada "imaginaire" par le commissaire Adamsberg, et qui ont toutes un rapport avec l'altérité culturelle et linguistique telle qu'elle apparaît dans la partie canadienne du roman. Il faut tout d'abord remarquer que le roman met en scène une confrontation de différentes variétés de français – le français de France dit "normé" et le québécois, mais pas seulement – d'une façon qui met en scène et tout à la fois relativise les rapports hiérarchiques entre ces variantes ; ensuite il apparaît que cette confrontation des deux variantes du français s'articule à des stéréotypes culturels qui sont rappelés dans le roman mais qui sont aussi mis à distance ; enfin cette question du langage sera réexaminée à travers le thème du réalisme linguistique et culturel, à rattacher à la place du texte dans le genre policier.

Le rôle des différentes variantes du français dans ce roman a fait l'objet d'une étude assez développée par Kathleen Shields, dont la démonstration suivante va largement s'inspirer. Cette étude fait ressortir que dans un contexte national encore très marqué par une approche idéologique de la langue française, et mettant en avant une promotion de la langue française dans une visée universaliste, le roman de Fred Vargas met en scène la rencontre des Français et des Canadiens dans un contexte particulier puisque la supériorité culturelle supposée des Français ("le vieux pays", comme le dit un personnage p. 151) est en butte à la supériorité technologique des Canadiens qui ressort de leur maîtrise des relevés d'empreintes génétiques. Ainsi, la scène de la présentation des deux équipes qui vont travailler ensemble dans le roman insiste sur la persistance et le renversement des préjugés et stéréotypes hiérarchiques :

> However, there are important differences on both sides, since the French team's cultural superiority might tempt them to laugh at the Canadians and the Canadians' scientific superiority might lead them to mock the French. The underlying point is that cultural superiority is similar wherever it is to be encountered and needs to be mocked, whether it is linguistic or technological. (Shields, p. 206)[3]

---

[3] Je traduis ici, comme par la suite, les citations de K. Shields : "Cependant, des différences importantes subsistent des deux côtés, puisque les Français, en raison

Où l'on voit que l'on est bien toujours le colonisé – culturel ou technologique – d'un autre… Cette déconstruction des hiérarchies se poursuit sur le plan linguistique dans la mesure où le français parlé par Adamsberg s'oppose en termes d'images au français canadien, mais aussi dans la mesure où cette opposition cache une certaine complémentarité :

> Parisian and Canadian French are paired and contrasted throughout, serving as foils for each other. The Canadian French is rich in metaphor, idioms and catchphrases all rooted in the physical and geographical realities of the continent, whereas the Parisian French is equally stylized, as a plain language from which these features are lost or banished. This is particularly so in the case of Adamsberg from whose speech all visual images are repressed, only to resurface in his dreams and nightmares. (Shields, p. 209)[4]

Cette complémentarité permet en effet à Fred Vargas de dédramatiser la confrontation hiérarchisée entre les deux variantes du français, notamment par l'humour et les recours à la traduction "facétieuse" de certains québécismes, voire par l'adoption par Adamsberg de ces expressions (notamment celles qui renvoient à la sincérité et à l'absence d'arrière-pensées, par exemple "je n'ai pas de porte de derrière" signifiant la sincérité de ses propos). Comme le dit l'un des personnages canadiens, "ici, on n'a pas d'histoire mais on a de la géographie" : quel meilleur moyen de suggérer que ce qui manque à Adamsberg, grand marcheur, les lieux à arpenter pour dénouer son destin, il les trouvera au Canada ?

Cette complémentarité culturelle et linguistique ne va pas sans une mise en scène de ce qui contrarie les rapports sociaux entre les porteurs de ces deux variantes linguistiques, c'est-à-dire un certain bagage de stéréotypes culturels associés à l'autre francophone. Pour le Canadien il s'agit avant tout de l'association à un passé "livresque" le plus souvent

---

de leur supériorité culturelle, peuvent être tentés de railler les Canadiens, tout comme les Canadiens, forts de leur supériorité scientifique, pourraient se moquer des Français. Ce qui est implicite ici c'est qu'il est nécessaire de relativiser cette question de la supériorité culturelle, peu importe de quel côté elle se trouve, et peu importe qu'elle soit de nature linguistique ou technologique."

[4] "Tout au long du texte, le français parisien et canadien sont associés et différenciés, ils assurent une fonction de faire-valoir l'un pour l'autre. Le français canadien regorge de métaphores, de formules idiomatiques et de phrases fétiches, qui sont toutes ancrées dans la réalité physique et géographique du continent, alors que le français parisien, tout aussi stylisé, est dénué de ces traits caractéristiques. Ce contraste se remarque tout particulièrement dans le discours d'Adamsberg duquel est bannie toute image visuelle ; ces images refont cependant surface dans ses rêves et ses cauchemars."

synonyme d'artificialité et d'un manque de spontanéité. Ainsi de cet échange entre Adamsberg et un Canadien francophone :

> – T'es du vieux pays ? Français, hein ?
> – Oui.
> – Comment je le sais ? dit l'homme en riant cette fois, et en s'approchant d'Adamsberg. Parce que quand tu parles, je crois pas t'entendre, je crois te lire. Tu fais-tu quoi par-là? Tu vas aux hommes ? (p. 151)

De même, le lieutenant Retancourt expliquant à Adamsberg son projet pour berner les autorités de la GRC (Gendarmerie Royale Canadienne) fait reposer celui-ci sur une vision très stéréotypée et pétrie de préjugés culturels. Quand elle explique la raison pour laquelle elle pense que son plan fonctionnera, elle se fonde sur un "puritanisme culturel" qui dissuadera les enquêteurs de la fouiller si elle leur fait face en peignoir :

> – Les Québécois sont pudiques et réservés, dit-elle. Pas de femmes nues sur les couvertures de journaux ou sur les rives des lacs. C'est là-dessus qu'on table, sur leur pudeur. En revanche, dit-elle en se tournant vers Adamsberg, vous et moi devrons la laisser de côté. Ce ne sera pas le moment d'être prudes. Et si vous l'êtes, rappelez-vous seulement que vous jouez votre tête. (p. 254)

Bien sûr, cette mise en scène des préjugés culturels n'est pas à prendre au pied de la lettre. Ce que Fred Vargas cherche à montrer c'est le caractère éminemment problématique de ces représentations stéréotypées. Le français de France n'est pas davantage le médium par excellence d'une supériorité culturelle ou intellectuelle que le français canadien n'est le langage de la pruderie morale, et c'est à ce type de constructions imaginaires que le texte nous renvoie pour les déconstruire.

Prenons un dernier exemple de cette déconstruction, cité par Kathleen Shields également. Lorsque le texte s'attarde sur le lac Pink et sa créature mystérieuse, les deux niveaux du lac renvoient potentiellement à ces deux plans d'approche de la réalité, l'intuitif et le rationnel, le pratique et l'abstrait – deux niveaux qui renvoient aussi aux stéréotypes nationaux :

> The lake is described as "un lac vivant posé sur un lac mort", a living lake on top of a dead one. The two types of waters in the lake can be read as a metaphor for the non-translatability, incomprehension and lack of connection between obsessive dreams and rational science. In terms of the quest structure of the thriller they reveal the lack of connection in Adamsberg's mind between the nightmarish living present of the serial

killing and the historical evidence needed to make sense of it. (Shields, p. 212)[5].

La résolution de l'intrigue criminelle vient donc établir une connexion entre ces différents champs de l'expérience et proposer ce que Shields appelle un humanisme nouveau qui prend l'aspect d'un syncrétisme culturel, d'une combinaison entre culture scientifique et intuition.

Pour finir, la question du réalisme linguistique semble résumer de façon assez pertinente le propos de Fred Vargas sur les transferts culturels "bénéfiques" qui s'opèrent dans l'intrigue. Nous avons vu que le roman ne cherche pas à adopter un point de vue documentaire – et donc réaliste – sur la question du langage. Il y a "trop" de québécismes pour maintenir l'illusion mimétique de la réalité diégétique – comme le dit une internaute canadienne à propos de l'écriture de ce roman, c'est *too much*. Mais ce refus du réalisme prend tout son sens dans le rapport à l'altérité ; il s'agit sans doute de sur-jouer cette altérité pour finalement pointer une résolution du conflit dans l'imaginaire.

Cette résolution imaginaire nous rappelle plusieurs éléments à la fois sur l'écriture spécifique de Vargas et sur le genre policier, en lien avec la question de la marge et du territoire. Premièrement, cette altérité n'est pas totalement "explicable", ou intégrable, dans le "système Adamsberg". Le texte insiste d'ailleurs beaucoup sur le désarroi constant du commissaire au cours de l'intrigue. La marge n'est donc pas toujours assimilée au territoire, et une partie des événements qui se déroulent dans cet ailleurs canadien est vouée à l'oubli, voire au refoulement (c'est le cas pour la relation qu'entretient Adamsberg avec Noëlla, la jeune femme que Fulgence veut le faire accuser d'avoir tuée). En d'autres termes, le genre policier n'est certes pas le lieu contemporain de la clairvoyance et de la délimitation non-problématique des frontières entre conscient et inconscient. Une marge du réel demeure donc inassimilée. Deuxièmement, cette excentricité et cette vulnérabilité de l'enquêteur viennent nous rappeler au contraire que le genre policier a souvent servi, étonnamment, de contrepied à un rationalisme radical – notamment par le biais des nombreuses parodies policières qui sont presque contemporaines de son

---

[5] "Le lac est décrit comme "un lac vivant posé sur un lac mort". Les deux niveaux aquatiques du lac peuvent se lire comme l'expression métaphorique d'une déconnexion entre des rêves obsédants et une science rationnelle, comme l'image du non-sens et de l'intraduisible. Dans le contexte de l'enquête policière ils révèlent dans l'esprit d'Adamsberg une déconnexion entre le présent cauchemardesque des meurtres en série et les témoignages issus du passé qu'il est nécessaire d'exhumer pour comprendre le présent."

émergence (que l'on songe à Maurice Leblanc et à *Arsène Lupin contre Herlock Sholmès* paru en 1908). Le vagabondage et l'amateurisme d'Adamsberg, sa capacité à se laisser porter par les événements, sont donc dans le droit fil d'une lecture plus ou moins décalée du genre (représentée aussi parfois par l'écriture d'un Daniel Pennac), qui actualise le potentiel comique du genre. Enfin, ce roman de Vargas vient nous rappeler la pertinence contemporaine du récit policier dans la mesure où il présente une image de la marge et de l'ailleurs comme toujours étrangère, en opposition avec une standardisation mondialisée de rapports sociaux. Dans ces trois domaines – prédominance de l'inconscient chez Adamsberg, dimension parodique du texte envers le genre, et persistance de l'altérité du réel – le roman de Vargas, malgré certaines limites, met bien en scène une rencontre avec un ailleurs, inventé certes, mais fortement significatif au regard du concept si mobile de marginalité.

Primary sources

Vargas, F. 2004. *Sous les Vents de* Neptune, Paris : Viviane Hamy.

Other references

Dadoun, R. 1983. Un "sublime amour" de Sherlock Holmes et de Sigmund Freud. *Littérature*, n° 49, pp. 69-76.
Dubois, J. 1992. *Le roman policier ou la modernité*, Paris : Nathan.
Shields, K. 2010. Representations of the French Language in the Detective Novel S*ous les vents de Neptune* by Fred Vargas. *French Cultural Studies*, vol. 21, n° 3.
Vincent, N. 2014. Écrire dans la variante de l'autre : le cas de *Sous les vents de Neptune* de Fred Vargas. *Continents Manuscrits*, vol. 2, http://coma.revues.org/317.

CONTRIBUTORS

ALESSANDRA BONAZZI is associate professor at University of Bologna in Italy (Department of Philosophy and Communication). She teaches Geography of Communication, Cultural Geography and Geography of Cultures. Her recent research focuses on the relationship between geographical space and cultural imaginaries (Forthcoming: "L'Arte della fuga e l'Idea del Nord: Glenn Gould e il contrappunto cartografico del paesaggio artico"; "Il paesaggio e il *Dispatrio:* Luigi Meneghello *bricoleur* in diaspora").

MARIE-LAURE BOUDREAU is a native of Îles-de-la-Madeleine, Québec, Canada. She holds a Baccalaureate in Music from Université de Montréal, and a Master in French from University of Louisiana at Lafayette. She is currently a Ph.D. candidate in Francophone Studies at UL Lafayette (United States). Her dissertation research examines the relationship between Cajun and Creole traditional music and new media. She is also a musician and songwriter herself.

JÉRÔME CABOT is PhD in French Literature and maître de conférences (associate professor) at Institut National Universitaire Champollion, in Albi (France). He's the director of the professional Baccalaureate Degree (Licence) "Cultural development in rural territories". His research deals with 20th Century literature, aesthetics of reception, discourse analysis, reported speeches, and the relationship between Novel and the social world. He's also a poet and performer in slam poetry, interested in creative research.

ROSA CATALÀ MARTICELLA holds a PhD in Geography and a Master in Planning and Environmental Management from University of Barcelona (Spain). She teaches Geography and History at a secondary school and collaborates with a research group which works in didactic experiences from Literature. Her main research field is focused in the study of interactions between Literature and Geography. Her PhD Thesis is entitled *Geography as a descriptive narrative and as a pedagogy of our world. A case study of the landscape literature of Josep Pla.*

FRANCK CHIGNIER-RIBOULON is a full Professor at University Clermont Auvergne (UCA) in Clermont-Ferrand (France). He's a geographer, working on social, economic and political issues in the research center UMR Territoires. For a long time, he worked on urban neighborhood in decline, currently his studies are more on rural (re-)development and regional minorities' questions. His last books were *Architecture symbolique et renouveau d'espaces marginalises* (edited, 2014) and *Les quartiers disqualifiés français* (2014).

PIERRE COUTURIER is maître de conférences (associate professor) at University Clermont Auvergne (UCA), in Clermont-Ferrand (France) and member of the research center UMR Territoires, PhD of Geography. His research mobilizes critical currents of social sciences to question social and territorial ties that are built in resistance to the injunctions of capitalist productivism, of the material and cultural consumerism, of planning policies and their justification schemes.

MARIA DASCA BATALLA, is Lecturer in Catalan Studies at Harvard University (United States), PhD in Literature. Her teaching experiences involves Iberian Cultures and Literatures as well as Catalan and Spanish as a Foreign Language. Her research interests include Contemporary Novel, Translation Studies and Cultural Transfer. Her last book is *Entenebrats. Literatura catalana i bogeria* [Catalan literature and mental disease], Barcelona, Publicacions de l'Abadia de Montserrat, 2016.

OKSANA DOGNON is a PhD Candidate in Communication at University of Burgundy (France) and in Conflict Analysis and Resolution at NSU - Nova Southwestern University (United States). She holds a Master Degree in Criminology and Criminal Justice from University of Nebraska, Omaha (United States). Her research interests include criminology, criminal justice, fictional crime, Russian organized crime and mafia, Russian and Hollywood cinema, aesthetic of mafia, media criminalization, fictional crime and media influence on the public, Death Penalty and its media representation. Currently she is a 2nd Dan black belt and instructor in Taekwondo.

MAURICETTE FOURNIER holds a PhD in Geography, and she is maître de conférences (associate professor) at University Clermont Auvergne (UCA), in Clermont-Ferrand (France) and member of the research center UMR Territoires. She's the director of the Master "Social innovation and territorial development". Her recent research focuses on cultural geography, with a particular interest on literary geography and geography of literature. In connection with these questions, she led several research programs in cooperation with local authorities (*Imaginaire des lieux : littérature, régionalité et attractivité des territoires* [Imaginary places: literature, regionality and attractiveness of territories] (2012-2016); « *Itinéraire littéraire en Bourbonnais - Constitution d'un réseau de coopération pour la valorisation des patrimoines littéraires et des écrivains* [Literary Route in Bourbonnais - Creation of a cooperation network for the valorization of literary heritages and writers] (2015-2017). She wrote about fifty articles for journals or book chapters. She edited also several collective books and thematic issues of journals: *Labellisation et mise en marque des territoires* [Labeling and marking the territories], 2014; *Cartographier les récits* [Mapping Stories], 2016; « Geography, Literature, Territories », special issue of the journal *Territoires en Mouvement,* n°31, 2016.

CHRISTOPHE GELLY is Professor of British and American literature and film studies at University Clermont Auvergne (UCA), and director of the Presses Universitaires Blaise Pascal (PUBP) in Clermont-Ferrand (France). He has worked mainly on film genre, film noir, adaptation and has published two book-length studies on Arthur Conan Doyle (*Le Chien des Baskerville: Poétique du roman policier chez Conan Doyle*, Lyon, Presses Universitaires de Lyon, collection Champ Anglophone, 2005) and Raymond Chandler (*Raymond Chandler — Du roman noir au film noir*, Paris, Michel Houdiard, 2009), and co-edited a book on reception theories in cinema and literature (*Approaches to film and reception theories / Cinéma et théories de la réception —Etudes et panorama critique*, Christophe Gelly et David Roche [eds.], Clermont-Ferrand, Presses Universitaires Blaise Pascal, 2012). He currently orients his research on cinema theory at large.

EKATERINA ISAEVA holds a PhD in Linguistics. She is a full-time professor at the Department of European languages of Russian State University for Humanities (RGGU) in Moscow (Russia). Since 1999 she has also been occupying the position of the Director of the "Moscow-Quebec" center for education, research and culture. Prof. Isaeva has authored 60 papers and articles on linguistics and culture. Her research interests include verbal-cultural representation of Image, Concept and Value.

ANNIE JOUAN-WESTLUND is Professor of French in the Department of World Languages, Literatures and Cultures at Cleveland State University (United States). She received her doctoral degree from the University of

Wisconsin-Madison. She is specialized in the study of contemporary French autobiography/autofiction with a strong interest in the risk implied in writing the self. He recent research focuses on cultural representations of France and the United States in literature, cinema and the media. She published book chapters and articles on the works of Simone de Beauvoir, Serge Doubrovsky, George Sand, Annie Ernaux, Yamina Benguigui, Andreï Makine, Stephen Clarke, Adam Gopnik, Jean-Benoit Nadeau and films by Mathieu Kassovitz, Sylvain Chomet, Denis Chouinard, Bertrand Tavernier, Nicolas Philibert, Laurent Cantet and Philippe Faucon. She is the author of a forthcoming interview with Pierre Jourde entitled « Écriture du territoire et territoire de l'écriture » in *Nouvelles Francographies 6.*

PIERRE-MATHIEU LE BEL is PhD of Geography, specialized in social and cultural geography. He received his doctoral degree from the University of Ottawa (Canada). He is currently a research professional for the research center UMR Territoires and part-time lecturer at University Clermont-Auvergne (UCA) in Clermont-Ferrand (France). He published a book on representations of Montreal in contemporary novels entitled *Montreal et la métropolisation, une géographie romanesque* (Triptyque, 2012) and has written a number of articles in literary geography. He also works on heritage and citizen participation, usually with a critical geography approach.

MARINA MARENGO is geographer and Professor of Geography at the University of Genua (Italy). She teaches Geography, Social Geography and Cultural Geography. In 1990 she took her PhD in Urban and Regional Geography (Rome, Department of University and Scientific Research). In 2001 she took her Doctorat Es Lettres (University of Lausanne). She has worked mainly on migratory phenomena and interculturality (particularly in Italy, Canada and Switzerland), gender studies, local sustainable development (particularly applied to networks of associations and public sector), methodology of geography and fieldwork research in social sciences, cultural geography. Her recent research focuses on literary geography, with a particular interest on french popular literature.

ANTOINE MARTY is geographer. He obtained in 2014 a double Master Degree (Master DYNamiques des Territoires et Aménagement Rural (DYNTAR) and Master Territoires, Acteurs, Modélisation (TAM) at University Clermont Auvergne (UCA). He's currently working as a project manager for the housing environment and the town planning for the Community of Agglomeration of Bourges (France).

AURORE MIRLOUP is PhD of Geography and member of the research center UMR Territoires, in Clermont-Ferrand (France). Her thesis deals with the relationship between literary heritage and territorial attractivness. More specifically, it develops a typology and a socio-spatial analysis of writers' houses, routes and literary trails. Aurore Mirloup is also an agricultural engineer. She worked on several research programs in tourism and territorial development. She is currently a research professional and she is working as a project manager in a consulting firm.

MARIE PASCAL holds a PhD in Québec literature and cinema (University of Toronto, Canada). She completed a double M.A. in France (Université Blaise Pascal, Clermont-Ferrand) in 2010, in English and Francophone studies. Her research interests are Québec literature and films, and she focuses on figures of excluded others in the Arts and Cultures. Her most recently published works are: « Clown et masque: deux figures d'altérité dans le roman migrant *Le Pavillon des miroirs* de Sergio Kokis », *Études Françaises*, PUM, volume 51, n°3, Fall 2015 ; « Une odyssée de parias: la tétralogie *Le Sang des promesses* (W. Mouawad) et ses deux adaptations cinématographiques », LiCArC, Classiques Garnier, June 2016; and « Entre anomie et obscurantisme religieux : la littérature québécoise comme relecture sociologique d'un siècle », Contact +, n°78, June-July-August 2017.

NORA SEMMOUD is Professor of Geography and Planning at the University of Tours (France). She is specially engaged in the team EMAM (Équipe Monde arabe et Méditerranée) about the spacial and social inqualities, into the laboratory "CITERES" (Cités, Territoires, Sociétés). The social reception of urbanism, at the heart of its work, refers to analysis of the « entre-deux », between the public urban action and the practices of their recipients, in a variety of contexts (Arabic world and specially Algeria, but also France and Poland).

JOAN TORT DONADA, geographer and Professor of Geography at University of Barcelona (Spain). His research interests encompass Regional Studies, Landscape, Toponymy, Epistemology of Geography, Urban and Rural Planning, and Geographical Research in Literature. He has a particular interest in the study of place names and the relationship between names and human experience of world – the subject of his doctoral thesis in Geography –. He has led various research projects aiming to tackle the analysis of regions and landscapes in Spain as cultural constructions, and the study of what he calls 'the memory of the territory'.

FLORENCE TROIN is Research Engeener in Cartography in the laboratory "CITERES" (Cités, Territoires, Sociétés) at the University of Tours (France). She has been involved in the researchs of the team EMAM (Équipe Monde arabe et Méditerranée) for more than fifteen years, ensuring also the editorialy coordination of the journal *Les Cahiers d'EMAM*. At the same time, she has invested the field of the relationships between geography and litterature, in producing some "mappings" of novels. On this subject, one of her latest papers was "Une expérience de cartographie stimulante : révéler des dimensions cachées à l'intérieur des récits policiers. *"L'Ombre du vent* de C.R. Zafón et la *trilogie Fabio Montale* de J.-C. Izzo", in Fournier (ed), *Cartographier les récits* [Mapping Stories], 2016